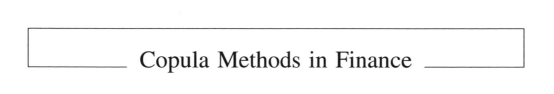

Copula Methods in Finance

Wiley Finance Series

Copula Methods in Finance

Umberto Cherubini
Elisa Luciano
and
Walter Vecchiato

John Wiley & Sons, Ltd

This publication is designed to provide accurate and authoritative information in regard to the subject matter covered. It is sold on the understanding that the Publisher is not engaged in rendering professional services. If professional advice or other expert assistance is required, the services of a competent professional should be sought.

Other Wiley Editorial Offices

John Wiley & Sons Inc., 111 River Street, Hoboken, NJ 07030, USA

Jossey-Bass, 989 Market Street, San Francisco, CA 94103-1741, USA

Wiley-VCH Verlag GmbH, Boschstr. 12, D-69469 Weinheim, Germany

John Wiley & Sons Australia Ltd, 33 Park Road, Milton, Queensland 4064, Australia

John Wiley & Sons (Asia) Pte Ltd, 2 Clementi Loop #02-01, Jin Xing Distripark, Singapore 129809

John Wiley & Sons Canada Ltd, 22 Worcester Road, Etobicoke, Ontario, Canada M9W 1L1

Wiley also publishes its books in a variety of electronic formats. Some content that appears in print may not be available in electronic books.

Library of Congress Cataloging-in-Publication Data

Cherubini, Umberto.
  Copula methods in finance / Umberto Cherubini, Elisa Luciano, and Walter Vecchiato.
    p. cm.
ISBN 0-470-86344-7 (alk. paper)
  1. Finance–Mathematical models. I. Luciano, Elisa. II. Vecchiato, Walter. III. Title.

HG106.C49 2004
332′.01′519535 – dc22
                                                                          2004002624

British Library Cataloguing in Publication Data

A catalogue record for this book is available from the British Library

ISBN 10: 0-470-86344-7 (HB)   ISBN 13: 978-0-470-86344-2 (HB)

Typeset in 10/12pt Times by Laserwords Private Limited, Chennai, India
Printed and bound in Great Britain by TJ International, Padstow, Cornwall, UK
This book is printed on acid-free paper responsibly manufactured from sustainable forestry
in which at least two trees are planted for each one used for paper production.

Contents

Preface

Copula functions represent a methodology which has recently become the most significant new tool to handle in a flexible way the comovement between markets, risk factors and other relevant variables studied in finance. While the tool is borrowed from the theory of statistics, it has been gathering more and more popularity both among academics and practitioners in the field of finance principally because of the huge increase of volatility and erratic behavior of financial markets. These new developments have caused standard tools of financial mathematics, such as the Black and Scholes formula, to become suddenly obsolete. The reason has to be traced back to the overwhelming evidence of non-normality of the probability distribution of financial assets returns, which has become popular well beyond the academia and in the dealing rooms. Maybe for this reason, and these new environments, non-normality has been described using curious terms such as the "smile effect", which traders now commonly use to define strategies, and the "fat-tails" problem, which is the major topic of debate among risk managers and regulators. The result is that nowadays no one would dare to address any financial or statistical problem connected to financial markets without taking care of the issue of departures from normality.

For one-dimensional problems many effective answers have been given, both in the field of pricing and risk measurement, even though no model has emerged as the heir of the traditional standard models of the Gaussian world.

On top of that, people in the field have now begun to realize that abandoning the normality assumption for multidimensional problems was a much more involved issue. The multidimensional extension of the techniques devised at the univariate level has also grown all the more as a necessity in the market practice. On the one hand, the massive use of derivatives in asset management, in particular from hedge funds, has made the non-normality of returns an investment tool, rather than a mere statistical problem: using non-linear derivatives any hedge fund can design an appropriate probability distribution for any market. As a counterpart, it has the problem of determining the joint probability distribution of those exposures to such markets and risk factors. On the other hand, the need to reach effective diversification has led to new investment products, bound to exploit the credit risk features of the assets. It is particularly for the evaluation of these new products, such as securitized assets (asset-backed securities, such as CDO and the like) and basket credit derivatives (nth to default options) that the need to account for comovement among non-normally distributed variables has become an unavoidable task.

Copula functions have been first applied to the solution of these problems, and have been later applied to the multidimensional non-normality problem throughout all the fields in mathematical finance. In fact, the use of copula functions enables the task of specifying the marginal distributions to be decoupled from the dependence structure of variables. This allows us to exploit univariate techniques at the first step, and is directly linked to non-parametric dependence measures at the second step. This avoids the flaws of linear correlation that have, by now, become well known.

This book is an introduction to the use of copula functions from the viewpoint of mathematical finance applications. Our method intends to explain copulas by means of applications to major topics such as asset pricing, risk management and credit risk analysis. Our target is to enable the readers to devise their own applications, following the strategies illustrated throughout the book. In the text we concentrate all the information concerning mathematics, statistics and finance that one needs to build an application to a financial problem. Examples of applications include the pricing of multivariate derivatives and exotic contracts (basket, rainbow, barrier options and so on), as well as risk-management applications. Beyond that, references to financial topics and market data are pervasively present throughout the book, to make the mathematical and statistical concepts, and particularly the estimation issues, easier for the reader to grasp.

The audience target of our work consists of academics and practitioners who are eager to master and construct copula applications to financial problems. For this applied focus, this book is, to the best of our knowledge, the first initiative in the market. Of course, the novelty of the topic and the growing number of research papers on the subject presented at finance conferences all over the world allows us to predict that our book will not remain the only one for too long, and that, on the contrary, this topic will be one of the major issues to be studied in the mathematical finance field in the near future.

Outline of the book

Chapter 1 reviews the state of the art in asset pricing and risk management, going over the major frontier issues and providing justifications for introducing copula functions.

Chapter 2 introduces the reader to the bivariate copula case. It presents the mathematical and probabilistic background on which the applications are built and gives some first examples in finance.

Chapter 3 discusses the flaws of linear correlation and highlights how copula functions, along with non-parametric association measures, may provide a much more flexible way to represent market comovements.

Chapter 4 extends the technical tools to a multivariate setting. Readers who are not already familiar with copulas are advised to skip this chapter at first reading (or to read it at their own risk!).

Chapter 5 explains the statistical inference for copulas. It covers both methodological aspects and applications from market data, such as calibration of actual risk factors comovements and VaR measurement. Here the readers can find details on the classical estimation methods as well as on most recent approaches, such as the conditional copula.

Chapter 6 is devoted to an exhaustive account of simulation algorithms for a large class of multivariate copulas. It is enhanced by financial examples.

Chapter 7 presents credit risk applications, besides giving a brief introduction to credit derivative markets and instruments. It applies copulas to the pricing of complex credit structures such as basket default swaps and CDOs. It is shown how to calibrate the pricing model to market data. Its sensitivity with respect to the copula choice is accounted for in concrete examples.

Chapter 8 covers option pricing applications. Starting from the bivariate pricing kernel, copulas are used to evaluate counterparty risk in derivative transactions and bivariate rainbow options, such as options to exchange. We also show how the barrier option pricing problem can be cast in a bivariate setting and can be represented in terms of copulas. Finally, the estimation and simulation techniques presented in Chapters 5 and 6 are put at work to solve the evaluation problem of a multivariate basket option.

List of Common Symbols and Notations

$\square$ = end of proof

N = the set of natural numbers

$I = [0, 1]$ the unit interval of the real line

$\Re = (-\infty, +\infty)$ the real line

$\Re^* = [-\infty, +\infty]$ the extended real line

$\Re^{*+} = [0, +\infty]$ the non-negative extended real line

$\Re^{*+} \setminus \{0\} = (0, +\infty]$ the positive extended real line

$[a, b] \times [c, d]$ = Cartesian product of the intervals $[a, b]$, $[c, d]$

$$\Re^n = \underbrace{(-\infty, +\infty) \times (-\infty, +\infty) \times \cdots \times (-\infty, +\infty)}_{n \text{ times}}$$

the n-dimensional Euclidean vector space

$$\Re^{*n} = \underbrace{[-\infty, +\infty] \times [-\infty, +\infty] \times \cdots \times [-\infty, +\infty]}_{n \text{ times}}$$

the n-dimensional extended Euclidean vector space

$$I^n = \underbrace{[0, 1] \times [0, 1] \times \cdots \times [0, 1]}_{n \text{ times}} \text{ unit cube in } R^n, n \geqslant 2$$

$\mathbf{x} = [x_1 x_2 \ldots x_n]^T$ n-dimensional (column) vector

$\mathbf{x}'$ = the transpose of the vector $\mathbf{x}$

C = copula function

$\mathcal{C}$ = subcopula function

ϕ = generator of an Archimedean copula

$\phi^{[-1]}$ = pseudo-inverse of ϕ

$F(x, y)$ = bivariate distribution function (cumulative probability function) of the random vector $[X, Y]$, computed at (x, y)

F_i = univariate distribution function (cumulative probability function) of the ith random variable

F_i^{-1} = generalized inverse of F_i

Dom F = the domain of the F function

Ran F = the range of the F function

$$f_i = \text{density of } F_i \text{ (if it exists)}$$
$$C^\infty = \text{the space of functions } f : R \to R$$
$$\text{with derivatives of all orders}$$
$$L^2 = \text{the space of random variables with finite first two}$$
$$\text{moments}$$
$$C^+ = \text{upper Fréchet bound}$$
$$C^- = \text{lower Fréchet bound (copula for } n = 2)$$
$$C^\perp = \text{product copula}$$
$$\overline{C} = \text{survival copula}$$
$$C = \text{joint survivor or survival function}$$
$$\tilde{C} = \text{co-copula}$$
$$\mathbf{1}_{\{E\}} = \text{indicator function of the event } E$$

$$\mathrm{sgn}(x) = \begin{cases} -1 & x < 0 \\ 0 & x = 0 \\ 1 & x > 0 \end{cases} \quad \text{signum function}$$

a.e. = almost everywhere (other than in a set of Lebesgue measure zero)

a.s. = almost surely

c.d.f. = cumulative distribution function

d.o.f. = degrees of freedom

i.i.d. = independent identically distributed

l.h.s. = left-hand side

p.d.f. = probability distribution function

r.h.s. = right-hand side

r.v. = random variable

w.r.t. = with respect to

iff = if and only if

monotone increasing = monotone strictly increasing

monotone non-decreasing = monotone weakly increasing

$\equiv$ = equal by definition

$\sim$ = equal in distribution

$E(X)$ = the expectation of the r.v. X

$\mathrm{Var}(X)$ = its variance

1
Derivatives Pricing, Hedging and Risk Management:
The State of the Art

1.1 INTRODUCTION

The purpose of this chapter is to give a brief review of the basic concepts used in finance for the purpose of pricing contingent claims. As our book is focusing on the use of copula functions in financial applications, most of the content of this chapter should be considered as a prerequisite to the book. Readers who are not familiar with the concepts exposed here are referred for a detailed treatment to standard textbooks on the subject. Here our purpose is mainly to describe the basic tools that represent the state of the art of finance, as well as general problems, and to provide a brief, mainly non-technical, introduction to copula functions and the reason why they may be so useful in financial applications. It is particularly important that we address three hot issues in finance. The first is the non-normality of returns, which makes the standard Black and Scholes option pricing approach obsolete. The second is the incomplete market issue, which introduces a new dimension to the asset pricing problem – that of the choice of the right pricing kernel both in asset pricing and risk management. The third is credit risk, which has seen a huge development of products and techniques in asset pricing.

This discussion would naturally lead to a first understanding of how copula functions can be used to tackle some of these issues. Asset pricing and risk evaluation techniques rely heavily on tools borrowed from probability theory. The prices of derivative products may be written, at least in the standard complete market setting, as the discounted expected values of their future pay-offs under a specific probability measure derived from non-arbitrage arguments. The risk of a position is instead evaluated by studying the negative tail of the probability distribution of profit and loss. Since copula functions provide a useful way to represent multivariate probability distributions, it is no surprise that they may be of great assistance in financial applications. More than this, one can even wonder why it is only recently that they have been discovered and massively applied in finance. The answer has to do with the main developments of market dynamics and financial products over the last decade of the past century.

The main change that has been responsible for the discovery of copula methods in finance has to do with the standard hypothesis assumed for the stochastic dynamics of the rates of returns on financial products. Until the 1987 crash, a normal distribution for these returns was held as a reasonable guess. This concept represented a basic pillar on which most of modern finance theory has been built. In the field of pricing, this assumption corresponds to the standard Black and Scholes approach to contingent claim evaluation. In risk management, assuming normality leads to the standard parametric approach to risk measurement that has been diffused by J.P. Morgan under the trading mark of RiskMetrics since 1994, and is still in use in many financial institutions: due to the assumption of normality, the approach only relies on volatilities and correlations among the returns on the assets in the portfolio. Unfortunately, the assumption of normally distributed returns has been severely challenged by the data and the reality of the markets. On one hand, even evidence on the returns of standard financial products such as stocks and bonds can be easily proved to be at odds with this assumption. On the other hand, financial innovation has spurred the development of products that are specifically targeted to provide non-normal returns. Plain vanilla options are only the most trivial example of this trend, and the development of the structured finance business has made the presence of non-linear products, both plain vanilla and exotic, a pervasive phenomenon in bank balance sheets. This trend has even more been fueled by the pervasive growth in the market for credit derivatives and credit-linked products, whose returns are inherently non-Gaussian. Moreover, the task to exploit the benefits of diversification has caused both equity-linked and credit-linked products to be typically referred to baskets of stocks or credit exposures. As we will see throughout this book, tackling these issues of non-normality and non-linearity in products and portfolios composed by many assets would be a hopeless task without the use of copula functions.

1.2   DERIVATIVE PRICING BASICS: THE BINOMIAL MODEL

Here we give a brief description of the basic pillar behind pricing techniques, that is the use of risk-neutral probability measures to evaluate contingent claims, versus the objective measure observed from the time series of market data. We will see that the existence of such risk measures is directly linked to the basic pricing principle used in modern finance to evaluate financial products. This requirement imposes that prices must ensure that arbitrage gains, also called "free lunches", cannot be obtained by trading the securities in the market. An arbitrage deal is a trading strategy yielding positive returns at no risk. Intuitively, the idea is that if we can set up two positions or trading strategies giving identical pay-offs at some future date, they must also have the same value prior to that date, otherwise one could exploit arbitrage profits by buying the cheaper and selling the more expensive before that date, and unwinding the deal as soon as they are worth the same. Ruling out arbitrage gains then imposes a relationship among the prices of the financial assets involved in the trading strategies. These are called "fair" or "arbitrage-free" prices. It is also worth noting that these prices are not based on any assumption concerning utility maximizing behavior of the agents or equilibrium of the capital markets. The only requirement concerning utility is that traders "prefer more to less", so that they would be ready to exploit whatever arbitrage opportunity was available in the market. In this section we show what the no-arbitrage principle implies for the risk-neutral measure and the objective measure in a discrete setting, before extending it to a continuous time model.

The main results of modern asset pricing theory, as well as some of its major problems, can be presented in a very simple form in a binomial model. For the sake of simplicity, assume that the market is open on two dates, t and T, and that the information structure of the economy is such that, at the future time T, only two states of the world $\{H, L\}$ are possible. A risky asset is traded on the market at the current time t for a price equal to $S(t)$, while at time T the price is represented by a random variable taking values $\{S(H), S(L)\}$ in the two states of the world. A risk-free asset gives instead a value equal to 1 unit of currency at time T no matter which state of the world occurs: we assume that the price at time t of the risk-free asset is equal to B. Our problem is to price another risky asset taking values $\{G(H), G(L)\}$ at time T. As we said before, the price $g(t)$ must be consistent with the prices $S(t)$ and B observed on the market.

1.2.1 Replicating portfolios

In order to check for arbitrage opportunities, assume that we construct a position in Δ_g units of the risky security $S(t)$ and Π_g units of the risk-free asset in such a way that at time T

$$\Delta_g S(H) + \Pi_g = G(H)$$
$$\Delta_g S(L) + \Pi_g = G(L)$$

So, the portfolio has the same value of asset G at time T. We say that it is the "replicating portfolio" of asset G. Obviously we have

$$\Delta_g = \frac{G(H) - G(L)}{S(H) - S(L)}$$
$$\Pi_g = \frac{G(L)S(H) - G(H)S(L)}{S(H) - S(L)}$$

1.2.2 No-arbitrage and the risk-neutral probability measure

If we substitute Δ_g and Π_g in the no-arbitrage equation

$$g(t) = \Delta_g S(t) + B\Pi_g$$

we may rewrite the price, after naive algebraic manipulation, as

$$g(t) = B[QG(H) + (1 - Q)G(L)]$$

with

$$Q \equiv \frac{S(t)/B - S(L)}{S(H) - S(L)}$$

Notice that we have

$$0 < Q < 1 \Leftrightarrow S(L) < \frac{S(t)}{B} < S(H)$$

It is straightforward to check that if the inequality does not hold there are arbitrage opportunities: in fact, if, for example, $S(t)/B \leqslant S(L)$ one could exploit a free-lunch by borrowing and buying the asset. So, in the absence of arbitrage opportunities it follows that $0 < Q < 1$, and Q is a probability measure. We may then write the no-arbitrage price as

$$g(t) = BE_Q[G(T)]$$

In order to rule out arbitrage, then, the above relationship must hold for all the contingent claims and the financial products in the economy. In fact, even for the risky asset S we must have

$$S(t) = BE_Q[S(T)]$$

Notice that the probability measure Q was recovered from the no-arbitrage requirement only. To understand the nature of this measure, it is sufficient to compute the expected rate of return of the different assets under this probability. We have that

$$E_Q\left[\frac{G(T)}{g(t)} - 1\right] = E_Q\left[\frac{S(T)}{S(t)} - 1\right] = \frac{1}{B} - 1 \equiv i$$

where i is the interest rate earned on the risk-free asset for an investment horizon from t to T. So, under the measure Q all of the risky assets in the economy are expected to yield the same return as the risk-free asset. For this reason such a measure is called *risk-neutral* probability.

Alternatively, the measure can be characterized in a more technical sense in the following way. Let us assume that we measure each risky asset in the economy using the risk-free asset as numeraire. Recalling that the value of the riskless asset is B at time t and 1 at time T, we have

$$\frac{g(t)}{B(t)} = E_Q\left[\frac{G(T)}{B(T)}\right] = E_Q[G(T)]$$

A process endowed with this property (i.e. $z(t) = E_Q(z(T))$) is called a *martingale*. For this reason, the measure Q is also called an *equivalent martingale measure* (EMM).[1]

1.2.3 No-arbitrage and the objective probability measure

For comparison with the results above, it may be useful to address the question of which constraints are imposed by the no-arbitrage requirements on expected returns under the objective probability measure. The answer to this question may be found in the well-known *arbitrage pricing theory* (APT). Define the rates of return of an investment on assets S and g over the horizon from t to T as

$$i_g \equiv \frac{G(T)}{g(t)} - 1 \qquad i_S \equiv \frac{S(T)}{S(t)} - 1$$

and the rate of return on the risk-free asset as $i \equiv 1/B - 1$.

The rate of returns on the risky assets are assumed to be driven by a linear data-generating process

$$i_g = a_g + b_g f \qquad i_S = a_S + b_S f$$

where the risk factor f is taken with zero mean and unit variance with no loss of generality.

---

[1] The term *equivalent* is a technical requirement referring to the fact that the risk-neutral measure and the objective measure must agree on the same subset of zero measure events.

Of course this implies $a_g = E(i_g)$ and $a_S = E(i_S)$. Notice that the expectation is now taken under the original probability measure associated with the data-generating process of the returns. We define this measure P. Under the same measure, of course, b_g and b_S represent the standard deviations of the returns. Following a standard no-arbitrage argument we may build a zero volatility portfolio from the two risky assets and equate its return to that of the risk-free asset. This yields

$$\frac{a_S - i}{b_S} = \frac{a_g - i}{b_g} = \lambda$$

where λ is a parameter, which may be constant, time-varying or even stochastic, but has to be the same for all the assets. This relationship, that avoids arbitrage gains, could be rewritten as

$$E(i_S) = i + \lambda b_S \qquad E(i_g) = i + \lambda b_g$$

In words, the expected rate of return of each and every risky asset under the objective measure must be equal to the risk-free rate of return plus a risk premium. The risk premium is the product of the volatility of the risky asset times the market price of risk parameter λ. Notice that in order to prevent arbitrage gains the key requirement is that the market price of risk must be the same for all of the risky assets in the economy.

1.2.4 Discounting under different probability measures

The no-arbitrage requirement implies different restrictions under the objective probability measures. The relationship between the two measures can get involved in more complex pricing models, depending on the structure imposed on the dynamics of the market price of risk. To understand what is going on, however, it may be instructive to recover this relationship in a binomial setting. Assuming that P is the objective measure, one can easily prove that

$$Q = P - \lambda \sqrt{P(1 - P)}$$

and the risk-neutral measure Q is obtained by shifting probability from state H to state L.

To get an intuitive assessment of the relationship between the two measures, one could say that under risk-neutral valuation the probability is adjusted for risk in such a way as to guarantee that all of the assets are expected to yield the risk-free rate; on the contrary, under the objective risk-neutral measure the expected rate of return is adjusted to account for risk. In both cases, the amount of adjustment is determined by the market price of risk parameter λ.

To avoid mistakes in the evaluation of uncertain cash flows, it is essential to take into consideration the kind of probability measure under which one is working. In fact, the discount factor applied to expected cash flows must be adjusted for risk if the expectation is computed under the objective measure, while it must be the risk-free discount factor if the expectation is taken under the risk-neutral probability. Indeed, one can also check that

$$g(t) = \frac{E[G(T)]}{1 + i + \lambda b_g} = \frac{E_Q[G(T)]}{1 + i}$$

and using the wrong interest rate to discount the expected cash flow would get the wrong evaluation.

1.2.5 Multiple states of the world

Consider the case in which three scenarios are possible at time T, say $\{S(HH), S(HL), S(LL)\}$. The crucial, albeit obvious, thing to notice is that it is not possible to replicate an asset by a portfolio of only two other assets. To continue with the example above, whatever amount Δ_g of the asset S we choose, and whatever the position of Π_g in the risk-free asset, we are not able to perfectly replicate the pay-off of the contract g in all the three states of the world: whatever replicating portfolio was used would lead to some *hedging error*. Technically, we say that contract g is not *attainable* and we have an *incomplete market* problem. The discussion of this problem has been at the center of the analysis of modern finance theory for some years, and will be tackled in more detail below. Here we want to stress in which way the model above can be extended to this multiple scenario setting. There are basically two ways to do so. The first is to assume that there is a third asset, whose pay-off is independent of the first two, so that a replicating portfolio can be constructed using three assets instead of two. For an infinitely large number of scenarios, an infinitely large set of independent assets is needed to ensure perfect hedging. The second way to go is to assume that the market for the underlying opens at some intermediate time τ prior to T and the underlying on that date may take values $\{S(H), S(L)\}$. If this is the case, one could use the following strategy:

- Evaluate $g(\tau)$ under both scenarios $\{S(H), S(L)\}$, yielding $\{g(H), g(L)\}$: this will result in the computation of the risk-neutral probabilities $\{Q(H), Q(L)\}$ and the replicating portfolios consisting of $\{\Delta_g(H), \Delta_g(L)\}$ units of the underlying and $\{\Pi_g(H), \Pi_g(L)\}$ units of the risk-free asset.
- Evaluate $g(t)$ as a derivative product giving a pay-off $\{g(H), g(L)\}$ at time τ, depending on the state of the world: this will result in a risk-neutral probability Q, and a replicating portfolio with Δ_g units of the underlying and Π_g units of the risk-free asset.

The result is that the value of the product will be again set equal to its replicating portfolio

$$g(t) = \Delta_g S(t) + B\Pi_g$$

but at time τ it will be *rebalanced*, depending on the price observed for the underlying asset. We will then have

$$g(H) = \Delta_g(H) S(H) + B\Pi_g(H)$$
$$g(L) = \Delta_g(L) S(L) + B\Pi_g(L)$$

and both the position on the underlying asset and the risk-free asset will be changed following the change of the underlying price. We see that even though we have three possible scenarios, we can replicate the product g by a replicating portfolio of only two assets, thanks to the possibility of changing it at an intermediate date. We say that we follow a *dynamic* replication trading strategy, opposed to the *static* replication portfolio of the simple example above. The replication trading strategy has a peculiar feature: the value of the replicating portfolio set up at t and re-evaluated using the prices of time τ is, in any circumstances, equal to that of the new replicating portfolio which will be set up at time τ. We have in fact that

$$\Delta_g S(H) + \Pi_g = g(H) = \Delta_g(H) S(H) + B\Pi_g(H)$$

$$\Delta_g S(L) + \Pi_g = g(L) = \Delta_g(L) S(L) + B\Pi_g(L)$$

This means that once the replicating portfolio is set up at time t, no further expense or withdrawal will be required to rebalance it, and the sums to be paid to buy more of an asset will be exactly those made available by the selling of the other. For this reason the replicating portfolio is called *self-financing*.

1.3   THE BLACK–SCHOLES MODEL

Let us think of a multiperiod binomial model, with a time difference between one date and the following equal to h. The gain or loss on an investment on asset S over every period will be given by

$$S(t + h) - S(t) = i_S(t) S(t)$$

Now assume that the rates of return are serially uncorrelated and normally distributed as

$$i_S(t) = \mu^* + \sigma^* \varepsilon(t)$$

with μ^* and σ^* constant parameters and $\varepsilon(t) \sim N(0, 1)$, i.e. a series of uncorrelated standard normal variables. Substituting in the dynamics of S we get

$$S(t + h) - S(t) = \mu^* S(t) + \sigma^* S(t) \varepsilon(t)$$

Taking the limit for h that tends to zero, we may write the stochastic dynamics of S in continuous time as

$$dS(t) = \mu S(t) \, dt + \sigma S(t) \, dz(t)$$

The stochastic process is called *geometric brownian motion*, and it is a specific case of a *diffusive* process. $z(t)$ is a Wiener process, defined by $dz(t) \sim N(0, dt)$ and the terms $\mu S(t)$ and $\sigma S(t)$ are known as the *drift* and *diffusion* of the process. Intuitively, they represent the expected value and the volatility (standard deviation) of instantaneous changes of $S(t)$.

Technically, a stochastic process in continuous time $S(t), t \leqslant T$, is defined with respect to a filtered probability space $\{\Omega, \Im_t, P\}$, where $\Im_t = \sigma(S(u), u \leqslant t)$ is the smallest σ-field containing sets of the form $\{a \leqslant S(u) \leqslant b\}, 0 \leqslant u \leqslant t$: more intuitively, $\Im_t$ represents the amount of information available at time t.

The increasing σ-fields $\{\Im_t\}$ form a so-called filtration F:

$$\Im_0 \subset \Im_1 \subset \cdots \subset \Im_T$$

Not only is the filtration increasing, but $\Im_0$ also contains all the events with zero measure; and these are typically referred to as "the usual assumptions". The increasing property corresponds to the fact that, at least in financial applications, the amount of information is continuously increasing as time elapses.

A variable observed at time t is said to be measurable with respect to $\Im_t$ if the set of events, such that the random variable belongs to a Borel set on the line, is contained in $\Im_t$, for every Borel set: in other words, $\Im_t$ contains all the amount of information needed to recover the value of the variable at time t. If a process $S(t)$ is measurable with respect to $\Im_t$ for all $t \geqslant 0$, it is said to be adapted with respect to $\Im_t$. At time t, the values of a variable at any time $\tau > t$ can instead be characterized only in terms of the last object, i.e. the probability measure P, conditional on the information set $\Im_t$.

In this setting, a diffusive process is defined, assuming that the limit of the first and second moments of $S(t+h) - S(t)$ exist and are finite, and that finite jumps have zero probability in the limit. Technically,

$$\lim_{h \to 0} \frac{1}{h} E\left[S(t+h) - S(t) \mid S(t) = S\right] = \mu(S, t)$$

$$\lim_{h \to 0} \frac{1}{h} E\left[\left[S(t+h) - S(t)\right]^2 \mid S(t) = S\right] = \sigma^2(S, t)$$

and

$$\lim_{h \to 0} \frac{1}{h} \Pr\left(|S(t+h) - S(t)| > \varepsilon \mid S(t) = S\right) = 0$$

Of course the moments in the equations above are tacitly assumed to exist. For further and detailed discussion of the matter, the reader is referred to standard textbooks on stochastic processes (see, for example, Karlin & Taylor, 1981).

1.3.1 Ito's lemma

A paramount result that is used again and again in financial applications is Ito's lemma. Say $y(t)$ is a diffusive stochastic process

$$dy(t) = \mu_y \, dt + \sigma_y \, dz(t)$$

and $f(y, t)$ is a function differentiable twice in the first argument and once in the second. Then f also follows a diffusive process

$$df(y, t) = \mu_f \, dt + \sigma_f \, dz(t)$$

with drift and diffusion terms given by

$$\mu_f = \frac{\partial f}{\partial t} + \frac{\partial f}{\partial y} \mu_y + \frac{1}{2} \frac{\partial^2 f}{\partial y^2} \sigma_y^2$$

$$\sigma_f = \frac{\partial f}{\partial y} \sigma_y$$

Example 1.1 Notice that, given

$$dS(t) = \mu S(t)\, dt + \sigma S(t)\, dz(t)$$

we can set $f(S, t) = \ln S(t)$ to obtain

$$d\ln S(t) = (\mu - \tfrac{1}{2}\sigma^2)\, dt + \sigma dz(t)$$

If μ and σ are constant parameters, it is easy to obtain

$$\ln S(\tau) \mid \Im_t \sim N(\ln S(t) + (\mu - \tfrac{1}{2}\sigma^2)(\tau - t), \sigma^2(\tau - t))$$

where $N(m, s)$ is the normal distribution with mean m and variance s. Then, $\Pr(S(\tau) \mid \Im_t)$ is described by the lognormal distribution.

It is worth stressing that the *geometric brownian motion* assumption used in the Black–Scholes model implies that the log-returns on the asset S are normally distributed, and this is the same as saying that their volatility is assumed to be constant.

1.3.2 Girsanov theorem

A second technique that is mandatory to know for the application of diffusive processes to financial problems is the result known as the Girsanov theorem (or Cameron–Martin–Girsanov theorem). The main idea is that given a Wiener process $z(t)$ defined under the filtration $\{\Omega, \Im_t, P\}$ we may construct another process $\tilde{z}(t)$ which is a Wiener process under another probability space $\{\Omega, \Im_t, Q\}$. Of course, the latter process will have a drift under the original measure P. Under such measure it will be in fact

$$d\tilde{z}(t) = dz(t) + \gamma\, dt$$

for γ deterministic or stochastic and satisfying regularity conditions. In plain words, changing the probability measure is the same as changing the drift of the process.

The application of this principle to our problem is straightforward. Assume there is an opportunity to invest in a *money market mutual fund* yielding a constant instantaneous risk-free yield equal to r. In other words, let us assume that the dynamics of the investment in the risk-free asset is

$$dB(t) = rB(t)$$

where the constant r is also called the interest rate intensity ($r \equiv \ln(1 + i)$). We saw before that under the objective measure P the no-arbitrage requirement implies

$$E\left[\frac{dS(t)}{S(t)}\right] = \mu\, dt = (r + \lambda\sigma)\, dt$$

where λ is the market price of risk. Substituting in the process followed by $S(t)$ we have

$$dS(t) = (r + \lambda\sigma) S(t) \, dt + \sigma S(t) \, dz(t)$$
$$= S(t) (r \, dt + \sigma (dz(t) + \lambda \, dt))$$
$$= S(t) (r \, dt + \sigma \, d\widetilde{z}(t))$$

where $d\widetilde{z}(t) = dz(t) + \lambda \, dt$ is a Wiener process under some new measure Q. Under such a measure, the dynamics of the underlying is then

$$dS(t) = rS(t) \, dt + \sigma S(t) \, d\widetilde{z}(t)$$

meaning that the instantaneous expected rate of the return on asset $S(t)$ is equal to the instantaneous yield on the risk-free asset

$$E_Q \left[\frac{dS(t)}{S(t)} \right] = r \, dt$$

i.e. that Q is the so-called risk-neutral measure. It is easy to check that the same holds for any derivative written on $S(t)$. Define $g(S, t)$ the price of a derivative contract giving pay-off $G(S(T), T)$. Indeed, using Ito's lemma we have

$$dg(t) = \mu_g g(t) \, dt + \sigma_g g(t) \, dz(t)$$

with

$$\mu_g g = \frac{\partial g}{\partial t} + \frac{\partial g}{\partial S} (r + \lambda\sigma) S(t) + \frac{1}{2} \frac{\partial^2 g}{\partial S^2} \sigma^2(t) S^2$$

$$\sigma_g g = \frac{\partial g}{\partial S} \sigma$$

Notice that under the original measure we then have

$$dg(t) = \left[\frac{\partial g}{\partial t} + \frac{\partial g}{\partial S} \mu S(t) + \frac{1}{2} \frac{\partial^2 g}{\partial S^2} \sigma^2(t) S^2 \right] dt + \frac{\partial g}{\partial S} \sigma \, dz(t)$$

However, the no-arbitrage requirement implies

$$\mu_g g = \frac{\partial g}{\partial t} + \frac{\partial g}{\partial S} (r + \lambda\sigma) S(t) + \frac{1}{2} \frac{\partial^2 g}{\partial S^2} \sigma^2(t) S^2 = rg + \lambda \frac{\partial g}{\partial S} \sigma$$

so it follows that

$$\frac{\partial g}{\partial t} + \frac{\partial g}{\partial S} rS(t) + \frac{1}{2} \frac{\partial^2 g}{\partial S^2} \sigma^2(t) S^2 = rg$$

This is the fundamental partial differential equation (PDE) of the Black–Scholes model. Notice that by substituting this result into the risk-neutral dynamics of g under measure Q we get

$$dg(t) = rg(t) \, dt + \frac{\partial g}{\partial S} \sigma \, d\widetilde{z}(t)$$

and the product g is expected to yield the instantaneous risk-free rate. We reach the conclusion that under the risk-neutral measure Q

$$E_Q\left[\frac{dS(t)}{S(t)}\right] = E_Q\left[\frac{dg(t)}{g(t)}\right] = r\,dt$$

that is, all the risky assets are assumed to yield the instantaneous risk-free rate.

1.3.3 The martingale property

The price of any contingent claim g can be recovered solving the fundamental PDE. An alternative way is to exploit the martingale property embedded in the measure Q. Define Z as the value of a product expressed using the riskless money market account as the numeraire, i.e. $Z(t) \equiv g(t)/B(t)$. Given the dynamics of the risky asset under the risk-neutral measure Q we have that

$$dS(t) = rS(t)\,dt + \sigma S(t)\,d\widetilde{z}(t)$$

$$dB(t) = rB(t)\,dt$$

and it is easy to check that

$$dZ(t) = \sigma Z(t)\,d\widetilde{z}(t)$$

The process $Z(t)$ then follows a martingale, so that $E_Q(Z(T)) = Z(t)$. This directly provides us with a pricing formula. In fact we have

$$Z(t) = \frac{g(S,t)}{B(t)} = E_Q(Z(T)) = E_Q\left(\frac{G(S,T)}{B(T)}\right)$$

Considering that $B(T)$ is a deterministic function, we have

$$g(S,t) = \frac{B(t)}{B(T)}E_Q(G(S,T)) = \exp(-r(T-t))\,E_Q(G(S,T))$$

The price of a contingent claim is obtained by taking the relevant expectation under the risk-neutral measure and discounting it back to the current time t. Under the assumption of log-normal distribution of the future price of the underlying asset S, we may recover for instance the basic Black–Scholes formula for a plain vanilla call option

$$\text{CALL}(S,t;K,T) = S(t)\,\Phi(d_1) - \exp[-r(T-t)]\,K\Phi(d_2)$$

$$d_1 = \frac{\ln(S(t)/K) + \left(r + \sigma^2/2\right)(T-t)}{\sigma\sqrt{T-t}}$$

$$d_2 = d_1 - \sigma\sqrt{T-t}$$

where $\Phi(x)$ is the standard normal distribution function evaluated at x

$$\Phi(x) = \frac{1}{2\pi}\int_{-\infty}^{x}\exp\left[-\frac{u^2}{2}\right]du$$

The formula for the put option is, instead,

$$\text{PUT}(S, t; K, T) = -S(t)\,\Phi(-d_1) + \exp[-r(T-t)]\,K\Phi(-d_2)$$

Notice that a long position in a call option corresponds to a long position in the underlying and a debt position, while a long position in a put option corresponds to a short position in the underlying and an investment in the risk-free asset. As $S(t)$ tends to infinity, the value of a call tends to that of a long position in a forward and the value of the put tends to zero; as $S(t)$ tends to zero, the value of the put tends to the value of a short position in a forward and the price of the call option tends to zero.

The sensitivity of the option price with respect to the underlying is called *delta* (Δ) and is equal to $\Phi(d_1)$ for the call option and $\Phi(d_1) - 1$ for the put. The sensitivity of the delta with respect to the underlying is called *gamma* (Γ), and that of the option price with respect to time is called *theta* (Θ). These derivatives, called the *greek letters*, can be used to approximate, in general, the value of any derivative contract by a Taylor expansion as

$$g(S(t+h), t+h) \simeq g(S(t), t) + \Delta_g(S(t+h) - S(t))$$
$$+ \tfrac{1}{2}\Gamma_g(S(t+h) - S(t))^2 + \Theta_g h$$

Notice that the *greek letters* are linked one to the others by the *fundamental PDE* ruling out arbitrage. Indeed, this condition can be rewritten as

$$\Theta_g + \Delta_g r S(t) + \tfrac{1}{2}\Gamma_g \sigma^2(t) S^2 - rg = 0$$

1.3.4 Digital options

A way to understand the probabilistic meaning of the Black–Scholes formula is to compute the price of digital options. Digital options pay a fixed sum or a unit of the underlying if the underlying asset is above some strike level at the exercise date. Digital options, which pay a fixed sum, are called *cash-or-nothing* (CoN) options, while those paying the asset are called *asset-or-nothing* (AoN) options. Under the log-normal assumption of the conditional distribution of the underlying held under the Black–Scholes model, we easily obtain

$$\text{CoN}(S, t; K, T) = \exp[-r(T-t)]\,\Phi(d_2)$$

The asset-or-nothing price can be recovered by arbitrage observing that at time T

$$\text{CALL}(S, T; K, T) + K\,\text{CoN}(S, T; K, T) = \mathbf{1}_{\{S(T)>K\}}S(T) = \text{AoN}(S, T; K, T)$$

where $\mathbf{1}_{\{S(T)>K\}}$ is the indicator function assigning 1 to the case $S(T) > K$. So, to avoid arbitrage we must have

$$\text{AoN}(S, t; K, T) = S(t)\,\Phi(d_1)$$

Beyond the formulas deriving from the Black–Scholes model, it is important to stress that this result – that a call option is the sum of a long position in a digital *asset-or-nothing* option and a short position in K *cash-or-nothing* options – remains true for all the option pricing models. In fact, this result directly stems from the no-arbitrage requirement imposed in the asset pricing model. The same holds for the result (which may be easily verified) that

$$- \exp\left[r\left(T - t\right)\right] \frac{\partial \text{CALL}(S, t; K, T)}{\partial K} = \Phi\left(d_2\right) = \Pr\left(S\left(T\right) > K\right)$$

where the probability is computed under measure Q. From the derivative of the call option with respect to the strike price we can then recover the risk-neutral probability of the underlying asset.

1.4 INTEREST RATE DERIVATIVES

The valuation of derivatives written on fixed income products or interest rates is more involved than the standard Black–Scholes model described above, even though all models are based on the same principles and techniques of arbitrage-free valuation presented above. The reason for this greater complexity is that the underlying asset of these products is the curve representing the discounting factors of future cash-flows as a function of maturity T. The discount factor $D(t, T)$ of a unit cash-flow due at maturity T, evaluated at current time t, can be represented as

$$D\left(t, T\right) = \exp\left[-r\left(t, T\right)\left(T - t\right)\right]$$

where $r\left(t, T\right)$ is the continuously compounded spot rate or yield to maturity. Alternatively, the discount factor can be characterized in terms of forward rates, as

$$D\left(t, T\right) = \exp\left[-\int_t^T f\left(t, u\right) du\right]$$

Term structure pricing models are based on stochastic representations of the spot or forward yield curve.

1.4.1 Affine factor models

The classical approach to interest rate modeling is based on the assumption that the stochastic dynamics of the curve can be represented by the dynamics of some risk factors. The yield curve is then recovered endogenously from their dynamics. The most famous models are due to Vasicek (1977) and Cox, Ingersoll and Ross (1985). They use a single risk factor, which is chosen to be the intercept of the yield curve – that is, the instantaneous interest rate. While this rate was assumed to be constant under the Black–Scholes framework, now it is assumed to vary stochastically over time, so that the value of a European contingent claim g, paying $G(T)$ at time T, is generalized to

$$g\left(t\right) = E_Q\left[\exp\left[-\int_t^T r\left(u\right) du\right] G\left(T\right) \mid \Im_t\right]$$

where the expectation is again taken under the risk-neutral measure Q. Notice that for the discount factor $D\left(t, T\right)$ we have the pay-off $D\left(T, T\right) = 1$, so that

$$D\left(t, T\right) = E_Q\left[\exp\left[-\int_t^T r\left(u\right) du\right] \mid \Im_t\right]$$

We observe that even if the pay-off is deterministic, the discount factor is stochastic, and it is a function of the instantaneous interest rate $r(t)$. Let us assume that the dynamics of $r(t)$ under the risk-neutral measure is described by the diffusion process

$$dr(t) = \mu_r \, dt + \sigma_r \, d\widetilde{z}(t)$$

and let us write the dynamics of the discount factor, under the same measure Q, as

$$dD(t, T) = r(t) D(t, T) \, dt + \sigma_T D(t, T) \, d\widetilde{z}(t)$$

where σ_T is the volatility of instantaneous percentage changes of the discount factor. Applying Ito's lemma we have

$$r(t) D(t, T) = \frac{\partial D(t, T)}{\partial t} + \mu_r \frac{\partial D(t, T)}{\partial r} + \frac{1}{2} \sigma_r^2 \frac{\partial^2 D(t, T)}{\partial r^2}$$

which is a partial differential equation ruling out arbitrage opportunities.

It may be proved that in the particular case in which

$$\mu_r = \alpha + \beta r$$
$$\sigma_r^2 = \gamma + \zeta r$$

that is, in the case in which both the drift and the instantaneous variance are linear in the risk factor, the solution is

$$D(t, T) = \exp[A(T - t) - M(T - t) r(t)]$$

These models are called *affine factor models*, because interest rates are affine functions of the risk factor.

The general shape of the instantaneous drift used in one-factor affine models is $\mu_r = k(\theta - r)$, so that the interest rate is recalled toward a long run equilibrium level θ: this feature of the model is called *mean reversion*. Setting $\zeta = 0$ and $\gamma > 0$ then leads to the Vasicek model, in which the conditional distribution of the instantaneous interest rate is normal. Alternatively, assuming $\zeta > 0$ and $\gamma = 0$ then leads to the famous Cox, Ingersoll and Ross model: the stochastic process followed by the instantaneous interest rate is a *square root* process, and the conditional distribution is non-central chi-square. The case in which $\zeta > 0$ and $\gamma > 0$ is a more general process studied in Pearson and Sun (1994). Finally, the affine factor model result was proved in full generality with an extension to an arbitrary number of risk factors by Duffie and Kan (1996).

Looking at the solution for the discount factor $D(t, T)$, it is clear that the function $M(T - t)$ is particularly relevant, because it represents its sensitivity to the risk factor $r(t)$. In fact, using Ito's lemma we may write the dynamics of $D(t, T)$ under the risk-neutral measure as

$$dD(t, T) = r(t) D(t, T) \, dt + \sigma_T M(T - t) D(t, T) \, d\widetilde{z}(t)$$

1.4.2 Forward martingale measure

Consider now the problem of pricing a contingent claim whose pay-off is a function of the interest rate. Remember that, differently from the Black–Scholes framework, the discount factor to be applied to the contingent claim is now stochastic and, if the underlying is an interest rate sensitive product, it is not independent from the pay-off. The consequence is that the discount factor and the expected pay-off under the risk-neutral measure cannot be factorized. To make a simple example, consider a call option written on a zero coupon bond maturing at time T, for strike K and exercise time τ. We have:

$$\text{CALL}\,(D\,(t,T)\,,t;\tau,K) = E_Q\left[\exp\left[-\int_t^\tau r\,(u)\,du\right]\max\left[D\,(\tau,T)-K,0\right]\|\,\Im_t\right]$$

$$\neq E_Q\left[\exp\left[-\int_t^\tau r\,(u)\,du\right]\Big\|\,\Im_t\right]$$

$$E_Q\left[\max\left[D\,(\tau,T)-K,0\right]\|\,\Im_t\right]$$

and the price cannot be expressed as the product of the discount factor $D\,(t,\tau)$ and the expected pay-off. Factorization can, however, be achieved through a suitable change of measure.

Consider the discount factors evaluated at time t for one unit of currency to be received at time τ and T respectively, with $\tau < T$. Their dynamics under the risk-neutral measure are

$$dD\,(t,T) = r\,(t)\,D\,(t,T)\,dt + \sigma_T D\,(t,T)\,d\widetilde{z}\,(t)$$

$$dD\,(t,\tau) = r\,(t)\,D\,(t,\tau)\,dt + \sigma_\tau D\,(t,\tau)\,d\widetilde{z}\,(t)$$

We can define $D\,(t,\tau,T)$ as the *forward price* set at time t for an investment starting at time τ and yielding one unit of currency at time T. A standard no-arbitrage argument yields

$$D\,(t,\tau,T) = \frac{D\,(t,T)}{D\,(t,\tau)}$$

The dynamics of the forward price can be recovered by using Ito's division rule.

Remark 1.1 [*Ito's division rule*]   Assume two diffusive processes $X\,(t)$ and $Y\,(t)$ following the dynamics

$$dX\,(t) = \mu_X X\,(t)\,dt + \sigma_X X\,(t)\,dz\,(t)$$

$$dY\,(t) = \mu_Y Y\,(t)\,dt + \sigma_Y Y\,(t)\,dz\,(t)$$

Then, the process $F\,(t) \equiv X\,(t)\,/\,Y\,(t)$ follows the dynamics

$$dF\,(t) = \mu_F F\,(t)\,dt + \sigma_F F\,(t)\,dz\,(t)$$

with

$$\sigma_F = \sigma_X - \sigma_Y$$

$$\mu_F = \mu_X - \mu_Y - \sigma_F \sigma_Y$$

Applying this result to our problem yields immediately

$$dD(t, \tau, T) = -\sigma_F \sigma_\tau D(t, \tau, T) \, dt + \sigma_F D(t, \tau, T) \, d\widetilde{z}(t)$$

$$\sigma_F = \sigma_T - \sigma_\tau$$

We may now use the Girsanov theorem to recover a new measure Q_τ under which $d\widehat{z} = d\widetilde{z} - \sigma_\tau dt$ is a Wiener process. We have then

$$dD(t, \tau, T) = \sigma_F D(t, \tau, T) \, d\widehat{z}(t)$$

and the forward price is a martingale. Under such a measure, the forward price of any future contract is equal to the expected spot value. We have

$$D(t, \tau, T) = E_{Q_\tau}[(D(\tau, \tau, T)) \mid \Im_t] = E_{Q_\tau}[(D(\tau, T)) \mid \Im_t]$$

and the measure Q_τ is called the *forward martingale measure*. This result, which was first introduced by Geman (1989) and Jamshidian (1989), is very useful to price interest rate derivatives. In fact, consider a derivative contract g, written on $D(t, T)$, promising the pay-off $G(D(\tau, T), \tau)$ at time τ. As $g(t)/D(t, \tau)$ is a martingale, we have immediately

$$g(D(t, \tau, T), t) = P(t, \tau) E_{Q_\tau}[G(D(\tau, T), \tau) \mid \Im_t]$$

and the factorization of the discount factor and expected pay-off is now correct.

To conclude, the cookbook recipe emerging from the forward martingale approach is that the forward price must be considered as the underlying asset of the derivative contract, instead of the spot.

1.4.3 LIBOR market model

While the standard classical interest rate pricing models are based on the dynamics of instantaneous spot and forward rates, the market practice is to refer to observed interest rates for investment over discrete time periods. In particular, the reference rate mostly used for short-term investments and indexed products is the 3-month LIBOR rate. Moreover, under market conventions, interest rates for investments below the one-year horizon are computed under simple compounding. So, the LIBOR interest rate for investment from t to T is defined as

$$L(t, T) = \frac{1}{T - t} \left(\frac{1}{D(t, T)} - 1 \right)$$

The corresponding forward rate is defined as

$$L(t, \tau, T) = \frac{1}{T - \tau} \left(\frac{1}{D(t, \tau, T)} - 1 \right) = \frac{1}{T - \tau} \left(\frac{D(t, \tau)}{D(t, T)} - 1 \right)$$

Notice that, under the forward martingale measure Q_T, we have immediately

$$L(t, \tau, T) = E_{Q_T}[L(\tau, \tau, T) \mid \Im_t] = E_{Q_T}[L(\tau, T) \mid \Im_t]$$

The price of a floater, i.e. a bond whose coupon stream is indexed to the LIBOR, is then evaluated as

$$\text{FLOATER}(t, t_N) = \sum_{j=1}^{N} \delta_i E_Q[D(t, t_j)L(t_{j-1}, t_j) \mid \Im_t] + P(t, t_N)$$

$$= \sum_{j=1}^{N} \delta_i D(t, t_j) E_{Q_{t_j}}[L(t_{j-1}, t_j) \mid \Im_t] + P(t, t_N)$$

$$= \sum_{j=1}^{N} D(t, t_j)\delta_i L(t, t_{j-1}, t_j) + P(t, t_N)$$

where the set $\{t, t_1, t_2, \ldots, t_N\}$ contains the dates at which a coupon is reset and the previous one is paid and $\delta_j = t_j - t_{j-1}$. Consider now a stream of call options written on the index rate for each coupon period. This product is called a *cap*, and the price is obtained, assuming a strike rate L_{CAP}, from

$$\text{CAP}(t, t_1, t_N) = \sum_{j=2}^{N} \delta_i E_Q[D(t, t_j) \max(L(t_{j-1}, t_j) - L_{\text{CAP}}), 0 \mid \Im_t]$$

$$= \sum_{j=2}^{N} \delta_i D(t, t_j) E_{Q_{t_j}}[\max(L(t_{j-1}, t_j) - L_{\text{CAP}}), 0 \mid \Im_t]$$

and each call option is called *caplet*. By the same token, a stream of put options are called *floor*, and are evaluated as

$$\text{FLOOR}(t, t_1, t_N) = \sum_{j=1}^{N} \delta_2 D(t, t_j) E_{Q_{t_j}}[\max(L_{\text{FLOOR}} - L(t_{j-1}, t_j)), 0 \mid \Im_t]$$

where L_{FLOOR} is the strike rate. The names *cap* and *floor* derive from the results, which may be easily verified

$$L(t_j, t_{j-1}) - \text{CAPLET}(t_j, t_{j-1}) = \min(L(t_{j-1}, t_j), L_{\text{CAP}})$$

$$L(t_j, t_{j-1}) + \text{FLOORLET}(t_j, t_{j-1}) = \max(L(t_{j-1}, t_j), L_{\text{FLOOR}})$$

Setting a cap and a floor amounts to building a *collar*, that is a band in which the coupon is allowed to float according to the interest rate. The price of each caplet and floorlet can then be computed under the corresponding forward measure. Under the assumption that each forward rate is log-normally distributed, we may again recover a pricing formula largely used in the market, known as Black's formula.

$$\text{CAPLET}(t; t_j, t_{j-1}) = D(t, t_j) E_{Q_{t_j}}[\max(L(t_{j-1}, t_j) - L_{\text{CAP}}), 0 \mid \Im_t]$$

$$= D(t, t_j)\{E_{Q_{t_j}}[L(t_{j-1}, t_j) \mid \Im_t]N(d_1) - L_{\text{CAP}}N(d_2)\}$$

$$= D(t, t_j)L(t, t_{j-1}, t_j)N(d_1) - D(t, t_j)L_{\text{CAP}}N(d_2)$$

$$d_1 = \frac{\ln(L(t, t_{j-1}, t_j)/L_{CAP}) + \sigma_j^2(t_j - t)}{\sigma_j\sqrt{t_j - t}}$$

$$d_2 = d_1 - \sigma_j\sqrt{t_j - t}$$

where σ_j is the instantaneous volatility of the logarithm of the forward rate $L\left(t, t_{j-1}, t_j\right)$. The floorlet price is obtained by using the corresponding put option formula

$$\text{FLOORLET}(t; t_j, t_{j-1}) = -D(t, t_j)L(t, t_{j-1}, t_j)N(-d_1) + D(t, t_j)L_{CAP}N(-d_2)$$

$$d_1 = \frac{\ln(L(t, t_{j-1}, t_j)/L_{FLOOR}) + \sigma_j^2(t_j - t)}{\sigma_j\sqrt{t_j - t}}$$

$$d_2 = d_1 - \sigma_j\sqrt{t_j - t}$$

1.5 SMILE AND TERM STRUCTURE EFFECTS OF VOLATILITY

The Black–Scholes model, which, as we saw, can be applied to the pricing of contingent claims on several markets, has been severely challenged by the data. The contradiction emerges from a look at the market quotes of options and a comparison with the implied information, that is, with the dynamics of the underlying that would make these prices consistent. In the Black–Scholes setting, this information is collected in the same parameter, volatility, which is assumed to be constant both across time and different states of the world. This parameter, called *implied* volatility, represents a sufficient statistic for the risk-neutral probability in the Black–Scholes setting: the instantaneous rate of returns on the assets are in fact assumed normal and with first moments equal to the risk-free rate. Contrary to this assumption, implied volatility is typically different both across different strike prices and different maturities. The first evidence is called the *smile* effect and the second is called the *volatility term structure*.

Non-constant implied volatility can be traced back to market imperfections or it may actually imply that the stochastic process assumed for the underlying asset is not borne out by the data, namely that the rate of return on the assets is not normally distributed. The latter interpretation is indeed supported by a long history of evidence on non-normality of returns on almost every market. This raises the question of which model to adopt to get a better fit of the risk-neutral distribution and market data.

1.5.1 Stochastic volatility models

A first approach is to model volatility as a second risk factor affecting the price of the derivative contract. This implies two aspects, which may make the model involved. The first is the dependence structure between volatility and the underlying. The second is that the risk factor represented by volatility must be provided with a market price, something that makes the model harder to calibrate.

A model that is particularly easy to handle, and reminds us of the Hull and White (1987) model, could be based on the assumption that volatility risk is not priced in the market, and volatility is orthogonal to the price of the underlying. The idea is that conditional on a given volatility parameter taking value s, the stochastic process followed by the underlying asset follows a geometric brownian motion. The conditional value of the call would then yield the standard Black–Scholes solution. As volatility is stochastic and is not known at the time of evaluation, the option is priced by integrating the Black–Scholes formula times the volatility density across its whole support. Analytically, the pricing formula for a call option yields, for example,

$$\text{CALL}\,(S(t), t, \sigma(t); K, T) = \int_0^\infty \text{CALL}_{\text{BS}}\,(S, t; \sigma(t) = s, K, T)\, q_\sigma\,(s \mid \Im_t)\, \mathrm{d}s$$

where CALL_{BS} denotes the Black–Scholes formula for call options and $q_\sigma\,(s \mid \Im_t)$ represents the volatility conditional density.

Extensions of this model account for a dependence structure between volatility and the underlying asset. A good example could be to model instantaneous variance as a square root process, to exploit its property to be defined on the non-negative support only and the possibility, for some parameter configurations, of making zero volatility an *inaccessible barrier*. Indeed, this idea is used both in Heston (1993) and in Longstaff and Schwartz (1992) for interest rate derivatives.

1.5.2 Local volatility models

A different idea is to make the representation of the diffusive process more general by modeling volatility as a function of the underlying asset and time. We have then, under the risk-neutral measure

$$\mathrm{d}S\,(t) = rS\,(t)\, \mathrm{d}t + \sigma\,(S, t)\, S\,(t)\, \mathrm{d}\widetilde{z}\,(t)$$

The function $\sigma\,(S, t)$ is called the *local volatility surface* and should then be calibrated in such a way as to produce the smile and volatility term structure effects actually observed on the market. A long-dated proposal is represented by the so-called *constant elasticity of variance* (CEV) models, in which

$$\mathrm{d}S\,(t) = rS\,(t)\, \mathrm{d}t + \sigma S\,(t)^\alpha\, \mathrm{d}\widetilde{z}\,(t)$$

Alternative local volatility specifications were proposed to comply with techniques that are commonly used by practitioners in the market to fit the smile. An idea is to resort to the so-called *mixture of log-normal* or *shifted log-normal* distributions. Intuitively, this approach leads to closed form valuations. For example, assuming that the risk-neutral probability distribution Q is represented by a linear combination of n log-normal distributions Q_j

$$Q\,(S\,(T) \mid \Im_t) = \sum_{j=1}^n \lambda_j Q_j\,(X_j\,(T) \mid \Im_t)$$

where X_j are latent random variables drawn from log-normal distributions Q_j, corresponding to geometric brownian motions with volatility σ_j. It may be checked that the price of a call option in this model can be recovered as

$$\text{CALL}\,(S(t), t; K, T) = \sum_{j=1}^n \lambda_j \text{CALL}_{\text{BS}}\,(X_j, t; K, T)$$

Brigo and Mercurio (2001) provide the corresponding local volatility specification corresponding to this model, obtaining

$$dS(t) = rS(t)\,dt + \sqrt{\frac{\sum_{j=1}^{n} \sigma_j^2 \lambda_j q_j(X_j(T) \mid \mathfrak{I}_t)}{\sum_{j=1}^{n} \lambda_j q_j(X_j(T) \mid \mathfrak{I}_t)}} \, S(t)\,d\widetilde{z}(t)$$

where $q_j\left(X_j(T) \mid \mathfrak{I}_t\right)$ are the densities corresponding to the distribution functions Q_j. Once the mixture weights λ_j are recovered from observed plain vanilla option prices, the corresponding dynamics of the underlying asset under the risk-neutral measure can be simulated in order to price exotic products.

1.5.3 Implied probability

A different idea is to use non-parametric techniques to extract general information concerning the risk-neutral probability distribution and dynamics implied by observed options market quotes. The concept was first suggested by Breeden and Litzenberger (1978) and pushes forward the usual implied volatility idea commonly used in the Black–Scholes framework. This is the approach that we will use in this book.

The basic concepts stem from the martingale representation of option prices. Take, for example, a call option

$$\text{CALL}(S, t; K, T) = \exp[-r(T-t)]\,E_Q[\max(S(T) - K, 0)]$$

By computing the derivative of the pricing function with respect to the strike K we easily obtain

$$\frac{\partial \text{CALL}(S, t; K, T)}{\partial K} = -\exp[-r(T-t)](1 - Q(K \mid \mathfrak{I}_t))$$

where $Q(K \mid \mathfrak{I}_t)$ is the conditional distribution function under the risk-neutral measure. Defining

$$\overline{Q}(K \mid \mathfrak{I}_t) \equiv 1 - Q(K \mid \mathfrak{I}_t)$$

that is, the probability corresponding to the complementary event $\Pr(S(T) > K)$, we may rewrite

$$\overline{Q}(K \mid \mathfrak{I}_t) = -\exp[r(T-t)]\frac{\partial \text{CALL}(S, t; K, T)}{\partial K}$$

So, the risk-neutral probability of exercise of the call option is recovered from the forward value of the derivative of the call option, apart from a change of sign. The result can be immediately verified in the Black–Scholes model, where we easily compute $\overline{Q}(K \mid \mathfrak{I}_t) = N(d_2(K))$.

Remark 1.2 Notice that by integrating the relationship above from K to infinity, the price of the call option can also be written as

$$\text{CALL}(S, t; K, T) = \exp[-r(T-t)]\int_K^\infty \overline{Q}(u \mid \mathfrak{I}_t)\,du$$

where we remark that the cumulative probability, rather than the density, appears in the integrand. As we will see, this pricing representation will be used again and again throughout this book.

Symmetric results hold for put prices which, in the martingale representation, are written as

$$\text{PUT}(S, t; K, T) = \exp[-r(T - t)] E_Q[\max(K - S(T), 0)]$$

Computing the derivative with respect to the strike and reordering terms we have

$$Q(K \mid \Im_t) = \exp[r(T - t)] \frac{\partial \text{PUT}(S, t; K, T)}{\partial K}$$

that is, the implied risk-neutral distribution. Again, we may check that, under the standard Black–Scholes setting, we obtain

$$Q(K \mid \Im_t) = N(-d_2(K)) = 1 - N(d_2(K))$$

Furthermore, integrating from zero to K we have

$$\text{PUT}(S, t; K, T) = \exp[-r(T - t)] \int_0^K Q(u \mid \Im_t)\, \mathrm{d}u$$

Finally, notice that the density function can be obtained from the second derivatives of the put and call prices. We have

$$q(K \mid \Im_t) \equiv \frac{\partial Q(K \mid \Im_t)}{\partial K} = \exp[r(T - t)] \frac{\partial^2 \text{PUT}(S, t; K, T)}{\partial K^2}$$

$$q(K \mid \Im_t) = -\frac{\partial \overline{Q}(K \mid \Im_t)}{\partial K} = \exp[r(T - t)] \frac{\partial^2 \text{CALL}(S, t; K, T)}{\partial K^2}$$

The strength of these results stems from the fact that they directly rely on the no-arbitrage requirement imposed by the martingale relationship. In this sense, they are far more general than the assumptions underlying the Black–Scholes setting. Indeed, if the assumptions behind the Black–Scholes model were borne out by the data, the results above would be of little use, as all the information sufficient to characterize the risk-neutral distribution would be represented by the volatility implied by the prices. If the price distribution is not lognormal, these results are instead extremely useful, enabling one to extract the risk-neutral probability distribution, rather that its moments, directly from the option prices.

1.6   INCOMPLETE MARKETS

The most recent challenge to the standard derivative pricing model, and to its basic structure, is represented by the *incomplete market* problem. A brief look over the strategy used to recover the *fair price* of a derivative contract shows that a crucial role is played by the assumption that the future value of each financial product can be *exactly* replicated by some trading strategy. Technically, we say that each product is *attainable* and the market is *complete*. In other words, every contingent claim is endowed with a *perfect hedge*. Both in the binomial and in the continuous time model we see that it is this assumption that leads to two strong results. The first is a unique risk-neutral measure and, through that, a unique price for each and every asset in the economy. The second is that this price is obtained with no reference to any preference structure of the agents in the market, apart from the very weak (and realistic) requirement that they "prefer more to less".

Unfortunately, the completeness assumption has been fiercely challenged by the market. Every trader has always been well aware that *no perfect hedge exists*, but the structure of derivatives markets nowadays has made consideration of this piece of truth unavoidable. Structured finance has brought about a huge proliferation of customized and exotic products. Hedge funds manufacture and manage derivatives on exotic markets and illiquid products to earn money from their misalignment: think particularly of long–short and relative value hedge fund strategies. Credit derivatives markets have been created to trade protection on loans, bonds, or mortgage portfolios. All of this has been shifting the core of the derivatives market away from the traditional underlying assets traded on the organized markets, such as stocks and government bonds, toward contingent claims written on illiquid assets. The effect has been to make the problem of finding a *perfect hedge* an impossible task for most of the derivative pricing applications, and the assumption of complete markets an unacceptable approximation. The hot topic in derivative pricing is then which hedge to choose, facing the reality that no hedging strategy can be considered completely safe.

1.6.1 Back to utility theory

The main effect of accounting for market incompleteness has been to bring utility theory back in derivative pricing techniques. Intuitively, if no perfect hedge exists, every replication strategy is a lottery, and selecting one amounts to defining a preference ranking among them, which is the main subject of utility theory. In a sense, the ironic fate of finance is that the market incompleteness problem is bringing it back from a preference-free paradigm to a use of utility theory very similar to early portfolio theory applications: this trend is clearly witnessed by terms such as "minimum variance hedging" (Follmer & Schweitzer, 1991). Of course, we know that the minimum variance principle is based on restrictive assumptions concerning both the preference structure and the distributional properties of the hedging error. One extension is to use more general expected utility representations, such as exponential or power preferences, to select a specific hedging strategy and the corresponding martingale measure (Frittelli, 2000).

A question that could also be useful to debate, even though it is well beyond the scope of this book, is whether the axiomatic structure leading to the standard expected utility framework is flexible enough and appropriate to be applied to the hedging error problem. More precisely, it is well known that standard expected utility results rest on the so-called independence axiom, which has been debated and criticized in decision theory for decades, and which seems particularly relevant to the problem at hand. To explain the problem in plain words, consider you prefer hedging strategy A to another denoted B ($A \succeq B$). The independence axiom reads that you will also prefer $\alpha A + (1 - \alpha) C$ to $\alpha B + (1 - \alpha) C$ for every $\alpha \in [0, 1]$, and for whatever strategy C. This is the crucial point: the preference structure between two hedging strategies is preserved under a mixture with any other third strategy, and if this is not true the expected utility results do not carry over. It is not difficult to argue that this assumption may be too restrictive, if, for example, one considers a hedging strategy C counter-monotone to B and orthogonal to A. Indeed, most of the developments in decision theory were motivated by the need to account for the possibility of hedging relationships among strategies, that are not allowed for under the standard expected utility framework. The solutions proposed are typically the restriction of the independence axiom to a subset of the available strategies. Among them, an interesting choice is to restrict C to the set of so-called *constant acts*, which in our application means a strategy yielding a risk-free return. This was proposed by Gilboa and Schmeidler (1989) and leads to a decision strategy called *Maximin Expected Utility* (MMEU). In intuitive terms, this strategy can be described as one taking into account the worst possible probability scenario for every possible event. As we are going to see in the following paragraph, this worst probability scenario corresponds to what in the mathematics of incomplete market pricing are called *super-replication* or *super-hedging* strategies.

1.6.2 Super-hedging strategies

Here we follow Cherubini (1997) and Cherubini and Della Lunga (2001) in order to provide a general formal representation of the incomplete market problem, i.e. the problem of pricing a contingent claim on an asset that cannot be exactly replicated. In this setting, a general contingent claim $g(S, t)$ with pay-off $G(S, T)$, can be priced computing

$$g(S, t) = \exp[-r(T - t)] E_Q [G(S, T) ; Q \in \wp \mid \Im_t]$$

where E_Q represents the expectation with respect to a conditional risk-neutral measure Q. Here and in the following we focus on the financial meaning of the issue and assume that the technical conditions required to ensure that the problem is well-defined are met (the readers are referred to Delbaen & Schachermayer, 1994, for details). The set $\wp$ contains the risk-neutral measures and describes the information available on the underlying asset. If it is very precise, and the set $\wp$ contains a single probability measure, we are in the standard complete market pricing setting tackled above. In the case in which we do not have precise information – for example, because of limited liquidity of the underlying – we have the problem of choosing a single probability measure, or a pricing strategy. Therefore, in order to price the contingent claim g in this incomplete market setting, we have to define: (i) the set of probability measures $\wp$ and (ii) a set of rules describing a strategy to select the appropriate measure and price. As discussed above, one could resort to expected utility to give a preference rank for the probabilities in the set, picking out the optimal one. As an alternative, or prior to that, one could instead rely on some more conservative strategy, selecting a range of prices: the bounds of this range would yield the highest and lowest price consistent with the no-arbitrage assumption, and the replicating strategies corresponding to these bounds are known as *super-replicating* portfolios. In this case we have

$$g^-(S, t) = \exp[-r(T - t)] \inf E_Q [G(S, T) ; Q \in \wp \mid \Im_t]$$
$$g^+(S, t) = \exp[-r(T - t)] \sup E_Q [G(S, T) ; Q \in \wp \mid \Im_t]$$

More explicitly, the lower bound is called the *buyer price* of the derivative contract g, while the upper bound is denoted the *seller price*. The idea is that if the price were lower than the buyer price, one could buy the contingent claim and go short a replicating portfolio ending up with an arbitrage gain. Conversely, if the price were higher than the maximum, one could short the asset and buy a replicating portfolio earning a safe return. Depending on the definition of the set of probability measures, one is then allowed to recover different values for long and short positions. Notice that this does not hold for models that address the incomplete market pricing problem in a standard expected utility setting, in which the selected measure yields the same value for long and short positions.

Uncertain probability model

The most radical way to address the problem of super-replication is to take the worst possible probability scenario for every event. To take the simplest case, that of a call digital option paying one unit of currency at time T if the underlying asset is greater than or equal to K, we have

$$DC^- (S, t) = \exp [-r (T - t)] \inf E_Q \left[\mathbf{1}_{S(T) \geqslant K}; Q \in \wp \mid \Im_t \right]$$

$$= \exp [-r (T - t)] \inf \left[\overline{Q} (K); Q \in \wp \mid \Im_t \right] \equiv B (t, T) \overline{Q}^-$$

$$DC^+ (S, t) = \exp [-r (T - t)] \sup E_Q \left[\mathbf{1}_{S(T) \geqslant K}; Q \in \wp \mid \Im_t \right]$$

$$= \exp [-r (T - t)] \sup E_Q \left[\overline{Q} (K); Q \in \wp \mid \Im_t \right] \equiv B (t, T) \overline{Q}^+$$

where we recall the definition $\overline{Q} (K) \equiv 1 - Q (K)$ and where the subscripts '+' and '−' stand for the upper and lower value of $\overline{Q} (K)$.

Having defined the pricing bounds for the digital option, which represents the pricing kernel of any contingent claim written on asset S, we may proceed to obtain pricing bounds for call and put options using the integral representations recovered in section 1.5.3. Remember in fact that the price of a European call option C under the martingale measure Q may be written in very general terms as

$$\text{CALL} (S, t; K, T) = \exp [-r (T - t)] \int_K^\infty \overline{Q} (u \mid \Im_t) \, du$$

We know that if the kernel were the log-normal distribution, the equation would yield the Black–Scholes formula. Here we want instead to use the formula to recover the pricing bounds for the option. The buyer price is then obtained by solving the problem

$$\text{CALL}^- (S, t; K, T) = \exp [-r (T - t)] \int_K^\infty \overline{Q}^- (u) \, du$$

By the same token, the seller price is obtained from

$$\text{CALL}^+ (S, t; K, T) = \exp [-r (T - t)] \int_K^\infty \overline{Q}^+ (u) \, du$$

and represents the corresponding upper bound for the value of the call option in the most general setting.

The same could be done for the European put option with the same strike and maturity. In this case we would have

$$\text{PUT} (S, t; K, T) = \exp [-r (T - t)] \int_0^K Q (u \mid \Im_t) \, du$$

for any conditional measure $Q \in \wp$ and the pricing bounds would be

$$\text{PUT}^- (S, t; K, T) = \exp[-r(T - t)] \int_0^K Q^- (u \mid \Im_t) \, du$$

$$\text{PUT}^+ (S, t; K, T) = \exp[-r(T - t)] \int_0^K Q^+ (u \mid \Im_t) \, du$$

where $Q^- (u)$ and $Q^+ (u)$ have the obvious meanings of the lower and upper bound of the probability distribution for every u. Notice that whatever pricing kernel, Q in the $\wp$ set has to be a probability measure, so it follows that $Q(u) + \overline{Q}(u) = 1$. This implies that we must have

$$Q^- (u) + \overline{Q}^+ (u) = 1$$
$$Q^+ (u) + \overline{Q}^- (u) = 1$$

In the case of incomplete markets, in which the set $\wp$ is not a singleton, we have $Q^- (u) < Q^+ (u)$, which implies

$$Q^- (u) + \overline{Q}^- (u) = Q^- (u) + \left[1 - Q^+ (u) \right] < 1$$

and the measure Q^- is sub-additive. In the same way, it is straightforward to check that

$$Q^+ (u) + \overline{Q}^+ (u) > 1$$

and the measure Q^+ is super-additive.

So, if we describe the probability set as above, the result is that the buyer and seller prices are integrals with respect to non-additive measures, technically known as *capacities*. The integrals defined above are well defined even for non-additive measures, in which case they are known in the literature as *Choquet integrals*. This integral is in fact widely used in the modern decision theory trying to amend the standard expected utility framework: lotteries are ranked using capacities instead of probability measures and expected values are defined in terms of Choquet integrals rather than Lebesgue integrals, as is usual in the standard expected utility framework.

Example 1.2 [*Fuzzy measure model*]   A particular parametric form of the approach above was proposed by Cherubini (1997) and Cherubini and Della Lunga (2001). The idea is drawn from fuzzy measure theory: the parametric form suggested is called Sugeno fuzzy measure. Given a probability distribution Q and a parameter $\lambda \in \Re_+$, define

$$\overline{Q}^- (u) = \frac{1 - Q(u)}{1 + \lambda Q(u)} \qquad \overline{Q}^+ (u) = \frac{1 - Q(u)}{1 + \lambda^* Q(u)}$$

with

$$\lambda^* = -\frac{\lambda}{1 + \lambda}$$

It may be easily checked that the measure $\overline{Q}^-$ is sub-additive, and $\overline{Q}^+$ is the dual super-additive measure in the sense described above.

The pricing bounds for call options are then recovered as discussed above based on any choice of the reference probability distribution Q. If the pricing kernel is chosen to be log-normal, we obtain

$$\text{CALL}^-(S, t; K, T) = \exp[-r(T - t)] \int_{d_2}^{\infty} \frac{\Phi(u)}{1 + \lambda \Phi(-u)} du$$

$$\text{CALL}^+(S, t; K, T) = \exp[-r(T - t)] \int_{d_2}^{\infty} \frac{\Phi(u)}{1 + \lambda^* \Phi(-u)} du$$

Notice that in the case $\lambda = \lambda^* = 0$ the model yields the Black–Scholes formula. For any value $\lambda > 0$, the model yields buyer and seller prices. The discount (premium) applied to buyer (seller) prices is higher the more the option is *out-of-the-money*.

Uncertain volatility model

An alternative strategy to address the incomplete market problem would be to define a set of risk-neutral dynamics of the underlying asset, rather than the set of risk-neutral measures. A typical example is to assume that the volatility parameter is not known exactly, and is considered to be included in a given interval. Assume further that the stochastic process followed by the underlying asset is a geometric brownian motion. Under any risk-neutral measure Q we have

$$dS(t) = rS(t) \, dt + \sigma S(t) \, d\widetilde{z}$$

and we assume that $\sigma \in [\sigma^-, \sigma^+]$. This model is called the *uncertain volatility model* (UVM) and is due to Avellaneda, Levy and Parás (1995) and Avellaneda and Parás (1996).

Working through the solution as in the standard Black–Scholes framework, assume to build a dynamic hedged portfolio. Notice that if we knew the exact value of the σ parameter, the delta hedging strategy could be designed precisely, enabling perfect replication of the contingent claim. Unfortunately, we are only allowed to know the interval in which the true volatility value is likely to be located, and we are not aware of any probability distribution about it. Assume that we take a conservative strategy designing the hedging policy under the worst possible volatility scenario. Avellaneda, Levy and Parás (1995) show that this leads to the pricing formula

$$\frac{\partial g}{\partial t} + \frac{1}{2} \sigma^2 S^2(t) \left[\frac{\partial^2 g}{\partial S^2} \right]^+ + rS \frac{\partial g}{\partial S} - rg = 0$$

with

$$\left[\frac{\partial^2 g}{\partial S^2} \right]^+ = \begin{Bmatrix} \sigma^- & (\partial^2 g / \partial S^2) > 0 \\ \sigma^+ & (\partial^2 g / \partial S^2) < 0 \end{Bmatrix}$$

Notice that the partial differential equation is a modified non-linear version of the Black–Scholes no-arbitrage condition. The non-linearity is given by the fact that the multiplicative term of the second partial derivative is a function of the sign of the second partial derivative. This equation was denoted the BSB (Black, Scholes & Barenblatt) fundamental equation. The solution has to be carried out numerically except in trivial cases in which it may be proved that the solution is globally convex or concave, when it obviously delivers the same results as the standard Black–Scholes model. Notice also that in this approach, as in the previous uncertain probability model, the result yields different values for long and short positions.

1.7 CREDIT RISK

The recent developments of the market have brought about a large increase of credit risk exposures and products. On the one hand, this has been due to the massive shift of the investment practices from standard stocks and bonds products toward the so-called *alternative investments*. This shift has been motivated both by the quest for portfolio diversification and the research of higher returns in a low interest rate period. Moreover, another face of credit risk has become increasingly relevant along with the progressive shift from the classical standard intermediation business toward structured finance products, and the need to resort to *over-the-counter* (OTC) transactions to hedge the corresponding exposure. Contrary to what happens in derivatives transactions operated in *futures-style* organized markets, OTC deals involve some credit risk, as the counterparty in the contract may default by the time it has to honor its obligations. The credit-risk feature involved in derivative contracts is known as *counterparty risk*, and has been getting all the more relevant in the risk management debate.

A very general way to represent the pay-off of a *defaultable* contingent claim – that is, a contract in which the counterparty may go bankrupt – is

$$G\,(S,T)\,[1 - \mathbf{1}_{\{\text{DEF}\}}(T)\text{LGD}]$$

where $\mathbf{1}_{\{\text{DEF}\}}$ is the indicator function denoting the default of the counterparty by time T and LGD is the *loss given default* figure, also defined as $\text{LGD} \equiv 1 - \text{RR}$, that is one minus the *recovery rate*. In very general terms, the value of the contract at time t is computed under the risk-neutral measure as

$$E_Q\left[\exp\left[-\int_t^T r\,(u)\,\mathrm{d}u\right]G\,(S,T)\,[1 - \mathbf{1}_{\{\text{DEF}\}}\text{LGD}]\right]$$

Notice that there are three risk factors involved in this representation: (i) market risk due to fluctuations of the underlying asset S; (ii) interest rate risk due to changes in the discount factor; and (iii) credit risk due to the event of default of the counterparty. We will see that evaluating defaultable contingent claims in this framework crucially involves the evaluation of the dependence structure among the sources of risk involved. Fortunately, we know that one of the sources may be made orthogonal by the change in measure corresponding to the bond numeraire (*forward martingale measure*). In this case we have

$$D\,(t,T)\,E_{Q_T}[G\,(S,T)\,[1 - \mathbf{1}_{\{\text{DEF}\}}\text{LGD}]]$$

and the credit risk problem is intrinsically bivariate, involving the dependence structure between the underlying dynamics and default of the counterparty.

The standard credit risk problem that we are used to think of is only the simplest case in this general representation. Setting in fact $G(S, T) = 1$ we have the standard defaultable bond pricing problem. In the discussion below, we will first address this topic, before extending it to the case in which the defaultable security is a derivative contract. Dealing with the simplest case will enable us to stress that credit risk itself is similar to an exposure in the derivative market. Curiously enough, it can be seen as a position in an option, following the so-called structural approach, or as a position with the same features as an interest rate derivative, according the so-called reduced form approach.

1.7.1 Structural models

Structural models draw the main idea from the pioneering paper by Merton (1974). Assume that an entrepreneur is funding a project whose value is $V(t)$ with debt issued in the form of a zero coupon bond with a face value of $\overline{DD}$. The debt is reimbursed at time T. If at that date the value of the asset side of the firm is high enough to cover the value of debt, the nominal value is repaid and equityholders get the remaining value. If instead the value of the firm is not sufficient to repay the debt, it is assumed that the debtholders take over the firm at no cost, and stockholders get zero (a feature called *limited liability*). The pay-off value of debt at maturity is then $\min(\overline{DD}, V(T))$, while the value of equity is what is left after bondholders have been repaid (we say stockholders are *residual claimants*).

$$C(T) = \max(V(T) - \overline{DD}, 0)$$

The value of equity capital is then the value of a call option written on the asset value of the firm for a strike equal to the face value of the debt. Notice that the value of debt at the same date can be decomposed alternatively as

$$DD(T) = V(T) - \max(V(T) - \overline{DD}, 0)$$

or

$$DD(T) = \overline{DD} - \max(\overline{DD} - V(T), 0)$$

The latter representation is particularly instructive. The value of defaultable debt is the same as that of default-free debt plus a short position in a put option written on the asset value of the firm for a strike equal to the face value of debt. Notice that if put–call parity holds we have

$$V(T) = \max(V(T) - \overline{DD}, 0) + \overline{DD} - \max(\overline{DD} - V(T), 0)$$

and the value of the firm is equal to the value of equity, the call option, plus the value of debt, in turn decomposed into default-free debt minus a put option. This result is known in the corporate finance literature as the *Modigliani–Miller* theorem. Let us remark that it is not a simple accounting identity, but rather a separation result: it means that the value of the asset side of a firm is invariant under different funding policies; to put it another way, following an increase in the amount of nominal debt its value increases exactly by the same amount as the decrease in the value of equity. It is well known that this is only true under very restrictive assumptions, such as the absence of taxes and bankruptcy costs, or agency costs. Accounting for all of these effects would imply a break-up of the relationship above, and the choice of the amount of debt would have a feedback effect on the output of the firm.

Apart from such possible complications, it is clear that option theory could be applied to recover both the value of debt and equity, and to decompose debt into the default-free part and the credit risk premium.

Assume that the asset side of the firm $V(t)$ follows a geometric brownian motion, so that under the risk-neutral measure we have

$$dV(t) = rV(t) \, dt + \sigma_V V(t) \, d\tilde{z}(t)$$

Then, the standard Black–Scholes formula can be applied to yield the value of equity C

$$C(t) = V(t) \Phi(d_1) - \exp(-r(T-t)) \overline{DD} \Phi(d_2)$$

$$d_1 = \frac{\ln(V(t)/\overline{DD}) + (r + \sigma_V^2/2)(T-t)}{\sigma_V \sqrt{T-t}}$$

$$d_2 = d_1 - \sigma_V \sqrt{T-t}$$

and the value of debt DD is recovered as

$$DD(t) = V(t) - [V(t)\Phi(d_1) - \exp(-r(T-t))\overline{DD}\Phi(d_2)]$$

$$= \Phi(-d_1)V(t) + \exp(-r(T-t))\overline{DD}\Phi(d_2)$$

Notice that, by adding and subtracting $\exp(-r(T-t))\overline{DD}$ we can rewrite the value as

$$DD(t) = \exp(-r(T-t))\overline{DD} - \left[-V(t)\Phi(-d_1) + \exp(-r(T-t))\overline{DD}\Phi(-d_2)\right]$$

and we recognize the short position in the put option representing credit risk.

The result could be rewritten by defining the underlying asset of the option in percentage terms, rather than in money amounts. For this reason, we introduce

$$d = \frac{\exp(-r(T-t))\overline{DD}}{V(t)}$$

which is called by Merton *quasi-debt-to-firm-value ratio* or *quasi-leverage*. The *quasi* term is motivated by the fact that the debt is discounted using the risk-free rate rather than the defaultable discount factor. We have

$$DD(t) = \exp(-r(T-t))\overline{DD}\left\{1 - \left[-\frac{1}{d}\Phi(-d_1) + \Phi(-d_2)\right]\right\}$$

$$d_1 = \frac{\ln(1/d) + \sigma_V^2/2(T-t)}{\sigma_V \sqrt{T-t}}$$

$$d_2 = d_1 - \sigma_V \sqrt{T-t}$$

Remembering that the probability of exercise of a put option is equal to $\Phi(-d_2)$, a modern way to rewrite the formula above would be

$$DD(t) = \exp(-r(T-t))\,\overline{DD}\left\{1 - \Phi(-d_2)\left[1 - \frac{1}{d}\frac{\Phi(-d_1)}{\Phi(-d_2)}\right]\right\}$$

$$= \exp(-r(T-t))\,\overline{DD}\,\{1 - Dp * LGD\}$$

where Dp stands for default probability and LGD is the *loss given default* figure in this model.

$$Dp = \Phi(-d_2)$$

$$LGD = 1 - \frac{1}{d}\frac{\Phi(-d_1)}{\Phi(-d_2)}$$

Notice that both the default probability and the loss given default are dependent on the quasi leverage d.

Finally, in order to account for different maturities, credit risk can be represented in terms of credit spreads as

$$r^*(t,T) - r = -\frac{\ln\left\{1 - \Phi(-d_2)\left[1 - \frac{1}{d}\frac{\Phi(-d_1)}{\Phi(-d_2)}\right]\right\}}{T-t}$$

$$= -\frac{\ln\{1 - Dp * LGD\}}{T-t}$$

where $r^*(t,T)$ is the yield to maturity of the defaultable bond.

While the original model is based on very restrictive assumptions, some extensions have been proposed to make it more realistic. In particular, the extension to defaultable coupon bond debt was handled in Geske (1977), while the possibility of default events prior to maturity as well as the effects of debt seniority structures was tackled in Black and Cox (1976). Finally, the effects of bankruptcy costs, strategic debt servicing behavior and absolute priority violations were taken into account in Anderson and Sundaresan (1996) and Madan and Unal (2000).

Structural models represent a particularly elegant approach to defaultable bond evaluation and convey the main idea that credit risk basically amounts to a short position in an option. Unfortunately, the hypothesis that both the recovery rate and default probability depend on the same state variable, i.e. the value of the firm, may represent a serious drawback to the flexibility of the model, overlooking other events that may trigger default. As a result, the credit spreads that are generated by this model consistently with reasonable values of asset volatility turn out to be much smaller than those actually observed on the market. Furthermore, the fact that the value of the asset is modeled as a diffusive process observed in continuous time gives a typical hump-shaped credit spread curve (in the usual case with $d < 1$) with zero intercept: technically speaking this is due to the fact that default is a *predictable* event with respect to the information set available at any time t. Three different ways have been suggested to solve this problem: the first is to include a jump in the process followed by the value of assets (Zhou, 1996); the second is to assume that the value of the underlying is not observable in continuous time (Duffie & Lando, 2001); the third is to assume that the default barrier is not observed at any time t (the CreditGrades approach followed by Finger et al., 2002).

1.7.2 Reduced form models

A more radical approach to yield a flexible parametric representation for the credit spreads observed in the market is to model default probability and loss given default separately. By contrast with structural models, this approach is called the reduced form.

Assuming the recovery rate to be exogenously given, the most straightforward idea is to model the default event as a Poisson process. We know that the probability distribution of this process is indexed by a parameter called *intensity* (or hazard rate): for this reason, these models are also called *intensity based*. If γ is the intensity of the Poisson process representing default, the probability that this event will not occur by time T is described by the function

$$\Pr(\tau > T) = \exp\left[-\gamma(T - t)\right]$$

where we assume $\tau > t$, that is, the firm is not in default as of time t. Assume that under the risk-neutral measure Q we have

$$E_Q[1 - \mathbf{1}_{\text{DEF}}] \equiv \Pr(\tau > T) = \exp\left[-\gamma(T - t)\right]$$

and that the default event is independent of interest rate fluctuations. Furthermore, let us assume that the recovery rate RR is equal to zero, so that the whole principal is lost in case of default. Under these assumptions, the price of a defaultable zero-coupon bond maturing at time T is simply

$$DD(t, T; \text{RR} = 0) = D(t, T) E_Q[1 - \mathbf{1}_{\text{DEF}}]$$
$$= D(t, T) \exp\left[-\gamma(T - t)\right]$$

and the credit spread is obtained as

$$r^{\star}(t, T; \text{RR} = 0) - r(t, T) \equiv \left(-\frac{\ln DD(t, T; \text{RR} = 0)}{T - t}\right) - \left(-\frac{\ln D(t, T)}{T - t}\right) = \gamma$$

In this special case the credit spread curve is flat and equal to the intensity figure of the default process.

In the more general case of a positive recovery rate $\text{RR} \equiv 1 - \text{LGD}$, assumed to be non-stochastic, we have instead

$$DD(t, T; \text{RR}) = D(t, T) E_Q[1 - \mathbf{1}_{\text{DEF}}\text{LGD}]$$
$$= D(t, T) E_Q[(1 - \mathbf{1}_{\text{DEF}}) + \text{RR}\mathbf{1}_{\text{DEF}}]$$
$$= D(t, T) \left\{\text{RR} + (1 - \text{RR}) E_Q[(1 - \mathbf{1}_{\text{DEF}})]\right\}$$
$$= D(t, T) \text{RR} + (1 - \text{RR}) D(t, T) E_Q[(1 - \mathbf{1}_{\text{DEF}})]$$
$$= D(t, T) \text{RR} + (1 - \text{RR}) DD(t, T; \text{RR} = 0)$$

So, the value of the defaultable bond is recovered as a portfolio of an investment in the default-free bond, and one in a defaultable bond with the same default probability and recovery rate zero.

In terms of credit spreads we have

$$r^*(t, T; \text{RR}) - r(t, T) = -\frac{\ln\{\text{RR} + (1 - \text{RR}) \exp[-\gamma(T - t)]\}}{T - t}$$

Notice that in this case the term structure of the credit spreads is not flat, even though the intensity is still assumed constant.

A natural extension of the model is to assume the intensity to be stochastic. In this case, the default event is said to follow what is called a *Cox process*. The survival probability of the obligor beyond time T is determined as

$$E_Q[1 - \mathbf{1}_{\text{DEF}}] \equiv \Pr(\tau > T) = E_Q\left[\exp\left[-\int_t^T \gamma(u)\, du\right]\right]$$

It is easy to see that, from a mathematical point of view, the framework is much the same as that of interest rate models. These techniques can then be directly applied to the evaluation of credit spreads.

Affine intensity

As an example, assume that the instantaneous intensity $\gamma(t)$ follows a diffusive process dynamics under the risk neutral measure Q

$$d\gamma(t) = k(\bar{\gamma} - \gamma(t))\, dt + \sigma \gamma^\alpha\, d\widetilde{w}$$

For $\alpha = 0, 1$ we know that the model is affine and we know that the solution to

$$E_Q[1 - \mathbf{1}_{\text{DEF}}] = E_Q\left[\exp\left[-\int_t^T \gamma(u)\, du\right]\right]$$

is

$$E_Q\left[\exp\left[-\int_t^T \gamma(u)\, du\right]\right] = \exp\left[A(T - t) + M(T - t)\gamma(t)\right]$$

The value of a defaultable discount bond is then

$$DD(t, T; \text{RR}) = D(t, T)\text{RR} + (1 - \text{RR})DD(t, T; \text{RR} = 0)$$

$$= D(t, T)\{\text{RR} + (1 - \text{RR}) \exp[A(T - t) + M(T - t)\gamma(t)]\}$$

Notice that using the framework of the forward martingale measure we can easily extend the analysis to the case of correlation between interest rate and credit risk. In fact, we leave the reader to check that the dynamics of the default intensity under such measure, which we denoted Q_T, is

$$d\gamma(t) = \left[k(\bar{\gamma} - \gamma(t)) - \sigma_T \sigma \gamma^\alpha\right] dt + \sigma \gamma^\alpha dw^*$$

where we recall that σ_T is the instantaneous volatility of the default free zero-coupon bond with maturity T. Using the dynamics above one can compute or simulate the price from

$$DD(t, T; \text{RR}) = D(t, T)\,\text{RR} + (1 - \text{RR})\,D(t, T)\,E_{Q_T}\left[\exp\left[-\int_t^T \gamma(u)\,du\right]\right]$$

A final comment is in order concerning the recovery rate. Extensions of the model refer to a stochastic recovery rate. Of course, the extension is immediate as long as one is willing to assume that the recovery rate is independent of the default intensity and interest rate. In this case the expected value is simply substituted for the deterministic value assumed in the analysis above. Obviously, as the support of the recovery rate is in the unit interval, one has to choose a suitable probability distribution, which typically is the Beta. Accounting for recovery risk, however, has not been investigated in depth.

Finally, consider that the choice of the amount with respect to which the recovery rate is computed may be relevant for the analysis. There are three possible choices. The first is to measure recovery rate with respect to the nominal value of the principal, as supposed in Jarrow and Turnbull (1995) and Hull and White (1995). The second choice is to compute it with respect to the market value of debt right before default, as in Duffie and Singleton (1998). The last one, which is much more common in practice, is to compute it with respect to principal plus accrued interest. Notice that with the last choice, we get the unfortunate result that the value of a coupon bond cannot be decomposed into a stream of defaultable zero-coupon bonds, and the analysis may turn out to be much more involved.

1.7.3 Implied default probabilities

A look at the models above shows that credit risk is evaluated drawing information from different markets, in particular the equity market, for structural models, and the corporate bond market, for reduced form models. Nowadays more information is implied in other markets, such as the credit derivatives markets. A question is how to extract and combine information from all of these markets to determine the *implied* risk-neutral default probability concerning a particular obligor. Here we give a brief account of the different choices available.

Stock markets

A first choice, implicit in structural models, is to draw information from the equity market. Taking the standard Merton model we have that

$$C(t) = V(t)\,\Phi(d_1) - \exp(-r(T - t))\,\overline{DD}\,\Phi(d_2)$$

where $C(t)$ is the value of equity. As we know, this is a standard application of the Black–Scholes formula, and we are interested in recovering the probability of exercise $\Phi(d_2)$. Let us remark that this probability is referred to the event that the option representing equity ends up in the money, so that the company does not default. Default probability is then $1 - \Phi(d_2) = \Phi(-d_2)$. The main difference with respect to the Black–Scholes framework is that in this case not only the volatility of the underlying asset σ_V, but also its current value $V(t)$, cannot be observed on the market. What we observe instead is the value of equity $C(t)$. Some other piece of information is needed to close the model. A possible solution is to resort to some estimate of the volatility of equity, σ_C, which can be obtained from the historical time series of prices or from the options traded on the stock. From Ito's lemma, we know that volatility of equity must satisfy

$$\sigma_C = \sigma_V \Phi(d_1) \frac{V(t)}{C(t)}$$

This equation, along with the Black–Scholes formula above, constitutes a non-linear system of two equations in two unknowns that can be solved to yield the values of $V(t)$ and σ_C implied by market prices. The default probability is then recovered, under the risk-neutral measure, as

$$\Phi(-d_2) = \Phi\left(-\frac{\ln\left(V(T)/\overline{DD}\right) + \left(r - \sigma_V^2/2\right)(T-t)}{\sigma_V\sqrt{T-t}}\right)$$

The default probability under the objective measure can be recovered by simply substituting the actual drift μ_V of the asset value of the firm. The latter can be estimated either from historical data or by resorting to the no-arbitrage relationship $\mu_V = r + \lambda\sigma_V$, where λ is the market price of risk.

The solution described above is used in the very well known application of structural models employed by KMV, a firm specialized in supplying default probability estimates about many companies across the world, and recently purchased by Moody's. We know that a serious flaw of the Merton approach is that it underestimates the default probability. The key KMV idea is to apply the argument of the default probability function, which they denote *distance to default*

$$-\frac{\ln\left(V(T)/\overline{DD}\right) + \left(\mu_V - \sigma_V^2/2\right)(T-t)}{\sigma_V\sqrt{T-t}}$$

to fit the empirical distribution of actual historical defaults.

Example 1.3 Based on Standard and Poor's statistics for the year 2001, the leverage figures of AA and BBB industrial companies were equal to 26.4% and 41%. Using these figures, an interest rate equal to 4% and a volatility of the asset side equal to 25% for both firms, we compute a risk-neutral default probability over five years equal to 0.69% and 4.71% respectively. Assuming a market price of risk equal to 6%, the corresponding objective probabilities are 0.29% and 2.42% for the AA and the BBB firm.

Corporate bond markets

Reduced form models suggest that the information about default is in the observed prices of corporate bonds. Given the zero-coupon-bond yield curve of debt issues from a single obligor, and given a recovery rate figure RR we know that

$$DD(t, T; RR) = D(t, T)RR + (1 - RR)DD(t, T; RR = 0)$$

Furthermore, we know that the value of the zero-coupon with recovery rate zero implied in this price is

$$DD(t, T; RR = 0) = D(t, T) \Pr(\tau > T)$$

where again we assume that interest rate risk and default risk are orthogonal. The implied survival probability is then obtained from defaultable and non-defaultable bond prices as

$$\Pr(\tau > T) = \frac{DD(t, T; RR)/D(t, T) - RR}{1 - RR}$$

Alternatively, a common practice in the market is to refer to asset swap spreads as representative of the credit spread of a specific issue. To get the main idea behind this practice, consider a defaultable coupon bond issued at par with coupon equal to r^*. We know that if the bond issued were default-free, it could be swapped at the swap rate SR. We remind the reader that the swap rate is defined as the coupon that equals the value of the fixed leg to that of the floating one in a plain vanilla swap. So, the defaultable cash flow r^* can be swapped against a stream of floating payments plus a spread equal to the difference between the coupon and the swap rate. The advantage of using the asset swap spread is that it conveys information on the riskiness of the individual bond, rather than a whole set of bonds issued by the same entity, while the main flaw is that it may represent other sources of risk, beyond that of default, linked to specific features of the issue, particularly its liquidity. Furthermore, by its very nature it is not well suited to represent the term structure of default risk and credit spreads. Typically, then, the asset swap spread is used to represent a flat credit spread and default intensity curve.

Credit default swap markets

The process of financial innovation that has characterized the recent development credit market has offered new tools to extract market information on the default risk of the main obligors. Credit derivative products, which are used to transfer credit risk among financial institutions, represent a natural source of information concerning the default risk. In particular, credit default swaps represent a very liquid market to extract such information. A credit default swap is a contract in which one counterparty *buys protection* from the other against default of a specific obligor, commonly denoted *name*. The buyer of protection promises periodic payments of a fixed coupon until the end of the contract or default of the *name*. The seller of protection agrees to refund the loss on the assets of a *name* if default occurs, either by buying its obligations at par (*physical settlement*) or by cash refund of the loss on them (*cash settlement*). As in a standard swap, its value at origin is zero.

Assuming, for the sake of simplicity, that no payment is made in case of default for the coupon period in which the credit event occurs, the credit default swap coupon for maturity t_N is defined from

$$\text{LGD} \sum_{i=1}^{N-1} D(t, t_i) \left(\overline{Q}(t_i) - \overline{Q}(t_{i+1}) \right) = c_N \sum_{i=1}^{N-1} D(t, t_i) \overline{Q}(t_{i+1})$$

where c_N are the credit default swap spreads observed on the market, $\overline{Q}(t_i)$ is the survival probability of the obligor beyond time t_i and the loss given default figure is supposed to be non-stochastic. Notice that the term structure of survival probabilities can be recovered by means of a *bootstrap* algorithm. The credit default swap rates are sorted from short to long maturities. Then, for maturity t_1 we have

$$\overline{Q}(t_1) = \frac{\text{LGD}}{c_1 + \text{LGD}}$$

and for any other maturity t_N, $N \geqslant 2$, one can compute

$$\overline{Q}(t_N) = \frac{c_{N-1} - c_N}{D(t, t_N)(c_N + \text{LGD})} \sum_{i=1}^{N-1} D(t, t_i)\overline{Q}(t_i) + \overline{Q}(t_{N-1}) \frac{\text{LGD}}{c_N + \text{LGD}}$$

Alternatively, one can assume that the coupon of the period in which the underlying credit defaults is paid at the end of the period. In this case, the credit default swap is defined as

$$\text{LGD} \sum_{i=1}^{N-1} D(t, t_i)\left(\overline{Q}(t_i) - \overline{Q}(t_{i+1})\right) = c_N \sum_{i=1}^{N-1} D(t, t_i)\overline{Q}(t_i)$$

The bootstrap procedure now yields

$$\overline{Q}(t_1) = 1 - \frac{c_1}{\text{LGD}}$$

and

$$\overline{Q}(t_N) = \frac{c_{N-1} - c_N}{D(t, t_N)\text{LGD}} \sum_{i=1}^{N-1} D(t, t_i)\overline{Q}(t_{i-1}) + \overline{Q}(t_{N-1})\left(1 - \frac{c_N}{\text{LGD}}\right)$$

1.7.4 Counterparty risk

Credit risk is not only a feature of standard corporate or defaultable bonds. It is also an element that should be taken into account in the evaluation of any contractual exposure to a counterparty. Derivative contracts may generate such credit risk exposures, particularly in transactions on the OTC market, that, as we have noticed above, represent the main development of the derivative industry.

The pay-off of a defaultable, or as termed in the literature, *vulnerable* derivative, is defined as

$$G(S, T)\left[1 - \mathbf{1}_{\text{DEF}}(T)\text{LGD}\right]$$

Of course the dependence structure between the pay-off and the default event may be particularly relevant, and will be the object of some of the applications presented in this book. However, even assuming independence of the two risk factors, some important effects of counterparty risk on the evaluation of derivative contracts can be noticed.

The first, obvious, point is that accounting for counterparty risk leads to a discount in the value of the derivative, with respect to its default-free value. Even under independence, the value of the derivative contract is obtained under the risk-neutral valuation measure as

$$D(t, T)E_Q[G(S, T)] - D(t, T)E_Q[G(S, T)]E_Q[\mathbf{1}_{\text{DEF}}(T)\text{LGD}]$$

that is, the value of the default-free derivative minus the product of such value times the default probability and the loss given default figure.

Both the approaches described above to represent credit risk can be exploited to evaluate the discount to be applied to a derivative contract in order to account for counterparty risk. So, under a structural model one could have

$$D(t, T) E_Q [G(S, T)] \left[1 - \Phi(-d_2) \left[1 - \frac{1}{d} \frac{\Phi(-d_1)}{\Phi(-d_2)} \right] \right]$$

while an intensity based model would yield

$$D(t, T) E_Q [G(S, T)] \left[1 - (1 - \exp(-\gamma(T - t))) \text{LGD} \right]$$

The second point to realize is that even though market and credit risk are orthogonal, they must be handled jointly in practice. If one overlooks counterparty risk in evaluating a vulnerable derivative, one obtains the wrong price and the wrong hedging policy, ending up with an undesired market risk.

The third point to notice is that counterparty risk generally turns linear derivatives into non-linear ones. To make the point clear, consider the simplest example of a linear vulnerable derivative, i.e. forward contract. Assume that counterparty A is long in the contract, and counterparty B is short. The delivery price is the forward price F: we remind the reader that the forward price is the delivery value that equals to zero the value of a forward contract at the origin. Assume now that the two counterparties have default probabilities $Q_A(T)$ and $Q_B(T)$ and zero recovery rates, and that the time of default is independent of the underlying asset of the forward contract. Notice that the default risk of counterparty A is relevant only if the contract ends up in the money for counterparty B, that is, if $S(T) < F$, while default of counterparty B is relevant only if the long counterparty ends up with a gain, that is, if $S(T) > F$. The value of the forward contract is then

$$E_Q \left[(S(T) - F) \mathbf{1}_{\{S(T) > F\}} \right] \overline{Q}_B(T) + E_Q \left[(S(T) - F) \mathbf{1}_{\{S(T) < F\}} \right] \overline{Q}_A(T)$$

where we remind that $\overline{Q}_A(T)$ and $\overline{Q}_B(T)$ are the survival probabilities beyond time T. Notice that linearity of the product is broken unless $\overline{Q}_A(T) = \overline{Q}_B(T)$. Even in the latter case, the delta of the contract would not be equal to 1, but would rather be equal to the survival probability of the two counterparties.

1.8 COPULA METHODS IN FINANCE: A PRIMER

Up to this point, we have seen that the three main frontier problems in derivative pricing are the departure from normality, emerging from the smile effect, market incompleteness, corresponding to hedging error, and credit risk, linked to the bivariate relationship in OTC transactions. Copula functions may be of great help to address these problems. As we will see, the main advantage of copula functions is that they enable us to tackle the problem of specification of marginal univariate distributions separately from the specification of market comovement and dependence. Technically, we will see in Chapter 3 that the term "dependence" is not rigorously correct, because, strictly speaking, dependence is a concept limited to positive comovement of a set of variables. However, we will stick to the term "dependence" throughout most of this book because it is largely diffused both among practitioners in the financial markets and academics in statistics and finance. We will instead insist again and again on the distinction between the concept of dependence, defined in this broad sense, and the concept of linear correlation, which is used by quantitative analysts in most of the financial institutions in the world. In fact, we will show that the concept of dependence embedded in copula functions is much more general than the standard linear correlation concept, and it is able to capture non-linear relationships among the markets.

1.8.1 Joint probabilities, marginal probabilities and copula functions

To give an intuitive grasp of the use of copula functions in finance, consider a very simple product, a bivariate digital option. This option pays one unit of currency if two stocks or indexes are above or below a pair of strike price levels. Options like these are very often used in structured finance, particularly index-linked products: examples are digital bivariate notes and, more recently, Altiplano notes.

As an example, assume a product written on the Nikkei 225 and S&P 500 indexes which pays, at some exercise date T, one unit if both are lower than some given levels K_{NKY} and K_{SP}. According to the basic pricing principles reviewed in this chapter, the price of this digital put option in a complete market setting is

$$DP = \exp\left[-r\left(T - t\right)\right] Q\left(K_{NKY}, K_{SP}\right)$$

where $Q\left(K_{NKY}, K_{SP}\right)$ is the joint risk-neutral probability that both the Japanese and US market indexes are below the corresponding strike prices.

How can we recover a price consistent with market quotes? The first requirement that may come to mind is to ensure that the price is consistent with the market prices for plain vanilla options on each of the two indexes. Say, for example, we can recover, using some of the models or techniques described in this chapter, the risk-neutral probability Q_{NKY} that the Nikkei index at time T will be below the level K_{NKY}. We can do the same with the S&P 500 index, recovering probability Q_{SP}. In financial terms, we are asking what is the forward price of univariate digital options with strikes K_{NKY} and K_{SP}; in statistical terms, what we are estimating from market data are the marginal risk-neutral distributions of the Nikkei and the S&P indexes.

In order to compare the price of our bivariate product with that of the univariate ones, it would be great if we could write the price as

$$DP = \exp\left[-r\left(T - t\right)\right] Q\left(K_{NKY}, K_{SP}\right) = \exp\left[-r\left(T - t\right)\right] C\left(Q_{NKY}, Q_{SP}\right)$$

with $C\left(x, y\right)$ a bivariate function.

Without getting involved in heavy mathematics, we can also discover the general requirements that the function $C\left(x, y\right)$ must satisfy in order to be able to represent a joint probability distribution. Beyond the basic requirement that the output of the function must be in the unit interval, as it must represent a probability, three requirements immediately come to mind. The first: if one of the two events has zero probability, the joint probability that both events occur must also be zero. So, if one of the arguments of $C\left(x, y\right)$ is equal to 0 the function must return 0. On the contrary, if one event will occur for sure, the joint probability that both the events will take place corresponds to the probability that the second event will be observed. This leads to the second technical requirement that if one of the arguments $C(x, y)$ is equal to 1 the function must yield the other argument. Finally, it is intuitive to require that if the probabilities of both the events increase, the joint probability should also increase, and for sure it cannot be expected to decrease. Technically, this implies a third requirement for the function $C(x, y)$, that must be increasing in the two arguments (2-increasing is approximately the correct term: you will learn more on this in Chapter 2). We have just described the three requirements that enable us to define $C(x, y)$ as a copula function.

If we go back to our pricing problem, that's where copula functions come in: they enable us to express a joint probability distribution as a function of the marginal ones. So, the bivariate product is priced consistently with information stemming from the univariate ones. Beyond the intuitive discussion provided here, this opportunity rests on a fundamental finding, known as Sklar's theorem. This result states that any joint probability distribution can be written in terms of a copula function taking the marginal distributions as arguments and that, conversely, any copula function taking univariate probability distributions as arguments yields a joint distribution.

1.8.2 Copula functions duality

Consider now a bivariate digital call option. Differently from the digital put option, it pays one unit of currency if both the Nikkei 225 and the S&P 500 indexes are above the strike levels K_{NKY} and K_{SP}. The relevant probability in this case is

$$DC = \exp[-r(T - t)] \overline{Q}(K_{NKY}, K_{SP})$$

Analogously to the approach above, the copula function method enables us to recover a copula function $\overline{C}(v, z)$ such that

$$DC = \exp[-r(T - t)] \overline{Q}(K_{NKY}, K_{SP})$$
$$= \exp[-r(T - t)] \overline{C}[\overline{Q}(K_{NKY}), \overline{Q}(K_{SP})]$$

The new copula function $\overline{C}(v, z)$ is known as *survival copula*. Readers will learn from the mathematical treatment in Chapter 2 that the survival copula is related to the copula function by the relationship

$$\overline{C}[\overline{Q}(K_{NKY}), \overline{Q}(K_{SP})] = 1 - Q(K_{NKY}) - Q(K_{SP}) + C[Q(K_{NKY}), Q(K_{SP})]$$

Readers can also check, as will be discussed in detail in Chapter 8, that the relationship above corresponds to a requirement to rule out arbitrage opportunities.

1.8.3 Examples of copula functions

Let us start with the simplest example of a copula function. This obviously corresponds to the simplest hypothesis corresponding to the comovements of the Japanese and the US markets. Assume, to keep things simple, that the two markets are independent. In this case we know from basic statistics that the joint probability corresponds to the product of the marginal probabilities, and we have

$$DP = \exp[-r(T - t)] Q(K_{NKY}, K_{SP}) = \exp[-r(T - t)] Q_{NKY} Q_{SP}$$

So, $C(x, y) = xy$, also known as the product copula, is the first function we are able to build and use to price our bivariate option.

The next question is what would happen if the two markets were perfectly positively or negatively correlated. The answer to this question requires us to draw from more advanced statistics, referring to the so-called *Fréchet bounds*. The joint probability is constrained within the bounds

$$\max(Q_{NKY} + Q_{SP} - 1, 0) \leqslant Q(K_{NKY}, K_{SP}) \leqslant \min(Q_{NKY}, Q_{SP})$$

Moreover, the upper bound corresponds to the case of perfect positive dependence between the two markets and the lower bound represents perfect negative dependence. We can therefore check the impact of perfect positive dependence on the value of the bivariate product by computing

$$DP = \exp[-r(T - t)] Q(K_{NKY}, K_{SP}) = \exp[-r(T - t)] \min(Q_{NKY}, Q_{SP})$$

So, $C(x, y) = \min(x, y)$ is another copula function, known as the maximum copula. The minimum copula will instead correspond to the case of perfect negative dependence and to the Fréchet lower bound $C(x, y) = \max(x + y - 1, 0)$ yielding

$$DP = \exp[-r(T - t)] Q(K_{NKY}, K_{SP})$$
$$= \exp[-r(T - t)] \max(Q_{NKY} + Q_{SP} - 1, 0)$$

We have then recovered copula functions corresponding to the extreme cases of independence and perfect dependence. Moving one step forward, we could try to build a copula function accounting for imperfect dependence between the two markets. The first idea would be to try a linear combination of the three cases above, obtaining

$$C(Q_{NKY}, Q_{SP}) = \beta \max(Q_{NKY} + Q_{SP} - 1, 0) + (1 - \alpha - \beta) Q_{NKY} Q_{SP}$$
$$+ \alpha \min(Q_{NKY}, Q_{SP})$$

with $0 \leqslant \alpha, \beta \leqslant 1$ and $\alpha + \beta = 1$. Copula functions obtained in this way define the so-called Fréchet family of copula functions.

Other ways of obtaining copula functions are more involved and less intuitive. For example, consider taking a function $\varphi(.)$ satisfying some technical conditions that will be discussed in more detail throughout the book. If we define

$$C(Q_{NKY}, Q_{SP}) = \varphi^{[-1]} [\varphi(Q_{NKY}) + \varphi(Q_{SP})]$$

we obtain copula functions. Copulas constructed in this way are called Archimedean copulas and are largely used in actuarial science.

As a final idea, one could try to generalize and make more flexible the standard setting under which most of the results in finance were obtained under the Black–Scholes theory. This corresponds to normal distribution of the returns, which in this case is extended to multivariate normality. From this perspective, a particularly useful result is that the joint standard normal distribution computed in the inverse of the arguments satisfies the requirements of a copula function. We may then price our bivariate claim using

$$DP = \exp[-r(T - t)]\Phi[\Phi^{-1}(Q_{NKY}), \Phi^{-1}(Q_{SP}); \rho]$$

where $\Phi(x, y; \rho)$ is the standard bivariate normal distribution with correlation parameter ρ. This example is particularly useful to highlight the main advantage from the use of copula functions. Notice in fact that in this way we may preserve the dependence structure typical of a multivariate normal distribution by modifying **only** the marginal distributions, which may be allowed to display skewness and fat-tails behavior consistently with the data observed from the market.

1.8.4 Copula functions and market comovements

As we have already seen from the examples, copula functions provide a way to represent the dependence structure between markets and risk factors, while preserving the specification of the marginal distribution of each and every one of them. Representing market comovements in a world in which the marginal distribution of returns is not normal raises problems that may be new for many scholars and practitioners in finance.

The main result is that linear correlation, which represents the standard tool used in the dealing rooms and risk management units to measure the comovement of markets may turn out to be a flawed instrument in the presence of a non-normal return. Linear correlation between the rate of returns r_{NKY} and r_{SP} in our two markets may be written as

$$\text{corr}(r_{NKY}, r_{SP}) = \frac{\text{cov}(r_{NKY}, r_{SP})}{\sigma_{NKY}\sigma_{SP}}$$

$$= \frac{1}{\sigma_{NKY}\sigma_{SP}} \int_{-\infty}^{\infty} \int_{-\infty}^{\infty} [Q(x, y) - Q_{NKY}Q_{SP}] \, dx \, dy$$

where σ_{NKY} and σ_{SP} represent volatilities. Notice that the correlation depends on the marginal distributions of the returns. The maximum value it can achieve can be computed by substituting the upper Fréchet bound in the formula

$$\text{corr}_{max}(r_{NKY}, r_{SP})$$

$$= \frac{1}{\sigma_{NKY}\sigma_{SP}} \int_{-\infty}^{\infty} \int_{-\infty}^{\infty} [\min(Q_{NKY}, Q_{SP}) - Q_{NKY}Q_{SP}] \, dx \, dy$$

and the value corresponding to perfect negative correlation is obtained by substituting the lower bound

$$\text{corr}_{min}(r_{NKY}, r_{SP})$$

$$= \frac{1}{\sigma_{NKY}\sigma_{SP}} \int_{-\infty}^{\infty} \int_{-\infty}^{\infty} [\max(Q_{NKY} + Q_{SP} - 1, 0) - Q_{NKY}Q_{SP}] \, dx \, dy$$

Of course everyone would expect these formulas to yield $\text{corr}_{max} = 1$ and $\text{corr}_{min} = -1$. The news is that this is not true in general. Of course, that is what we are used to expect in a world of normal returns. The result would also hold in the more general case of elliptic distributions, but not for other arbitrary choices. Looking at the problem from a different viewpoint, correlation is an effective way to represent comovements between variables if they are linked by linear relationships, but it may be severely flawed in the presence of non-linear links. Readers may check this in the simple case of a variable z normally distributed and z^2 which is obviously perfectly correlated with the first one, but has a chi-squared distribution.

So, using linear correlation to measure the comovements of markets in the presence of non-linear relationships may be misleading because it may not cover the whole range from -1 to $+1$ even though two markets are moved by the same factor, and so are perfectly dependent.

The alternative offered by statistics to this shortcoming is the use of non-parametric dependence measures, such as Spearman's ρ_S and Kendall's τ. The non-parametric feature of these measures means that they do not depend on the marginal probability distributions. It does not come as a surprise, then, that these measures are directly linked to the copula function. In particular, it may be proved that the following relationships hold

$$\rho_S = 12 \int_0^1 \int_0^1 C(u, v) \, \mathrm{d}u \mathrm{d}v - 3$$

$$\tau = 4 \int_0^1 \int_0^1 C(u, v) \, \mathrm{d}C(u, v) - 1$$

Notice that the specific shape of the marginal probability distributions does not enter these relationships. Furthermore, it may be proved that substituting the maximum and minimum copulas in these equations gives values of 1 and -1 respectively. Differently from the linear correlation measure, then, if the two variables (markets in our case) are perfectly dependent we expect to observe figures equal to 1 for Spearman's ρ_S and Kendall's τ, while a score -1 corresponds to perfect negative dependence.

The relationship between non-parametric dependence measures and copula functions can also be applied to recover a first calibration technique of the copula function itself. In some cases the relationship between these non-parametric statistics and the parameters of the copula function may also be particularly easy. One of the easiest, that we report as an example, is the relationship between the copula functions of the Fréchet family and Spearman's ρ_S. We have in fact

$$\rho_S = \alpha - \beta$$

where the parameters α, β are reported in the definition of the Fréchet family given above.

1.8.5 Tail dependence

The departure from normality in a multivariate system and the need to represent the comovement of markets as closely as possible raises a second dimension of the problem. We know that non-normality at the univariate level is associated with skewness and leptokurtosis phenomena, and what is known as the *fat-tail* problem. In a multivariate setting, the *fat-tail* problem can be referred both to the marginal univariate distributions or to the joint probability of large market movements. This concept is called *tail dependence*. Intuitively, we may conceive markets in which the marginal distributions are endowed with *fat tails*, but extreme market movements are orthogonal, or cases in which the returns on each market are normally distributed, but large market movements are likely to occur together. The use of copula functions enables us to model these two features, *fat tails* and *tail dependence*, separately.

To represent tail dependence we consider the likelihood that one event with probability lower than v occurs in the first variable, given that an event with probability lower than v occurs in the second one. Concretely, we ask which is the probability to observe, for example, a crash with probability lower than $v = 1\%$ in the Nikkei 225 index, given that a crash with probability lower than 1% has occurred in the S&P 500 index. We have

$$\lambda\left(v\right) \equiv \Pr(Q_{\text{NKY}} \leqslant v \mid Q_{\text{SP}} \leqslant v)$$
$$= \frac{\Pr(Q_{\text{NKY}} \leqslant v, Q_{\text{SP}} \leqslant v)}{\Pr(Q_{\text{SP}} \leqslant v)}$$
$$= \frac{C\left(v, v\right)}{v}$$

If we compute this dependence measure far in the lower tail, that is, for very small values of v, we obtain the so-called *tail index*, in particular the *lower* tail index

$$\lambda_{\text{L}} \equiv \lim_{v \to 0^+} \frac{C\left(v, v\right)}{v}$$

It may be easily verified that the tail index is zero for the product copula and 1 for the maximum copula. Along the same lines, one can also recover the tail dependence for the *upper* tail index. Analogously, using the duality among copulas described above, we have

$$\lambda_{\text{U}} = \lim_{v \to 1^-} \lambda_v \equiv \lim_{v \to 1^-} \frac{\Pr(\overline{Q}_{\text{NKY}} > v, \overline{Q}_{\text{SP}} > v)}{\Pr(\overline{Q}_{\text{SP}} > v)}$$
$$= \lim_{v \to 1^-} \frac{1 - 2v + C\left(v, v\right)}{1 - v}$$

and this represents the probability that price booms may occur at the same time in the US and Japanese markets.

1.8.6 Equity-linked products

Here we give a brief preview of applications to equity-linked products, beyond the simple multivariate digital options seen above. Consider a simple case of a rainbow option, such as, for example, a call option on the minimum between two assets. These derivatives are largely used in structured finance. An example is a class of products, known as Everest notes, whose coupon at the given time T is determined by computing, for example,

$$\text{coupon}\left(T\right) = \max\left[\min\left(\frac{S_{\text{NKY}}\left(T\right)}{S_{\text{NKY}}\left(0\right)}, \frac{S_{\text{SP}}\left(T\right)}{S_{\text{SP}}\left(0\right)}\right) - 1, 0\right]$$

where S_{NKY} and S_{SP} are the values of the Nikkei 225 and the S&P 500 indexes and time
0 is the initial date of the contract. At any time $0 < t < T$, the value of the coupon will
be computed as a call option with strike on the minimum between two assets whose initial
value was 1. The strike price is set equal to 1. We will see in Chapter 8 that the price
of options like these can be computed using copula functions. Here we just convey the
intuition by working the argument backward. Assume that you have a price function for the
rainbow option above

$$\text{CALL}\,[s_{NKY}\,(t)\,, s_{SP}\,(t)\,;\,K,\,T]$$

$$= \exp\,[-r\,(T - t)]\,E_Q\,[\max\,(\min\,(s_{NKY}\,(T)\,, s_{SP}\,(T)) - K, 0)\mid \Im_t]$$

where we have simplified the notation defining $s_{NKY}\,(t)$ and $s_{SP}\,(t)$, the values of the indexes
rescaled with respect to their levels at time 0. Of course in our case we also have $K = 1$.
Applying what we know about implied risk-neutral probability we have

$$\Pr\,(\min\,(s_{NKY}\,(T)\,, s_{SP}\,(T)) > 1 \mid \Im_t) = \Pr\,(s_{NKY}\,(T) > 1, s_{SP}\,(T) > 1 \mid \Im_t)$$

$$= \overline{Q}\,(1, 1 \mid \Im_t)$$

$$= -\exp\,[r\,(T - t)]\,\frac{\partial \text{CALL}}{\partial K}$$

Using copula functions we obtain

$$\overline{Q}\,(1, 1 \mid \Im_t) = \overline{C}\,\left(\overline{Q}_{NKY}\,(1)\,, \overline{Q}_{SP}\,(1) \mid \Im_t\right) = -\exp\,[r\,(T - t)]\,\frac{\partial \text{CALL}}{\partial K}$$

By integrating from the strike $K = 1$ to infinity we have

$$\text{CALL}\,(s_{NKY}\,(t)\,, s_{SP}\,(t)\,;\,K,\,T) = \int_1^\infty \overline{C}\,\left(\overline{Q}_{NKY}\,(\eta)\,, \overline{Q}_{SP}\,(\eta) \mid \Im_t\right)\,d\eta$$

and the call option is written in terms of copula functions. Much more about applications
and cases like these and techniques by which closed form solutions may also be recovered
is reported in Chapter 8.

1.8.7 Credit-linked products

The vast majority of copula function applications have been devoted to credit risk and
products whose pay-off depends on the performance of a basket of obligations from several
obligors (*names*). In order to illustrate the main choices involved, we describe the application
to a standard problem, that is the pricing of a *first-to-default swap*. This product is a credit
derivative, just like the credit default swap described above, with the difference that the
counterparty offering protection pays a sum, for example a fixed amount, at the first event
of default out of a basket of credit exposures.

   To see how the pricing problem of a first-to-default derivative leads to the use of copula
functions consider a product that pays one unit of currency if at least one out of two
credit exposures defaults by time T. It is clear that the risk-neutral probability of paying

the protection is equal to that of the complement to the event that a credit exposure goes bankrupt – that is, the case that both names will survive beyond time T. Formally,

$$\text{FTD} = \exp\left[-r\left(T - t\right)\right]\left[1 - \Pr\left(\tau_1 > T, \tau_2 > T \mid \Im_t\right)\right]$$

where FTD denotes *first-to-default*, τ_i, $i = 1, 2$ denote the default times of the two names. It is then immediate to write the price in terms of copula functions

$$\text{FTD} = \exp\left[-r\left(T - t\right)\right]\left[1 - \overline{C}\left(\overline{Q}_1\left(T\right), \overline{Q}_2\left(T\right) \mid \Im_t\right)\right]$$

Using the duality relationship between a copula function and its survival copula we obtain

$$\text{FTD} = \exp\left[-r\left(T - t\right)\right]\left[Q_1\left(T\right) + Q_2\left(T\right) - C\left(Q_1\left(T\right), Q_2\left(T\right) \mid \Im_t\right)\right]$$

and the value of the product is negatively affected by the dependence between the defaults of the two names. This diversification effect may be appraised computing the case of perfect positive dependence

$$\text{FTD}_{\text{max}} = \exp\left[-r\left(T - t\right)\right]\left[Q_1\left(T\right) + Q_2\left(T\right) - \min\left(Q_1\left(T\right), Q_2\left(T\right) \mid \Im_t\right)\right]$$
$$= \exp\left[-r\left(T - t\right)\right]\left[\max\left(Q_1\left(T\right), Q_2\left(T\right) \mid \Im_t\right)\right]$$

and that corresponding to independence

$$\text{FTD}_{\perp} = \exp\left[-r\left(T - t\right)\right]\left[Q_1\left(T\right) + Q_2\left(T\right) - Q_1\left(T\right) Q_2\left(T\right) \mid \Im_t\right]$$
$$= \exp\left[-r\left(T - t\right)\right]\left[Q_1\left(T\right) + \overline{Q}_1\left(T\right) Q_2\left(T\right), \mid \Im_t\right]$$

So, as the value of the copula function increases with dependence, the value of the first-to-default product decreases.

Of course one could consider reconducting the analysis to the multivariate normal distribution, by using structural models to specify the marginal distributions and the Gaussian copula to represent dependence

$$C\left(Q_1\left(T\right), Q_2\left(T\right) \mid \Im_t\right) = \Phi\left[\Phi^{-1}\left(Q_1\left(T\right)\right), \Phi^{-1}\left(Q_2\left(T\right)\right); \rho\right]$$

where $\Phi^{-1}\left(Q_i\left(T\right)\right)$, $i = 1, 2$ denote the inverse of marginal default probabilities consistent with both the leverage figures of the names and volatilities of their assets, while ρ is the correlation between the assets. In this approach, which is used for example in CreditMetrics, the correlation figure is recovered either from equity correlation or by resorting to the analysis of industrial sector comovements.

Example 1.4 Consider a first-to-default option written on a basket of two names, rated AA and BBB. Under the contract, the counterparty selling protection will pay 1 million euros if one of the names defaults over a 5-year period. We saw in a previous example that the leverage figures of AA and BBB industrial companies were equal to 26.4% and 41%. Under the risk-neutral probability measure, assuming the risk-free rate flat at 4% and a volatility of the asset side equal to 25% for both the firms, we obtained 0.69% and 4.71% default probabilities respectively. The maximum value of the first-to-default can be immediately computed as

$$\text{FTD}_{\max} = 1\,000\,000\exp[-0.04(5)]\,[0.0471] = 38\,562$$

If one assumes independence between the two credit risks, we obtain instead

$$\text{FTD}_{\perp} = 1\,000\,000\exp[-0.04(5)]\,[0.0069 + 0.9931(0.0471)] = 43\,945$$

Finally, assuming a Gaussian copula with an asset correlation equal to 20%, the value "in fashion" in the market at the time we are writing, we obtain a joint default probability of 0.088636%. The price of the first-to-default swap is then

$$\text{FTD} = 1\,000\,000\exp[-0.04(5)]\,[0.0471 + 0.0069 - 0.00088636] = 43\,486$$

Besides this case, it is easy to see why copula functions may be particularly useful in this case. If, for example, we choose to model the distribution of the time to default as in reduced form models, rather than the structure of the firm as in structural models, it is clear that the assumption of normality can no longer be preserved. In this case the marginal distributions are obviously non-Gaussian since they are referred to default times and are naturally defined on a non-negative support. Nevertheless, we may conceive applications that may involve features from both structural and reduced form models. For example, the joint default probability may be specified by using a reduced form model for the marginals and the structural model for the dependence structure. We may write

$$C(Q_1(T), Q_2(T) \mid \Im_t) = \Phi[\Phi^{-1}(1 - \exp(-\gamma_1(T - t))), \Phi^{-1}(1 - \exp(-\gamma_2(T - t))); \rho]$$

where γ_i, $i = 1, 2$ denote the default intensities of the two names and now, differently from the fully structural model quoted above, ρ is correlation between the default times. Notice that in this way we may mix information stemming from different sources, such as equity market for the specification of the dependence structure, and corporate bond or credit default bond markets for the marginal distributions. We now give a simple example of this flexibility, but, again, this has to be taken only as an appetizer to invite readers to get into the details of the matter, which will be covered in the rest of the book.

Example 1.5 Consider a 5-year first-to-default option written on a basket of two names, namely Deutsche Telecom and Dresdner Bank. The nominal value is 1 million euros. The information we have is that the default probability of DT, bootstrapped from a credit default swap, is 12.32%. As for Dresdner, we know that the asset swap spread for a 5-year bond is 75 bp. This allows us to compute a default probability of $[1 - \exp(-0.0075(5))] = 3.6806\%$. We assume that the correlation between the default times is 50% and that the copula is Gaussian. So, we first compute $\Phi^{-1}(12.32\%) = -1.15926$. Analogously, we have for Dresdner $\Phi^{-1}(3.6806\%) = -1.788967169$. The joint default probability is computed from

$$C(Q_1(T), Q_2(T) \mid \Im_t) = \Phi(\Phi^{-1}(3.6806\%), \Phi^{-1}(12.32\%); 50\%)$$

$$= \Phi(-1.788967169, -1.15926; 50\%) = 1.729\%$$

The price of the first-to-default is then

$$\text{FTD} = 1\,000\,000\exp\left[-0.04(5)\right][0.03606 + 0.1232 - 0.01729] = 116\,240$$

Notice that the value obtained is very close to the case of perfect default dependence, which would obviously cost 123 200, and the basket of names of the first-to-default in this example is definitely undiversified.

2

Bivariate Copula Functions

This chapter introduces the notion of a copula function and its probabilistic interpretation, which allows us to consider it a "dependence function" (Deheuvels, 1978). It also examines the survival copula and density notions, together with the canonical representation and, lastly, the use of copulas in setting probability bounds for sums of random variables. It collects a number of financial applications, which will be further developed in the following chapters. The examples are mainly intended to make the reader aware of the usefulness of copulas in extending financial modeling beyond the Black–Scholes world. All the proofs are in the Appendix (see page 87).

We take for granted that the reader is familiar with the notions of the (right continuous) **joint distribution function** (or **joint cumulative distribution function** or **joint c.d.f.**) $F(x, y)$ **of a couple of random variables (r.v.s)** X and Y, as well as with their **marginal distribution functions** (or **d.f.s** or **margins**) $F_i(t)$, $i = 1, 2$. We define the **generalized inverse** of a distribution function as[1]

$$F_i^{-1}(t) = \inf\{u : F_i(u) \geqslant t, 0 < t < 1\}$$

2.1 DEFINITION AND PROPERTIES

The section is organized as follows: first we present subcopulas, provide an example and list a number of subcopula properties. Then we define copulas, as introduced by Sklar[2] (1959) and link them to distributions of uniform random variates.

To start with, we need the notions of groundedness and the 2-increasing property, which allow copulas to respect the distribution function properties.

Definition 2.1 Let us consider two non-empty subsets A_1 and A_2 of $\Re^*$ and a function $G : A_1 \times A_2 \to \Re$. Denote with a_i the least element of A_i, $i = 1, 2$. The function G is named **grounded** if, for every (v, z) of $A_1 \times A_2$,

$$G(a_1, z) = 0 = G(v, a_2)$$

---

[1] Evidently, this notion reduces to the usual inverse function one if F_i is increasing.

[2] Copulas were introduced by Sklar (1959): important developments in the theory are due to Schweizer and Sklar (1974, 1983), who studied them in the context of probabilistic metric spaces, and to Schweizer and Wolff (1981). Independent, early work is due also to Hoeffding (1940), Kimeldorf and Sampson (1975), Deheuvels (1978, 1979). Related problems, such as the characterization of the Fréchet class or the definition of measures of dependence, date back to the 1950s (see, respectively, Fréchet (1951) and Rényi (1959)): they were later related with and merged in the theory of copulas, as we will illustrate in the text. For "a historical overview and rather personal account" see Schweizer (1991).

Definition 2.2 $G : A_1 \times A_2 \to \Re$ is called **2-increasing** if for every rectangle $[v_1, v_2] \times [z_1, z_2]$ whose vertices lie in $A_1 \times A_2$, such that $v_1 \leqslant v_2, z_1 \leqslant z_2$

$$G(v_2, z_2) - G(v_2, z_1) - G(v_1, z_2) + G(v_1, z_1) \geqslant 0 \qquad (2.1)$$

The l.h.s. of (2.1) measures the mass or area, according to the function G, of the rectangle $[v_1, v_2] \times [z_1, z_2]$. Then, 2-increasing functions assign non-negative mass to every rectangle in their domain.

The above definitions allow us to define subcopulas.

Definition 2.3   A two-dimensional subcopula C is a real function defined on $A \times B$, where A and B are non-empty subsets of $I = [0, 1]$, containing both 0 and 1:

$$C : A \times B \to \Re$$

(i) grounded ($C(v, 0) = C(0, z) = 0$)
(ii) such that

$$C(v, 1) = v, \qquad C(1, z) = z$$

for every (v, z) of $A \times B$
(iii) 2-increasing

Example 2.1   Set $A = B = I$ and consider the function $C(v, z) = \max(v + z - 1, 0)$. Since $\max(z - 1, 0) = \max(v - 1, 0) = 0$, C is grounded. Property (ii) is satisfied, since $\max(z, 0) = z, \max(v, 0) = v$. C is also 2-increasing, since $z_1 \leqslant z_2$ implies

$$\max(v_2 + z_1 - 1, 0) - \max(v_1 + z_1 - 1, 0)$$
$$\leqslant \max(v_2 + z_2 - 1, 0) - \max(v_1 + z_2 - 1, 0) \qquad (2.2)$$

Rearranging we get (2.1). The function $\max(v + z - 1, 0)$ on I^2 is therefore a subcopula.

Remark 2.1   The above function is still a subcopula if, instead of setting $A = B = I$, one sets $A = B = \{0\} \cup \left[\frac{1}{2}, 1\right]$.

As a general rule, the 2-increasing property neither implies nor is implied by the non-decreasing property in each argument[3]: however, 2-increasing functions which are also grounded, such as subcopulas, are non-decreasing in each place.

Theorem 2.1   A function $G(v, z) : A_1 \times A_2 \to \Re$ grounded and 2-increasing is non-decreasing in both v and z.

It follows from properties (i), (ii) of the subcopula definition, together with Theorem 2.1, that:

---

[3] Examples of 2-increasing functions which are not non-decreasing in each argument (and vice versa) are given for instance by Schweizer and Sklar (1983, section 6.1).

Corollary 2.1   For every (v, z) of $A \times B$

$$0 \leqslant \mathcal{C}(v, z) \leqslant 1$$

Another property of subcopulas is (uniform) continuity, which in turn will prove to be useful for the so-called section (and differentiability) properties.

Theorem 2.2 $\mathcal{C}$ is uniformly continuous on $A \times B$.

Indeed, as a consequence of Theorems 2.1 and 2.2 we get

Corollary 2.2   For a given subcopula, the functions W and V defined – for $k \in B$, $K \in A$ – as follows:

$$W_k(x) = \mathcal{C}(x, k)$$

$$V_K(x) = \mathcal{C}(K, x)$$

are non-decreasing and uniformly continuous.

These functions are called, respectively, the **horizontal** and **vertical** sections of the subcopula $\mathcal{C}$. The section properties entail the following.

Theorem 2.3   In the interior of $A \times B$, both partial derivatives of the $\mathcal{C}$ function, $\partial \mathcal{C} / \partial v$, $\partial \mathcal{C} / \partial z$, exist almost everywhere and take values in I.

Example 2.2   The partial derivatives of the subcopula in Example 2.1 exist whenever $v + z - 1 \neq 0$, i.e. $z \neq 1 - v$. Since $\max(v + z - 1, 0) = v + z - 1$ whenever $z > 1 - v$, they are

$$\frac{\partial \mathcal{C}}{\partial v} = \frac{\partial \mathcal{C}}{\partial z} = \begin{cases} 0 & z < 1 - v \\ 1 & z > 1 - v \end{cases}$$

Having given the definition of the two-dimensional subcopula and its main properties, we are now in a position to define two-dimensional copulas.[4]

Definition 2.4 (Sklar, 1959)   A two-dimensional copula C is a two-dimensional subcopula with $A = B = I$.

The subcopula of Example 2.1 is actually a copula.

First of all, let us notice that, from the definition, copulas are joint distribution functions of standard uniform random variates:

$$C(v, z) = \Pr(U_1 \leqslant v, U_2 \leqslant z)$$

---

[4] In the rest of the chapter we will omit the term "two-dimensional" while referring to subcopulas and copulas, since the definition of n-dimensional subcopulas and copulas is deferred until Chapter 4.

The following probabilities of uniform variates can then be written via copulas:

$$\Pr(U_1 \leqslant v, U_2 > z) = v - C(v, z)$$

$$\Pr(U_1 > v, U_2 \leqslant z) = z - C(v, z)$$

$$\Pr(U_1 \leqslant v \mid U_2 \leqslant z) = C(v, z)/z$$

$$\Pr(U_1 \leqslant v \mid U_2 > z) = \frac{v - C(v, z)}{1 - z}$$

$$C_{1|2}(v, z) \equiv \Pr(U_1 \leqslant v \mid U_2 = z) = \lim_{\Delta z \to 0+} \frac{C(v, z + \Delta z) - C(v, z)}{\Delta z} = \frac{\partial C(v, z)}{\partial z}$$

$$C_{2|1}(v, z) \equiv \Pr(U_2 \leqslant z \mid U_1 = v) = \frac{\partial C(v, z)}{\partial v}$$

Second, we know from elementary probability theory that the **probability-integral trans-forms** of the r.v.s X and Y, $X \to F_1(X)$, $Y \to F_2(Y)$, are distributed as standard uniform U_i, $i = 1, 2$:

$$F_1(X) \sim U_1, \qquad F_2(Y) \sim U_2$$

Analogously, the transforms according to F_i^{-1} of standard uniforms are distributed according to F_i:

$$F_i^{-1}(U_i) \sim F_i$$

Since copulas are joint distribution functions of standard uniforms, a copula computed at $F_1(x)$, $F_2(y)$ gives a joint distribution function at (x, y):

$$C(F_1(x), F_2(y)) = \Pr(U_1 \leqslant F_1(x), U_2 \leqslant F_2(y))$$

$$= \Pr\left(F_1^{-1}(U_1) \leqslant x, F_2^{-1}(U_2) \leqslant y\right)$$

$$= \Pr(X \leqslant x, Y \leqslant y)$$

$$= F(x, y) \qquad (2.3)$$

This anticipates part of the link between distribution functions and copulas, which will be the content of Sklar's theorem. Before studying the latter, let us introduce the bounds for copulas, analogous to the Fréchet bounds for distribution functions.

2.2 FRÉCHET BOUNDS AND CONCORDANCE ORDER

It is straightforward to demonstrate that subcopulas are bounded:

Theorem 2.4   Subcopulas satisfy the following inequality:

$$\max(v + z - 1, 0) \leqslant \mathcal{C}(v, z) \leqslant \min(v, z) \qquad (2.4)$$

for every point $(v, z) \in A \times B$.

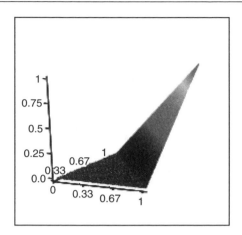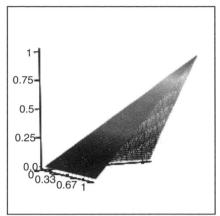

Figure 2.1 Minimum (left) and maximum (right) copulas

When $(v, z) \in I^2$, so that C becomes a copula, the bounds in (2.4) are copulas too: in the remainder of the section we will consider this case. The lower bound is denoted by C^-, and called **the minimum copula**; the upper bound is denoted by C^+, and called **the maximum copula**. They are represented in Figure 2.1.

From Theorem 2.4 and continuity it follows that the graph of each copula is "a continuous surface over the unit square that contains the skew quadrilateral whose vertices are $(0, 0, 0)$, $(1, 0, 0)$, $(1, 1, 1)$ and $(0, 1, 0)$. This surface is bounded below by the two triangles that together make up the surface of C^- and above by the two triangles that make up the surface of C^+" (Schweizer, 1991), as in Figure 2.2.

Theorem 2.4 has consequences on the so-called **level curves** of the copula $C(v, z)$, i.e. the set of points of I^2 such that $C(v, z) = \mathcal{K}$, with $\mathcal{K}$ constant:

$$\left\{ (v, z) \in I^2 : C(v, z) = \mathcal{K} \right\}$$

The level curves of the minimum and maximum copulas are

$$\{(v, z) : \max(v + z - 1, 0) = \mathcal{K}\}, \quad \mathcal{K} \in I$$
$$\{(v, z) : \min(v, z) = \mathcal{K}\}, \quad \mathcal{K} \in I \tag{2.5}$$

They are represented in the plane (v, z) respectively by segments parallel to the line $z = -v$, and kinked lines (see Figure 2.3).

It follows from the previous theorem that, for fixed $\mathcal{K}$, the level curve of each C stays in the triangle formed by the level sets (2.5). As $\mathcal{K}$ increases, the triangle is shifted upwards.

We will see below that level curves play an important role in financial applications of copulas, both for the simple evaluation of relationships between financial asset returns and for value-at-risk trade-off assessment.

The existence of the lower and upper bounds also suggests the following definition of **concordance order**:

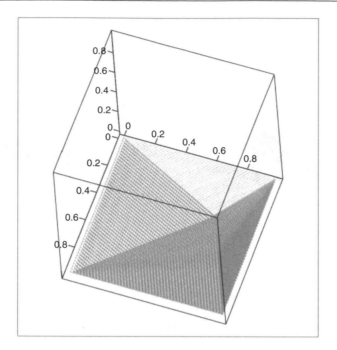

Figure 2.2   The pyramid is the region in which the copula graph is always included

Figure 2.3   Level curves of the minimum (left) and maximum (right) copulas

Definition 2.5   The copula C_1 is smaller than the copula C_2 — written as $C_1 \prec C_2$ — iff

$$C_1(v, z) \leqslant C_2(v, z)$$

for every $(v, z) \in I^2$.

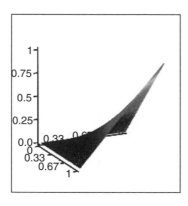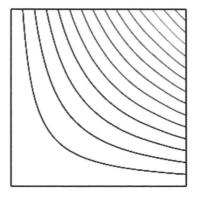

Figure 2.4 The product copula and its level curves

The order so defined is only partial, since not all copulas can be compared. In order to present some examples of concordance order, let us also define the **product copula**, represented in Figure 2.4, as

$$C^{\perp}(v, z) = vz$$

Example 2.3 One can easily verify that any convex linear combination of C^- and C^+ is a copula. Consider, for instance, the case

$$C = \tfrac{1}{3}C^- + \tfrac{2}{3}C^+$$

It is possible to find points in I^2 where $C \geqslant C^{\perp}$, as well as points where $C < C^{\perp}$, so that the two are not comparable. In particular

$$\tfrac{1}{3}\max(v + z - 1, 0) + \tfrac{2}{3}\min(vz) > vz$$

when $v = z = \tfrac{1}{2}$, while the opposite inequality holds for $v = \tfrac{1}{4}$, $z = \tfrac{3}{4}$.

We will encounter one-parameter families of copulas – to be defined exactly below – which are totally ordered. The order will depend on the value of the parameter: in particular, a family will be positively (negatively) ordered iff, denoting with C_α and C_β the copulas with parameter values α and β respectively, $C_\alpha(v, z) \prec C_\beta(v, z)$ whenever $\alpha \leqslant \beta$ ($\alpha \geqslant \beta$). For positively (negatively) ordered families, the level curves of C_α stay above those of C_β.

Example 2.4 One can easily demonstrate – using the definition – that, for every $p \in I$

$$C(v, z) = pC^- + (1 - p)C^{\perp}$$

is a copula. Since $C^- \prec C^{\perp}$, for $p_1 \geqslant p_2$ we have

$$(p_1 - p_2) C^- - (p_1 - p_2)C^{\perp} \leqslant 0$$

Rearranging:

$$p_1 C^- + (1 - p_1) C^\perp \leqslant p_2 C^- + (1 - p_2) C^\perp$$

which shows that the copula family under examination is negatively ordered with respect to the constant p.

2.3   SKLAR'S THEOREM AND THE PROBABILISTIC INTERPRETATION OF COPULAS

The point of departure for financial applications of copulas is their probabilistic interpretation, i.e. the relationship between copulas and distribution functions of r.v.s. This relationship is essentially contained in Sklar's theorem, which says that not only are copulas joint distribution functions, as argued in (2.3), but the converse also holds true: joint distribution functions can be rewritten in terms of the marginals and a (unique) subcopula, which in turn can be extended (not uniquely, in general) to a copula. Therefore, "much of the study of joint distribution functions can be reduced to the study of copulas" (Schweizer, 1991).

The presentation is organized as follows: in section 2.3.1 we state Sklar's theorem. In section 2.3.2 we present a corollary of Sklar's theorem, which permits us to reconstruct the subcopula mentioned in the theorem. In section 2.3.3 we comment on the modeling flexibility given by the theorem. Section 2.3.4 provides some financial applications.

2.3.1   Sklar's theorem

Consider a probability space $(\Omega, \Im, P)$, with Ω a non-empty set, $\Im$ a sigma algebra on Ω and P a probability measure on $\Im$. Let X and Y be two (Borel-measurable) r.v.s on $(\Omega, \Im, P)$ with values in $\Re^*$, the extended real line. Let also F, F_1 and F_2 be their joint and marginal distribution functions. As usual, the r.v.s are said to be continuous when their d.f.s are.

Theorem 2.5 (Sklar, 1959)   Let $F_1(x)$, $F_2(y)$ be (given) marginal distribution functions. Then, for every $(x, y) \in \Re^{*2}$:

  (i) if C is any subcopula whose domain contains Ran $F_1 \times$ Ran F_2,

$$\mathcal{C}(F_1(x), F_2(y))$$

   is a joint distribution function with margins $F_1(x)$, $F_2(y)$;
 (ii) conversely, if $F(x, y)$ is a joint distribution function with margins $F_1(x)$, $F_2(y)$, there exists a unique subcopula $\mathcal{C}$, with domain Ran $F_1 \times$ Ran F_2, such that

$$F(x, y) = \mathcal{C}(F_1(x), F_2(y)) \tag{2.6}$$

   If $F_1(x)$, $F_2(y)$ are continuous, the subcopula is a copula; if not, there exists a copula C such that

$$C(v, z) = \mathcal{C}(v, z)$$

   for every $(v, z) \in$ Ran $F_1 \times$ Ran F_2.

Example 2.5 Consider the copula in Example 2.1, defined on Ran $F_1 \times$ Ran F_2. The function

$$C(F_1(x), F_2(y)) = \max(F_1(x) + F_2(y) - 1, 0)$$

is a joint distribution function if F_1 and F_2 are marginal, since:

(i) it is defined for every $(x, y) \in \Re^{*2}$

(ii) it is 2-increasing:

$$\max(F_1(x_2) + F_2(y_2) - 1, 0) - \max(F_1(x_2) + F_2(y_1) - 1, 0)$$

$$- \max(F_1(x_1) + F_2(y_2) - 1, 0) + \max(F_1(x_1) + F_2(y_1) - 1, 0) \geqslant 0$$

(iii) it is grounded:

$$\max(F_1(-\infty) + F_2(y) - 1, 0) = 0$$

$$\max(F_1(x) + F_2(-\infty) - 1, 0) = 0$$

(iv) it gives:

$$C(F_1(+\infty), F_2(+\infty)) = \max(1, 1) = 1$$

(v) it is right continuous, since F_1 and F_2 are. Its margins are

$$C(F_1(x), F_2(+\infty)) = \max(F_1(x), 0) = F_1(x)$$

$$C(F_1(+\infty), F_2(y)) = \max(F_2(y), 0) = F_2(y)$$

This verifies part (i) of the theorem. As for part (ii), consider for instance two standard uniform r.v.s:

$$F_1(x) = \begin{cases} 0 & x < 0 \\ x & 0 \leqslant x \leqslant 1 \\ 1 & x > 1 \end{cases}$$

and analogously for y. Suppose that their joint distribution function for $\inf(x, y) > 0$ is

$$F(x, y) = \max(\inf(x, 1) + \inf(y, 1) - 1, 0) \tag{2.7}$$

and 0 otherwise. Since F_1 and F_2 are continuous, there exists a unique copula C such that

$$F(x, y) = C(F_1(x), F_2(y))$$

This is exactly the copula of Example 2.1.

If $F_1(x), F_2(y)$ are not continuous, uniqueness of the copula C, which extends the sub-copula $\mathcal{C}$, is not guaranteed. If, for instance, Ran $F_1 \times$ Ran F_2 is a singleton, every copula that has the same value as $\mathcal{C}$ at that point satisfies the theorem. We can also provide the following example.

Example 2.6   Let us consider the following distributions:

$$F(x, y) = \begin{cases} 0 & x \text{ or } y < 0 \\ \frac{1}{2}(\inf(x, 1) + \inf(y, 1)) & 0 \leqslant x, y \leqslant 1 \end{cases}$$

$$F_1(x) = \begin{cases} 0 & x < 0 \\ \frac{1}{2}(x + 1) & 0 \leqslant x \leqslant 1 \\ 1 & x > 1 \end{cases}$$

$$F_2(y) = \begin{cases} 0 & y < 0 \\ \frac{1}{2}(y + 1) & 0 \leqslant y \leqslant 1 \\ 1 & y > 1 \end{cases}$$

For them, the subcopula of Remark 2.1 satisfies the second part of Sklar's theorem on $A = B = \{0\} \cup \left[\frac{1}{2}, 1\right]$, as one can easily verify from the fact that for $\frac{1}{2} \leqslant x, y \leqslant 1$,

$$F(x, y) = \tfrac{1}{2}(x + y) = \max(\tfrac{1}{2}(x + 1) + \tfrac{1}{2}(y + 1) - 1, 0) = C(F_1(x), F_2(y))$$

This subcopula can be extended to I^2 either using the copula of Example 2.1, or the following one, suggested by Deheuvels (1978):

$$C(v, z) = \begin{cases} 2v(z - \frac{1}{2}) & 0 \leqslant v \leqslant \frac{1}{2}, \frac{1}{2} \leqslant z \leqslant 1 \\ 2z(v - \frac{1}{2}) & \frac{1}{2} \leqslant v \leqslant 1, 0 \leqslant z \leqslant \frac{1}{2} \\ 0 & v \leqslant \frac{1}{2}, z \leqslant \frac{1}{2} \end{cases}$$

Non-uniqueness arises from the fact that Y and X are not continuous and Ran $F_1(x) =$ Ran $F_2(y) = \{0\} \cup \left[\frac{1}{2}; 1\right]$.

According to Sklar's theorem, while writing

$$F(x, y) = C(F_1(x), F_2(y))$$

one splits the joint probability into the marginals and a copula, so that the latter only represents the "association" between X and Y. **Copulas separate marginal behavior, as represented by the F_i, from the association**: at the opposite, the two cannot be disentangled in the usual representation of joint probabilities via distribution functions. For this reason, copulas are called also **dependence functions** (Deheuvels, 1978). We refer to the possibility of writing the joint cumulative probability in terms of the marginal ones as the **probabilistic interpretation of copulas**.

Remark 2.2   Evidently, Sklar's theorem entails:

$$\Pr(X \leqslant x, Y > y) = F_1(x) - C(F_1(x), F_2(y))$$
$$\Pr(X > x, Y \leqslant y) = F_2(y) - C(F_1(x), F_2(y))$$

$$\Pr(X \leqslant x \mid Y \leqslant y) = C(F_1(x), F_2(y))/F_2(y)$$

$$\Pr(X \leqslant x \mid Y > y) = F_1(x) - C(F_1(x), F_2(y))/(1 - F_2(y))$$

$$\Pr(X \leqslant x \mid Y = y) = C_{1|2}(F_1(x), F_2(y)) = \frac{\partial C(v, z)}{\partial z}\bigg| v = F_1(x), z = F_2(y)$$

As a consequence of Sklar's theorem, the minimum and maximum copulas C^-, C^+ are named respectively the **Fréchet lower and upper bounds**: using Sklar's result, the inequality $C^- \leqslant C \leqslant C^+$ can be rewritten as

$$\max(F_1(x) + F_2(y) - 1, 0) \leqslant F(x, y) \leqslant \min(F_1(x), F_2(y)) \tag{2.8}$$

which is the well-known **Fréchet–Hoeffding inequality** for distribution functions.

2.3.2 The subcopula in Sklar's theorem

It follows as a corollary of Sklar's theorem that the subcopula that allows the representation (2.6) can be reconstructed from the margins and the joint distribution by inversion. Using the generalized inverse concept, we can state that

Corollary 2.3 Under the hypotheses of part (ii) of Sklar's theorem the (unique) subcopula C: Ran $F_1 \times$ Ran $F_2 \to I$ such that

$$F(x, y) = C(F_1(x), F_2(y))$$

for every (x, y) in $\Re^{*2}$ is

$$C(v, z) = F\left(F_1^{-1}(v), F_2^{-1}(z)\right)$$

Evidently, if Ran $F_1 =$ Ran $F_2 = I$, the previous subcopula is a copula.

Example 2.7 Suppose, in part (ii) of Sklar's theorem, that X and Y are exponential random variables

$$F_1(x) = 1 - \exp(-\lambda_1 x)$$

$$F_2(y) = 1 - \exp(-\lambda_2 y)$$

for $x > 0$, $y > 0$, $\lambda_1, \lambda_2 > 0$. Suppose also that their joint distribution is

$$F(x, y) = \max(1 - \exp(-\lambda_1 x) - \exp(-\lambda_2 y), 0) \tag{2.9}$$

Then, since

$$F_1^{-1}(v) = -\ln(1 - v)/\lambda_1 \tag{2.10}$$

and an analogous expression holds for z, the copula C such that

$$C(F_1(x), F_2(y)) = C(1 - \exp(-\lambda_1 x), 1 - \exp(-\lambda_2 y))$$

$$= \max(1 - \exp(-\lambda_1 x) - \exp(-\lambda_2 y), 0)$$

is

$$F\left(F_1^{-1}(v), F_2^{-1}(z)\right) = F\left(-\ln(1-v)/\lambda_1, -\ln(1-z)/\lambda_2\right)$$

$$= \max\left(1 - \exp(\ln(1-v)) - \exp\left(\ln\left(1-z\right)\right), 0\right)$$

$$= \max(v + z - 1, 0)$$

i.e. the copula of Example 2.1.

Corollary 2.3 states that the construction via Sklar's theorem exhausts the so-called **Fréchet class**, i.e. the class of joint distribution functions which have F_1 and F_2 as margins (Fréchet, 1935, 1951; Hoeffding, 1940).

2.3.3 Modeling consequences

The separation between marginal distributions and dependence explains the modeling flexibility given by copulas, which has a number of theoretical and practical applications. Before explaining them, let us introduce the following remark.

Remark 2.3 In Examples 2.5 and 2.7 above, the association between the r.v.s X and Y was encapsulated in the copula $C(v, z) = \max(v + z - 1, 0)$. As argued in Chapter 1 and in section 2.4.2 below, this copula represents perfect negative dependence. The marginal behavior was uniform in Example 2.5, exponential in Example 2.7: as a consequence, in the two examples the same copula gave different joint distributions, (2.7) and (2.9) respectively.

The first part of Sklar's theorem allows us to construct bivariate distributions in a straightforward, flexible way: simply "plug" a couple of univariate margins into a function which satisfies the subcopula definition. This contrasts with the "traditional" way to construct multivariate distributions, which suffers from the restriction that the margins are usually of the same type, i.e. the corresponding random variables are a linear affine transform of each other. With the copula construction we are allowed to start from marginals of different types.

Example 2.8 Using the product copula and the marginal of X of Example 2.5, i.e. exponential, assume Y to be a (central) Student r.v., with υ degrees of freedom (d.o.f.). Formally, this means that:

$$F_2(y) = t_\upsilon(y) = \int_{-\infty}^y \frac{\Gamma((\upsilon+1)/2)}{\sqrt{\pi\upsilon}\Gamma(\upsilon/2)} \left(1 + \frac{s^2}{\upsilon}\right)^{-\frac{\upsilon+1}{2}} ds$$

where Γ is the usual Euler function. Then the joint distribution function, according to Sklar's theorem, is:

$$F(x, y) = [1 - \exp(\lambda_1 x)] \int_{-\infty}^y \frac{\Gamma((\upsilon+1)/2)}{\sqrt{\pi\upsilon}\Gamma(\upsilon/2)} \left(1 + \frac{s^2}{\upsilon}\right)^{-\frac{\upsilon+1}{2}} ds$$

Consider now, with the same marginals, the following function, which, as the readers can check, satisfies the copula definition[5]:

$$\mathring{C}(v, z) = \begin{cases} vz^{1-r}, & v \leqslant z \\ v^{1-r}z, & v > z \end{cases}$$

Then Sklar's theorem allows us to state that also $\mathring{C}(F_1(x), F_2(y))$ is a distribution function:

$$\mathring{F}(x, y) = \begin{cases} [1 - \exp(\lambda_1 x)] \left[\int_{-\infty}^{y} \frac{\Gamma((v+1)/2)}{\sqrt{\pi v}\Gamma(v/2)} \left(1 + \frac{s^2}{v}\right)^{-\frac{v+1}{2}} ds \right]^{1-r}, & (x, y) \in A \\ [1 - \exp(\lambda_1 x)]^{1-r} \int_{-\infty}^{y} \frac{\Gamma((v+1)/2)}{\sqrt{\pi v}\Gamma(v/2)} \left(1 + \frac{s^2}{v}\right)^{-\frac{v+1}{2}} ds, & (x, y) \notin A \end{cases}$$

where the region A is defined by

$$x \leqslant -\frac{1}{\lambda_1} \ln \left[1 - \int_{-\infty}^{y} \frac{\Gamma((v+1)/2)}{\sqrt{\pi v}\Gamma(v/2)} \left(1 + \frac{s^2}{v}\right)^{-\frac{v+1}{2}} ds \right]$$

We have been able, through copulas, to construct joint distributions for X and Y, even if they had marginals of different types. These distribution functions encapsulate different assumptions on the dependence between X and Y: in particular, the former, F, represents independence, since it is the product of the marginals, while the latter, $\mathring{F}$, does not, unless $r = 0$.

In the previous example, we could continue to generate joint distribution functions from the given marginals as long as we could produce copula functions, even though we started from marginals of different types. *A fortiori*, the result would have obtained with marginals of the same type.

When modeling from the **theoretical point of view** then, copulas allow a double "infinity" of degrees of freedom, or flexibility:

 (i) define the appropriate marginals and
(ii) choose the appropriate copula.

This flexibility holds also when modeling from the **practical** (or estimation) **point of view**, since the separation between marginal distributions and dependence suggests that we should decompose any estimation problem into two steps: the first for the marginals and the second for the copula. We will return to this issue in Chapter 5.

2.3.4 Sklar's theorem in financial applications: toward a non-Black–Scholes world

This section presents some applications of Sklar's theorem, as well as of the other copula properties listed above, to option pricing and credit risk evaluation: by so doing, it develops the examples in the primer of Chapter 1. It also provides an example in market risk evaluation.

---

[5] It is the so-called Cuadras–Augé one.

Bivariate digital option pricing

Let us consider two (univariate) put digital options, which pay 1 unit of account iff the underlying asset is at or below the strike at maturity T. Suppose that the riskless interest rate is zero. If we denote by X and Y the prices of the underlyings at maturity, and by K and k their strikes, it is known from martingale pricing theory that (in a complete, arbitrage-free market) the option prices are:

$$\Pr(X \leqslant K) = F_1(K)$$

$$\Pr(Y \leqslant k) = F_2(k)$$

The so-called bivariate put digital option, which pays one unit of account iff both X and Y are at or below the strike, has price

$$\Pr(X \leqslant K, Y \leqslant k) = F(K, k)$$

According to Sklar's theorem, it is always possible to represent this price in terms of the single digital prices:

$$F(K, k) = C(F_1(K), F_2(k))$$

and the representation is unique on Ran $F_1 \times$ Ran F_2. It is unique *tout court* if X and Y are continuous.

If the riskless interest rate is different from zero, then the price at 0 is $B(0, T)C(F_1(K), F_2(k))$ where $B(0, T)$ is the discount factor from T to 0, so that $C(F_1(K), F_2(k))$ is the forward price.

Assume now that X and Y are log-normally distributed, with log returns, $\ln(X/X_0)$ and $\ln(Y/Y_0)$, normal with mean $\left(r - \frac{1}{2}\sigma_X^2\right)T$, $\left(r - \frac{1}{2}\sigma_Y^2\right)T$ and variance $\sigma_X^2 T$, $\sigma_Y^2 T$ respectively, as in the (risk-neutralized) Black–Scholes model. We have

$$\Pr(X \leqslant K) = F_1(K) = \Phi\left(-\frac{\ln(X_0/K) + \left(r - \frac{1}{2}\sigma_X^2\right)T}{\sigma_X \sqrt{T}}\right) \equiv \Phi(-d_{2X}(K))$$

$$\Pr(Y \leqslant k) = F_2(k) = \Phi\left(-\frac{\ln(Y_0/k) + \left(r - \frac{1}{2}\sigma_Y^2\right)T}{\sigma_Y \sqrt{T}}\right) \equiv \Phi(-d_{2Y}(k))$$

and therefore

$$\Pr(X \leqslant K, Y \leqslant k) = F(K, k) = C(F_1(K), F_2(k)) = C(\Phi(-d_{2X}(K)), \Phi(-d_{2Y}(k)))$$

Suppose, for instance, that $K = 2$, $k = \frac{1}{2}$, $X_0 = Y_0 = 1$, $r - \frac{1}{2}\sigma_X^2 = r - \frac{1}{2}\sigma_Y^2 = 0$, $\sigma_X = \sigma_Y = 0.2$, $T = 5$, so that

$$-d_{2X}(K) = 1.55, \qquad -d_{2Y}(k) = -1.55$$

Then the forward bivariate digital price is

$$F(2, \tfrac{1}{2}) = C(\Phi(1.55), \Phi(-1.55)) = C(0.9394, 0.0606)$$

If in addition we assume $C = C^-$, then the forward price becomes

$$\max\left(\Phi(1.55) + \Phi(-1.55) - 1, 0\right) = \max(0.9394 + 0.0606 - 1, 0) = 0$$

If instead we assume $C = C^+$, we obtain

$$\min(\Phi(1.55), \Phi(-1.55)) = \min(0.9394, 0.0606) = 0.0606$$

and it follows from the Fréchet inequality that

$$0 \leqslant C(0.9394, 0.0606) \leqslant 0.0606$$

In particular, if we assume independence between the two returns, we have argued in Chapter 1 and will see below that $C = C^{\perp}$. The forward digital price is

$$\Phi(1.55)\Phi(-1.55) = 0.0569$$

However, the natural extension of the Black–Scholes model to a bivariate setting consists in assuming jointly normal returns. In we assume that $\ln\left(X/X_0\right)$ and $\ln\left(Y/Y_0\right)$ are not only marginally, but also jointly normally distributed, with correlation coefficient ρ, Corollary 2.3 permits us to state that their copula is the so-called Gaussian one, defined as:

$$C^{\mathrm{Ga}}(v, z) = \int_{-\infty}^{\Phi^{-1}(v)} \int_{-\infty}^{\Phi^{-1}(z)} \frac{1}{2\pi\sqrt{1-\rho^2}} \exp\left(\frac{2\rho s\omega - s^2 - \omega^2}{2\left(1-\rho^2\right)}\right) ds\, d\omega$$

Using the copula framework, the no-arbitrage forward price of the bivariate digital option is

$$\Pr\left(X \leqslant K, Y \leqslant k\right) = F(K, k) = C^{\mathrm{Ga}}(\Phi(-d_{2X}(K)), \Phi(-d_{2Y}(k)))$$

$$= \int_{-\infty}^{-d_{2X}(K)} \int_{-\infty}^{-d_{2Y}(k)} \frac{1}{2\pi\sqrt{1-\rho^2}} \exp\left(\frac{2\rho s w - s^2 - w^2}{2\left(1-\rho^2\right)}\right) ds\, dw$$

If $K = 2$, $k = \frac{1}{2}$, as previously assumed, and $\rho = 20\%$, the price turns out to be

$$F\left(2, \tfrac{1}{2}\right) = \int_{-\infty}^{1.55} \int_{-\infty}^{-1.55} \frac{1}{2\pi\sqrt{1-0.2^2}} \exp\left(\frac{0.4sw - s^2 - w^2}{2\left(1-0.2^2\right)}\right) ds\, dw = 0.886$$

If, in the previous case, we use a copula other than the Gaussian one, this means that, via copulas, we are extending bivariate financial modeling beyond Black–Scholes. Consider, for instance, two stock indices, DAX 30 and FTSE 100. Assume that they are marginally normal. Using a daily time series from January 2, 1999, to March 27, 2000, one can argue that their (daily) variances are respectively $\sigma_X^2 = 0.0147$ and $\sigma_Y^2 = 0.01197$, while, considering the riskless rate on the euro zone, $\mu_X = r - \frac{1}{2}\sigma_X^2 = 0.0013$ and $\mu_Y = r - \frac{1}{2}\sigma_Y^2 = 0.0004$.

Cherubini and Luciano (2002a) argue that for these indices the "best fit" copula, starting from a selection of three, is the so-called Frank copula[6]:

$$C^A(v, z) = -\frac{1}{\alpha} \ln \left(1 + \frac{(\exp(-\alpha v) - 1)(\exp(-\alpha z) - 1)}{\exp(-\alpha) - 1} \right) \tag{2.11}$$

Under this copula, the no-arbitrage forward price of the bivariate digital option is

$$\Pr(X \leqslant K, Y \leqslant k) = F(K, k) = C^A(\Phi(-d_{2X}(K)), \Phi(-d_{2Y}(k)))$$

$$= -\frac{1}{\alpha} \ln \left\{ 1 + \frac{[\exp(-\alpha \Phi(-d_{2X}(K))) - 1][\exp(-\alpha \Phi(-d_{2Y}(k))) - 1]}{\exp(-\alpha) - 1} \right\}$$

If $K = 2$, $k = \frac{1}{2}$, $X_0 = Y_0 = 1$, $T = 5$ and, as turns out from the estimates in Cherubini and Luciano (2002a), $\alpha = 4.469$, the price becomes

$$F(2, \tfrac{1}{2}) = -\frac{1}{4.469} \ln \left\{ 1 + \frac{\begin{array}{c}[\exp(-4.469\Phi(-d_{2X}(2))) - 1] \\ \times [\exp(-4.469\Phi(-d_{2Y}(1/2))) - 1]\end{array}}{\exp(-4.469) - 1} \right\}$$

$$= 0.0231$$

The copula approach then has allowed us, starting from marginally normal returns (with no joint behavior hypothesis) to obtain bounds for the bivariate digital price, then (under joint normality) to reconstruct the Black–Scholes price, and finally to price the derivative under the "best fit" dependence function choice.

Credit risk evaluation

We have seen in Chapter 1 that, in Merton's (1974) structural approach to credit risk, a firm defaults if its asset value falls below the debt at maturity of the latter, T. Denote with V and W the asset values at debt maturity of two firms and assume them to be log-normal: $\ln(V/V_0)$ and $\ln(W/W_0)$ are normal, with risk neutral means $(r - \sigma_V^2/2)T$, $(r - \sigma_W^2/2)T$ and variances $\sigma_V^2 T$, $\sigma_W^2 T$ respectively. Then, the probability that each firm defaults at time T, if $D_V(D_W) \in \Re$ is its debt, is

$$\Pr(V \leqslant D_V) = \Phi\left(-\frac{\ln(V_0/D_V) + (r - \sigma_V^2/2)T}{\sigma_V \sqrt{T}}\right) \equiv \Phi(-d_{2V}(V_0))$$

$$\Pr(W \leqslant D_W) = \Phi\left(-\frac{\ln(W_0/D_W) + (r - \sigma_W^2/2)T}{\sigma_W \sqrt{T}}\right) \equiv \Phi(-d_{2W}(W_0))$$

---

[6] Please note that in the original paper the current assumption on the marginals is abandoned.

and the risk-neutral joint default probability $\Pr(V \leqslant D_V, W \leqslant D_W)$ can always be written, according to Sklar's theorem, as

$$C\left(\Phi\left(-d_{2V}(V_0)\right), \Phi\left(-d_{2W}(W_0)\right)\right)$$

Suppose, for instance, that the two firms have debts equal to $D_V = 0.5$, $D_W = 0.7$, and $V_0 = W_0 = 1$, $\mu_V = \mu_W = 0$, $\sigma_V = \sigma_W = 0.2$, $T = 5$, so that $-d_{2V}(V_0) = -1.55$, $-d_{2W}(W_0) = -0.797$. Then

$$\Phi(-d_{2V}(V_0)) = 0.0606, \qquad \Phi(-d_{2V}(W_0)) = 0.2126$$

and the joint default probability is

$$\Pr(V \leqslant 0.5, W \leqslant 0.7) = C(0.0606, 0.2126)$$

If $C = C^-$, then the probability becomes 0; if $C = C^+$, then it is 0.0606. As an immediate application of Fréchet inequality, no matter which is the dependence function chosen, the joint default probability always stays between the C^- and C^+ values:

$$0 \leqslant C(0.0606, 0.2126) \leqslant 0.0606$$

In particular, if $C = C^\perp$, then it is 0.0129.

If the returns on the two firms are jointly normal at T, in addition to being marginally normal, we are again in the Black–Scholes framework. The joint default probability at time T, since the copula for the firms' values and returns is the same,[7] is the Gaussian one:

$$H(D_V, D_W) = \Pr(V \leqslant D_V, W \leqslant D_W) = C^{\text{Ga}}\left(\Phi\left(-d_{2V}(V_0)\right), \Phi\left(-d_{2W}(W_0)\right)\right)$$

Suppose, for instance, that the asset returns have a correlation coefficient $\frac{1}{2}$, while the outstanding debts are 0.5 and 0.7, as above: the joint default probability is

$$H(0.5, 0.7) = \int_{-\infty}^{-1.55} \int_{-\infty}^{-0.0797} \frac{1}{2\pi\sqrt{1-0.5^2}} \exp\left(\frac{sw - s^2 - w^2}{2\left(1 - 0.5^2\right)}\right) \mathrm{d}s\mathrm{d}w = 0.0069$$

The extension of the Black–Scholes framework in the default context could proceed along the same lines of the bivariate option example: assume a copula different from the Gaussian one, even if the marginals are Gaussians.

In order to make the reader aware of the full flexibility of copulas however, let us explore a totally different way to obtain joint default probabilities via copulas. In contrast with the Merton's case, let us consider historical default probabilities, following Luciano and Marena (2003).

As is well known, rating agencies provide tables (see Table 2.1), such as those of S&P, reported below, which give the marginal default probabilities $F_i(t)$ for different maturities and depending on the rating of the issuer:

---

[7] The result is straightforward in the example, when one switches from returns to values, and will be proved in general for increasing transforms in section 2.4.3 below.

Table 2.1 Historically observed default probabilities, source: S&P, 2000

	Rating			
Maturity	AAA	AA	A	BBB
1	0.00%	0.01%	0.04%	0.22%
2	0.00%	0.04%	0.11%	0.50%
3	0.03%	0.09%	0.19%	0.79%
4	0.06%	0.16%	0.32%	1.30%
5	0.10%	0.25%	0.49%	1.80%
7	0.26%	0.53%	0.83%	2.73%
8	0.40%	0.63%	1.01%	3.10%
9	0.45%	0.70%	1.21%	3.39%
10	0.51%	0.79%	1.41%	3.68%
15	0.51%	1.07%	1.83%	4.48%

We can immediately use these marginal default probabilities in a copula representation of the joint default probability

$$\Pr(T_1 \leqslant t, T_2 \leqslant t) = C(F_1(t), F_2(t))$$

Consider, for instance, an AAA and a simple A obligor, and focus attention on the maturities $t = 1, 5, 10, 15$:

$$F(1, 1) = C(0\%, 0.04\%)$$

$$F(5, 5) = C(0.1\%, 0.49\%)$$

$$F(10, 10) = C(0.51\%, 1.41\%)$$

$$F(15, 15) = C(0.51\%, 1.83\%)$$

For each specific copula choice, we can easily evaluate the joint default probability, by simple substitution.

Also, by choosing a single-parameter copula, such as the Gaussian or Frank defined above, we can study the behavior of the joint probability with respect to the parameter choice: since the copula represents dependence, its parameter, in analogy with the Gaussian case, must give a measure of how much the random variables in the copula (the times to default, here) "move together".[8] Let us denote as $d(F_1(t), F_2(t), \alpha)$ the joint default probability as a function of the parameter value:

$$d(F_1(t), F_2(t), \alpha) = C(F_1(t), F_2(t); \alpha)$$

and consider a Frank copula.

When α, the association parameter, varies from 1 to 25, we get the increasing behavior of the joint default probabilities illustrated in Figure 2.5.

---

[8] This concept will be clarified and made exact in Chapter 3.

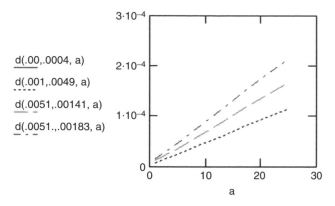

Figure 2.5 Joint default probabilities between an AAA and an A obligor, as a function of dependence (a = α in the text), over 1, 5, 10, 15 years (lines from bottom to top), Frank copula

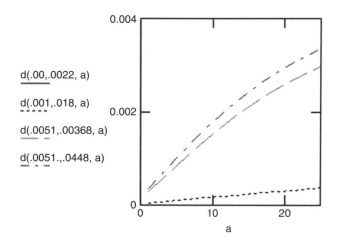

Figure 2.6 Joint default probabilities between an AAA and a BBB obligor, as a function of dependence (a = α in the text), over 1, 5, 10, 15 years (lines from bottom to top), Frank copula

Figure 2.6 presents analogous results, for an AAA and a BBB obligor.

A comparison between the two figures permits us to verify that the increase of the probabilities is much less pronounced in the second case than in the first: the greater the rating class distance between the counterparties, the less increase we notice in the joint default probability. This happens homogeneously across maturities.

In the bivariate option example the use of copulas permitted us to abandon the Black–Scholes assumption and to adopt the "best fit" model for joint behavior. Here, even without aiming at best fitting the joint model (due to the generality of the marginals), we obtained a sensitivity analysis with respect to the copula parameter, which, as claimed above, must represent the "dependence" between the underlying random variables. This will be the object of Chapter 3.

VaR computation

Copulas have been applied to the measurement of market risk, in particular to the assessment of the Value at Risk (VaR) of a portfolio. Let us recall that, for a given confidence level θ, VaR is the level under which returns will fall only with probability θ. If we denote as Z the portfolio return over a given horizon T, VaR is the threshold such that:

$$\Pr(Z \leqslant \mathrm{VaR}_Z) = \theta$$

Equivalently, using the distribution function of Z, $\mathfrak{H}(z)$, VaR can be defined as the solution z^* of the equation $\mathfrak{H}(z^*) = \theta$. In turn, the distribution function $\mathfrak{H}$ can be written via copulas, as follows. Consider a portfolio of two assets. Let X and Y be their continuous returns, over a common horizon T, and let $\beta \in (0, 1)$ be the weight of X. The portfolio return is $Z = \beta X + (1 - \beta) Y$, with distribution function

$$\mathfrak{H}(z) = \Pr(Z \leqslant z) = \Pr(\beta X + (1 - \beta) Y \leqslant z)$$

$$= \int_{-\infty}^{+\infty} \Pr\left(X \leqslant \frac{1}{\beta}z - \frac{1-\beta}{\beta}y, Y = y\right) f_2(y)\mathrm{d}y$$

$$= \int_{-\infty}^{+\infty} C_{1|2}\left(F_1\left(\frac{1}{\beta}z - \frac{1-\beta}{\beta}y\right), F_2(y)\right) f_2(y)\mathrm{d}y \qquad (2.12)$$

where the conditional probability assessment via $C_{1|2}$, introduced in Remark 2.2, has been used.

Suppose, as in Luciano and Marena (2003), that the returns on two assets X and Y have been estimated to be distributed according to a Student's t, with 5 and 6 d.o.f. respectively. Formally, we have

$$F_1(x) = \int_{-\infty}^{x} \frac{\Gamma(3)}{\Gamma(5/2)\sqrt{5\pi}} \left(1 + \frac{u^2}{5}\right)^{-3} \mathrm{d}u$$

$$F_2(y) = \int_{-\infty}^{y} \frac{\Gamma(7/2)}{\Gamma(3)\sqrt{6\pi}} \left(1 + \frac{u^2}{6}\right)^{-7/2} \mathrm{d}u$$

where Γ is the usual Euler function.

Assume that the Frank copula represents their association, and let $\alpha = -3$, so as to consider a case of negative "dependence" between the two assets, which hedge each other.

By letting the allocation weight vary from 10% to 90%, and considering both the level of confidence (loc) 95% and the 99% one, formula (2.12) gives the values at risk shown in Table 2.2.

Three facts are evident from Table 2.2: first, as usual, diversification pays, since when the allocation weight gets closer to 50% the VaR decreases, for given level of confidence; second, due to the fat-tailed nature of the returns, the VaR increases substantially with the loc, for given allocation weight; third, for symmetric weights (for instance $\beta = 10\%$, $1 - \beta = 90\%$ and $\beta = 90\%$, $1 - \beta = 10\%$), the VaR is greater when β increases, since X is riskier than Y (the variance of a Student's t is $\upsilon/(\upsilon - 2)$, where υ is the number of d.o.f.).

Table 2.2 VaR for the bivariate portfolio of page 68, as a function of β and the loc, Students's t marginals, Frank copula

β	10%	25%	50%	75%	90%
loc 95%	−1.670	−1.332	−1.093	−1.379	−1.735
loc 99%	−2.726	−2.197	−1.792	−2.344	−2.917

Table 2.3 VaR for the bivariate portfolio of page 68, as a function of β and the loc, normal marginals, Frank copula

β	10%	25%	50%	75%	90%
loc 95%	−1.735	−1.373	−1.105	−1.453	−1.835
loc 99%	−2.459	−1.983	−1.622	−2.093	−2.599

Table 2.4 VaR for the bivariate portfolio of page 68, as a function of β and the loc, Students's t marginals, product copula

β	10%	25%	50%	75%	90%
loc 95%	−1.757	−1.549	−1.422	−1.590	−1.818
loc 99%	−2.823	−2.451	−2.217	−2.587	−3.011

The copula approach then allows us to compute the VaRs for a portfolio with a non-normal joint distribution, and to study its sensitivity with respect to the portfolio mix. We could also study the sensitivity with respect to the copula parameter, as we did in the credit risk case.

Moreover, the copula approach has still its double "infinity" of d.o.f. to be exploited: it permits us either (i) to change the marginals while keeping the copula fixed or (ii) to change the copula while keeping the marginals fixed.

In the first case, suppose you want to eliminate the fat-tails effect of the Student's t, and consider the returns as being normal, with zero mean and the same standard deviations as above (1.291 for X and 1.225 for Y). The VaRs are shown in Table 2.3.

At the loc 99%, the VaR values for each allocation weight are smaller in absolute value than in Table 2.2, since we no longer have fat tails. However, for the very nature of the tails, this effect shows up only at the higher quantile.

In the second case, keep the marginals fixed (Student's t) and assume independence between the returns, i.e. a product copula.[9] We get Table 2.4.

As expected, the VaR values for each couple loc–allocation weight are greater (in absolute value) than in Table 2.2, since the two assets no longer hedge.

To conclude, the copula approach to VaR permits us to avoid the usual assumption of marginal and joint normality. For the marginals, one can indeed use in (2.12) any choice of F_1, F_2, so as to take into account, as above, fat tails. For the copula, functions with

---

[9] As we will argue in Chapter 3, the Frank copula also degenerates into the product one when the parameter goes to zero.

so-called upper (or lower) tail dependency (see the next chapter) have been suggested. The very powerfulness of the copula approach, however, consists in separating the marginal and dependence effects, as the example, as well as the previous pricing and credit risk ones, shows.

2.4 COPULAS AS DEPENDENCE FUNCTIONS: BASIC FACTS

Since copulas are dependence functions, they permit us to characterize independence and perfect dependence in a straightforward way. Since they separate the marginal behavior from dependence itself, they turn out to be invariant w.r.t. increasing the transform of the (continuous) r.v.s X and Y. Let us analyze these features separately.

In order not to be obliged to distinguish the (unique) copula of X and Y on Ran $F_1 \times$ Ran F_2 from its (non-unique) extension to the whole of I^2, in this section we assume that X and Y are continuous random variates.

2.4.1 Independence

Recall that X and Y are independent r.v.s iff $F(x, y) = F_1(x)F_2(y)$. It is evident that Sklar's theorem entails

Corollary 2.4 The r.v.s X and Y are independent iff they have the product copula $C^{\perp}$.

2.4.2 Comonotonicity

Two r.v.s are comonotone or countermonotone – and therefore perfectly dependent – iff their copula is respectively the upper and lower Fréchet bound. To make this statement precise, let us recall the following.

Definition 2.6 The set $A \subset \Re^{*2}$ is said to be comonotic iff, for any (x_1, y_1), (x_2, y_2) in A, either

$$\begin{cases} x_1 \leqslant y_1 \\ x_2 \leqslant y_2 \end{cases} \quad \text{or} \quad \begin{cases} x_1 \geqslant y_1 \\ x_2 \geqslant y_2 \end{cases}$$

Definition 2.7 A random vector (X, Y) is **comonotonic** or **perfectly positively dependent** iff there exists a comonotonic set $A \subset \Re^{*2}$ such that

$$\Pr((X, Y) \in A) = 1$$

Loosely said, a couple of comonotonic random variates has outcomes that are ordered componentwise: realizations for which X is higher, have Y higher too. The comonotonic property can be characterized in a number of equivalent ways, as the following theorem, which appears up to point 5 also in Dhaene et al. (2002), shows:

Theorem 2.6 A random vector (X, Y), with marginal distribution functions F_1, F_2 and joint distribution $F(x, y)$ is comonotonic iff one of the following (equivalent) statements holds:

(1) (X, Y) has comonotonic support
(2) (Hoeffding, 1940; Fréchet, 1951) for every $(x, y) \in \Re^{*2}$

$$F(x, y) = \min(F_1(x), F_2(y))$$

(3) $C(v, z) = C^+(v, z)$
(4) (Hoeffding, 1940; Fréchet, 1951) (X, Y) is distributed as $(F_1^{-1}(U), F_2^{-1}(U))$, where U is a standard uniform random variate
(5) (X, Y) is distributed as $(F_1^{-1}(F_2(Y)), F_2^{-1}(F_1(X)))$

It follows that

Corollary 2.5 If $F_1 = F_2$, then X and Y are comonotonic iff they are equal a.s.

A symmetric definition for countermonotonic or perfectly negatively dependent random variates can be given as:

Definition 2.8 The set $A \subset \Re^{*2}$ is said to be countermonotonic iff, for any (x_1, y_1), (x_2, y_2) in A, either

$$\begin{cases} x_1 \leqslant y_1 \\ x_2 \geqslant y_2 \end{cases} \quad \text{or} \quad \begin{cases} x_1 \geqslant y_1 \\ x_2 \leqslant y_2 \end{cases}$$

Definition 2.9 A random vector (X, Y) is **countermonotonic** or **perfectly negatively dependent** iff there exists a countermonotonic set $A \subset \Re^{*2}$ such that

$$\Pr((X, Y) \in A) = 1$$

The following theorem can be easily demonstrated.

Theorem 2.7 A random vector (X, Y), with marginal distribution functions F_1, F_2 and joint distribution $F(x, y)$ is countermonotonic iff one of the following (equivalent) statements holds:

(1) (X, Y) has countermonotonic support
(2) (Hoeffding, 1940; Fréchet, 1951) for every $(x, y) \in \Re^{*2}$

$$F(x, y) = \max(F_1(x) + F_2(y) - 1, 0)$$

(3) $C(v, z) = C^-(v, z)$
(4) (Hoeffding, 1940; Fréchet, 1951) (X, Y) is distributed as $(F_1^{-1}(U), 1 - F_2^{-1}(U))$, where U is a standard uniform random variate
(5) (X, Y) is distributed as $(F_1^{-1}(1 - F_2(Y)), F_2^{-1}(1 - F_1(X)))$

Example 2.9 The r.v.s in Example 2.7 have the C^- copula: the previous theorem entails that $Y = F_2^{-1}(1 - F_1)$ a.s.
Recalling that X and Y are exponential, with the inverse (2.10), we have

$$Y = -\ln(1 - \exp(-\lambda_1 X))/\lambda_2$$

2.4.3 Monotone transforms and copula invariance

Copulas of increasing or decreasing transforms of (continuous) r.v.s are easily written in terms of the copula of X and Y: in particular, copulas are invariant w.r.t. increasing transforms.

Let $\alpha_i : \mathfrak{R}^* \to \mathfrak{R}$, $i = 1, 2$, be two functions, increasing a.s. It is known from elementary probability theory that the margins of the r.v.s $\alpha_1(X)$, $\alpha_2(Y)$ are transformations of the corresponding F_i, i.e.

$$\alpha_1(X) \sim F_1\left(\alpha_1^{-1}\right), \quad \alpha_2(Y) \sim F_2\left(\alpha_2^{-1}\right)$$

Let us denote the margins $F_i\left(\alpha_i^{-1}\right)$ as H_i. The following theorem holds:

Theorem 2.8 (Schweizer & Wolff, 1976, 1981)   Let X, Y be continuous random variables with marginal distribution functions F_1, F_2 and copula C. If α_1, α_2 are two transformations, increasing (a.s.), the r.v.s $\alpha_1(X)$, $\alpha_2(Y)$, which have marginal distribution functions $H_1 = F_1\left(\alpha_1^{-1}\right)$, $H_2 = F_2\left(\alpha_2^{-1}\right)$ and joint one H

$$H(u, t) = \Pr(\alpha_1(X) \leqslant u, \alpha_2(Y) \leqslant t)$$

have copula C too:

$$H(u, t) = C(H_1(u), H_2(t))$$

Loosely speaking, copulas are invariant w.r.t. increasing transformations, even though the latter act differently on X and Y ($\alpha_1 \neq \alpha_2$).

Example 2.10   Consider two standard normals X and Y and let their dependence be represented by the Gaussian copula. If we consider now the increasing transforms $U = \exp(X)$, $T = \exp(Y)$, which we know to be log-normally distributed, we can state, according to Theorem 2.8, that they still have the Gaussian copula. Therefore, their joint distribution function is

$$H(u, t) = C^{Ga}(H_1(u), H_2(t)) = C^{Ga}(\Phi(\ln u), \Phi(\ln t))$$

Conversely, if one starts with X and Y log-normally distributed, so that $U = \ln X$ and $T = \ln Y$ are standard normal, and assumes the Gaussian copula for X and Y, then the joint distribution of U and T, according to Theorem 2.8, is

$$H(u, t) = C^{Ga}(\dot{H}_1(u), \dot{H}_2(t)) = C^{Ga}(\vec{\Phi}(e^u), \vec{\Phi}(e^t))$$

where $\vec{\Phi}$ is the log-normal distribution function with parameters $(0, 1)$, and $\dot{H}_1$ and $\dot{H}_2$ are the margins of U and T.

Analogously, one could demonstrate that for α_1 increasing a.s. and α_2 decreasing a.s., ceteris paribus,

$$H(u, t) = H_1(u) - C(H_1(u), 1 - H_2(t))$$

For α_1 decreasing and α_2 increasing (both a.s.)

$$H(u, t) = H_2(t) - C(1 - H_1(u), H_2(t))$$

while for both α_1 and α_2 decreasing (both a.s.)

$$H(u, t) = H_1(u) + H_2(t) - 1 + C(1 - H_1(u), 1 - H_2(t)) \qquad (2.13)$$

From the behavior of the copula w.r.t. increasing or decreasing transforms, and in particular from the fact that "the copula is invariant while the margins can be changed at will", a number of theoretical and applicative consequences follow.

From the theoretical point of view, it follows that "any functional or 'property' of the joint distribution function of (two) r.v.s that is invariant under strictly increasing transformations of the r.v.s is a functional or 'property' of their copula (and independent of the individual distributions ...). Thus ... it is natural to use any measure of distance between surfaces as a measure of dependence for pairs of r.v.s" (Schweizer & Sklar, 1983): this is the core of the definition of concordance between r.v.s, which we will discuss in the next chapter.

From the point of view of applications, the comonotonicity property, together with invariance, allows us to fully exploit the copula tool to enlarge financial modeling. An example is presented in the next section.

2.4.4   An application: VaR trade-off

Let us introduce an example in which the copula technique itself suggests an economic evaluation, the trade-off between values at risk.

Let us consider, as in Cherubini and Luciano (2001), the returns on two stock indices, namely the FTSE 100 and the S&P 100. Starting from their daily closing prices from January 3, 1995 to April 20, 2000, compute the empirical marginal distributions of their log returns X and Y, i.e. their cumulated frequencies. Let us denote them as $F_1(x_i)$, $F_2(y_i)$, $i = 1, 2, \ldots, n$ respectively.

As a first step, determine the level curves of the two indices, returns, using the minimum, product and maximum copula. Recalling the definition, they are respectively the loci of points

$$\{(v, z) : \max(v + z - 1, 0) = \mathcal{K}\}, \quad \mathcal{K} \in I$$

$$\{(v, z) : vz = \mathcal{K}\}, \quad \mathcal{K} \in I$$

$$\{(v, z) : \min(v, z) = \mathcal{K}\}, \quad \mathcal{K} \in I$$

As the readers learned from Theorems 2.6 and 2.7, the first copula – and then the first level curves – apply if (and only if) the returns on the FTSE and S&P are countermonotonic, the second if (and only) they are independent, the third if (and only if) they are comonotonic.

Cherubini and Luciano (2001) also computed some level curve values using the Clayton copula, defined as

$$C^C(v, z) = \max\left[\left(v^{-\alpha} + z^{-\alpha} - 1 \right)^{-1/\alpha}, 0 \right] \qquad (2.14)$$

They adopted the parameter value $\alpha = \frac{1}{2}$, since this was demonstrated to be the "best fit" one. Under the Clayton choice, with parameter value $\frac{1}{2}$, the level curves have equation:

$$\{(v, z) : (v^{-1/2} + z^{-1/2} - 1)^{-2} = \mathcal{K}\}, \quad \mathcal{K} \in I$$

As a second step, use the empirical marginals in order to reconstruct the return values corresponding to the (v, z) couples of each curve, by (generalized) inversion: $F_1^{-1}(v) = \inf_i \{x_i : F_1(x_i) \geqslant v\}$, and analogously for Y. By so doing, one obtains the probability level curves

$$\{(x, y) : F(x, y) = C(F_1(x), F_2(y)) = \mathcal{K}\%\}$$

For a given value of the FTSE return (on the abscissa axis), the latter represent the return on the S&P which gives a joint distribution value of $\mathcal{K}\%$, i.e. such that the joint probability of occurrence of smaller or equal returns is $\mathcal{K}\%$.

Figure 2.7 presents the level curves of the minimum, product, maximum and fitted Clayton copulas for $\mathcal{K} = 1\%$, i.e. it represents the couples

$$\{(x, y) : \max(F_1(x) + F_2(y) - 1, 0) = 1\%\}$$

$$\{(x, y) : F_1(x)F_2(y) = 1\%\}$$

$$\{(x, y) : \min(F_1(x), F_2(y)) = 1\%\}$$

$$\{(x, y) : (F_1(x)^{-1/2} + F_2(y)^{-1/2} - 1)^{-2} = 1\%\}$$

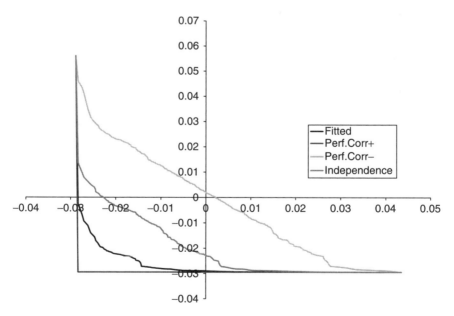

Figure 2.7 Level curves for returns on FTSE and S&P 100, corresponding to the (fitted) Clayton copula, the maximum one (perfect positive correlation), the minimum one (perfect negative correlation) and the product (independence) one

The top right line in the figure corresponds to the countermonotonic case, while the bottom left line corresponds to the comonotonic one: evidently, it is higher in the countermonotonic than in the comonotonic case, since in the former the two indices are perfect hedges, but in the second not at all. The independence case is between the two, and to the right of the fitted one, since, as we remarked above, positively ordered families (such as the Clayton) have level curves that shift upwards as the parameter decreases.

Using these curves, we can answer the following question: which are the levels x and y (respectively) of the DAX and FTSE returns, to be interpreted as (percentage) VaRs, that will be trespassed only with (joint) probability 1%? The level curves of the previous figure give these thresholds for the two assets, and therefore represent the VaR trade-off between the British and USA markets. As Cherubini and Luciano (2001) remark, "the closer the trade-off line to the lower region of the triangle, the higher the 'correlation' between losses: in this case, the joint probability cannot be affected by moving capital from one desk to another. On the contrary, if the trade-off line is close to the upper region of the triangle, we have negative dependence, and the losses of the two business units tend to offset each other. Finally, if the trade-off schedule is close to the independence line, trading-off capital from one desk to another is made possible by diversification. The case of our application is (...) close to the independence schedule."

2.5   SURVIVAL COPULA AND JOINT SURVIVAL FUNCTION

This section introduces the notions of survival copula and joint survival function, it discusses the relationships between them and applies them to the evaluation of the distribution functions of maxima and minima of two r.v.s. A financial application follows. Let us introduce the following definition.

Definition 2.10   The survival copula associated with the copula C, is

$$\overline{C}(v, z) = v + z - 1 + C(1 - v, 1 - z)$$

It is easy to verify that $\overline{C}$ has the copula properties. Once computed in $(1 - v, 1 - z)$, it represents the probability that two standard uniform variates with copula C be greater than v, z respectively, since

$$\overline{C}(1 - v, 1 - z) = 1 - v + 1 - z - 1 + C(v, z)$$

$$= 1 - \Pr(U_1 \leqslant v) + 1 - \Pr(U_2 \leqslant z) - 1 + \Pr(U_1 \leqslant v, U_2 \leqslant z)$$

$$= \Pr(U_1 > v) + \Pr(U_2 > z) - 1 + \Pr(U_1 \leqslant v, U_2 \leqslant z)$$

$$= \Pr(U_1 > v, U_2 > z)$$

Since $\overline{C}$ is a copula, it stays within the Fréchet bounds:

$$C^- \prec \overline{C} \prec C^+$$

In addition, it can be easily verified that in the minimum, product and maximum case, copulas and survival copulas coincide:

$$\overline{C}^- = C^-, \quad \overline{C}^\perp = C^\perp, \quad \overline{C}^+ = C^+$$

Sklar's theorem can be restated in terms of survival copula: to this end, given the random variables X and Y, let us consider

$$\overline{F}(x, y) = \Pr(X > x, Y > y) \tag{2.15}$$

and denote as $\overline{F}_i$ the complement to one of F_i. Notice that, as is known from elementary probability, $\overline{F}$ can be written in terms of F as $1 - F_1(x) - F_2(y) + F(x, y)$. It follows that:

$$\overline{F}(x, y) = \overline{F}_1(x) + \overline{F}_2(y) - 1 + C(1 - \overline{F}_1(x), 1 - \overline{F}_2(y)) \tag{2.16}$$

Sklar's theorem guarantees the existence of a subcopula, the survival one, unique on Ran $\overline{F}_1 \times$ Ran $\overline{F}_2$, such that the probability (2.15) can be represented in terms of $\overline{F}_1(x)$, $\overline{F}_2(y)$, i.e. $\overline{F}(x, y) = C(\overline{F}_1(x), \overline{F}_2(y))$. Before introducing it, let us notice that in the Actuarial (reliability theory) field $\overline{F}_1(x)$ is named the **marginal survival probability** or **survival function** of X: it represents the probability of survivalship of the agent (respectively, component) of age X beyond x. Since the probability (2.15) represents the **joint survival probability** or **survival function** of X and Y respectively beyond time x and y, the copula which represents it in terms of the marginal survival probabilities or survival distribution functions of the two agents or components separately, $\overline{F}_1(x)$ and $\overline{F}_2(y)$, is named **survival copula**. With this terminology, we have:

Theorem 2.9 Let $\overline{F}_1(x)$, $\overline{F}_2(y)$ be (given) marginal survival functions. Then, for every $(x, y) \in \Re^{*2}$:

(i) if C is any subcopula whose domain contains Ran $\overline{F}_1 \times$ Ran $\overline{F}_2$,

$$C(\overline{F}_1(x), \overline{F}_2(y))$$

 is a joint survival function with margins $\overline{F}_1(x)$, $\overline{F}_2(y)$;
(ii) conversely, if $\overline{F}(x, y)$ is a joint survival function with margins $\overline{F}_1(x)$, $\overline{F}_2(y)$, there exists a unique subcopula C, with domain Ran $\overline{F}_1 \times$ Ran $\overline{F}_2$, such that

$$\overline{F}(x, y) = C(\overline{F}_1(x), \overline{F}_2(y)) \tag{2.17}$$

If $F_1(x)$, $F_2(y)$ are continuous, the subcopula is a copula; if not, there exists a copula C such that

$$C(v, z) = C(v, z)$$

for every $(v, z) \in$ Ran $\overline{F}_1 \times$ Ran $\overline{F}_2$.

Remark 2.4 By comparing Definition 2.10 and formula (2.13) one can notice that the joint distribution function of two decreasing transforms of given r.v.s is represented through their survival copula.

It is also possible to express, via survival copula, the conditional probability

$$\Pr(U_1 > v \mid U_2 > z) = \frac{1 - v - z + C(v, z)}{1 - z} = \frac{\overline{C}(1 - v, 1 - z)}{1 - z}$$

and therefore

$$\Pr(X > x \mid Y > y) = \frac{\overline{C}(\overline{F}_1(x), \overline{F}_2(y))}{\overline{F}_2(y)}$$

It is customary to distinguish the survival copula from the joint survival function for uniform variates:

Definition 2.11 The **joint survival** or **survival function for (standard) uniform variates** U_1, U_2 with copula C, denoted as $\not\!C$, represents, if evaluated at (v, z), the joint probability that (U_1, U_2) be greater than v and z respectively:

$$\not\!C(v, z) = \Pr(U_1 > v, U_2 > z) \tag{2.18}$$

It follows from the definition that

$$\not\!C(v, z) = 1 - v - z + C(v, z) = \overline{C}(1 - v, 1 - z)$$

Comparing (2.18) and (2.16), it can easily be argued that, in terms of joint survival function for uniform variates, the survival probability $\overline{F}(x, y)$ can be written as

$$\overline{F}(x, y) = \not\!C(F_1(x), F_2(y))$$

Definition 2.12 Together with the survival copula, we define also the **co-copula**

$$C^*(v, z) = 1 - C(1 - v, 1 - z)$$

and the **dual of the copula**

$$\tilde{C}(v, z) = v + z - C(v, z)$$

Remark 2.5 Both the co-copula and the dual are not copulas[10], since the former fails to have property (i) in the subcopula definition, while the latter fails to be 2-increasing

---

[10] As concerns the co-copula, one can notice that $C^{**} = C$ and that the co-copulas of the Fréchet bounds and the product copula are respectively

$$C^{-*} = \min(v + z, 1)$$

$$C^{\perp *} = v + z - vz$$

$$C^{+*} = \max(v, z)$$

As concerns the dual, it coincides with the co-copula in the bounds and product case. In addition, every dual copula satisfies the following inequality:

$$\tilde{C}^+ \prec \tilde{C}^\perp \prec \tilde{C}^-$$

since $C_1 \prec C_2$ implies $\tilde{C}_1 \succ \tilde{C}_2$ and vice versa.

(see Schweizer and Sklar, 1983, lemma 6.4.2). However, they represent respectively the probability that either $X > x$ or $Y > y$, and the probability that either $X \leqslant x$ or $Y \leqslant y$:

$$\Pr(X > x \text{ or } Y > y) = C^*(1 - F_1(x), 1 - F_2(y)) \qquad (2.19)$$

$$\Pr(X \leqslant x \text{ or } Y \leqslant y) = \tilde{C}(F_1(x), F_2(y)) \qquad (2.20)$$

In addition, they have the following property, which will be used in Chapter 8: the dual of the survival copula is the co-copula. Substituting for the definition in fact it is easy to show that

$$\tilde{\tilde{C}}(v, z) = 1 - C(1 - v, 1 - z) = C^*(v, z)$$

Example 2.11   Consider two independent r.v.s, with copula $C(v, z) = vz$. It follows that

$$\mathcal{C} = (1 - v)(1 - z)$$

$$C^* = z + v - vz = 1 - \mathcal{C}$$

$$\tilde{C} = z + v - vz$$

from which it is evident, as mentioned above, that $C^* = \tilde{C}$.

There are several concepts that may be expressed in terms of copulas, survival copulas and survival functions for uniform variates. For example, the c.d.f. for **minima or maxima** of two random variables is easily expressed in terms of copula.

In fact, denote $m = \min(X, Y)$ and $M = \max(X, Y)$. Let F_m and F_M be the d.f.s of the minimum and maximum respectively.

We have, for maxima:

$$\begin{aligned} F_M(a) = \Pr(M \leqslant a) = \Pr(X \leqslant a, Y \leqslant a) = F(a, a) = \\ = C(F_1(a), F_2(a)) \end{aligned}$$

and, for minima:

$$\begin{aligned} F_m(a) = \Pr(m \leqslant a) = 1 - \Pr(m > a) \\ = 1 - \Pr(X > a, Y > a) \\ = 1 - \mathcal{C}(F_1(a), F_2(a)) = \\ = 1 - \overline{C}(\overline{F}_1(a), \overline{F}_2(a)) \end{aligned}$$

where, clearly, the point a has to be well chosen in the Ran F_1, Ran F_2.

2.5.1   An application: default probability with exogenous shocks

Consider the survivalship of two firms, whose default or survival time is denoted as X and Y, and let them be subject to three shocks, two idiosyncratic ones and the latter common to both firms. Let us assume that the shocks follow three independent Poisson processes with parameters λ_1, λ_2 and λ_{12}, where the index denotes the firm/s on which the shock has effect: this means that the times of occurrence of the shocks, denoted respectively as Z_1, Z_2, Z_{12}, are independent and exponential, with parameters λ_1, λ_2 and λ_{12} respectively. Their distribution functions, denoted as G_1, G_2, G_{12}, are:

$$G_1(z_1) = 1 - \exp(-\lambda_1 z_1)$$

$$G_2(z_2) = 1 - \exp(-\lambda_2 z_2)$$

$$G_{12}(z_{12}) = 1 - \exp(-\lambda_{12} z_{12})$$

If the shocks ever occur, the corresponding firm defaults, so that

$$X = \min(Z_1, Z_{12}), \qquad Y = \min(Z_2, Z_{12})$$

The probability that X survives beyond x, $\overline{F}_1(x)$, is

$$\overline{F}_1(x) = \Pr(X > x) = \Pr(Z_1 > x, Z_{12} > x)$$
$$= \overline{G}_1(x)\overline{G}_{12}(x) = \exp(-(\lambda_1 + \lambda_{12})x) \tag{2.21}$$

Analogously for Y:

$$\overline{F}_2(y) = \exp(-(\lambda_2 + \lambda_{12})y) \tag{2.22}$$

The probability that both survive beyond x and y respectively, $\overline{F}(x, y)$, is

$$\overline{F}(x, y) = \Pr(X > x, Y > y) = \Pr(\min(Z_1, Z_{12}) > x, \min(Z_2, Z_{12}) > y)$$
$$= \Pr(Z_1 > x)\Pr(Z_2 > y)\Pr(Z_{12} > \max(x, y))$$
$$= \exp(-\lambda_1 x)\exp(-\lambda_2 y)\exp(-\lambda_{12}\max(x, y))$$
$$= \exp(-(\lambda_1 + \lambda_{12})x - (\lambda_2 + \lambda_{12})y + \lambda_{12}\min(x, y)) \tag{2.23}$$

Substituting for (2.21) and (2.22) we get

$$\overline{F}(x, y) = \overline{F}_1(x)\overline{F}_2(y)\min(\exp(\lambda_{12}x), \exp(\lambda_{12}y))$$

In turn, having defined

$$m = \frac{\lambda_{12}}{\lambda_1 + \lambda_{12}}, \qquad n = \frac{\lambda_{12}}{\lambda_2 + \lambda_{12}}$$

we recognize that

$$\exp(\lambda_{12}x) = \overline{F}_1(x)^{-m}, \qquad \exp(\lambda_{12}y) = \overline{F}_2(y)^{-n}$$

so that the survival probability is

$$\overline{F}(x, y) = \overline{F}_1(x)\overline{F}_2(y) \min \left\{ \left[\overline{F}_1(x)\right]^{-m}, \left[\overline{F}_2(y)\right]^{-n} \right\}$$

$$= \min \left\{ \left[\overline{F}_2(y)\right] \left[\overline{F}_1(x)\right]^{1-m}, \left[\overline{F}_1(x)\right] \left[\overline{F}_2(y)\right]^{1-n} \right\} \tag{2.24}$$

It is easy to verify that this joint survival probability can be written in terms of the one of X and Y, $\overline{F}(x, y) = \overline{C}(\overline{F}_1(x), \overline{F}_2(y))$, using the following survival copula, named after Marshall and Olkin (1967a, b):

$$\overline{C}^{MO}(v, z) = \min(v^{1-m}z, vz^{1-n}) = \begin{cases} v^{1-m}z, & v^m \geqslant z^n \\ vz^{1-n}, & v^m < z^n \end{cases}$$

The joint survival probability beyond time t for instance is:

$$\overline{F}(t, t) = \overline{C}^{MO}(\overline{F}_1(t), \overline{F}_2(t))$$

$$= \min \left\{ \left[\overline{F}_2(t)\right] \left[\overline{F}_1(t)\right]^{1-m}, \left[\overline{F}_1(t)\right] \left[\overline{F}_2(t)\right]^{1-n} \right\} \tag{2.25}$$

and the corresponding default probability is:

$$\Pr(X \leqslant t, Y \leqslant t) = \overline{C}^{MO}(\overline{F}_1(t), \overline{F}_2(t)) - 1 + F_1(t) + F_2(t)$$

Suppose for instance that the two firms belong to the chemical and food sector respectively, and that the three shocks are, respectively, of the chemical sector, the food one, and of the economy as a whole. Let the expected time of occurrence of the three shocks be respectively 2, 1 and 4 years, which implies[11] $\lambda_1 = 0.5$, $\lambda_2 = 1$, $\lambda_{12} = 0.25$. It follows that the survival probability of the two firms beyond x and y respectively is

$$\overline{F}_1(x) = \exp(-(\lambda_1 + \lambda_{12})x) = \exp(-0.75x)$$

$$\overline{F}_2(y) = \exp(-1.25y) \tag{2.26}$$

while their joint survival probability, according to the Marshall–Olkin model, is

$$\overline{C}^{MO}(\overline{F}_1(x), \overline{F}_2(y)) = \min \left\{ \left[\exp(-1.25y)\right] \left[\exp(-0.5x)\right], \left[\exp(-0.75x)\right] \left[\exp(-y)\right] \right\}$$

$$= \begin{cases} \exp(-1.25y - 0.5x), & x \leqslant y \\ \exp(-0.75x - y), & x > y \end{cases}$$

since $m = 1/3$, $n = 1/5$. The joint survival probability beyond $x = y = t = 3$ years for instance is

$$\overline{C}^{MO}(\overline{F}_1(3), \overline{F}_2(3)) = \exp(3(-1.25 - 0.5)) = 0.5248\%$$

---

[11] For an exponential r.v. the expected value is the reciprocal of the intensity.

2.6 DENSITY AND CANONICAL REPRESENTATION

This section introduces the notion of density and canonical representation of a copula, together with those of its absolutely continuous and singular components.

Copulas, similarly to distribution functions, admit the notion of density:

Definition 2.13 The density $c(v, z)$ associated to a copula $C(v, z)$ is

$$c(v, z) = \frac{\partial^2 C(v, z)}{\partial v \partial z}$$

Theorem 2.10 The density exists a.e. in the interior of I^2 and is non-negative.

Example 2.12 The density of the Gaussian copula is

$$\frac{1}{\sqrt{1 - \rho^2}} \exp\left(\frac{\zeta_1^2 + \zeta_2^2}{2} + \frac{2\rho\zeta_1\zeta_2 - \zeta_1^2 - \zeta_2^2}{2\left(1 - \rho^2\right)} \right) \tag{2.27}$$

where $\zeta_1 := \Phi^{-1}(v)$, $\zeta_2 := \Phi^{-1}(z)$. This is represented, for $\rho = 0.5$, in Figure 2.8.

The density can be used in order to define the absolutely continuous component and the singular component of C, denoted as A_C and S_C, as follows (Nelsen, 1999):

$$A_C(v, z) = \int_0^v \int_0^z \frac{\partial^2 C(u, t)}{\partial u \partial t} du dt$$

$$S_C(v, z) = C(v, z) - A_C(v, z)$$

In turn, a copula for which $C = A_C$ on I^2 is called **absolutely continuous**, while it is called **singular** if $C = S_C$ on I^2. In the latter case $c = 0$ a.e. A copula that is neither absolutely

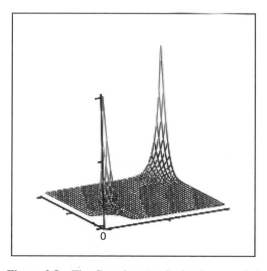

Figure 2.8 The Gaussian copula density, $\rho = 0.5$

continuous nor singular, $C = A_C + S_C$, is said to have **an absolutely continuous and a singular component**.

Non-negativity of the density permits us to ascertain the 2-increasing property in a straightforward way, if C is absolutely continuous:

Example 2.13 Suppose that we want to verify that the function

$$h(v, z) := \int_{-\infty}^{\Phi^{-1}(v)} \int_{-\infty}^{\Phi^{-1}(z)} \frac{1}{2\pi\sqrt{1 - \rho^2}} \exp\left(\frac{2\rho s w - s^2 - w^2}{2(1 - \rho^2)} \right) ds dw$$

is actually a copula. It is easy to check that

  (i) $h(0, z) = h(v, 0) = 0$
 (ii) $h(1, z) = z, h(v, 1) = v$
(iii) $C = A_C$, $\frac{\partial^2 h(v,z)}{\partial v \partial z} \geqslant 0 : h$ is absolutely continuous, with non-negative mixed second partial derivative, which means that it is 2-increasing
 (iv) Dom $h = I^2$

It follows that h is a copula.

Each copula induces a probability measure on I^2, which is nothing other than the C-mass of section 2.1, definition 2.2. The C-measure of the absolute component is $A_C(1, 1)$, while the one of the singular component is $S_C(1, 1)$.

Example 2.14 The product copula $C^\perp = vz$ is absolutely continuous, since for every $(v, z) \in I^2$

$$A_C = \int_0^v \int_0^z \frac{\partial^2 ut}{\partial u \partial t} du dt = \int_0^v \int_0^z du dt = vz = C^\perp$$

The Fréchet upper bound C^+ is singular, since for every (u, t)

$$\frac{\partial^2 C^+(u, t)}{\partial u \partial t} = 0$$

Consequently

$$A_C = \int_0^v \int_0^z \frac{\partial^2 C^+}{\partial u \partial t} du dt = 0 \neq C^+$$

Analogously for the Fréchet lower bound.

To end up with, consider the Marshall–Olkin copula of section 2.5.1. It is shown in Nelsen (1999) that, since

$$\frac{\partial^2 C^{MO}(u, t)}{\partial u \partial t} \begin{cases} u^{-m}, & u^m \geqslant t^n \\ t^{-n}, & u^m < t^n \end{cases}$$

then

$$A_C = C^{MO} - \mu \min(v^m, z^n)^{1/\mu}$$

where

$$\mu \equiv \frac{mn}{m + n - mn}$$

It follows that

$$S_C = C - A_C = \mu \min(v^m, z^n)^{1/\mu}$$

The Marshall–Olkin copula has then both an absolutely continuous and a singular component. The C-measure of the former is

$$A_C(1, 1) = C^{MO}(1, 1) - \mu \min(1, 1)^{1/\mu} = 1 - \mu$$

while that of the latter is μ.

Notice that for continuous random vectors, the copula density is related to the density of the distribution F, denoted as f. More precisely, it is equal to the ratio of the joint density f to the product of the marginal densities f_i, $i = 1, 2$:

$$c(F_1(x), F_2(y)) = \frac{f(x, y)}{f_1(x) f_2(y)} \tag{2.28}$$

since by Sklar's theorem the following **canonical representation** holds[12]:

$$f(x, y) = c(F_1(x), F_2(y)) f_1(x) f_2(y) \tag{2.29}$$

In the continuous random vector case, the density of the survival distribution, $\overline{F}(x, y)$, coincides with the distribution function one, $f(x, y)$. Indeed, the survival copula density, defined as

$$\overline{c}(v, z) = \frac{\partial^2 \overline{C}(v, z)}{\partial v \partial z}$$

---

[12] In fact, remembering that the probability integral transforms are uniform ($U_1 = F_1(X)$ and $U_2 = F_2(Y)$), we have $X = F_1^{-1}(U_1)$ and $Y = F_2^{-1}(U_2)$. Since for continuous random variates these transformations are strictly increasing and continuous

$$c(u_1, u_2) = f(F_1^{-1}(u_1), F_2^{-1}(u_2)) \cdot \det \begin{bmatrix} \partial X / \partial U_1 & \partial X / \partial U_2 \\ \partial Y / \partial U_1 & \partial Y / \partial U_2 \end{bmatrix}$$

$$= \frac{f(F_1^{-1}(u_1), F_2^{-1}(u_2))}{f_1(F_1^{-1}(u_1)) \cdot f_2(F_2^{-1}(u_2))}$$

From the above expression it is clear also that the copula density takes value equal to 1 everywhere when the original r.v.s are independent.

exists a.e. and is such that $\bar{c}(v, z) = c(1 - v, 1 - z)$. It is related to the density of the survival distribution $\bar{F}$, f, by the relationship

$$f(x, y) = \bar{c}(1 - F_1(x), 1 - F_2(y)) f_1(x) f_2(y)$$

so that

$$c(F_1(x), F_2(y)) = \bar{c}(1 - F_1(x), 1 - F_2(y))$$

The canonical representation is very useful when, for a given multivariate distribution and given marginals, one wants to know the copula that "couples" those marginals. Consider, for instance, the following example.

Example 2.15 Let X and Y be standard Gaussian, with standard normal joint distribution. Let their correlation coefficient be ρ. We want to know which copula "couples" their marginal distributions.

We know that the density of the joint distribution is

$$\frac{1}{2\pi \sqrt{1 - \rho^2}} \exp \left(\frac{2\rho st - s^2 - t^2}{2 \left(1 - \rho^2\right)} \right)$$

Using (2.28) one gets the copula density (2.27) and, consequently, the Gaussian copula.

The canonical representation will play also a fundamental role in the estimation procedures for copulas, treated in Chapter 5.

2.7 BOUNDS FOR THE DISTRIBUTION FUNCTIONS OF SUM OF R.V.S

A question that is connected to the copula definition and appears frequently in financial applications is the evaluation of bounds for the distribution function of the sum of two r.v.s.

More precisely, let X and Y be r.v.s with distribution functions F_1 and F_2, and denote with F_S the distribution function of their sum. We want to find distribution functions F_L and F_M such that, for every $s \in \Re^*$

$$F_L(s) = \inf_{F \in \mathcal{F}} F_S(s) \tag{2.30}$$

$$F_M(s) = \sup_{F \in \mathcal{F}} F_S(s) \tag{2.31}$$

where $\mathcal{F}$ is the Fréchet class which has F_1 and F_2 as marginals.

The question, posed by Kolmogorov, has been addressed in Moynihan, Schweizer and Sklar (1978), Frank, Nelsen and Schweizer (1987) and Makarov (1981). It is solved by the distribution functions

$$F_L(s) = \sup_{x \in \Re^*} \max \{F_1(x) + F_2(s - x) - 1, 0\} = \sup_{x \in \Re^*} C^-(F_1(x), F_2(s - x)) \tag{2.32}$$

$$F_M(s) = \inf_{x \in \Re^*} \min \{F_1(x) + F_2(s - x), 1\} \tag{2.33}$$

The bounds are the best possible in the sense of stochastic dominance, as argued by Frank, Nelsen and Schweizer (1987). For a.s. positive random variables, they can be improved only if there exists a copula C_-, smaller than the copula of X and Y, different from the minimum copula:

$$C^- \prec C_- \prec C$$

Explicit, analytical representations for the bounds exist when X and Y belong to the same "family", such as the normal, uniform, Cauchy, (even shifted) exponential or – under some restrictions on the parameters – (even shifted) Pareto.

Example 2.16   For the exponential family

$$F_1(x) = 1 - \exp(-\lambda_1 x), \quad \lambda_1 > 0 \tag{2.34}$$

$$F_2(y) = 1 - \exp(-\lambda_2 y), \quad \lambda_2 > 0 \tag{2.35}$$

Frank, Nelsen and Schweizer (1987) compute the bounds as follows:

$$F_L(s) = 1 - \exp\left[-\frac{\lambda_1 \lambda_2}{\lambda_1 + \lambda_2} \left(s - \left(\frac{\lambda_1 + \lambda_2}{\lambda_1 \lambda_2} \right) \log \left(\frac{\lambda_1 + \lambda_2}{\lambda_1 \lambda_2} \right) \right. \right.$$

$$\left. \left. - \frac{1}{\lambda_1} \log(\lambda_1) - \frac{1}{\lambda_2} \log(\lambda_2) \right) \right]$$

$$\Gamma_M(s) = 1 - \exp\left(-s \min(\lambda_1, \lambda_2) \right)$$

Apart from these analytical cases, Williamson and Downs (1990) give numerical algorithms for the computation of (2.32) and (2.33). The algorithms provide the value at the point u of the generalized inverse of F_L and F_M, $F_L^{-1}(u)$ and $F_M^{-1}(u)$, as follows:

$$F_L^{-1}(u) = \inf_{t \in [u,1]} \left[F_1^{-1}(t) + F_2^{-1}(u - t + 1) \right]$$

$$F_M^{-1}(u) = \sup_{t \in [0,u]} \left[F_1^{-1}(t) + F_2^{-1}(u - t) \right]$$

2.7.1   An application: VaR bounds

As we showed above, copulas have been applied to the measurement of market risk, in particular to the assessment of the Value at Risk (VaR) of a portfolio. Suppose that we have estimated the marginal distribution of two assets in a portfolio and want to "know" the portfolio VaR without introducing any assumption on their copula. It follows from (2.30), (2.31), i.e. from the fact that $F_L(s) \leqslant F_S(s) \leqslant F_M(s)$ for every s, that for any confidence level θ

$$\mathrm{VaR}_M(\theta) \leqslant \mathrm{VaR}_S(\theta) \leqslant \mathrm{VaR}_L(\theta) \tag{2.36}$$

where VaR_M and VaR_L are the VaRs corresponding to the distributions F_M and F_L. The latter distributions then provide respectively a lower and an upper bound for the VaR: the lower bound in particular is interesting, from the point of view of risk management, since it is the "worst possible outcome", with the given level of confidence. Opposite to intuition,

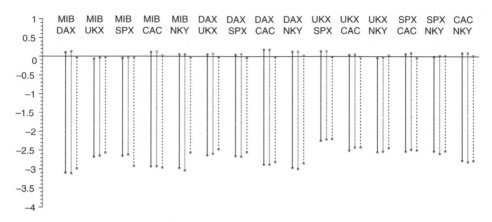

Figure 2.9 VaR bounds at the 95% level of confidence for equally weighted portfolios of couples of selected stock indices. The first line represents the bounds obtained from the empirical quantiles while the second and third lines represent the bounds from EVT estimated quantiles and from Student's *t* estimated quantiles respectively

Table 2.5 Comparison between the expected number of exceedances (1st row) and the actual ones (2nd to 5th column) for couples of selected stock indices, together with their p-values

	Var at 95% level		Var at 99% level	
	E Lower Bound	E Normal VaR	E Lower Bound	E Normal VaR
Expected	35		7	
MIB-DAX	28	65	4	30
	(0.11)	(0.00)	(0.12)	(0.00)
MIB-UKX	31	56	9	29
	(0.24)	(0.00)	(0.23)	(0.00)
MIB-SPX	18	58	5	23
	(0.00)	(0.00)	(0.22)	(0.00)
MIB-CAC	26	61	7	25
	(0.06)	(0.00)	(0.49)	(0.00)
DAX-UKX	32	62	8	33
	(0.29)	(0.00)	(0.36)	(0.00)
DAX-SPX	21	62	6	28
	(0.01)	(0.00)	(0.35)	(0.00)
DAX-CAC	31	64	6	35
	(0.24)	(0.00)	(0.35)	(0.00)
UKX-SPX	27	57	6	30
	(0.08)	(0.00)	(0.35)	(0.00)
UKX-CAC	31	60	10	30
	(0.24)	(0.00)	(0.13)	(0.00)
SPX-CAC	23	56	6	28
	(0.02)	(0.00)	(0.35)	(0.00)

the lower bound VaR_M does not correspond to the maximum copula, i.e. to the case in which portfolio returns are comonotone, even if no hedging is possible in this case.

The following numerical example is provided in Luciano and Marena (2002a,b): they consider the time series of daily closing prices of MIB 30, DAX, UKX, SPX, CAC, NKY, from December 30, 1994, to April 20, 2000. They compute the marginal empirical distributions and fit to the data both an Extreme Value Theory distribution[13] and a Student's t distribution. For each couple of indices, and assuming an equally weighted portfolio, $S = 0.5X + 0.5Y$, they evaluate the 95% daily VaR bounds corresponding to the three different choices for the marginals, using the numerical procedure in Williamson and Downs (1990). The results are collected in Figure 2.9.

They also compare the appropriateness of the lower bound with respect to that of the VaR obtained under the so-called normal approach, i.e. assuming both the marginal and joint return distribution to be normal (by estimating the mean, variances and covariances of the indices). In order to assess the appropriateness, they perform backtesting of the VaR, both at the 95% and 99% loc. In turn, backtesting consists in computing the number of loss exceedances with respect to the VaR and in comparing it with its expectation: a number of actual exceedances smaller than the expected one signals an overconservative VaR, while a number greater than the expected one signals an overoptimistic VaR. The results of the comparison are presented in Table 2.5 and show that the lower bound is not as overconservative as one could fear, while the normal VaR is excessively overoptimistic.

2.8 APPENDIX

This appendix collects the proofs of the theorems in this chapter (as for corollaries, only the corollary to Sklar's theorem is demonstrated).

Proof of Theorem 2.1 We demonstrate the property with reference to the first argument, v. More precisely, we show that $v_1 \leqslant v_2$ implies $G(v_1, x) \leqslant G(v_2, x)$ for every x in A_2.

From (2.1), the 2-increasing property of G, rearranging, gives

$$G(v_2, z_1) - G(v_1, z_1) \leqslant G(v_2, z_2) - G(v_1, z_2)$$

for every $z_2 \geqslant z_1$, i.e. the difference $G(v_2, x) - G(v_1, x)$ is a non-decreasing function of x. In particular,

$$G(v_2, a_2) - G(v_1, a_2) \leqslant G(v_2, x) - G(v_1, x) \tag{2.37}$$

for every $x \geqslant a_2$. Since $G(v_1, a_2) = G(v_2, a_2) = 0$, one gets $G(v_1, x) \leqslant G(v_2, x)$ for every x in A_2, as needed. $\square$

Proof of Theorem 2.2 We demonstrate that for every couple of points (v_1, z_1), (v_2, z_2) in $A \times B$, with $v_1 \lessgtr v_2, z_1 \lessgtr z_2$

$$|\mathcal{C}(v_2, z_2) - \mathcal{C}(v_1, z_1)| \leqslant |v_2 - v_1| + |z_2 - z_1| \tag{2.38}$$

---

[13] See, for instance, Embrechts, Klüppenberg and Mikosch (1997).

Starting from the difference on the l.h.s., subtracting and adding $C(v_1, z_2)$, and applying a basic property of absolute values, we have:

$$|C(v_2, z_2) - C(v_1, z_1)| \leqslant |C(v_2, z_2) - C(v_1, z_2)| + |C(v_1, z_2) - C(v_1, z_1)| \qquad (2.39)$$

If $v_1 \leqslant v_2$, it follows from Theorem 2.1 that $C(v_2, z_2) - C(v_1, z_2) \geqslant 0$, and from the 2-increasing property, applied to the rectangle $[v_1, v_2] \times [z_2, 1]$, that

$$C(v_2, 1) - C(v_2, z_2) - C(v_1, 1) + C(v_1, z_2) \geqslant 0$$

i.e.[14]

$$C(v_2, z_2) - C(v_1, z_2) \leqslant C(v_2, 1) - C(v_1, 1) = v_2 - v_1$$

For the same reasons, when $v_1 > v_2$, we have

$$C(v_2, z_2) - C(v_1, z_2) \leqslant 0$$

$$C(v_2, z_2) - C(v_1, z_2) \geqslant C(v_2, 1) - C(v_1, 1) = v_2 - v_1$$

Putting together the two cases:

$$|C(v_2, z_2) - C(v_1, z_2)| \leqslant |v_2 - v_1|$$

An analogous reasoning yields

$$|C(v_1, z_2) - C(v_1, z_1)| \leqslant |z_2 - z_1|$$

Substituting in (2.39) one gets (2.38).   □

Proof of Theorem 2.3   Existence follows from the fact that

$$\frac{\partial C(x, k)}{\partial v} = W_k'(x), \qquad \frac{\partial C(K, x)}{\partial z} = V_K'(x)$$

In turn, the sections are differentiables almost everywhere because they are monotone (non-decreasing). As for the values taken by the partial derivatives, consider $\partial C / \partial v$. The incremental ratio of W at x is

$$\frac{W_k(x + h) - W_k(x)}{h} = \frac{C(x + h, k) - C(x, k)}{h}$$

which, by uniform continuity, is not greater than one in absolute value. It follows that $|W_k'(x)| \leqslant 1$. In addition, $W_k'(x) \geqslant 0$ by monotonicity: as a consequence, $W_k'(x) \in I$.   □

---

[14] As in the proof of Theorem 2.1, we are using the fact that, when $v_1 \leqslant v_2$, $C(v_2, z_2) - C(v_1, z_2)$ is a non-decreasing function of z_2.

Proof of Theorem 2.4 L.h.s.: from the 2-increasing property, $\mathcal{C}(v_2, z_2) - \mathcal{C}(v_2, z_1) - \mathcal{C}(v_1, z_2) + \mathcal{C}(v_1, z_1) \geqslant 0$, choosing $v_2 = z_2 = 1$, we get $1 - \mathcal{C}(1, z_1) - \mathcal{C}(v_1, 1) + \mathcal{C}(v_1, z_1) \geqslant 0$, or $1 - z_1 - v_1 \geqslant -\mathcal{C}(v_1, z_1)$, which, being valid for every (v_1, z_1) in $A \times B$, can be rewritten as $\mathcal{C}(v, z) \geqslant v + z - 1$. Since at the same time Corollary 2.1 holds, we have the l.h.s. of the inequality. R.h.s.: it follows from property (ii) of the subcopula definition and Theorem 2.1, as applied to both arguments of $\mathcal{C}$. $\qquad\square$

Proof of Theorem 2.5 (Sklar's Theorem) We present a (partial) proof, following Schweizer and Sklar (1983). The proof is partial since we do not demonstrate an extension lemma, which is used in it.

An inequality for distribution functions involving their margins is used in the proof of Sklar's theorem. It is the second of the following lemmas, that concern grounded, 2-increasing functions with margins. The margins in turn are defined as follows:

Definition 2.14 The margins of a function $G: A_1 \times A_2 \to \Re$ are the functions $G_1(x): A_1 \to \Re$, defined as

$$G_1(x) = G(x, \overline{a}_2)$$

and $G_2(y): A_2 \to \Re$, defined as

$$G_2(y) = G(\overline{a}_1, y)$$

where $\overline{a}_i$ is the maximal element of A_i.

Evidently, marginal distribution functions of r.v.s are margins according to the previous definition.

Lemmas 2.1 and 2.2 apply.

Lemma 2.1 A function $G: A_1 \times A_2 \to \Re$ grounded, 2-increasing, with margins G_1 and G_2, is such that

$$|G(v_2, z) - G(v_1, z)| \leqslant |G_1(v_2) - G_1(v_1)|$$

for every couple of points (v_2, z), (v_1, z) belonging to Dom G,

$$|G(v, z_2) - G(v, z_1)| \leqslant |G_2(z_2) - G_2(z_1)|$$

for every couple of points (v, z_2), (v, z_1) belonging to Dom G.

Proof of Lemma 2.1 Consider first the case $v_2 > v_1$. Apply the 2-increasing property to the rectangle $[v_1, v_2] \times [z, \overline{a}_2]$

$$G(v_2, \overline{a}_2) - G(v_1, \overline{a}_2) - G(v_2, z) + G(v_1, z) \geqslant 0$$

By the definition of marginals, $G(v_2, \overline{a}_2) = G_1(v_2)$ and $G(v_1, \overline{a}_2) = G_1(v_1)$ and the previous inequality can be transformed into

$$G(v_2, z) - G(v_1, z) \leqslant G_1(v_2) - G_1(v_1)$$

In turn, by the non-decreasing property of G and G_1, this is equivalent to

$$|G(v_2, z) - G(v_1, z)| \leqslant |G_1(v_2) - G_1(v_1)|$$

If $v_2 < v_1$, the 2-increasing property entails

$$G(v_1, z) - G(v_2, z) \leqslant G_1(v_2) - G_1(v_1)$$

or

$$|G(v_2, z) - G(v_1, z)| \leqslant |G_1(v_2) - G_1(v_1)|$$

The two cases together give the first statement in the lemma. Analogously for the second assertion. $\square$

Lemma 2.2 For the function G of the previous lemma,

$$|G(v_1, z_1) - G(v_2, z_2)| \leqslant |G_1(v_1) - G_1(v_2)| + |G_2(z_1) - G_2(z_2)|$$

for every $(v_1, z_1), (v_2, z_2) \in \text{Dom } G$.

Proof of Lemma 2.2 It is sufficient to apply the previous lemma twice:

$$|G(v_2, z_2) - G(v_1, z_1)| \leqslant |G(v_2, z_2) - G(v_2, z_1)| + |G(v_2, z_1) - G(v_1, z_1)|$$
$$\leqslant |G_1(v_1) - G_1(v_2)| + |G_2(z_1) - G_2(z_2)|$$

$\square$

Using the previous lemmas, we can proceed to the proof of Sklar's theorem.

Proof of part (i) Let us demonstrate that, if $\text{Ran } F_1 \subset A$, $\text{Ran } F_2 \subset B$, the function $F(x, y)$ defined by

$$F(x, y) = \mathcal{C}(F_1(x), F_2(y))$$

- is a joint distribution function
- has margins F_1, F_2

As for the first assertion, let us check that

(1) $\text{Dom } F = \Re^{*2}$
(2) F is 2-increasing
(3) F is grounded
(4) $F(+\infty, +\infty) = 1$

Point (1) follows from the fact that Dom $F_i = \Re^*$, $i = 1, 2$; Ran $F_1 \subset A$; Ran $F_2 \subset B$.
Point (2) follows from the fact that C is 2-increasing, F_1 and F_2 are non-decreasing.
Point (3) is a consequence of the fact that

$$F(-\infty, y) = C(0, F_2(y)) = 0$$

$$F(x, -\infty) = C(F_1(x), 0) = 0$$

which in turn depends on F_1 and F_2 being marginal distribution functions and C being grounded.

Point (4) depends on property (ii) in the subcopula definition, which entails $F(+\infty, +\infty) = C(1, 1) = 1$.

As for the second assertion, let us check that the first margin of F, $F(x, +\infty)$, is actually the marginal distribution function $F_1(x)$: since $F(x, +\infty) = C(F_1(x), 1)$ and property (ii) in the subcopula definition holds, $F(x, +\infty) = F_1(x)$. Analogously for the second margin.

Proof of part (ii)   This requires the following lemma, which guarantees that every subcopula can be extended to a copula. The proof is in Schweizer and Sklar (1974).

Lemma 2.3 (Sklar, 1973)   Given any subcopula, there exists a copula C such that

$$C(v, z) = \mathcal{C}(v, z)$$

for every $(v, z) \in$ Dom $\mathcal{C}$.

Given the lemma, we can now proceed to:

Proof of part (ii)   Consider a joint distribution function $F(x, y)$ with margins F_1 and F_2 and two points (x_1, y_1), $(x_2, y_2) \in \Re^{*2}$. Suppose that

$$F_1(x_1) = F_1(x_2), \qquad F_2(y_1) = F_2(y_2)$$

Then $F(x, y)$ has the same value at the points (x_1, y_1), (x_2, y_2), since, by Lemma 2.2,

$$|F(x_1, y_1) - F(x_2, y_2)| \leqslant |F_1(x_1) - F_1(x_2)| + |F_2(y_1) - F_2(y_2)| = 0$$

Then, for every point (x, y), the value of F depends on $F_1(x)$, $F_2(y)$ only: otherwise stated, there is a unique function C, with Dom $C =$ Ran $F_1 \times$ Ran F_2, such that

$$F(x, y) = C(F_1(x), F_2(y))$$

The function under examination is a subcopula, since, on Ran $F_1 \times$ Ran F_2,

(i) it is grounded:

$$C(0, F_2(y)) = C(F_1(-\infty), F_2(y)) = F(-\infty, y) = 0$$

$$C(F_1(x), 0) = C(F_1(x), F_2(-\infty)) = F(x, -\infty) = 0$$

(ii) it has margins that are the identity function:

$$C(1, F_2(y)) = C(F_1(+\infty), F_2(y)) = F(+\infty, y) = F_2(y)$$

$$C(F_1(x), 1) = C(F_1(x), F_2(+\infty)) = F(x, +\infty) = F_1(x)$$

(iii) it is 2-increasing, as a consequence of the analogous property of distribution functions.

If $F_1(x)$, $F_2(y)$ are continuous, Dom $C = I^2$ and the subcopula is a copula. Otherwise, Sklar's lemma applies. □

Proof of Corollary 2.3 Consider the subcopula in part (ii) of Sklar's theorem and denote the value of $F_1(x)$ as v, and the value of $F_2(y)$ as z. Since F_1 and F_2 are margins of a distribution function, they are marginal distribution functions and therefore admit generalized inverses: $x = F_1^{-1}(v)$, $y = F_2^{-1}(z)$. Then

$$F(x, y) = F\left(F_1^{-1}(v), F_2^{-1}(z)\right)$$

$$C(F_1(x), F_2(y)) = C(v, z)$$

Substituting into (2.6) we obtain the statement of the corollary. □

Proof of Theorem 2.6 (1) → (2) Notice that

$$\Pr(X \leqslant x, Y \leqslant y) = \Pr((X, Y) \in A_1 \cap A_2) \tag{2.40}$$

where

$$A_1 := \{(s, t) \in A : s \leqslant x\}$$

$$A_2 := \{(s, t) \in A : t \leqslant y\}$$

The comonotonicity property of the support entails that either $A_1 \subset A_2$, so that $A_1 \cap A_2 = A_1$ and the probability in (2.40) is $F_1(x)$, or $A_1 \supset A_2$, so that $A_1 \cap A_2 = A_2$ and the probability in (2.40) is $F_2(y)$. In the first case $F_1(x) \leqslant F_2(y)$, in the second the opposite inequality holds. Property (2) follows.

(2) → (3) From Sklar's theorem.
(3) → (4) We want to show that

$$F(x, y) = C(F_1(x), F_2(y)) = \min(F_1(x), F_2(y))$$

implies

$$F(x, y) = \Pr(F_1^{-1}(U) \leqslant x, F_2^{-1}(U) \leqslant y)$$

The latter in fact is

$$\Pr(U \leqslant F_1(x), U \leqslant F_2(y)) = \Pr(U \leqslant \min(F_1(x), F_2(y)))$$

$$= \min(F_1(x), F_2(y))$$

(4) $\to$ (5) Since $X = F_1^{-1}(U)$, $U = F_1(X)$. Substituting into $Y = F_2^{-1}(U)$, we have $Y = F_2^{-1}(F_1(X))$. Conversely, since $Y = F_2^{-1}(U)$, $U = F_2(Y)$ and $X = F_1^{-1}(F_2(X))$.

(5) $\to$ (1) The set of possible outcomes, under (6), is

$$\left\{ (x, F_2^{-1}(F_1(x))) : x \in \Re^* \right\}$$

Since both F_1 and F_2 are marginal distributions, they are non-decreasing: as a consequence, both the above set and the couple (X, Y) are comonotonic. $\square$

An analogous technique applies to the **proof of Theorem 2.7**.

Proof of Theorem 2.8 Denote with $\check{C}$ the copula of $\alpha_1(X)$, $\alpha_2(Y)$. We are going to show that

$$\check{C}(v, z) = C(v, z)$$

for every (v, z) in $\Re^{*2}$. For fixed (v, z), take (x, y) such that $v = F_1(x)$, $z = F_2(y)$. Then

$$C(v, z) = C(F_1(x), F_2(y))$$

$$= F(x, y) = \Pr(X \leqslant x, Y \leqslant y)$$

$$= \Pr(\alpha_1(X) \leqslant \alpha_1(x), \alpha_2(Y) \leqslant \alpha_2(y)) = H(\alpha_1(x), \alpha_2(y))$$

$$= \check{C}(H_1(\alpha_1(x)), H_2(\alpha_2(y))) = \check{C}(F_1(x), F_2(y)) = \check{C}(v, z)$$

This, together with surjectivity of F_1, F_2, which in turn follows from their continuity, proves the theorem. $\square$

The **proof of Theorem 2.9** is analogous to the proof of Sklar's theorem.

The **proof of Theorem 2.10** requires the following lemma:

Lemma 2.4 The functions

$$\frac{\partial C(v, z)}{\partial v} : I \to I, \qquad \frac{\partial C(v, z)}{\partial z} : I \to I$$

are non-decreasing a.e. in the interior of I.

Proof of Lemma 2.4 The derivatives exist by Theorem 2.3; their non-decreasing behavior follows from the fact, exploited above, that, if $v_1 \leqslant v_2$, $C(v_2, z) - C(v_1, z)$ is a non-decreasing function of z. This means that

$$\frac{\partial (C(v_2, z) - C(v_1, z))}{\partial z}$$

is non-negative a.e., i.e. $\partial C(v_2, z)/\partial z \geqslant C(v_1, z)/\partial z$ when $v_1 \leqslant v_2$, or $\partial C/\partial z$ is non-decreasing a.e. in v (symmetrically for z). $\square$

Proof of Theorem 2.10 Since non-decreasing functions such as $\partial C/\partial v$ and $\partial C/\partial z$ are differentiable a.e., the density exists. Since the partial derivatives are non-decreasing, $c \geqslant 0$. $\square$

3
Market Comovements and Copula Families

This chapter discusses first the relationships between copula functions and association measures for couples of random variates, i.e. for financial applications, market indicators such as prices or returns. It then presents some well-known parametric families (or classes) of copula functions, for which the parameter value is directly related to one or more association measures. Due to their utility for financial applications – to be fully discussed after the estimation problem has been addressed (Chapter 5) – we present the following copula families: the Gaussian, the Student's t, the Fréchet, the Archimedean, the Marshall–Olkin.

3.1 MEASURES OF ASSOCIATION

Generally speaking, the random variates X and Y are said to be **associated** when they are not independent according to the characterization in section 2.4 of Chapter 2. However, there are a number of concepts of association. In the sequel, we will present some of these concepts, namely:

- concordance (as distinct from dependence), linear correlation, tail dependence, positive quadrant dependency

and some measures associated with them:

- Kendall's tau, Spearman's rho, the linear correlation coefficient, the indices of tail dependency.

All these measures are related to copulas since, in coupling a joint distribution function with its marginals, the copula "captures certain ... aspects of the relationship between the variates, from which it follows that (...) dependence concepts are properties of the copula" (Nelsen, 1991). As mentioned above, the same applies because of copula invariance with respect to increasing transformations.

From now on we will **assume that X and Y are continuous**.

3.1.1 Concordance

Concordance concepts, loosely speaking, aim at capturing the fact that the probability of having "large" (or "small") values of both X and Y is high, while the probability of having "large" values of X together with "small" values of Y – or vice versa – is low.

Geometrically, it looks at the probability mass associated with the upper and lower quadrants, as opposite to the one associated with the rest of the plane (x, y).

Formally, a measure of concordance between the r.v.s X and Y, with copula C, may be denoted by $M_{X,Y}$ or M_C. It is characterized by the following set of axiomatic properties (Scarsini, 1984):

Definition 3.1 $M_{X,Y} = M_C$ is a measure of concordance between the r.v.s X and Y – with copula C – iff

   (i) it is defined for every pair of r.v.s (completeness)
  (ii) it is a relative (or normalized) measure: $M_{X,Y} \in [-1, 1]$
 (iii) it is symmetric: $M_{X,Y} = M_{Y,X}$
  (iv) if X and Y are independent, then $M_{X,Y} = 0$
   (v) $M_{-X,Y} = M_{X,-Y} = -M_{Y,X}$
  (vi) it converges when the copula (pointwise)[1] does: if $\{(X_n, Y_n)\}$ is a sequence of continuous r.v.s with copula C_n, and

$$\lim_{n \to +\infty} C_n(v, z) = C(v, z) \quad \text{for every } (v, z) \in I^2$$

     then

$$\lim_{n \to +\infty} M_{X_n, Y_n} = M_{X,Y}$$

(vii) it respects concordance order: if $C_1 \prec C_2$, then $M_{C_1} \leqslant M_{C_2}$

This definition implies invariance with respect to increasing transformations and the existence of bounds for M in correspondence to comonotonicity and countermonotonicity.

Theorem 3.1   If $\alpha_i, i = 1, 2$, are a.s. increasing functions on Ran F_i, then $M_{X,Y} = M_{\alpha_1(X), \alpha_2(Y)}$.

Theorem 3.2   If X and Y are comonotone, $M_{X,Y} = 1$; if they are countermonotone, $M_{X,Y} = -1$.

Scarsini (1984) also proved that the following representation holds:

Theorem 3.3   Given a bounded, weakly monotone, odd function f, with Dom $f = \left[-\frac{1}{2}, \frac{1}{2}\right]$, then

$$k \iint_{I^2} f(v - \tfrac{1}{2}) f(z - \tfrac{1}{2}) \, dC(v, z) \tag{3.1}$$

where $k^{-1} = \int_I f^2(u - \frac{1}{2}) \, du$, is a concordance measure.

By specifying the function f, some very well-known measures of concordance can be obtained. For $f(u) = u$ one obtains Spearman's ρ_S, defined in the sequel; for $f(u) = \text{sgn}(u)$ Blomqvist's β, which is defined as

$$q = 4C(\tfrac{1}{2}, \tfrac{1}{2}) - 1 \tag{3.2}$$

Other popular concordance measures cannot be obtained from the above representation: this is the case of Kendall's τ, which will be discussed in the next section, or Gini's coefficient

---

[1] Please note that for bivariate copula functions, pointwise and uniform convergence coincide, due to uniform continuity.

γ, defined as

$$\gamma = 2 \iint_{I^2} (|v + z - 1| - |v - z|) \, dC(v, z) \tag{3.3}$$

It is interesting to notice that concordance measures have two features:

- Independency is a sufficient, but not a necessary condition for them to be equal to zero.
- They are distinct from **dependence** measures, as defined by Rényi (1959). Opposite to the former, the latter assume their minimum value when X and Y are independent, not when they are countermonotonic.

3.1.2 Kendall's τ

In this section we define Kendall's coefficient, first introduced – according to Nelsen (1991) – by Fechner around 1900, and rediscovered by Kendall (1938). We then interpret it, remark that it is a normalized expected value and give an alternative method to compute it for absolutely continuous copulas. Examples of computation, together with a discussion and some examples of estimation, conclude the section.

Definition 3.2 Kendall's *tau* for the r.v.s X and Y with copula C, denoted as τ or τ_C, is:

$$\tau = 4 \iint_{I^2} C(v, z) \, dC(v, z) - 1 \tag{3.4}$$

One can demonstrate that it measures the difference between the probability of concordance and the one of discordance for two independent random vectors, (X_1, Y_1) and (X_2, Y_2), each with the same joint distribution function F and copula C. The vectors are said to be concordant if $X_1 > X_2$ whenever $Y_1 > Y_2$, and $X_1 < X_2$ whenever $Y_1 < Y_2$; and discordant in the opposite case.[2] We have

Theorem 3.4 Given (X_1, Y_1) and (X_2, Y_2) i.i.d. with copula C,

$$\tau = \Pr((X_1 - X_2)(Y_1 - Y_2) > 0) - \Pr((X_1 - X_2)(Y_1 - Y_2) < 0) \tag{3.5}$$

We refer the reader to Scarsini (1984) for a proof of the fact that Kendall's τ satisfies axioms (i) to (vii) for a concordance measure. We stress only the fact that $-1 \leqslant \tau \leqslant 1$, and if we consider continuous random variables, the lower bound applies to countermonotonic r.v.s only, while the upper one applies to comonotonic ones only:

$$\tau = -1 \quad \text{iff } C = C^-$$
$$\tau = 1 \quad \text{iff } C = C^+$$

---

[2] In turn, the idea of using the concordance and discordance probabilities comes from the fact that probabilities of events involving only inequality relationships between two random variables are invariant with respect to increasing transformations. Measures based on these probabilities are then expected to satisfy axiom (vii) in the definition of measures of concordance.

Remark 3.1   One can also couple Theorem 3.2 with the fact that the double integral in the definition of τ is the expected value of the function $C(U_1, U_2)$, where both U_1 and U_2 are standard uniform and have joint distribution C:

$$\tau = 4E\left[C(U_1, U_2)\right] - 1$$

It follows that

$$-1 \leqslant 4E\left[C(U_1, U_2)\right] - 1 \leqslant 1$$

i.e. that Kendall's coefficient is a normalized expected value.

When the copula is absolutely continuous, the differential

$$dC = \frac{\partial^2 C}{\partial v \partial z}\, dv\, dz$$

can be substituted into the definition of τ (equation 3.4), in order to compute it. However, when C has both an absolutely continuous and a singular component, or is singular, the following theorem holds.

Theorem 3.5   Kendall's τ can be computed as:

$$\tau = 1 - 4 \iint_{I^2} \frac{\partial C(v, z)}{\partial v} \frac{\partial C(v, z)}{\partial z}\, dv\, dz \tag{3.6}$$

The equivalence of (3.4) and (3.6) follows from the following lemma (Nelsen, 1991):

Lemma 3.1   If C is a copula

$$\iint_{I^2} C(v, z)\, dC(v, z) + \iint_{I^2} \frac{\partial C(v, z)}{\partial v} \frac{\partial C(v, z)}{\partial z}\, dv\, dz = \tfrac{1}{2}$$

Example 3.1   Consider the product copula, for which we know from Example 2.14 that

$$\frac{\partial^2 C^\perp}{\partial v\, \partial z} = 1$$

It follows, according to the definition, that

$$\tau_{C^\perp} = 4 \iint_{I^2} vz\, dv\, dz - 1 = 0$$

Example 3.2   Consider the Marshall–Olkin copula defined in section 2.5.1, which is not absolutely continuous. Its partial derivatives exist whenever $v^m \neq z^n$ and

$$\frac{\partial C^{\mathrm{MO}}(v, z)}{\partial v} \frac{\partial C^{\mathrm{MO}}(v, z)}{\partial z} = \begin{cases} (1 - m)v^{1-2m}z, & v^m \geqslant z^n \\ (1 - n)vz^{1-2n}, & v^m < z^n \end{cases}$$

Therefore, one can compute

$$\iint_{I^2} \frac{\partial C(v,z)}{\partial v} \frac{\partial C(v,z)}{\partial z} \, dv \, dz = \tfrac{1}{4}(1-\mu)$$

and

$$\tau_{CMO} = \mu$$

which is the measure of the copula singular component.

It is easy to demonstrate, using (3.6), that

Theorem 3.6   The Kendall's τ of a copula and of its associated survival copula coincide:

$$\tau_C = \tau_{\overline{C}}$$

In order to estimate τ from a random sample of n pairs

$$(X_i, Y_i)$$

$i = 1, \ldots, n$, having defined the indicator variables

$$A_{ij} \equiv \operatorname{sgn}(X_i - X_j)(Y_i - Y_j)$$

as in Gibbons (1992), one can notice that

$$E(A_{ij}) = (+1)\Pr((X_i - X_j)(Y_i - Y_j) > 0) + (-1)\Pr((X_i - X_j)(Y_i - Y_j) < 0) = \tau$$

It follows that an unbiased estimator of Kendall's coefficient is the so-called **Kendall's sample τ**:

$$\frac{2}{n(n-1)} \sum_{i=1}^{n} \sum_{j>i} A_{ij} \tag{3.7}$$

The estimator can be demonstrated to be consistent too.

An application: Kendall's tau estimation for some financial indices and an FX rate

Let us consider[3] the time series of five assets, namely two stock indices (DAX 30 and S&P 500), two bond indices (the 10-year total return index for the German bond market and the corresponding index for the US market, GER10y and USA10y respectively) and one exchange rate, the DEM/USD. Namely, let us consider the weekly average data on their returns from January 1992 to June 2001, for a total of $n = 248$ observations. These data, which will be discussed and further used in Chapter 5 in order to illustrate the estimation methods for copulas, permit us to estimate Kendall's coefficient between the corresponding indices, using (3.7). The values obtained are given in Table 3.1.

---

[3] See Cazzulani, Meneguzzo and Vecchiato (2001).

Table 3.1 Sample Kendall's tau for selected assets, 01/92 to 06/01, weekly (average) data

	DAX 30	S&P 500	GER10y	USA10y	DEM/USD
DAX 30					
S&P 500	0.44				
GER10y	0.13	0.12			
USA10y	0.03	0.14	0.35		
DEM/USD	0.22	0.13	0.05	−0.11	

3.1.3 Spearman's ρ_S

In this section we define the Spearman coefficient, first proposed – according to Nelsen (1991) – in 1904. In analogy with what we did with Kendall's τ, we interpret the coefficient, remark that it is a normalized expected value and that it represents rank correlation. Examples of computation, together with a discussion and some examples of estimation, follow. A comment on the relationship between Kendall's τ and Spearman's ρ_S concludes the section.

Definition 3.3 Spearman's *rho* for r.v.s X and Y with copula C – denoted as ρ_S or ρ_{SC} – is:

$$\rho_S = 12 \iint_{I^2} C(v, z)\,dv\,dz - 3 = 12 \iint_{I^2} vz\,dC(v, z) - 3 \qquad (3.8)$$

This measure also exploits probabilities of concordance and discordance. It starts from three couples of i.i.d. random vectors, namely (X_1, Y_1), (X_2, Y_2) and (X_3, Y_3), with copula C. It is a multiple (because of normalization) of the difference between the probability of concordance and discordance for the vectors (X_1, Y_1), (X_2, Y_3), the latter being made up of independent r.v.s. Therefore, in the ρ_S case the probabilities of concordance and discordance are measured w.r.t. the independence case. We have:

Theorem 3.7 Given (X_1, Y_1), (X_2, Y_2), (X_3, Y_3), i.i.d. with copula C, then

$$\rho_S = 3\left[\Pr\left((X_1 - X_2)(Y_1 - Y_3) > 0\right) - \Pr\left((X_1 - X_2)(Y_1 - Y_3) < 0\right)\right] \qquad (3.9)$$

Substituting in the first definition, one can also write

$$\rho_{SC} = 12 \iint_{I^2} [C(v, z) - vz]\,dv\,dz$$

Remark 3.2 Since the integral transforms $U_1 = F_1(X)$, $U_2 = F_2(Y)$ are standard uniform, with joint distribution function C, the integral in the second form of Spearman's ρ_S Definition 3.3 is $E[U_1 U_2]$. As a consequence

$$\rho_S = 12E[U_1 U_2] - 3 = \frac{E[U_1 U_2] - \frac{1}{4}}{1/12}$$

Since $\frac{1}{2}$ and $\frac{1}{12}$ are the mean and variance of standard uniforms, it follows that

$$\rho_S = \frac{\mathrm{cov}\left(F_1(X), F_2(Y)\right)}{\sqrt{\mathrm{var}(F_1(X))\mathrm{var}(F_2(Y))}} \qquad (3.10)$$

We will define below such a ratio as the linear correlation coefficient between $F_1(X)$ and $F_2(Y)$: Spearman's ρ_S is therefore the **rank correlation**, in the sense of correlation of the integral transforms, of X and Y.

Also for Spearman's ρ_S one could demonstrate that it satisfies the definition of concordance measure and that it reaches its bounds iff X and Y are respectively countermonotonic and comonotonic continuous random variates:

$$\rho_S = -1 \quad \text{iff } C = C^-$$
$$\rho_S = 1 \quad \text{iff } C = C^+$$

As for computation, both the first and second formulas in Definition 3.3 can be fruitfully applied.

Example 3.3 Using the first or the second part of the definition, it is straightforward to show that Spearman's rho for the product copula is equal to zero:

$$\rho_{SC^\perp} = 12 \iint_{I^2} vz \, dv \, dz - 3 = 0$$

Example 3.4 In the Marshall–Olkin case, since

$$\iint_{I^2} C^{MO}(v, z) \, dv \, dz = \frac{1}{2} \frac{m+n}{2m + 2n - mn}$$

we have

$$\rho_{SC^{MO}} = 3 \frac{mn}{2m + 2n - mn}$$

It is easy to demonstrate, using the definition, that

Theorem 3.8 Spearman's ρ_S of a copula and its associated copula coincide:

$$\rho_{SC} = \rho_{S\overline{C}}$$

As far as estimation is concerned (see Gibbons, 1992), starting from a random sample of n pairs

$$(X_i, Y_i)$$

$i = 1, \ldots, n$, and recalling that ρ_S is the rank correlation, according to (3.10), one can switch to the ranks of the sample variates:

$$R_i \equiv \text{rank}(X_i), \qquad S_i \equiv \text{rank}(Y_i)$$

where the ranking has to be done in ascending order. By so doing, the following **Spearman's sample** ρ_S can be obtained:

$$\frac{\sum_{i=1}^n (R_i - \overline{R})(S_i - \overline{S})}{\sqrt{\sum_{i=1}^n (R_i - \overline{R})^2 \sum_{i=1}^n (S_i - \overline{S})^2}}$$

Taking into consideration the fact that the ranks of n data are the first n integer numbers, the above expression simplifies into either

$$12\frac{\sum_{i=1}^{n}(R_i - \overline{R})(S_i - \overline{S})}{n(n^2 - 1)}$$

or

$$1 - 6\frac{\sum_{i=1}^{n}(R_i - S_i)^2}{n(n^2 - 1)} \tag{3.11}$$

which has to be slightly modified, in applications, in order to take into account tied observations. The sample version of ρ_S so obtained is an unbiased estimator of the population one.

An application: Spearman's rho estimation for some financial indices and an FX rate

Using the same data as in the application of section 3.1.2, together with expression (3.11), the values for the rank correlation coefficient between the financial assets under examination, over the years 1992–2001, were obtained (see Table 3.2).

Table 3.2 Sample Spearman's rho for selected assets, 01/92 to 06/01, weekly (average) data

	DAX 30	S&P 500	GER10y	USA10y	DEM/USD
DAX 30	–				
S&P 500	0.67	–			
GER10y	0.20	0.18	–		
USA10y	0.04	0.13	0.49	–	
DEM/USD	0.31	0.19	0.06	−0.22	–

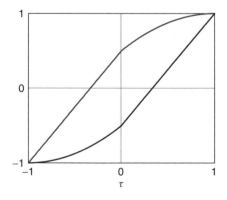

Figure 3.1 Spearman's ρ_S, as a function of Kendall's τ, for a given copula

Finally, one could wonder whether there exists a functional relationship between Kendall's τ and Spearman's ρ_S. Durbin and Stuart (1951) showed that (see Figure 3.1) for a given association between X and Y, i.e. for a given copula:

$$\left[\begin{array}{ll} \frac{3}{2}\tau - \frac{1}{2} \leqslant \rho_S \leqslant \frac{1}{2} + \tau - \frac{1}{2}\tau^2 & \tau \geqslant 0 \\ -\frac{1}{2} + \tau + \frac{1}{2}\tau^2 \leqslant \rho_S \leqslant \frac{3}{2}\tau + \frac{1}{2} & \tau < 0 \end{array} \right.$$

3.1.4 Linear correlation

For r.v.s belonging to L^2, concordance – in its loose significance – should be captured also by covariance. Since covariance is not a normalized or relative measure, however, the so-called Pearson product-moment or linear correlation coefficient has been introduced. We define it, show that it satisfies some of the axioms for a measure of concordance, and list five of its properties, which entail that it does not satisfy the remaining axioms. Last, we mention the estimation procedure and give an example.

In order to define linear correlation, let us denote by var(X) the variance of the r.v. X, and recall that a non-degenerate random variable has non-null variance.

Definition 3.4 For non-degenerate r.v.s X and Y belonging to L^2, the linear correlation coefficient ρ_{XY} is

$$\rho_{XY} = \frac{\text{cov}(X, Y)}{\sqrt{\text{var}(X)\text{var}(Y)}}$$

Theorem 3.9 The linear correlation coefficient satisfies axioms (i) to (v) and (vii) of the concordance measure definition.

Proof: It is evident that, if we exclude degenerate r.v.s, the linear correlation coefficient satisfies (i).

Axiom (ii) follows from the fact that $|\text{cov}(X, Y)| \leqslant \sqrt{\text{var}(X)\text{var}(Y)}$, while axiom (iii) depends on the symmetry of covariance, $\text{cov}(X, Y) = \text{cov}(Y, X)$.

Property (iv) follows from the fact that independence between X and Y implies $\text{cov}(X, Y) = 0$.

Property (v) is a consequence of the fact that if $Y = aX + b$ a.s., with $a \in \Re \setminus \{0\}$, $b \in \Re$, then $|\rho_{XY}| = 1$ and vice versa.[4]

As concerns property (vii), one needs Hoeffding's (1940) expression for covariance:

$$\text{cov}(X, Y) = \iint_D (F(x, y) - F_1(x)F_2(y)) \, dx \, dy \qquad (3.12)$$

where $D = \text{Dom } F_1 \times \text{Dom } F_2$.

---

[4] Since $r^2 = \{\text{var}(Y) - \min_{a,b} E[(Y - (aX + b))^2]\}/\text{var}(Y)$.

It follows from this and the Fréchet inequality that, if $C_1 \prec C_2$, and we denote as ρ_1 and ρ_2 the corresponding linear correlations, then from

$$\iint_D (C_1(F_1(x), F_2(y)) - F_1(x)F_2(y)) \, dx \, dy$$

$$\leqslant \iint_D (C_2(F_1(x), F_2(y)) - F_1(x)F_2(y)) \, dx \, dy$$

it follows that $\rho_1 \leqslant \rho_2$.   □

Nonetheless, the correlation coefficient does not satisfy axiom (vi) and therefore is not a measure of concordance. It satisfies instead the following properties, which entail that it violates Theorems 3.1 and 3.2.

Property 1 ρ_{XY} is invariant under linear increasing transformations, not under (non-linear) increasing transformations.

Proof: In order to prove the first fact, consider that

$$\rho_{aX+b,cY+d} = \text{sgn}(ac)\rho_{XY} \quad \text{for } a, c \in \Re \setminus \{0\}, b, d \in \Re$$

Linear increasing transforms produce $\text{sgn}(ac) = 1$ and $\rho_{aX+b,cY+d} = \rho_{XY}$.   □

In order to show that ρ_{XY} is not invariant under increasing, non-linear transforms, consider the following example:

Example 3.5   Start from two r.v.s X and Y jointly distributed as a bivariate standard normal, with correlation coefficient ρ_{XY}, and take their transforms according to the distribution function of the standard normal Φ, $\Phi(X)$ and $\Phi(Y)$. Computing the linear correlation coefficient between $\Phi(X)$ and $\Phi(Y)$ one gets

$$\rho_{\Phi(X),\Phi(Y)} = \frac{6}{\pi} \arcsin\left(\frac{\rho_{XY}}{2}\right) \tag{3.13}$$

In spite of reaching its bounds when X and Y are linear transformations of each other, ρ_{XY} does not necessarily reach its bounds when X and Y are comonotonic or countermonotonic, without being linearly related. Formally, it has the following property:

Property 2 ρ_{XY} is bounded

$$\rho_l \leqslant \rho_{XY} \leqslant \rho_u$$

where the bounds ρ_l and ρ_u are defined as

$$\rho_l = \frac{\iint_D \left(C^-(F_1(x), F_2(y)) - F_1(x)F_2(y)\right) dx \, dy}{\sqrt{\int_{\text{Dom}F_1} (x - EX)^2 \, dF_1(x) \int_{\text{Dom}F_2} (y - EY)^2 \, dF_2(y)}} \tag{3.14}$$

$$\rho_u = \frac{\iint_D \left(C^+(F_1(x), F_2(y)) - F_1(x)F_2(y)\right)}{\sqrt{\int_{\text{Dom}F_1} (x - EX)^2 \, dF_1(x) \int_{\text{Dom}F_2} (y - EY)^2 \, dF_2(y)}} \tag{3.15}$$

and are attained respectively when X and Y are countermonotonic and comonotonic.

Proof: The bounds for ρ_{XY} can be obtained from Hoeffding's (1940) expression for covariance, (3.12) above, together with the Fréchet inequality:

$$\iint_D \left(C^-(F_1(x), F_2(y)) - F_1(x)F_2(y)\right) \, dx \, dy \leqslant \text{cov}(X, Y)$$

$$\text{cov}(X, Y) \leqslant \iint_D \left(C^+(F_1(x), F_2(y)) - F_1(x)F_2(y)\right) \, dx \, dy$$

Dividing by the square root of the variances, the bounds are obtained. It is evident that they are attained when $C = C^-$ and $C = C^+$ respectively. $\qquad \square$

Property 3 ρ_{XY} for comonotone (countermonotone) random variables can be different from 1 (-1).

Proof: In order to show this, let us consider an example of comonotonicity, for which the linear correlation coefficient is bounded away from 1. Before doing that, remark however that the bounds in Property 2 depend on margins. The dependence of the bounds for ρ_{XY} on margins can *a priori* prevent the coefficient from being equal to 1 in absolute value for any pair of comonotone or countermonotone r.v.s. $\qquad \square$

As for the example, consider the following, due to Wang (1998):

Example 3.6 Let X and Y be two log-normal r.v.s, with parameters

$$(\mu_X, \sigma_X), \qquad (\mu_Y, \sigma_Y)$$

respectively. Computing α_l and α_u gives respectively:

$$\rho_l = \frac{\exp(-\sigma_X \sigma_Y) - 1}{\sqrt{(\exp(\sigma_X^2) - 1)(\exp(\sigma_Y^2) - 1)}} \leqslant 0$$

$$\rho_u = \frac{\exp(\sigma_X \sigma_Y) - 1}{\sqrt{(\exp(\sigma_X^2) - 1)(\exp(\sigma_Y^2) - 1)}} \geqslant 0$$

As argued by Georges et al. (2001), the lower bound tends to -1 when $\max(\sigma_X, \sigma_Y) \to 0$, while the upper bound is equal to 1 iff $\sigma_X = \sigma_Y$. When the two variances are different, the interval $[\rho_l, \rho_u]$ is different from $[-1, +1]$. Even worse, it may happen that the interval $[\rho_l, \rho_u]$ is very "small", since

$$\begin{aligned} \lim_{\max(\sigma_X, \sigma_Y) \to \infty} \rho_l = 0 \\ \lim_{|\sigma_X - \sigma_Y| \to \infty} \rho_u = 0 \end{aligned} \tag{3.16}$$

Example 3.7 To get a feeling of the phenomenon, consider for instance $\sigma_X = 0.4$, $\sigma_Y = 0.6$. In this case we get $\rho_l = -0.45$, $\rho_u = 0.57$. In addition, Figure 3.2 shows the whole behavior of the bounds, keeping σ_X fixed at the chosen value, 0.4, and letting σ_Y change.

An application: Stock indices correlation bounds

As an application of the linear correlation bounds concept, consider the following one, presented in Cherubini and Luciano (2002a). We want to determine the correlation bounds

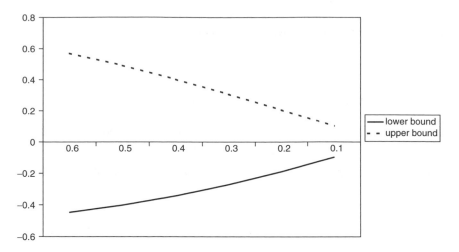

Figure 3.2 Bounds for linear correlation as a function of Y's volatility, volatility of $X = 0.4$, log-normal case

for the risk-neutral 3-month distributions of four stock indices, namely MIB 30, S&P 500, FTSE, DAX, using the time series of daily closing prices, from January 2, 1999 to March 27, 2000.

We first estimate the risk-neutral marginal distribution of each index using the European calls closing prices, as given by Bloomberg on March 27, 2000, for contracts with June expiration and different strikes. In doing this, we follow the approach in Shimko (1993), which exploits the seminal idea in Breeden and Litzenberger (1978), of reconstructing the distribution function of an underlying from the derivative of its European call price with respect to the strike.[5] If S is the underlying, with risk-neutral distribution F_S^*, $B(0, t)$ is the zero-coupon bond value for maturity t, $C(K, t)$ is the value of the call option on S with strike K and maturity t, it has been known since Breeden and Litzenberger (1978) that

$$F_S^*(K) = 1 + \frac{1}{B(0, t)} \frac{\partial C(K, t)}{\partial K}$$

Shimko superimposed on this idea the assumption of (conditionally) log-normal underlyings, where the conditioning is done with respect to the volatility, and of quadratic (implied) volatility function, $\sigma(K) = A_0 + A_1 K + A_2 K^2$. By so doing he obtained the following risk-neutral distribution function F_S of the underlying S:

$$F_S(s) = 1 + s\phi(D_2(s))\sqrt{t}(A_1 + 2A_2s) - \Phi(D_2(s)) \tag{3.17}$$

$$D_2(s) = \frac{\ln(S(0)/B(0, t)s)}{\sigma(s)\sqrt{t}} - \tfrac{1}{2}\sigma(s)\sqrt{t}$$

---

[5] The estimation technique for the marginals can be changed without modifying the bounds' existence and interpretation.

where $\phi(\cdot)$ and $\Phi(\cdot)$ are respectively the density and the distribution of the standard normal, $S(0)$ is the current value of the underlying, less the discounted dividends. We exploit his idea by first estimating the coefficients A_0, A_1, A_2 so as to minimize the squared differences between actual and theoretical implied volatility, $\sigma(K)$, on March 28. In order to obtain the whole indices' distributions (3.17) we then use, together with the coefficients so obtained, data on dividends and 3-month zero-coupon bond values from the same data source, in the same day. Finally, using the four marginals so obtained, we numerically compute the lower and upper Fréchet bounds for the joint distributions, C^- and C^+ evaluated at the marginal distribution values. Substituting them in (3.14) and (3.15) we recover the correlation bounds ρ_l and ρ_u in Figure 3.2.

As the readers can notice, these bounds are always of opposite sign but, at least for the first three pairs of indices, they are far from -1 and 1 respectively. The economic lesson we learn from the example is that for the Italian stock market, in the period under consideration, estimated correlation figures greater than (approximately) 0.7 in absolute value were inconsistent with the volatility smile. At the same time, estimated values close to (but smaller than) 0.7 were already very close to the maximum theoretical value: they had to be considered very high indeed, while usually a correlation close to 0.7 is not read as being very strong.

Recalling Theorems 2.6 and 2.7, we can state that, when $\rho = \rho_l$, one index is a decreasing function of the other, while when $\rho = \rho_u$ it is an increasing one, and the transformation functions are given in the aforementioned theorems. Applying and plotting them, for the case $X = DAX$, $Y = FTSE$, we obtain the relationships between the two indices shown in Figure 3.4, assuming extreme correlation between them.

Property 4 $\rho_{XY} = 0$ does not imply independence between X and Y, unless the latter are Gaussian.

Proof: If X and Y are Gaussian, $\rho_{XY} = 0$ implies $F(x, y) = F_1(x)F_2(y)$. This can be checked by substituting $\rho_{XY} = 0$ in the Gaussian expression for the joint distribution: as

Mib-S&P	Mib-FTSE	Mib-DAX	S&P-FTSE	S&P-DAX	FTSE-DAX
-0.673	-0.642	-0.678	-0.868	-0.9	-0.865
0.73	0.732	0.735	0.997	0.985	0.984

Figure 3.3 Linear correlation bounds for selected stock indices

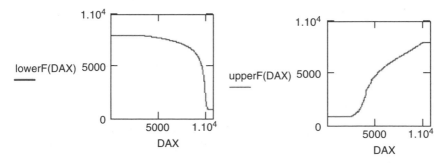

Figure 3.4 FTSE as a function of DAX, in the extreme correlation cases, lower F(DAX) & upper F(DAX)

usual, it is sufficient to prove the result for standardized normal variates. With $\rho_{XY} = 0$, the distribution of two standard jointly normal variables becomes

$$F(x, y) = \int_{-\infty}^{x} \int_{-\infty}^{y} \frac{1}{2\pi} \exp\left(\frac{-s^2 - t^2}{2}\right) \, ds \, dt$$

Since the marginal ones are $F_i = \Phi$, it is easy to see that $F(x, y) = F_1(x)F_2(y)$.

The same fact, that $\rho_{XY} = 0$ implies $F(x, y) = F_1(x)F_2(y)$, cannot be demonstrated in general: at the opposite, there are counterexamples, such as the one in the next property, in which, in spite of having $\rho_{XY} = 0$, one variable is a.s. a function of the other.   □

Property 5 $\rho_{XY} = 0$ does not mean that one r.v. cannot be almost surely a function of the other.

Proof: Nelsen (1999) defines the following copula

$$C(v, z) = \begin{cases} v & 0 \leqslant v \leqslant z/2 \leqslant \frac{1}{2} \\ z/2 & 0 \leqslant z/2 \leqslant v \leqslant 1 - z/2 \\ v + z - 1 & \frac{1}{2} \leqslant 1 - z/2 \leqslant v \leqslant 1 \end{cases}$$

Given this copula, $\text{cov}(U_1, U_2) = 0$, but

$$\Pr\left(U_2 = 1 - |2U_1 - 1|\right) = 1$$

The r.v.s U_1 and U_2 are uncorrelated, but one is a.s. a function of the other.   □

An application: Linear correlation estimation for some financial indices and an FX rate

Using the same data as in the application of section 3.1.2, the values in Table 3.3 were obtained for the correlation coefficient between the financial assets under examination over the years 1992–2001.

Table 3.3   Sample Pearson's linear correlation coefficient for selected assets, 01/92 to 06/01, weekly (average) data

	DAX 30	S&P 500	GER10y	USA10y	DEM/USD
DAX 30	–				
S&P 500	0.67	–			
GER10y	0.18	0.13	–		
USA10y	−0.02	0.13	0.50	–	
DEM/USD	0.30	0.14	0.06	−0.21	–

3.1.5   Tail dependence

Loosely said, bivariate tail dependence looks at concordance in the tail, or extreme, values of X and Y. Geometrically, it concentrates on the upper and lower quadrant tails of the joint distribution function.

Formally, having defined the joint survival function for uniform variates, $\bar{C}$, we have the following:

Definition 3.5 Let

$$\lim_{v \to 1^-} \frac{\bar{C}(v, v)}{1 - v} = \lambda_U$$

exist finite. C is said to have upper tail dependence iff $\lambda_U \in (0, 1]$, no upper tail dependence iff $\lambda_U = 0$. Analogously, let

$$\lim_{v \to 0^+} \frac{C(v, v)}{v} = \lambda_L$$

exist finite. C is said to have lower tail dependence iff $\lambda_L \in (0, 1]$, no lower tail dependence iff $\lambda_L = 0$.

In order to capture the correspondence between these definitions and the intuition above, recall that

$$\bar{C}(v, v) = \Pr(U_1 > v, U_2 > v)$$

so that the ratio $\bar{C}(v, v)/(1 - v)$ is the following conditional probability:

$$\frac{\bar{C}(v, v)}{1 - v} = \Pr(U_1 > v \mid U_2 > v) = \Pr(U_2 > v \mid U_1 > v)$$

Therefore

$$\lambda_U = \lim_{v \to 1^-} \Pr(U_1 > v \mid U_2 > v) = \lim_{v \to 1^-} \Pr(U_2 > v \mid U_1 > v)$$

and similarly for λ_L.

The value λ_U represents the limit of the conditional probability that the distribution function of X exceeds the threshold v, given that the corresponding function for Y does, when v tends to one (and therefore the r.v.s assume extreme or upper tail values). Analogously for λ_L.

Example 3.8 The copula $pC^+ + (1 - p)C^\perp$ has both upper and lower tail dependency, since in the upper tail

$$\frac{\bar{C}(v, v)}{1 - v} = \frac{1 - 2v + p \min(v, v) + (1 - p)v^2}{1 - v}$$

$$= \frac{1 - (2 - p)v + (1 - p)v^2}{1 - v}$$

and therefore

$$\lambda_U = \lim_{v \to 1^-} \frac{\bar{C}(v, v)}{1 - v} = p$$

In the lower tail

$$\frac{C(v, v)}{v} = \frac{p \min(v, v) + (1 - p)v^2}{v}$$

and therefore

$$\lambda_{\mathrm{L}} = \lim_{v \to 0^+} \frac{C(v, v)}{v} = p$$

The tail dependence and its coefficients in turn come from the fact that C^+ presents tail dependency, with both upper and lower index 1, while $C^\perp$ (as well as C^-) has neither lower nor upper tail dependency.

We can also introduce the coefficients of tail dependency for the survival copula $\overline{C}$:

$$\lim_{v \to 1^-} \frac{1 - 2v + \overline{C}(v, v)}{1 - v} = \overline{\lambda}_{\mathrm{U}}$$

$$\lim_{v \to 0^+} \frac{\overline{C}(v, v)}{v} = \overline{\lambda}_{\mathrm{L}}$$

if these limits are finite. The following property holds trivially:

Theorem 3.10   If $\overline{C}$ is the survival copula associated with C, then

$$\overline{\lambda}_{\mathrm{U}} = \lambda_{\mathrm{L}}$$

$$\overline{\lambda}_{\mathrm{L}} = \lambda_{\mathrm{U}}$$

Proof:

$$\lim_{v \to 1^-} \frac{1 - 2v + \overline{C}(v, v)}{1 - v} = \lim_{v \to 1^-} \frac{C(1 - v, 1 - v)}{1 - v}$$

implies $\overline{\lambda}_{\mathrm{U}} = \lambda_{\mathrm{L}}$. Symmetrically

$$\lim_{v \to 0^+} \frac{\overline{C}(v, v)}{v} = \lim_{v \to 0^+} \frac{2v - 1 + C(1 - v, 1 - v)}{v}$$

$$= \lim_{w \to 1^-} \frac{1 - 2w + C(w, w)}{1 - w}$$

gives $\overline{\lambda}_{\mathrm{L}} = \lambda_{\mathrm{U}}$.   □

3.1.6   Positive quadrant dependency

The concept of positive quadrant dependency (PQD), due to Lehmann (1966), can be expressed in terms of copulas as follows.

Definition 3.6   The r.v.s X and Y are positive quadrant dependent iff

$$C(v, z) \geqslant vz$$

for every $(v, z) \in I^2$.

Alternatively, using the concordance order between copulas, X and Y are PQD iff their copula is greater than that of the product:

$$C \succ C^{\perp}$$

Example 3.9 R.v.s with the copula $pC^{+} + (1 - p)C^{\perp}$, $p \in I$, are PQD, since

$$C^{+} \succ C^{\perp}$$

implies

$$pC^{+} + (1 - p)C^{\perp} \succ C^{\perp}$$

On the other hand, r.v.s with the copula $pC^{-} + (1 - p)C^{\perp}$, $p \in I$, are not PQD, since

$$C^{-} \prec C^{\perp}$$

implies

$$pC^{-} + (1 - p)C^{\perp} \prec C^{\perp}$$

In terms of distribution functions, PQD can be formalized as

$$F(x, y) \geqslant F_1(x)F_2(y) \quad \text{for every } (x, y) \in \Re^{*2}$$

the joint probability at each point must be not smaller than the independence one.

PQD implies the non-negativity of Kendall's τ, Spearman's ρ_S and of the linear correlation coefficient, since independent random variates, for which $C = C^{\perp}$, make these coefficients equal to zero, and the coefficients themselves respect concordance order.

By applying Bayes' rule the PQD inequality may be rewritten as:

$$\Pr(X \leqslant x | Y \leqslant y) \geqslant \Pr(X \leqslant x) \tag{3.18}$$

Hence, Lehmann's PQD condition may be strengthened by requiring the conditional probability to be a non-increasing function of y. This implies that the probability that the return X_t takes a small value does not increase as the value taken by the other return Y_t increases. This corresponds to a particular monotonicity in the tails.

Analogously, we say that a random variable X is *left tail decreasing* in Y, denoted by LTD$(X|Y)$, if

$$\Pr(X \leqslant x | Y \leqslant y) \text{ is a non-decreasing function of } y \text{ for all } x$$

This, in turn, is equivalent to the condition that, for all v in $[0, 1]$, $C(v, z)/z$ is a non-decreasing function in z, or:

$$\frac{\partial C(v, z)}{\partial z} \leqslant \frac{C(v, z)}{z} \quad \text{for almost all } z \tag{3.19}$$

3.2 PARAMETRIC FAMILIES OF BIVARIATE COPULAS

In this section we are going to present several **families** or **classes** of copulas. We will call **comprehensive** (Devroye, 1986) a copula family which encompasses the minimum, product and maximum one.

For each family, we give the copula definition and write down the density and conditional distribution via copula. We then discuss the concordance order and comprehensiveness properties of the family. Each family is characterized by a parameter or a vector of parameters. Whenever possible, the relationship between this parameter(s) and the measures of concordance or tail dependence defined above is clarified.

3.2.1 The bivariate Gaussian copula

Definition 3.7   The Gaussian copula is defined as follows:

$$C^{\text{Ga}}(v, z) = \Phi_{\rho_{XY}}\left(\Phi^{-1}(v), \Phi^{-1}(z)\right)$$

where $\Phi_{\rho_{XY}}$ is the joint distribution function of a bi-dimensional standard normal vector, with linear correlation coefficient ρ_{XY}, Φ is the standard normal distribution function. Therefore

$$\Phi_{\rho_{XY}}\left(\Phi^{-1}(v), \Phi^{-1}(z)\right)$$

$$= \int_{-\infty}^{\Phi^{-1}(v)} \int_{-\infty}^{\Phi^{-1}(z)} \frac{1}{2\pi\sqrt{1-\rho_{XY}^2}} \exp\left(\frac{2r_{XY}st - s^2 - t^2}{2\left(1 - \rho_{XY}^2\right)}\right) ds\, dt \qquad (3.20)$$

Since it is parametrized by the linear correlation coefficient, we can also write C_{ρ}^{Ga}. We have proved that it is actually a copula in Chapter 2 and we represent it and its level curves in Figure 3.5.

The following representation has been demonstrated by Roncalli (2002) to be equivalent to (3.20):

$$C^{\text{Ga}}(v, z) = \int_0^v \Phi\left(\frac{\Phi^{-1}(z) - \rho_{XY}\Phi^{-1}(t)}{\sqrt{1 - \rho_{XY}^2}}\right) dt \qquad (3.21)$$

In order to appreciate the effect of different correlation coefficients on the copula values, let us consider random samples from the Gaussian copula (Figure 3.6): the closer the samples are to a straight line (the main diagonal or the secondary one) the higher is (in absolute value) the correlation coefficient. The sign of the coefficient determines the diagonal on which the samples concentrate.

The **density** of C^{Ga} has been calculated in Chapter 2. By integrating the density, since the copula is absolutely continuous, the following, equivalent expression for the copula can

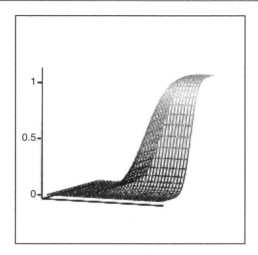

Figure 3.5   The Gaussian copula, $\rho = 0.5$

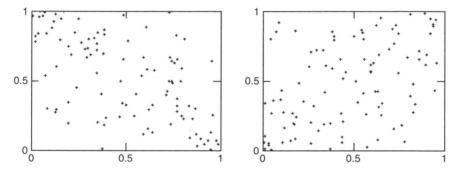

Figure 3.6   Random samples of (v, z) couples from a Gaussian copula, $\rho = 0.5$ (right) and $\rho = -0.5$ (left)

be obtained:

$$C^{\mathrm{Ga}}(v, z) = \int_0^v \int_0^z \frac{1}{\sqrt{1 - \rho_{XY}^2}} \exp\left(\frac{2r_{XY}xy - x^2 - y^2}{2\left(1 - \rho_{XY}^2\right)} + \frac{x^2 + y^2}{2} \right) \, \mathrm{d}s \, \mathrm{d}t$$

where $x = \Phi^{-1}(s)$, $y = \Phi^{-1}(t)$.

As for the **conditional distribution via copula**, from expression (3.21) one obtains:

$$C_{2|1}^{\mathrm{Ga}}(v, z) = \Phi\left(\frac{\Phi^{-1}(z) - \rho_{XY}\Phi^{-1}(v)}{\sqrt{1 - \rho_{XY}^2}} \right)$$

The reason why we start by analyzing this copula is that it may generate the Gaussian bivariate joint distribution function. Specifically, we have the following:

Proposition 3.1   The Gaussian copula generates the joint normal standard distribution function – via Sklar's theorem – iff the margins are standard normal.

Proof: Consider that

$$
C^{\mathrm{Ga}}(F_1(x), F_2(y)) = \int_{-\infty}^{x} \int_{-\infty}^{y} \frac{1}{2\pi\sqrt{1 - \rho_{XY}^2}} \exp\left(\frac{2r_{XY}st - s^2 - t^2}{2\left(1 - \rho_{XY}^2\right)} \right) ds\, dt
$$

iff $\Phi^{-1}(F_1(x)) = x$ and $\Phi^{-1}(F_2(y)) = y$, that is to say, iff $F_1 = F_2 = \Phi$. $\square$

For any other marginal choice, the Gaussian copula does not give a standard jointly normal vector. In order to have a visual representation of the phenomenon, and more generally of the effect of "coupling" the same copula with different marginals, let us consider the joint density functions in the following figures, obtained coupling the Gaussian copula with standard Gaussian margins (above) and with three Student's t d.o.f. (below); let us consider both the case $\rho = 0.2$ (in Figure 3.7) and $\rho = 0.9$ (in Figure 3.8).

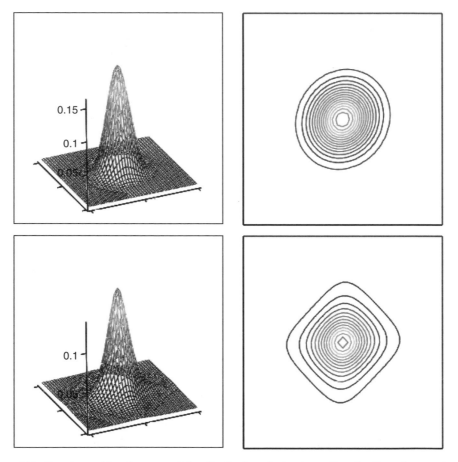

Figure 3.7 Density and level curves of the distribution obtained coupling the Gaussian copula with standard normal marginals (top) and 3-d.o.f. Student ones (bottom), $\rho = 0.2$

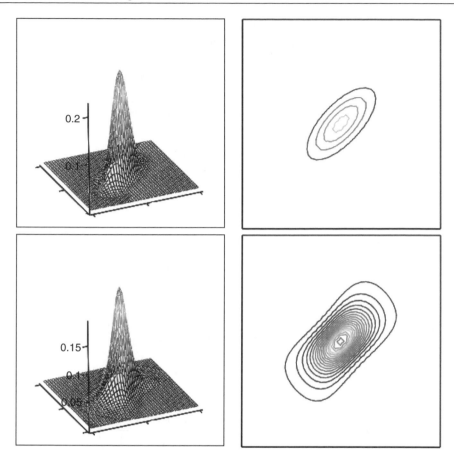

Figure 3.8 Density and level curves of the distribution obtained coupling the Gaussian copula with standard normal marginals (top) and 3-d.o.f. Student ones (bottom), $\rho = 0.9$

As expected, both in the positive and in the negative correlation cases, the same copula, together with different marginals, presents a different joint behavior, here synthesized by the density. In the specific case, the effect of marginal Student distributions is that of increasing the tail probabilities. In general, Figures 3.7 and 3.8 provide examples of the modeling flexibility obtained using copula functions instead of joint distribution functions: analogous effects could also be obtained by substituting different types of marginals in the other copulas. We will omit the corresponding diagrams in the next sections, but we strongly invite the readers to perform the substitutions and obtain the corresponding graphs.

As a consequence of the fact that it is parametrized by the linear correlation coefficient, which respects concordance order, the Gaussian copula is **positively ordered** with respect to the parameter:

$$C^{\mathrm{Ga}}_{\rho=-1} \prec C^{\mathrm{Ga}}_{\rho<0} \prec C^{\mathrm{Ga}}_{\rho=0} \prec C^{\mathrm{Ga}}_{\rho>0} \prec C^{\mathrm{Ga}}_{\rho=1}$$

Also, it is **comprehensive**: one in fact can verify that

$$C^{\mathrm{Ga}}_{\rho=-1} = C^- \quad \text{and} \quad C^{\mathrm{Ga}}_{\rho=1} = C^+$$

In addition, $C_{\rho=0}^{Ga} = C^{\perp}$. As for the measures of dependence, one can show, using the definition of Kendall's τ and Spearman's ρ_S, that

$$\tau = \frac{2}{\pi} \arcsin \rho \quad \text{and} \quad \rho_S = \frac{6}{\pi} \arcsin \frac{\rho}{2}$$

As for other types of dependence, it can be shown that Gaussian copulas have neither upper nor lower tail dependence, unless $\rho = 1$:

$$\lambda_U = \lambda_L = \begin{cases} 0 & \text{iff } \rho < 1 \\ 1 & \text{iff } \rho = 1 \end{cases}$$

They present PQD if $\rho \geqslant 0$.

3.2.2 The bivariate Student's t copula

Let $t_\upsilon : \mathfrak{R} \to \mathfrak{R}$ be the (central) univariate Student's t distribution function, with υ degrees of freedom (d.o.f.)[6]:

$$t_\upsilon(x) = \int_{-\infty}^{x} \frac{\Gamma((\upsilon+1)/2)}{\sqrt{\pi \upsilon} \Gamma(\upsilon/2)} \left(1 + \frac{s^2}{\upsilon}\right)^{-\frac{\upsilon+1}{2}} ds$$

where Γ is the usual Euler function. Let $\rho \in I$ and $t_{\rho,\upsilon}$ the bivariate distribution corresponding to t_υ:

$$t_{\rho,\upsilon}(x, y) = \int_{-\infty}^{x} \int_{-\infty}^{y} \frac{1}{2\pi \sqrt{1-\rho^2}} \left(1 + \frac{s^2 + t^2 - 2\rho st}{\upsilon(1-\rho^2)}\right)^{-\frac{\upsilon+2}{2}} ds \, dt$$

Definition 3.8 The bivariate Student's copula, $T_{\rho,\upsilon}$, is defined as

$$T_{\rho,\upsilon}(v, z) = t_{\rho,\upsilon}\left(t_\upsilon^{-1}(v), t_\upsilon^{-1}(z)\right)$$

$$= \int_{-\infty}^{t_\upsilon^{-1}(v)} \int_{-\infty}^{t_\upsilon^{-1}(z)} \frac{1}{2\pi \sqrt{1-\rho^2}} \left(1 + \frac{s^2 + t^2 - 2\rho st}{\upsilon(1-\rho^2)}\right)^{-\frac{\upsilon+2}{2}} ds \, dt$$

When the number of degrees of freedom diverges, the copula converges to the Gaussian one. For a limited number of degrees of freedom, however, the behavior of the two copulas is quite different, as the readers can appreciate comparing Figure 3.9, which presents random extractions from a 3-d.o.f. Student's copula, with the corresponding picture for the Gaussian copula (Figure 3.6). It is easy to remark that the Student copula presents more observations in the tails than the Gaussian one. Please notice also that this effect precedes the one exemplified by Figures 3.7 and 3.8, in which the different joint behavior was obtained – with the same copula – by changing the marginals. In concrete applications, both the copula and the marginal choice will be allowed, in sequential order.

---

[6] All odd moments of the distribution are zero due to symmetry; while the second moment exists if $\upsilon > 2$ and it is equal to $\upsilon/(\upsilon - 2)$; the fourth moment exists if $\upsilon > 4$ and its kurtosis is given by $3(\upsilon - 2)/(\upsilon - 4)$.

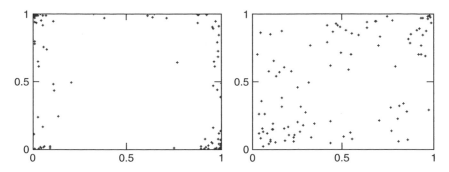

Figure 3.9   Random samples of (v, z) couples from a Student copula, $\rho = 0.5$ (right) and $\rho = -0.5$ (left), $\upsilon = 3$

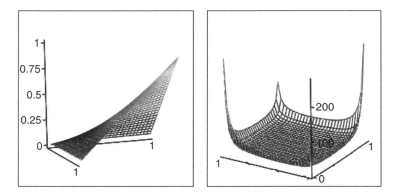

Figure 3.10   The Student copula (left) and its density (right), $\rho = 0.5$, $\upsilon = 3$

The Student's copula **density** is:

$$c_{\upsilon,\rho}^{S}(v, z) = \rho^{-\frac{1}{2}} \frac{\Gamma\left(\frac{\upsilon+2}{2}\right) \Gamma\left(\frac{\upsilon}{2}\right)}{\Gamma\left(\frac{\upsilon+1}{2}\right)^{2}} \frac{\left(1 + \frac{\varsigma_1^2 + \varsigma_2^2 - 2\rho\varsigma_1\varsigma_2}{\upsilon(1-\rho^2)}\right)^{-(\upsilon+2)/2}}{\prod\limits_{j=1}^{2}\left(1 + \frac{\varsigma_j^2}{\upsilon}\right)^{-(\upsilon+2)/2}}$$

where $\varsigma_1 = t_{\upsilon}^{-1}(v)$, $\varsigma_2 = t_{\upsilon}^{-1}(z)$, and the copula itself is absolutely continuous.

Since, as recalled by Roncalli (2002), given a couple of r.v.s (X, Y), jointly distributed as a Student's t, the conditional distribution of

$$\sqrt{\frac{\upsilon+1}{\upsilon+x^2}} \frac{Y - \rho x}{\sqrt{1-\rho^2}}$$

given $X = x$, is a Student's t with $\upsilon + 1$ degrees of freedom, the **conditional distribution via copula** $C_{2|1\upsilon,\rho}^{S}(v, z)$ is

$$C_{2|1\upsilon,\rho}^{S}(v, z) = t_{\upsilon+1}\left(\sqrt{\frac{\upsilon+1}{\upsilon+t_{\upsilon}^{-1}(v)^2}} \frac{t_{\upsilon}^{-1}(z) - \rho t_{\upsilon}^{-1}(v)}{\sqrt{1-\rho^2}}\right)$$

It follows that an equivalent expression for the bivariate Student's copula is

$$T_{\rho,\upsilon}(\upsilon, z) = \int_0^\upsilon t_{\upsilon+1}\left(\sqrt{\frac{\upsilon+1}{\upsilon+t_\upsilon^{-1}(s)^2}}\,\frac{t_\upsilon^{-1}(z) - \rho t_\upsilon^{-1}(s)}{\sqrt{1-\rho^2}}\right) ds$$

If $\upsilon > 2$, each margin admits a (finite) variance, $\upsilon/(\upsilon - 2)$, and ρ_{XY} can be interpreted as a linear correlation coefficient. The Student's copula is **positively ordered** w.r.t. ρ, for given degrees of freedom. It also reaches the lower and upper bound, since

$$C_{\upsilon,-1}^S = C^- \quad \text{and} \quad C_{\upsilon,1}^S = C^+$$

Nonetheless, $C_{\upsilon,0}^S \neq C^\perp$ for finite υ.

As for tail dependency, for finite υ

$$\lambda_U = \lambda_L = \begin{cases} > 0 & \text{iff } \rho > -1 \\ 0 & \text{iff } \rho = 1 \end{cases}$$

3.2.3   The Fréchet family

Definition 3.9   Fréchet (1958) introduced the following two-parameter copula family (Figure 3.11):

$$C^F(\upsilon, z) = p\max(\upsilon + z - 1, 0) + (1 - p - q)\upsilon z + q\min(\upsilon, z)$$
$$= pC^- + (1 - p - q)C^\perp + qC^+$$

where $p, q \in I, p + q \leqslant 1$.

The Fréchet copula **density** is

$$C^F(\upsilon, z) = 1 - p - q$$

It follows that this copula has an absolutely continuous and a singular component, if at least one between p and q is positive.

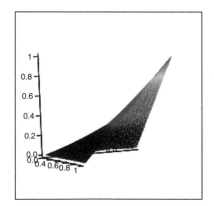 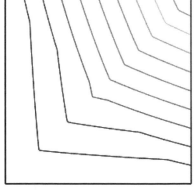

Figure 3.11   The Fréchet copula and its level curves, $p = 0.2, q = 0.5$

As for the **conditional probability via copula**, one can easily verify that

$$
C_{2|1}^F(v, z) = \begin{cases}
p + (1 - p - q)z + q & v + z - 1 > 0, \quad v < z \\
p + (1 - p - q)z & v + z - 1 > 0, \quad v > z \\
(1 - p - q)z & v + z - 1 < 0, \quad v > z \\
(1 - p - q)z + q & v + z - 1 < 0, \quad v < z
\end{cases}
$$

The Fréchet class is positively **ordered** with respect to q and negatively ordered with respect to p.

The class is **comprehensive**, since for $p = 1, q = 0$ it gives the Fréchet lower bound C^-, for $p = 0, q = 1$ it gives the upper, C^+, for $p = q = 0$ it collapses into the product copula $C^\perp$.

The relationship between the parameters of the Fréchet class and the concordance measures introduced above is (Nelsen, 1991):

$$
\tau = \frac{(q - p)(2 + p + q)}{3}
$$

$$
\rho_S = q - p
$$

which implies

$$
\begin{aligned}
\tau \leqslant \rho_S \leqslant -1 + \sqrt{1 + 3\tau} & \quad \text{when } \tau \geqslant 0 \\
1 - \sqrt{1 - 3\tau} \leqslant \rho_S \leqslant \tau & \quad \text{when } \tau < 0
\end{aligned}
$$

These bounds are stricter than those holding in general between τ and ρ_S.

In Figure 3.12 we depict the relationship between τ and ρ_S for the Fréchet family, together with the general one, already presented in Figure 3.1.

The Fréchet family reduces to the so-called **mixture copula** (Li, 2000), when either p or q are set to zero. In the former case, introduced by Konijn (1959), and presented as family B11 in Joe (1997)

$$
C_q^M(v, z) = (1 - q)vz + q \min(v, z) = (1 - q)C^\perp + qC^+
$$

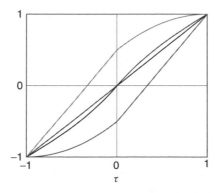

Figure 3.12 Spearman's ρ_S, as a function of Kendall's τ, for a given copula (external lines) and a given Spearman's copula (internal lines)

while in the second

$$C_p^{\mathrm{M}}(v, z) = (1 - p)vz + p \max(v + z - 1, 0) = (1 - p)C^{\perp} + pC^-$$

Opposite to C^{F}, C_q^{M} and C_p^{M} are not **comprehensive**. Nonetheless, the former includes the product and upper bound copula, respectively when $q = 0$ and $q = 1$. The latter includes the product and lower bound copula, respectively when $p = 0$ and $p = 1$.

As for the relationship between the parameters of the mixture copulas and the concordance measures, it is sufficient to substitute for $p = 0$ or $q = 0$ in the previous relationship: for positive dependence ($p = 0$) we have

$$\tau = \frac{q(2 + q)}{3} \quad \text{and} \quad \rho_S = q$$

and therefore

$$\tau = \rho_S \frac{2 + \rho_S}{3} \quad \text{and} \quad \rho_S = -1 + \sqrt{1 + 3\tau}$$

For negative dependence instead ($q = 0$)

$$\tau = -\frac{p(2 + p)}{3} \quad \text{and} \quad \rho_S = -p$$

so that

$$\tau = \rho_S \frac{2 - \rho_S}{3} \quad \text{and} \quad \rho_S = 1 - \sqrt{1 - 3\tau}$$

The relationship between τ and ρ_S, which is "narrowed" in the Fréchet family, reduces to a single value in the mixture family. In addition, the mixture copula reaches both the upper bound for ρ_S in the Fréchet copula in the positive case, and the lower bound in the negative case.

As for tail dependency, it is easy to show that for positive dependence[7]

$$\lambda_{\mathrm{U}} = \lambda_{\mathrm{L}} = q$$

so that the mixture copula presents tail dependence when $q > 0$. Symmetrically, it can be shown that for negative dependence

$$\lambda_{\mathrm{U}} = \lambda_{\mathrm{L}} = 0$$

so that the mixture copula presents no tail dependence in the presence of negative dependence.

3.2.4 Archimedean copulas

The class of Archimedean copulas has been named by Ling (1965), but it was recognized by Schweizer and Sklar (1961) in the study of t-norms. Before being introduced in Finance,

---

[7] See Example 3.8, where the notation was slightly different.

Archimedean copulas have been applied in the Actuarial field: the idea arose indirectly in Clayton (1978) and was developed in Oakes (1982), Cook and Johnson (1981). A survey of Actuarial applications is in Frees and Valdez (1998).

We divide the discussion of Archimedean copulas in three subsections: the first introduces them and their main properties, the second discusses dependence, the third presents different one-parameter families of Archimedean copulas. In the case of Archimedean copulas in fact, it is customary to use the term "class" for all of them, and to reserve "families" for some particular subclasses.

Definition and basic properties

Archimedean copulas may be constructed using a function $\phi : I \to \mathfrak{R}^{*+}$, continuous, decreasing, convex and such that $\phi(1) = 0$. Such a function ϕ is called a **generator**. It is called a strict generator whenever $\phi(0) = +\infty$. The behavior of the ϕ function is exemplified in Figure 3.13.

The **pseudo-inverse** of ϕ must also be defined, as follows:

$$\phi^{[-1]}(v) = \begin{cases} \phi^{-1}(v) & 0 \leqslant v \leqslant \phi(0) \\ 0 & \phi(0) \leqslant v \leqslant +\infty \end{cases}$$

This pseudo-inverse is such that, by composition with the generator, it gives the identity, as ordinary inverses do for functions with domain and range $\mathfrak{R}$:

$$\phi^{[-1]}(\phi(v)) = v \quad \text{for every } v \in I$$

In addition, it coincides with the usual inverse if ϕ is a strict generator.

Definition 3.10 Given a generator and its pseudo-inverse, an Archimedean copula C^A is generated as follows:

$$C^A(v, z) = \phi^{[-1]}(\phi(v) + \phi(z)) \tag{3.22}$$

If the generator is strict, the copula is said to be a strict Archimedean copula.

Let us recall the definition of Laplace transform:

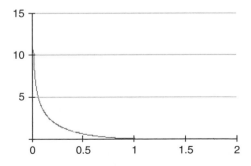

Figure 3.13   Generator of the Gumbel copula, $\alpha = 1.5$

Definition 3.11 The Laplace transform of a positive random variable γ, with distribution function F_γ, is defined as:

$$\tau(s) = E_\gamma\left(e^{-s\gamma}\right) = \int_0^{+\infty} e^{-st}\, dF_\gamma(t) \tag{3.23}$$

It is easy to show that the inverse of Laplace transforms gives strict generators: in order to generate Archimedean copulas then it is sufficient to start from the class of such transforms.

Archimedean copulas are easily verified to be symmetric, in the sense that

$$C^A(v, z) = C^A(z, v) \quad \text{for every } (v, z) \in I^2$$

They are also associative[8], i.e.

$$C^A(C^A(v, z), u) = C^A(v, C^A(z, u)) \quad \text{for every } (v, z, u) \in I^3$$

since both sides of the previous equality reduce to $\phi^{[-1]}\left(\phi(v) + \phi(z) + \phi(u)\right)$.

In addition, their level curves can be easily identified, since the condition

$$\{(v, z) \in I^2 : C(v, z) = K\}$$

in the Archimedean case becomes

$$\{(v, z) \in I^2 : \phi(v) + \phi(z) = \phi(K)\}$$

Therefore, for $K > 0$ the level curves consist of the couples

$$\{(v, z) \in I^2 : z = \phi^{[-1]}\left(\phi(K) - \phi(v)\right) = \phi^{-1}\left(\phi(K) - \phi(v)\right)\}$$

where we substituted the ordinary inverse for the pseudo one since $\phi(K) - \phi(v) \in [0, \phi(0))$.

For $K = 0$, the level curve can actually be a whole region in I^2, consisting of the so-called zero curve itself

$$\{(v, z) \in I^2 : z = \phi^{[-1]}\left(\phi(0) - \phi(v)\right) = \phi^{-1}\left(\phi(0) - \phi(v)\right)\}$$

and the so-called zero set of C, which is the region of I^2 between the axes of the Cartesian plane and the zero curve.

The following theorem is proved in Nelsen (1999):

Theorem 3.11 The level curves of an Archimedean copula (the zero curve included) are convex.

The **density** of Archimedean copulas is

$$C^A(v, z) = \frac{-\phi''(C(v, z))\phi'(v)\phi'(z)}{(\phi'(C(v, z)))^3} \tag{3.24}$$

---

[8] This justifies the relationship with t-norms: bi-dimensional copulas in fact are t-norms iff they are associative (see Schweizer, 1991). A further discussion of associative functions, copulas and t-norms is in Schweizer and Sklar (1983).

Dependency

Archimedean copulas are easily related to measures of association.

Genest and MacKay (1986) demonstrated that Kendall's τ is given by

$$\tau = 4 \int_I \frac{\phi(v)}{\phi'(v)} \, dv + 1 \tag{3.25}$$

where $\phi'(v)$ exists a.e., since the generator is convex. This makes Archimedean copulas easily amenable to estimation, as we will see in Chapter 5. Furthermore, conditions on the generators of two Archimedean copulas ϕ_1 and ϕ_2 can be given, which guarantee that the corresponding copulas are ordered in the same way as their association parameters (Genest & MacKay, 1986). If one denotes by C_i the copula corresponding to ϕ_i, $i = 1, 2$, then

$$C_1 \prec C_2 \leftrightarrow \tau_{C_1} \leqslant \tau_{C_2} \tag{3.26}$$

or, equivalently,

$$C_1 \prec C_2 \leftrightarrow \rho_{SC1} \leqslant \rho_{SC2} \tag{3.27}$$

Otherwise stated, the order between copulas is "measured" by either the Kendall or the Spearman association parameter. This is another "nice" feature of Archimedean copulas. As for tail dependency, the following result is demonstrated in Joe (1997):

Theorem 3.12 Let φ be a strict generator such that φ^{-1} belongs to the class of Laplace transforms of a.s. strictly positive r.v.s. If $\varphi'(0)$ is finite and different from zero, then

$$C(v, z) = \varphi^{-1}(\phi(v) + \phi(z))$$

does not have upper tail dependency. If instead C has upper tail dependency, then $1/\varphi'(0) = -\infty$ and the coefficient of upper tail dependency is

$$\lambda_U = 2 - 2 \lim_{s \to 0+} \frac{\varphi'(s)}{\varphi'(2s)}$$

The coefficient of lower tail dependency is

$$\lambda_L = 2 \lim_{s \to +\infty} \frac{\varphi'(s)}{\varphi'(2s)}$$

As for PQD, the relationship between this notion of dependency and Archimedean copulas relies on the following notion:

Definition 3.12 A function $h(t) : \Re \to \Re$ is said to be completely monotone on the interval J if it belongs to C^∞ and if in the interior of J derivatives alternate in sign:

$$(-1)^n \frac{d^n h(t)}{dt^n} \geqslant 0, \quad n = 0, 1, 2, \ldots$$

Notice that in particular such a function is non-negative ($h \geqslant 0$) and non-increasing ($h' \leqslant 0$). Given the notion of complete monotonocity, we have the following:

Theorem 3.13   If the inverse of a strict generator is completely monotone, then the corresponding copula entails PQD:

$$\varphi^{-1}(\phi(v) + \phi(z)) \geqslant vz$$

One-parameter Archimedean copulas

Among Archimedean copulas, we are going to consider in particular the one-parameter ones, which are constructed using a generator $\varphi_\alpha(t)$, indexed by the (real) parameter α. By choosing the generator, one obtains a subclass or family of Archimedean copulas. Table 3.4 describes some well-known families and their generators (for a more exhaustive list see Nelsen, 1999).

The Gumbel family has been introduced by Gumbel (1960). Since it has been discussed in Hougaard (1986), it is also known as the Gumbel–Hougaard family. Another important reference is Hutchinson and Lai (1990). It gives the product copula if $\alpha = 1$ and the upper Fréchet bound $\min(v, z)$ for $\alpha \to +\infty$. Figure 3.14 presents its behavior and some of its level curves in correspondence to $\alpha = 1.5$.

The Clayton family was first proposed by Clayton (1978), and studied by Oakes (1982, 1986), Cox and Oakes (1984), Cook and Johnson (1981, 1986). It is **comprehensive** and gives the product copula if $\alpha = 0$, the lower Fréchet bound $\max(v + z - 1, 0)$ when $\alpha = -1$, and the upper one for $\alpha \to +\infty$. Figure 3.15 presents its behavior and some of its level curves in correspondence to $\alpha = 6$.

To end up with, the Frank family, which appeared in Frank (1979), is discussed at length in Genest (1987). It reduces to the product copula if $\alpha = 0$, and reaches the lower and upper Fréchet bounds for $\alpha \to -\infty$ and $\alpha \to +\infty$, respectively. It is the only family for which both C and $\mathcal{C}$ are associative. Figure 3.16 presents its behavior and some of its level curves in correspondence to $\alpha = 0.5$.

The densities of the previous copulas, obtained via (3.24), are represented in Figure 3.17.

As for the relationship between the parameters of Archimedean copulas and measures of concordance, using formula (3.25) we get the results collected in Table 3.5 (see, e.g. Frees & Valdez, 1998).

Table 3.4   Some Archimedean copulas

Gumbel (1960)	
$\phi_\alpha(t)$	$(-\ln t)^\alpha$
range for α	$[1, +\infty)$
$C(v, z)$	$\exp\{-[(-\ln v)^\alpha + (-\ln z)^\alpha]^{1/\alpha}\}$
Clayton (1978)	
$\phi_\alpha(t)$	$\frac{1}{\alpha}(t^{-\alpha} - 1)$
range for α	$[-1, 0) \cup (0, +\infty)$
$C(v, z)$	$\max[(v^{-\alpha} + z^{-\alpha} - 1)^{-1/\alpha}, 0]$
Frank (1979)	
$\phi_\alpha(t)$	$-\ln \frac{\exp(-\alpha t)-1}{\exp(-\alpha)-1}$
range for α	$(-\infty, 0) \cup (0, +\infty)$
$C(v, z)$	$-\frac{1}{\alpha}\ln\left(1 + \frac{(\exp(-\alpha v)-1)(\exp(-\alpha z)-1)}{\exp(-\alpha)-1}\right)$

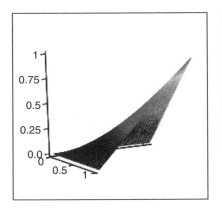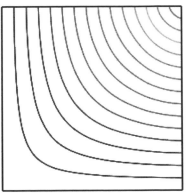

Figure 3.14 The Gumbel copula and its level curves, $\alpha = 1.5$

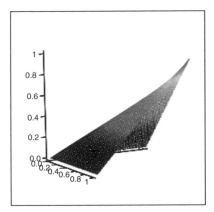

Figure 3.15 The Clayton copula and its level curves, $\alpha = 6$

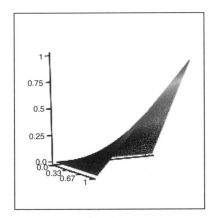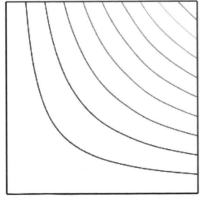

Figure 3.16 The Frank copula and its level curves, $\alpha = \frac{1}{2}$

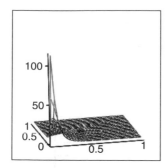 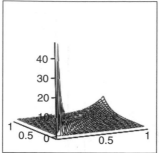 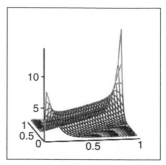

Figure 3.17 Densities of the Gumbel ($\alpha = 2$, left), the Clayton ($\alpha = 6$, center) and the Frank ($\alpha = 14.14$, right) copulas. All the parameters correspond to a Kendall's $\tau = 0.75$

Table 3.5 Association measures for some Archimedean copulas

Family	Kendall's τ	Spearman's ρ_S
Gumbel (1960)	$1 - \alpha^{-1}$	no closed form
Clayton (1978)	$\alpha/(\alpha + 2)$	complicated expression
Frank (1979)	$1 + 4\left[D_1(\alpha) - 1\right]/\alpha$	$1 - 12\left[D_2(-\alpha) - D_1(-\alpha)\right]/\alpha$

In Table 3.5 the concordance measures of the Frank copula require the computation of the so-called "Debye" functions, defined as

$$D_k(\alpha) = \frac{k}{\alpha^k} \int_0^\alpha \frac{t^k}{\exp(t) - 1}\, \mathrm{d}t, \quad k = 1, 2$$

For these functions, it follows from basic calculus that

$$D_k(-\alpha) = D_k(\alpha) + \frac{k\alpha}{k+1}$$

Table 3.5 allows us to remark that, with the exception of Spearman's ρ_S for the Gumbel case, the computation of the copula parameter from the association one is elementary and the relationship between the two is one-to-one.

An application: An Archimedean copula for international stock indices

Using the time series presented on page 105, whose size is reported in Figure 3.18, we estimated both Kendall's τ and Spearman's ρ_S, according to the methodology explained in the corresponding sections. The relationships between the copula parameter and the association measures in Table 3.5 then permitted us to compute the α value assuming a Gumbel, Clayton and Frank copula.

Once endowed with the parameter value, we are able to compute any joint probability between the stock indices: if for instance we consider the DAX–FTSE case and the Frank copula, we obtain the joint distribution and level curves shown in Figure 3.19.

	Sample Size	Kendall's tau	Spearman's rho	Gumbel's alpha	Clayton's alpha	Frank's alpha
Mib-S&P	306	0.372	0.548	1.593	1.185	3.789
Mib-FTSE	308	0.351	0.508	1.540	1.080	3.518
Mib-DAX	311	0.433	0.580	1.765	1.530	4.642
S&P-FTSE	304	0.581	0.772	2.387	2.774	7.445
S&P-DAX	306	0.646	0.846	2.828	3.657	9.317
FTSE-DAX	311	0.406	0.582	1.683	1.367	4.469

Figure 3.18 Estimated Kendall's τ, Spearman's ρ_S and α for MIB 30, S&P 500, FTSE, DAX, 1/2/99–3/27/00

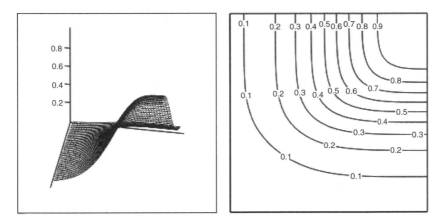

Figure 3.19 Joint distribution and level curves, DAX–FTSE

When, in particular, the relationship is monotonic, the family can be ordered not only according to the dependence parameter, as in (3.26) or (3.27) above, but also according to the α parameter: if the relationship is increasing, as in the Gumbel, Clayton and Frank cases, the following rule applies:

$$C_1 \prec C_2 \leftrightarrow \alpha_1 \leqslant \alpha_2$$

where α_i is the parameter corresponding to the copula C_i.

It follows that the Gumbel family can represent independence and "positive" dependence only, since the lower and upper bound for its parameter correspond to the product copula and the upper Fréchet bound. On the other hand, the Frank and Clayton family both cover the whole range of dependence.

As for tail dependency, applying Theorem 3.12 one can show that the Gumbel family has upper tail dependency, with

$$\lambda_U = 2 - 2^{1/\alpha}$$

The Clayton family has lower tail dependency for $\alpha > 0$, since

$$\lambda_L = 2^{-1/\alpha}$$

The Frank family has neither lower nor upper tail dependency.

The remarks on Table 3.5, together with the fact that the Frank and Clayton are **comprehensive**, so that they allow the maximum range of dependence, explain the relative popularity of the one-parameter families in the applied literature on copulas.

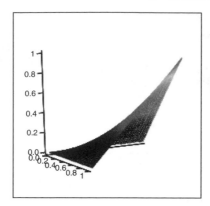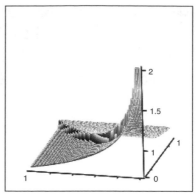

Figure 3.20 The Marshall–Olkin copula (left) and its density (right), $m = 0.2, n = 0.3$

3.2.5 The Marshall–Olkin copula

Definition 3.13 The Marshall–Olkin family (Marshall & Olkin, 1967a, b) is characterized by two parameters, m and n, belonging to I. It is defined as follows:

$$C^{MO}(v, z) = \min(v^{1-m}z, vz^{1-n}) = \begin{cases} v^{1-m}z, & v^m \geqslant z^n \\ vz^{1-n}, & v^m < z^n \end{cases} \qquad (3.28)$$

The copula **density** is

$$c^{MO}(v, z) = \begin{cases} (1-m)\, v^{-m}, & v^m > z^n \\ (1-n)z^{-n}, & v^m < z^n \end{cases}$$

and the copula itself has both an absolutely continuous and a singular component, whose mass is along the line $v^m = z^n$, in I^2. Both the copula and its density are represented in Figure 3.20.

As for the **conditional probability via copula**, one can easily verify that

$$C_{2|1}^{MO}(v, z) = \begin{cases} (1-m)\, v^{-m}z, & v^m > z^n \\ z^{1-n}, & v^m < z^n \end{cases}$$

The family is **positively ordered** w.r.t. each parameter. It can be noticed that when either m or n is set to zero, the product copula is obtained; when both parameters are equal to 1, the Marshall–Olkin copula gives the upper Fréchet bound. Therefore, this copula is not **comprehensive**.

As for its relationship with measures of concordance, we have (Nelsen, 1999):

$$\tau = \frac{mn}{m - mn + n} \quad \text{and} \quad \rho_S = \frac{3mn}{2m + 2n - mn}$$

This class of copulas presents upper tail dependency, with coefficient

$$\lambda_U = \min(m, n)$$

4

Multivariate Copulas

This chapter extends the results of Chapter 2 to the multidimensional case. For the sake of simplicity, we will omit the proofs, when the corresponding ones have been given in the previous chapter.

4.1 DEFINITION AND BASIC PROPERTIES

In the n-dimensional case, $n > 2$, the notions of groundedness and the n-increasing property are straightforward extensions of the definitions for the 2-dimensional case.

Let us recall that we denote vectors with bold letters: $\mathbf{u} = (u_1, u_2, \ldots, u_n)$.

Definition 4.1 Let the function $G : \mathfrak{R}^{*n} \to \mathfrak{R}$ have a domain $\text{Dom}\,G = A_1 \times A_2 \times \cdots \times A_n$, where the non-empty sets A_i have a least element a_i. The function G is said to be grounded iff it is null for every $\mathbf{v} \in \text{Dom}\,G$, with at least one index k such that $v_k = a_k$:

$$G(\mathbf{v}) = G(v_1, v_2, \ldots, v_{k-1}, a_k, v_{k+1}, \ldots, v_n) = 0$$

Let also the n-box A be defined as

$$A = [u_{11}, u_{12}] \times [u_{21}, u_{22}] \times \cdots \times [u_{n1}, u_{n2}]$$

with $u_{i1} \leqslant u_{i2}, i = 1, 2, \ldots, n$. An n-box is then the Cartesian product of n closed intervals.

Let us denote with $\mathbf{w}$ any vertex of A and with $\text{ver}(A)$ the set of all vertices of A: $\mathbf{w} \in \text{ver}(A)$ iff its ith component $w_i, i = 1, 2, \ldots, n$, is either equal to u_{i1} or to u_{i2}. Consider the product

$$\prod_{i=1}^{n} \text{sgn}(2w_i - u_{i1} - u_{i2})$$

Since each factor in the product is -1 if $w_i = u_{i1} < u_{i2}$, is equal to zero if $w_i = u_{i1} = u_{i2}$, and is $+1$ if $w_i = u_{i2} > u_{i1}$,

$$\prod_{i=1}^{n} \text{sgn}(2w_i - u_{i1} - u_{i2}) = \begin{cases} -1 & \text{if } u_{i1} \neq u_{i2}, \forall i, \sharp\{i : w_i = u_{i2}\} = 2m + 1 \\ 0 & \text{if } \exists\, i : u_{i1} = u_{i2} \qquad\qquad\qquad m \in N \\ +1 & \text{if } u_{i1} \neq u_{i2}, \forall i, \sharp\{i : w_i = u_{i1}\} = 2m \end{cases}$$

If $\text{ver}(A) \subset \text{Dom}\,G$, define the G-volume of A as the sum

$$\sum_{\mathbf{w} \in \text{ver}(A)} G(\mathbf{w}) \prod_{i=1}^{n} \text{sgn}(2w_i - u_{i1} - u_{i2}) \tag{4.1}$$

As in the bi-dimensional case, the sum (4.1) measures the mass or volume, according to the function G, of the n-box A.

We are now ready to define an n-increasing function:

Definition 4.2 The function $G : A_1 \times A_2 \times \cdots \times A_n \to \Re$ is said to be n-increasing if the G-volume of A is non-negative for every n-box A for which $\text{ver}(A) \subset \text{Dom } G$:

$$\sum_{\mathbf{w} \in \text{ver}(A)} G(\mathbf{w}) \prod_{i=1}^{n} \text{sgn}(2w_i - u_{i1} - u_{i2}) \geqslant 0$$

Grounded, n-increasing functions are non-decreasing with respect to all entries:

Theorem 4.1 A function $G : A_1 \times A_2 \times \cdots \times A_n \to \Re$ grounded and n-increasing is non-decreasing in each argument.

Proof: We are going to demonstrate that, if $(u_1, u_2, \ldots, u_{i-1}, x, u_{i+1}, \ldots, u_n) \in \text{Dom } G$, $(u_1, u_2, \ldots, u_{i-1}, y, u_{i+1}, \ldots, u_n) \in \text{Dom } G$ and $x \leqslant y$, then

$$G(u_1, u_2, \ldots, u_{i-1}, x, u_{i+1}, \ldots, u_n) \leqslant G(u_1, u_2, \ldots, u_{i-1}, y, u_{i+1}, \ldots, u_n) \qquad (4.2)$$

Consider the n-box

$$A = [a_1, u_1] \times [a_2, u_2] \times \cdots \times \left[a_{i-1}, u_{i-1}\right] \times \left[x, y\right] \times \left[a_{i+1}, u_{i+1}\right] \times \cdots \times [a_n, u_n]$$

Since G is grounded, the G-volume of A is

$$G(u_1, u_2, \ldots, u_{i-1}, y, u_{i+1}, \ldots, u_n) - G(u_1, u_2, \ldots, u_{i-1}, x, u_{i+1}, \ldots, u_n)$$

Since it is n-increasing, the volume is non-negative, i.e. (4.2) holds.   □

In order to characterize the copula, we use the notion of margins:

Definition 4.3 The k-dimensional margins of the function $G : A_1 \times A_2 \times \cdots \times A_n \to \Re$, for $1 \leqslant k \leqslant n, k \in N$, if each A_i is non-empty, are the functions $C_{i_1 i_2 \ldots i_k}(u_{i_1}, u_{i_2}, \ldots, u_{i_k}) : A_{i_1} \times A_{i_2} \times \cdots \times A_{i_k} \to \Re$ defined by

$$G_{i_1 i_2 \ldots i_k}(u_{i_1}, u_{i_2}, \ldots, u_{i_k}) = G(\bar{a}_1, \bar{a}_2, \ldots, u_{i_1}, \ldots, u_{i_2}, \ldots, u_{i_k} \ldots, \bar{a}_n) \qquad (4.3)$$

where $i_1 i_2 \ldots i_k$ is any selection of k indices (also non-consecutive) among the original n indices. In particular, we have:

Definition 4.4 The ith one-dimensional margin of the function $G : A_1 \times A_2 \times \cdots \times A_n \to \Re$, if each A_i is non-empty and we denote with $\bar{a}_i$ its maximal element, is the function $G_i(u) : A_i \to \Re$ defined by

$$G_i(u) = G(\bar{a}_1, \bar{a}_2, \ldots, \bar{a}_{i-1}, u, \bar{a}_{i+1}, \ldots, \bar{a}_n)$$

A grounded, n-increasing function with one-dimensional margins satisfies the following lemmas, which are used in the proof of the multidimensional version of Sklar's theorem:

Lemma 4.1   A function $G : A_1 \times A_2 \times \cdots \times A_n \to \Re$ grounded, n-increasing, with one-dimensional margins, is such that

$$G\left(\mathbf{u}^y\right) - G\left(\mathbf{u}^x\right) \leqslant G_i(y) - G_i(x) \quad \text{for every } 1 \leqslant i \leqslant n, \quad x < y$$

and

$$\mathbf{u}^y = (u_1, u_2, \ldots, u_{i-1}, y, u_{i+1}, \ldots, u_n) \in \mathrm{Dom}\, G$$
$$\mathbf{u}^x = (u_1, u_2, \ldots, u_{i-1}, x, u_{i+1}, \ldots, u_n) \in \mathrm{Dom}\, G$$

Lemma 4.2   For the function G of the previous lemma,

$$|G(\mathbf{u}) - G(\dot{\mathbf{u}})| \leqslant \sum_{i=1}^{n} |G_i(u_i) - G_i(\dot{u}_i)|$$

for every $\mathbf{u} = (u_1, u_2, \ldots, u_n)$, $\dot{\mathbf{u}} = (\dot{u}_1, \dot{u}_2, \ldots, \dot{u}_n) \in \mathrm{Dom}\, G$.

Given this terminology, the definition of n-dimensional subcopula and n-dimensional copula (from now on subcopula and copula respectively) is:

Definition 4.5   An n-dimensional subcopula is a function $\mathcal{C} : A_1 \times A_2 \times \cdots \times A_n \to \Re$, where, for each i, $A_i \subset I$ and contains at least 0 and 1, such that

  (i) $\mathcal{C}$ is grounded
 (ii) its one-dimensional margins are the identity function on I: $\mathcal{C}_i(u) = u, i = 1, 2, \ldots, n$
(iii) $\mathcal{C}$ is n-increasing

An n-dimensional subcopula for which $A_i = I$ for every i is a copula C.

It follows from this definition that

Theorem 4.2   For $n > 2$, $1 < k < n$, the k-dimensional margins of C are k-dimensional copulas.

Proof: We demonstrate that, when $A_i = I$ for every i, the function

$$C_{i_1 i_2 \ldots i_k}(u_{i_1}, u_{i_2}, \ldots, u_{i_k}) : I^k \to \Re$$

defined according to (4.3) is

  (i) grounded
 (ii) such that $C_i(u) = u, i = i_1, i_2, \ldots, i_k$
(iii) k-increasing

As for (i), groundedness, with at least one index i_j such that $u_{i_j} = a_{i_j}$, we have

$$C_{i_1 i_2 \ldots i_k}(u_{i_1}, u_{i_2}, \ldots, u_{i_k}) = C(\bar{a}_1, \bar{a}_2, \ldots, u_{i_1}, \ldots, u_{i_{j-1}}, a_{i_j}, u_{i_{j+1}}, \ldots, u_{i_k}, \bar{a}_n) = 0$$

since the vector $(\bar{a}_1, \bar{a}_2, \ldots, u_{i_1}, \ldots, u_{i_{j-1}}, a_{i_j}, u_{i_{j+1}}, \ldots, u_{i_k}, \bar{a}_n)$ has the feature of $\mathbf{v}$ in Definition 4.1.

As for (ii), it comes from the fact that one-dimensional margins for C are also one-dimensional margins for its k-dimensional margins.

Property (iii), k-increasingness is a consequence of the fact that the $C_{i_1 i_2 \ldots i_k}$-volume of each k-box

$$\left[u_{i_1 1}, u_{i_1 2}\right] \times \left[u_{i_2 1}, u_{i_2 2}\right] \times \cdots \times \left[u_{i_k 1}, u_{i_k 2}\right]$$

is the C-column of the n-box

$$[\bar{a}_1, \bar{a}_1] \times \cdots \times \left[u_{i_1 1}, u_{i_1 2}\right] \times \left[u_{i_2 1}, u_{i_2 2}\right] \times \cdots \times \left[u_{i_k 1}, u_{i_k 2}\right] \times \cdots \times [\bar{a}_n, \bar{a}_n]$$

which is non-negative because of n-increasingness. $\square$

Example 4.1   It is easy to verify that the function

$$C(\mathbf{u}) = \min(u_1, u_2, \ldots, u_n)$$

is an n-dimensional copula:

(i) $\min(u_1, u_2, \ldots, u_{i-1}, 0, u_{i+1}, \ldots, u_n) = 0, i = 1, 2, \ldots, n$
(ii) $\min(1, 1, \ldots, u_i, \ldots, 1) = u_i, i = 1, 2, \ldots, n$
(iii) $\displaystyle\sum_{\mathbf{w} \in \text{ver}(A)} \min(w_1, w_2, \ldots, w_n) \prod_{i=1}^{n} \text{sgn}(2w_i - u_{i1} - u_{i2}) \geqslant 0$

With the same technique we can verify that its margins are copulas, since for every k

$$C_{i_1 i_2 \ldots i_k}(u_{i_1}, u_{i_2}, \ldots, u_{i_k}) = \min(u_{i_1}, u_{i_2}, \ldots, u_{i_k})$$

As in the bi-dimensional case, from the characterization of C it follows that

- it is non-decreasing in each argument (Theorem 4.1)
- Ran $C = I$ (by (i)), $C(\mathbf{v}) = 0$ if there exists an index i such that $u_i = 0$; by (ii), if we denote by $\mathbf{e}^i$ the vector that has all entries equal to zero, apart from the ith, which is equal to 1, $C(\mathbf{v} + \mathbf{e}^i) = 1$. The two features, together with the fact that C is non-decreasing in each component, give the assertion about Ran C
- it is uniformly continuous (as a straightforward consequence of Lemma 4.2 above):

$$|C(\mathbf{u}) - C(\dot{\mathbf{u}})| \leqslant \sum_{i=1}^{n} |u_i - \dot{u}_i|$$

for every $\mathbf{u}, \dot{\mathbf{u}} \in I^n$
- it has mixed kth-order partial derivatives a.s., $1 \leqslant k \leqslant n$, and

$$0 \leqslant \frac{\partial^k C(\mathbf{u})}{\partial u_1 \partial u_2 \ldots \partial u_k} \leqslant 1$$

Example 4.2 For the copula in the previous example

- $x \leqslant y$ implies $\min(u_1, u_2, \ldots, u_{i-1}, x, u_{i+1}, \ldots, u_n) \leqslant \min(u_1, u_2, \ldots, u_{i-1}, y, u_{i+1}, \ldots, u_n)$
- $0 \leqslant \min(u_1, u_2, \ldots, u_n) \leqslant 1$:

$$|\min(u_1, u_2, \ldots, u_n) - \min(\dot{u}_1, \dot{u}_2, \ldots, \dot{u}_n)| \leqslant \sum_{i=1}^{n} |u_i - \dot{u}_i|$$

- the partial derivatives are

$$\frac{\partial C(\mathbf{u})}{\partial u_i} = \begin{cases} 1 & \text{if } u_i = \min(u_1, u_2, \ldots, u_n) \\ 0 & \text{otherwise} \end{cases}$$

and

$$\frac{\partial^k C(\mathbf{u})}{\partial u_1 \partial u_2 \ldots \partial u_k} = 0 \quad \text{for } k \geqslant 2$$

4.2 FRÉCHET BOUNDS AND CONCORDANCE ORDER: THE MULTIDIMENSIONAL CASE

It is straightforward to demonstrate that

Theorem 4.3 Every copula satisfies the following inequality:

$$\max(u_1 + u_2 + \cdots + u_n - 1, 0) \leqslant C(\mathbf{u}) \leqslant \min(u_1, u_2, \ldots, u_n)$$

for every $\mathbf{u} \in I^n$.

The upper bound still satisfies the definition of copula, and is denoted with C^+ (the maximum copula). However, as first noted by Féron (1956), the lower bound never satisfies the definition of copula for $n > 2$. This can be seen from the following:

Example 4.3 (Schweizer & Sklar, 1983) Consider the n-cube $\left[\frac{1}{2}, 1\right]^n$ and compute its volume according to the lower copula bound:

$$\max(1 + 1 + \cdots + 1 - n + 1, 0 - n) - n\max(\tfrac{1}{2} + 1 + \cdots + 1 - n + 1, 0)$$
$$+ \binom{n}{2}\max(\tfrac{1}{2} + \tfrac{1}{2} + 1 + \cdots + 1 - n + 1, 0) + \ldots$$
$$+ \max(\tfrac{1}{2} + \tfrac{1}{2} + \cdots + \tfrac{1}{2} - n + 1, 0)$$
$$= 1 - n/2 + 0 + \cdots + 0$$

Since for $n > 2$ the volume is negative ($n > 2 \Leftrightarrow 1 - n/2 < 0$), the lower bound cannot be a copula.

Nonetheless, the bound is the best possible: pointwise there always exists a copula that takes its value. Therefore, the latter copula is parametrized using the point for which it coincides with the Fréchet lower bound:

Theorem 4.4 (Sklar, 1998)   When $n > 2$, for every $\mathbf{u} \in I^n$ there exists a copula $C_\mathbf{u}$ such that

$$C_\mathbf{u}(\mathbf{u}) = \max(u_1 + u_2 + \cdots + u_n - 1, 0)$$

Proof: See Nelsen (1999).   □

The notion of order for n-dimensional copulas requires the introduction of the **survival function for n-dimensional vectors of uniform variates**, which will be discussed further in section 4.4:

Definition 4.6   The joint survival function for the vector $(U_1, U_2, \ldots, U_n)$ of (standard) uniform r.v.s with copula C, denoted as $\bar{\mathcal{C}}$, represents, when evaluated at $(u_1, u_2, \ldots, u_n)$, the joint probability that $(U_1, U_2, \ldots, U_n)$ be greater than $u_1, u_2, \ldots, u_n$:

$$\bar{\mathcal{C}}(u_1, u_2, \ldots, u_n) = \Pr[U_1 > u_1, U_2 > u_2, \ldots, U_n > u_n]$$

The following definition of **concordance order** between copulas can then be introduced:

Definition 4.7   The copula C_1 is smaller than the copula C_2 (written as $C_1 \prec C_2$) iff

$$C_1(\mathbf{u}) \leqslant C_2(\mathbf{u})$$

$$\bar{\mathcal{C}}_1(\mathbf{u}) \leqslant \bar{\mathcal{C}}_2(\mathbf{u})$$

for every $\mathbf{u} \in I^n$.

The order so defined is only partial, as in the bi-dimensional case.[1]

Example 4.4   We want to determine whether every three-dimensional copula is smaller than the maximum one, i.e. whether

$$C \prec C^+$$

for $n = 3$. Since Theorem 4.3 guarantees that, at any point in I^3, $C(\mathbf{u}) \leqslant C^+(\mathbf{u})$, we are left with testing whether $\bar{\mathcal{C}}(\mathbf{u}) \leqslant \bar{\mathcal{C}}^+(\mathbf{u})$. We will show in Example 4.5 below that when $n = 3$ the survival function is

$$\bar{\mathcal{C}}(u_1, u_2, u_3) = 1 - u_1 - u_2 - u_3 + C_{12}(u_1, u_2) + C_{13}(u_1, u_3)$$
$$+ C_{23}(u_2, u_3) - C(u_1, u_2, u_3)$$

It follows that $\bar{\mathcal{C}}(\mathbf{u}) \leqslant \bar{\mathcal{C}}^+(\mathbf{u})$ iff

$$1 - u_1 - u_2 - u_3 + C_{12}(u_1, u_2) + C_{13}(u_1, u_3) + C_{23}(u_2, u_3) - C(u_1, u_2, u_3)$$
$$\leqslant 1 - u_1 - u_2 - u_3 + \min(u_1, u_2) + \min(u_1, u_3) + \min(u_2, u_3) - \min(u_1, u_2, u_3)$$

---

[1] In the bi-dimensional case, the definition was reduced to the first inequality, since $C_1(v, z) \leqslant C_2(v, z)$ iff $\bar{\mathcal{C}}_1(v, z) \leqslant \bar{\mathcal{C}}_2(v, z)$ (due to the fact that $\bar{\mathcal{C}}_1(v, z) = 1 - v - z + C(v, z)$).

Since the two-dimensional margins are copulas, $C_{ij}(u_i, u_j) \leqslant \min(u_i, u_j)$ for any choice of indices; however, also

$$C(u_1, u_2, u_3) \leqslant \min(u_1, u_2, u_3)$$

and we cannot state that $\mathcal{C}(\mathbf{u}) \leqslant \mathcal{C}^+(\mathbf{u})$.

4.3 SKLAR'S THEOREM AND THE BASIC PROBABILISTIC INTERPRETATION: THE MULTIDIMENSIONAL CASE

In order to introduce Sklar's theorem, we take it for granted that the readers are familiar with the notion of n-dimensional joint distribution functions (or n-dimensional distribution functions or joint distribution functions) for r.v.s, whose one-dimensional margins are marginal distribution functions.

The following generalization to the n-dimensional case of Sklar's theorem guarantees that not only every subcopula is a joint distribution function, if its arguments are marginal distribution functions, but that the converse holds too. Every joint distribution function can be represented as a (unique) subcopula, which in turn can be extended (not uniquely, in general) to a copula. If the marginals are continuous, the extension is unique.

Theorem 4.5 Let $F_1(x_1)$, $F_2(x_2), \ldots, F_n(x_n)$ be (given) marginal distribution functions. Then, for every $\mathbf{x} = (x_1, x_2, \ldots, x_n) \in \Re^{*n}$:

(i) If $\mathcal{C}$ is any subcopula whose domain contains $\operatorname{Ran} F_1 \times \operatorname{Ran} F_2 \times \cdots \times \operatorname{Ran} F_n$,

$$\mathcal{C}(F_1(x_1), F_2(x_2), \ldots, F_n(x_n))$$

is a joint distribution function with margins $F_1(x_1)$, $F_2(x_2), \ldots, F_n(x_n)$.

(ii) Conversely, if F is a joint distribution function with margins

$$F_1(x_1), F_2(x_2), \ldots, F_n(x_n)$$

there exists a unique subcopula $\mathcal{C}$, with domain $\operatorname{Ran} F_1 \times \operatorname{Ran} F_2 \times \cdots \times \operatorname{Ran} F_n$, such that

$$F(\mathbf{x}) = \mathcal{C}(F_1(x_1), F_2(x_2), \ldots, F_n(x_n)) \tag{4.4}$$

If $F_1(x_1)$, $F_2(x_2), \ldots, F_n(x_n)$ are continuous, the subcopula is a copula; if not, there exists a copula C such that

$$C(u_1, u_2, \ldots, u_n) = \mathcal{C}(u_1, u_2, \ldots, u_n)$$

for every $(u_1, u_2, \ldots, u_n) \in \operatorname{Ran} F_1 \times \operatorname{Ran} F_2 \times \cdots \times \operatorname{Ran} F_n$.

The proof of the theorem in the n-dimensional case without the extension lemma is in Schweizer and Sklar (1983). The complete proof, i.e. with the extension lemma, was given independently by Moore and Spruill (1975), Deheuvels (1978) and Sklar (1996).

The following corollary holds:

Corollary 4.1   Under the hypotheses of part (ii) of Sklar's theorem, the (unique) subcopula C: Ran $F_1 \times$ Ran $F_2 \times \cdots \times$ Ran $F_n \to I$ such that

$$F(\mathbf{x}) = C(F_1(x_1), F_2(x_2), \ldots, F_n(x_n))$$

for every $\mathbf{x}$ in $\mathfrak{R}^{*n}$ is

$$C(\mathbf{u}) = F(F_1^{-1}(u_1), F_2^{-1}(u_2), \ldots, F_n^{-1}(u_n))$$

Otherwise stated, Corollary 4.1 states that the construction via Sklar's theorem exhausts the so-called **Fréchet class**, i.e. the class of joint distribution functions that have $F_1, F_2, \ldots, F_n$ as margins.

As in the bi-dimensional case, Sklar's theorem guarantees that the cumulative joint probability can be written (via an eventually non-unique copula) as a function of the cumulative marginal ones and vice versa

$$F(\mathbf{x}) = C(F_1(x_1), F_2(x_2), \ldots, F_n(x_n))$$

We say that the r.v.s in **X have the copula** C or that the latter is **the copula of X**. When needed, we denote the copula of $\mathbf{X} = [X_1 X_2 \ldots X_n]$ also as $C_{\mathbf{X}}$ or $C_{X_1 X_2 \ldots X_n}$. Also in the multidimensional case the possibility of writing the joint cumulative probability in terms of the marginal ones, i.e. the **basic probabilistic interpretation of copulas**, and the fact that multidimensional copulas are **dependence functions**, opens the way to a number of financial applications.

An application: Digital options with n underlyings

The copula application to bivariate option pricing in Chapter 2 can be extended to the n-dimensional case, as follows. Consider an n-variate bearish digital option, written on n underlyings, $X_1, \ldots, X_n$, with strikes $k_1, \ldots, k_n$ and expiration T. Under complete, arbitrage-free markets its forward price is the risk-neutral probability

$$\Pr(X_1 \leqslant k_1, \ldots, X_n \leqslant k_n) = F(k_1, \ldots, k_n)$$

According to the multivariate version of Sklar's theorem, it is always possible to represent this price in terms of the single digital prices, through a copula, unique on $\Pi_{i=1}^n$Ran F_i:

$$F(k_1, \ldots, k_n) = C(F_1(k_1), \ldots, F_n(k_n))$$

where the distribution functions F_i are those of the single underlyings X_i. If the latter have normal log returns, no matter how we want to model their dependency, we have in particular

$$F(k_1, \ldots, k_n) = C(\Phi(-d_{21}(k_1)), \ldots, \Phi(-d_{2n}(k_n))) \tag{4.5}$$

where

$$-d_{2i}(k_i) = -\frac{\ln(X_{i,0}/k_i) + \mu_{X_i}T}{\sigma_{X_i}\sqrt{T}}, \qquad \mu_{X_i} = r - \frac{\sigma_{X_i}^2}{2}$$

and r is the (instantaneous) riskless rate, assumed constant.

The basic probabilistic interpretation has at least two important consequences, which we are going to discuss in the rest of the section:

(1) r.v.s are independent iff on $\Pi_{i=1}^{n} \text{Ran } F_i$ their copula is the product one;
(2) the copulas of a.s. increasing or decreasing transforms of continuous r.v.s are easily written in terms of the copula of X and Y: in particular, copulas are invariant w.r.t. increasing transforms.

As for the characterization of independence via copulas, recall that the r.v.s in the vector $\mathbf{X}$ are independent iff $F(\mathbf{x}) = F_1(x_1) F_2(x_2) \ldots F_n(x_n)$, and define the **product copula** as

$$C^{\perp}(\mathbf{u}) = u_1 u_2 \ldots u_n$$

It is evident that Sklar's theorem entails

Corollary 4.2 The r.v.s in $\mathbf{X}$ are independent iff they have the product copula on $\Pi_{i=1}^{n} \text{Ran } F_i$.

As for the copulas of increasing or decreasing transforms of continuous r.v.s, the following theorem holds:

Theorem 4.6 (Schweizer & Wolff, 1976, 1981) Let the r.v.s in $\mathbf{X}$ be continuous with copula C. If $\alpha_1, \alpha_2, \ldots, \alpha_n$ are a.s. increasing transformations on $\alpha_i : \text{Ran } F_i \rightarrow \Re^*$, the r.v.s $\alpha_1(X_1), \alpha_2(X_2), \ldots, \alpha_n(X_n)$ – with marginals

$$H_1 = F_1(\alpha_1^{-1}), H_2 = F_2(\alpha_2^{-1}), \ldots, H_n = F_n(\alpha_n^{-1})$$

and joint distribution H – have copula C too:

$$C_{\alpha_1(X_1), \alpha_2(X_2), \ldots, \alpha_n(X_n)}(\mathbf{u}) = C_{X_1 X_2 \ldots X_n}(\mathbf{u})$$

for every $\mathbf{u} \in I^n$ or, equivalently:

$$H(\mathbf{u}) = C(H_1(u_1), H_2(u_2), \ldots, H_n(u_n))$$

Copulas are then invariant w.r.t. increasing transformations, even though the latter act differently on the components of $\mathbf{X}$.

Analogously, one could demonstrate that

Corollary 4.3 Under the hypotheses of Theorem 4.6, if α_1 is a.s. decreasing and $\alpha_2, \ldots, \alpha_n$ are a.s. increasing

$$C_{\alpha_1(X_1), \alpha_2(X_2), \ldots, \alpha_n(X_n)}(\mathbf{u}) = C_{\alpha_2(X_2), \ldots, \alpha_n(X_n)}(u_2, u_3, \ldots, u_n)$$
$$- C_{X_1, \alpha_2(X_2), \ldots, \alpha_n(X_n)}(1 - u_1, u_2, u_3, \ldots, u_n)$$

or, in terms of distribution functions:

$$H(\mathbf{u}) = C_{\alpha_2(X_2), \ldots, \alpha_n(X_n)}(H_2(u_2), \ldots, H_n(u_n))$$
$$- C_{X_1, \alpha_2(X_2), \ldots, \alpha_n(X_n)}(1 - H_1(u_1), H_2(u_2), \ldots, H_n(u_n))$$

where

$$C_{\alpha_2(X_2),\ldots,\alpha_n(X_n)} : I^{n-1} \to I$$

is the copula of $\alpha_2(X_2), \ldots, \alpha_n(X_n)$ (and consequently of $X_2 \ldots X_n$), while

$$C_{X_1,\alpha_2(X_2),\ldots,\alpha_n(X_n)}$$

is the copula of $X_1, \alpha_2(X_2), \ldots, \alpha_n(X_n)$ (and consequently of $X_1 X_2 \ldots X_n$):

$$C_{\alpha_2(X_2),\ldots,\alpha_n(X_n)}(u_2, u_3, \ldots, u_n) = C_{X_2,\ldots,X_n}(u_2, u_3, \ldots, u_n)$$

$$C_{X_1,\alpha_2(X_2),\ldots,\alpha_n(X_n)}(\mathbf{u}) = C_{X_1 X_2 \ldots X_n}(\mathbf{u})$$

For the three-dimensional case, for instance, we have, for α_1 decreasing and α_2, α_3 increasing

$$C_{\alpha_1(X_1),\alpha_2(X_2),\alpha_3(X_3)}(\mathbf{u}) = C_{\alpha_2(X_2),\alpha_3(X_3)}(u_2, u_3) - C_{X_1,\alpha_2(X_2),\alpha_3(X_3)}(1 - u_1, u_2, u_3)$$

$$= C_{X_2,X_3}(u_2, u_3) - C_{X_1 X_2, X_3}(1 - u_1, u_2, u_3)$$

Using recursively the corollary above, one can obtain the copula for the case in which two of the n functions α_i are decreasing, three are, and so on.

To conclude this section on the relationship between copula functions and r.v.s, let us notice that, as in the bi-dimensional case, multivariate copulas can be easily seen to be distribution functions of vectors of standard uniform random variables: for every $\mathbf{u} \in I^n$

$$C(\mathbf{u}) = \Pr(U_1 \leqslant u_1, \ldots, U_n \leqslant u_n)$$

The following remark extends to the multidimensional case:

Remark 4.1 The copula of the vector $\mathbf{X}$ is the joint distribution function of the probability-integral transforms of the functions F_i:

$$\Pr(F_1(X_1) \leqslant u_1, F_2(X_2) \leqslant u_2, \ldots, F_n(X_n) \leqslant u_n)$$

$$= \Pr\left(X_1 \leqslant F_1^{-1}(u_1), X_2 \leqslant F_2^{-1}(u_2), \ldots, X_n \leqslant F_n^{-1}(u_n)\right)$$

$$= C\left(F_1\left(F_1^{-1}(u_1)\right), F_2\left(F_2^{-1}(u_2)\right), \ldots, F_n\left(F_n^{-1}(u_n)\right)\right)$$

$$= C(u_1, u_2, \ldots, u_n)$$

4.3.1 Modeling consequences

In this section we revisit some examples of Chapter 2, in order to highlight that also in the multidimensional case the modeling consequence of the copula adoption is that of enlarging the pricing and risk evaluation possibilities beyond the Black–Scholes world.

An application: Digital options with log-normal underlyings

Let us consider the pricing of digital options with n underlyings on page 136, when the corresponding returns are assumed to be not only marginally normal, but also jointly normal, i.e. in the Black–Scholes world. In this case the joint risk-neutral distribution of the returns can be written via the Gaussian copula with Gaussian marginals, as in the bivariate case (see also section 8.1 below). The Gaussian copula in turn is defined as

$$C_R^{Ga}(\mathbf{u}) = \Phi_R\left(\Phi^{-1}(u_1), \Phi^{-1}(u_2), \ldots, \Phi^{-1}(u_n)\right)$$

$$= \int_{-\infty}^{\Phi^{-1}(u_1)} \cdots \int_{-\infty}^{\Phi^{-1}(u_n)} \frac{1}{(2\pi)^{\frac{n}{2}} |R|^{\frac{1}{2}}} \exp\left(-\frac{1}{2}\mathbf{x}^T R^{-1}\mathbf{x}\right) dx_1 \ldots dx_n$$

where Φ_R is the multivariate Gaussian distribution function with correlation matrix R. It follows from Theorem 4.6 that the price can be written in copula terms using the Gaussian copula too. More precisely, let the log returns of the underlyings, $\ln\left(X_i/X_{i,0}\right)$, be normal with risk-neutral mean $\mu_{X_i} = r - \frac{1}{2}\sigma_{X_i}^2$ and variance $\sigma_{X_i}^2$ per unit of time, so that the so-called standardized returns from 0 to T,

$$X\prime_i = \frac{\ln\left(X_i/X_{i,0}\right) - \mu_{X_i}T}{\sigma_{X_i}\sqrt{T}}$$

are standard normal. Assume them to be also jointly normal. Then the joint risk-neutral distribution of the underlyings, F, can be written as:

$$F(x_1, \ldots, x_n) = C_R^{Ga}(\Phi(x_1'), \ldots, \Phi(x_n'))$$

According to (4.5), the forward price of the n-variate bearish digital option is then:

$$F(k_1, \ldots k_n) = \int_{-\infty}^{-d_{21}} \cdots \int_{-\infty}^{-d_{2n}} \frac{1}{(2\pi)^{\frac{n}{2}} |R|^{\frac{1}{2}}} \exp\left(-\frac{1}{2}\mathbf{x}^T R^{-1}\mathbf{x}\right) dx_1 \ldots dx_n \qquad (4.6)$$

where

$$-d_{2i} = -d_{2i}(k_i) = \frac{\ln\left(k_i/X_{i,0}\right) - \mu_{X_i}T}{\sigma_{X_i}\sqrt{T}}$$

Suppose instead that the copula of the underlyings (or the returns) is a Student's T copula, an assumption that, as we will discuss in Chapter 5, seems much more appropriate in the financial domain. The Student's copula will be defined below to be

$$T_{R,\upsilon}(u_1, u_2, \ldots, u_n)$$

$$= \int_{-\infty}^{t_\upsilon^{-1}(u_1)} \int_{-\infty}^{t_\upsilon^{-1}(u_2)} \cdots \int_{-\infty}^{t_\upsilon^{-1}(u_n)} \frac{\Gamma\left(\frac{\upsilon+n}{2}\right) |R|^{-\frac{1}{2}}}{\Gamma\left(\frac{\upsilon}{2}\right)(\upsilon\pi)^{\frac{n}{2}}} \left(1 + \frac{1}{\upsilon}\mathbf{x}^T R^{-1}\mathbf{x}\right)^{-\frac{\upsilon+n}{2}} dx_1 dx_2 \ldots dx_n$$

where υ is, as usual, the number of degrees of freedom. Maintaining the marginal normality assumption on standardized returns, it follows from (4.5) that the digital option forward price is

$$F(k_1, \ldots, k_n) = \int_{-\infty}^{t_v^{-1}(\Phi(-d_{21}))} \int_{-\infty}^{t_v^{-1}(\Phi(-d_{22}))} \cdots \int_{-v}^{t_v^{-1}(\Phi(-d_{2n}))}$$

$$\frac{\Gamma\left(\frac{v+n}{2}\right) |R|^{-\frac{1}{2}}}{\Gamma\left(\frac{v}{2}\right)(v\pi)^{\frac{n}{2}}} \left(1 + \frac{1}{v} \mathbf{x}^T R^{-1} \mathbf{x}\right)^{-\frac{v+n}{2}} dx_1 dx_2 \ldots dx_n$$

Let us consider the following three assets: the DAX 30 index, the DEM/USD exchange rate and the 10-year total return index for the German bond market (GER10y). In the next chapter we will use weekly (average) data from January 1992 to June 2001, for a total of 248 observations, in order to fit a Gaussian copula to them. By so doing, we will obtain the following correlation matrix:

		DAX 30	DEM/USD	GER10y
$R =$	DAX 30	1		
	DEM/USD	0.3035	1	
	GER10y	0.1998	0.0551	1

Suppose that you want to price an at-the-money digital option on them, with one week to expiration. Using the same dataset, the initial levels of the three indices, and therefore the option strikes, were respectively $X_{1,0} = k_1 = 1603.620$, $X_{2,0} = k_2 = 1.547$, $X_{3,0} = k_3 = 7.37\%$. Consider also that the estimated standard deviations, over the same period, are $\sigma_{X_1} = 3.56\%$, $\sigma_{X_2} = 2.04\%$, $\sigma_{X_3} = 0.90\%$, while the riskless rate is $r = 3\%$, so that $\mu_{X_1} = 2.94\%$, $\mu_{X_2} = 2.98\%$, $\mu_{X_3} = 2.996\%$ and

$$-d_{21} = -\frac{\mu_{X_1}}{\sigma_{X_1}} = -0.8249, \qquad -d_{22} = -1.4604, \qquad -d_{23} = -3.3289$$

Using formula (4.6) we obtain the following price:

$$\int_{-\infty}^{-0.8249} \int_{-\infty}^{-1.46049} \int_{-\infty}^{-3.3289} \frac{1}{(2\pi)^{\frac{3}{2}} |R|^{\frac{1}{2}}} \exp(-\frac{1}{2} \mathbf{x}^T R^{-1} \mathbf{x}) \, dx_1 \, dx_2 \, dx_3 \qquad (4.7)$$

4.4 SURVIVAL COPULA AND JOINT SURVIVAL FUNCTION

This section introduces the notion of survival copula and recalls the joint survival function (for standard uniform r.v.s) copula given above. It discusses the relationships between them and applies them to the evaluation of the distribution functions of maxima and minima of $n > 2$ r.v.s.

Let us consider the probability:

$$\overline{F}(\mathbf{x}) = \Pr(X_1 > x_1, X_2 > x_2, \ldots, X_n > x_n) \qquad (4.8)$$

As in the bi-dimensional case, this probability is called the **joint survival probability** or **survival function** of the n agents or components X_i, while the **marginal survival**

probabilities or **survival functions** are:

$$\overline{F}_i(x_i) = \Pr(X_i > x_i)$$

The copula that represents the joint survival probability in terms of the survival probabilities of the n agents or components X_i separately is named the **survival copula**. The existence of the latter is guaranteed by the survival version of Sklar's theorem, which guarantees that there is a copula $\overline{C}$, unique on Ran $\overline{F}_1 \times$ Ran $\overline{F}_2 \times \cdots \times$ Ran $\overline{F}_n$, such that

$$\overline{F}(\mathbf{x}) = \overline{C}(\overline{F}_1(x_1), \overline{F}_2(x_2), \ldots, \overline{F}_n(x_n)) \tag{4.9}$$

Uniqueness *tout court* holds if the marginal survival probabilities are continuous. We are then allowed to introduce the following:

Definition 4.8 The survival copula of the r.v.s $X_1, X_2, \ldots, X_n$ is the copula $\overline{C}$, unique on Ran $F_1 \times$ Ran $F_2 \times \cdots \times$ Ran F_n, such that

$$\overline{F}(\mathbf{x}) = \overline{C}(\overline{F}_1(x_1), \overline{F}_2(x_2), \ldots, \overline{F}_n(x_n)) \tag{4.10}$$

Also in the multidimensional case it is customary to distinguish the survival copula from the **joint survival** or **survival function of n uniform variates**, defined above. In terms of the latter, the probability $\overline{F}(\mathbf{x})$ is simply

$$\overline{F}(\mathbf{x}) = \emptyset(F_1(x), F_2(x_2), \ldots, F_n(x_n))$$

Recalling that the probability integral transforms are uniformly distributed, and denoting with U_i the nth transform:

$$U_i = F_i(X_i)$$

one can also write $F_i(x_i) = u_i$ and $1 - \overline{F}_i(x_i) = u_i$; with this notation, it is very easy to find the **relationship between the survival copula and the survival function for uniform variates**. Since both can express the joint survival probability, $\overline{F}(\mathbf{x})$, respectively as

$$\overline{C}(\overline{F}_1(x_1), \overline{F}_2(x_2), \ldots, \overline{F}_n(x_n))$$

and

$$\emptyset(F_1(x), F_2(x_2), \ldots, F_n(x_n))$$

we have

$$\overline{C}(\overline{F}_1(x_1), \overline{F}_2(x_2), \ldots, \overline{F}_n(x_n)) = \emptyset(F_1(x), F_2(x_2), \ldots, F_n(x_n))$$
$$= \emptyset(1 - \overline{F}_1(x_1), 1 - \overline{F}_2(x_2), \ldots, 1 - \overline{F}_n(x_n))$$

It follows that the relationship between $\overline{C}$ and $\emptyset$ is

$$\overline{C}(u_1, u_2, \ldots, u_n) = \emptyset(1 - u_1, 1 - u_2, \ldots, 1 - u_n)$$

We are also interested in the **relationship between the survival copula and the copula**, since, differently from the bi-dimensional case, in the multidimensional one we do not define the former using the latter. Georges et al. (2001), adapting a result proved by Feller (1968), demonstrate the following theorems, which give the survival copula in terms of the copula and vice versa:

Theorem 4.7   The survival copula $\bar{C}$ can be written in terms of the corresponding copula C as follows:

$$\bar{C}(u_1, u_2, \ldots, u_n) = \not{C}(1 - u_1, 1 - u_2, \ldots, 1 - u_n)$$

$$= \sum_{i=0}^{n} \left[(-1)^i \sum_{\mathbf{w(u)} \in Z(n-i,n,1)} C(\mathbf{1 - w}) \right]$$

where $Z(n - i, n, 1)$ is the set of the $\binom{n}{i}$ possible vectors with $n - i$ components equal to 1, i equal to u_i, and

$$\mathbf{1 - w} \equiv (1 - w_1, \ldots, 1 - w_n)$$

Symmetrically, the copula C can be written in terms of the corresponding survival copula $\bar{C}$ as follows:

$$C(u_1, u_2, \ldots, u_n) = \sum_{i=0}^{n} \left[(-1)^i \sum_{\mathbf{w(u)} \in Z(n-i,n,1)} \bar{C}(\mathbf{1 - w}) \right]$$

Example 4.5   In the three-dimensional case, for instance, the previous theorem allows us, for a given copula, to obtain first the survival function and then the survival copula, as follows: we have the following representation for the survival function

$$\not{C}(u_1, u_2, u_3) = \sum_{i=0}^{3} \left[(-1)^i \sum_{\mathbf{w(u)} \in Z(3-i,3,1)} C(\mathbf{w}) \right]$$

$$= C(1, 1, 1) - C(u_1, 1, 1) - C(1, u_2, 1) - C(1, 1, u_3)$$

$$+ C(u_1, u_2, 1) + C(u_1, 1, u_3) + C(1, u_2, u_3) - C(u_1, u_2, u_3)$$

Exploiting the uniform margins property this becomes

$$\not{C}(u_1, u_2, u_3) = 1 - u_1 - u_2 - u_3 + C_{12}(u_1, u_2)$$

$$+ C_{13}(u_1, u_3) + C_{23}(u_2, u_3) - C(u_1, u_2, u_3)$$

where $C_{ij}, i = 1, 2, j = 2, 3$, are the two-dimensional margins of the copula. It follows that the survival copula is

$$\bar{C}(u_1, u_2, u_3) = \not{C}(1 - u_1, 1 - u_2, 1 - u_3)$$

$$= -2 + u_1 + u_2 + u_3 + C_{12}(1 - u_1, 1 - u_2)$$

$$+ C_{13}(1 - u_1, 1 - u_3) + C_{23}(1 - u_2, 1 - u_3)$$

$$- C(1 - u_1, 1 - u_2, 1 - u_3)$$

To conclude our discussion of the survival copula, we mention the following theorem, which gives – in terms of the copula of a random vector – the survival copula of certain transforms of its components. The theorem can be very useful for simulation issues.

Theorem 4.8   Let $X_1, X_2, \ldots, X_n$ be n r.v.s with continuous c.d.f.s $F_1, F_2, \ldots, F_n$ and copula C. We consider n continuous c.d.f.s $G_1, G_2, \ldots, G_n$ and we denote by T_j the r.v. $T_j = G_j^{-1}(1 - F_j(X_j))$. Then, the margins and the copula of the random vector $(T_1, T_2, \ldots, T_n)$ are respectively $G_1, G_2, \ldots, G_n$ and the survival copula $\overline{C}$ of C.

Proof: To prove that the margins are $G_1, G_2, \ldots, G_n$ is very simple since:

$$\Pr(T_j \leqslant t_j) = \Pr(G_j^{(-1)}(1 - F_j(X_j)) \leqslant t_j)$$

$$= 1 - \Pr(1 - F_j(X_j) \geqslant G_j(t_j)) = 1 - \Pr(F_j(X_j) \leqslant 1 - G_j(t_j))$$

$$= 1 - F_j \left(F_j^{(-1)} \left(1 - G_j(t_j) \right) \right) = G_j(t_j)$$

As for the copula, the fact that the copula of the random vector $(T_1, T_2, \ldots, T_n)$ is $\overline{C}$ depends on the theorem of Schweizer and Wolff (1976, 1981), because G_j^{-1} and $1 - F_j$ are respectively increasing and decreasing functions.

$\square$

As in the bi-dimensional case, distribution functions (d.f.s) for *minima* or *maxima* of n random variables are easily expressed in terms of their copula, survival copula or survival function. In fact, let us denote with m the minimum between the given r.v.s:

$$m = \min(X_1, X_2, \ldots, X_n)$$

and with M their maximum:

$$M = \max(X_1, X_2, \ldots, X_n)$$

Let F_m and F_M be the d.f.s of the minimum and maximum respectively. We have

for maxima:

$$F_M(a) = \Pr(M \leqslant a) = \Pr(X_1 \leqslant a, X_2 \leqslant a, \ldots, X_n \leqslant a) = F(a, a, \ldots, a) =$$

$$= C(F_1(a), F_2(a), \ldots, F_n(a))$$

for minima:

$$F_m(a) = \Pr(m \leqslant a) = 1 - \Pr(m > a)$$

$$= 1 - \Pr(X_1 > a, X_2 > a, \ldots, X_n > a)$$

$$= 1 - \overline{\mathcal{C}}(F_1(a), F_2(a), \ldots, F_n(a)) =$$

$$= 1 - \overline{C}(\overline{F}_1(a), \overline{F}_2(a), \ldots, \overline{F}_n(a))$$

This method may be extended to any order statistics involving the r.v.s $X_1, X_2, \ldots, X_n$ (Theorem 23 of Georges et al., 2001).

4.5 DENSITY AND CANONICAL REPRESENTATION OF A MULTIDIMENSIONAL COPULA

This section introduces the notions of density and canonical representation of a copula, together with those of the absolutely continuous and singular components.

Definition 4.9 The density $c(u_1, u_2, \ldots, u_n)$ associated to a copula $C(u_1, u_2, \ldots, u_n)$ is

$$c(u_1, u_2, \ldots, u_n) = \frac{\partial^n C(u_1, u_2, \ldots, u_n)}{\partial u_1 \ldots \partial u_n}$$

It exists a.e. in I^n, as noticed at the end of section 4.1.

The density can be used to define the absolutely continuous and singular components of C, denoted as A_C and S_C, as follows:

$$A_C(u_1, u_2, \ldots, u_n) = \int_0^{u_1} \int_0^{u_2} \ldots \int_0^{u_n} \frac{\partial^n C(s_1, s_2, \ldots, s_n)}{\partial s_1 \ldots \partial s_n} ds_1 \ldots ds_n$$

$$S_C(u_1, u_2, \ldots, u_n) = C(u_1, u_2, \ldots, u_n) - A_C(u_1, u_2, \ldots, u_n)$$

In turn, a copula for which $C = A_C$ on I^n is called **absolutely continuous**, while it is called **singular** if $C = S_C$ on I^n. It has both an **absolutely continuous and a singular component** if it belongs to neither the first nor the second class.

Each copula induces a probability measure on I^n, which is no other than the C-volume of section 4.1. The C-measure of the absolute component is $A_C(\mathbf{1})$, while that of the singular component is $S_C(\mathbf{1})$.

Example 4.6 The product copula $C^\perp = u_1 u_2 u_3$ is absolutely continuous, since

$$\frac{\partial^3 s_1 s_2 s_3}{\partial s_1 \partial s_2 \partial s_3} = 1$$

and for every $(u_1, u_2, u_3) \in I^3$

$$A_C = \int_0^{u_1} \int_0^{u_2} \int_0^{u_3} \frac{\partial^3 s_1 s_2 s_3}{\partial s_1 \partial s_2 \partial s_3} ds_1 ds_2 ds_3 = u_1 u_2 u_3 = C^\perp$$

The Fréchet upper bound C^+ is singular, since a.e.

$$\frac{\partial^3 C^+(u_1, u_2, u_3)}{\partial u_1 \, \partial u_2 \, \partial u_3} = \frac{\partial^3 \min(u_1, u_2, u_3)}{\partial u_1 \, \partial u_2 \, \partial u_3} = 0$$

Consequently

$$A_C = \int_0^{u_1} \int_0^{u_2} \int_0^{u_3} \frac{\partial^3 C^+}{\partial s_1 \partial s_2 \partial s_3} ds_1 ds_2 ds_3 = 0 \neq C^+$$

Finally, notice that for continuous random variables, the copula density is related to the density of the distribution F, denoted as f, by the **canonical representation**:

$$f(x_1, x_2, \ldots, x_n) = c(F_1(x_1), F_2(x_2), \ldots, F_n(x_n)) \cdot \prod_{j=1}^{n} f_j(x_j)$$

where

$$c(F_1(x_1), F_2(x_2), \ldots, F_n(x_n)) = \frac{\partial^n (C(F_1(x_1), F_2(x_2), \ldots, F_n(x_n)))}{\partial F_1(x_1) \partial F_2(x_2) \ldots \partial F_n(x_n)}$$

and f_j are the densities of the marginals

$$f_j(x_j) = \frac{\mathrm{d}F_j(x_j)}{\mathrm{d}x_j}$$

Also in the n-dimensional case the copula density is therefore equal to the ratio of the joint density f and the product of all marginal densities f_j. From this expression it is clear also that the copula density takes a value equal to 1 everywhere when the original r.v.s are independent.

The canonical representation is very useful in statistical estimation, in order to have a flexible representation for joint densities (mostly other than Gaussian, in financial applications), and in order to determine the copula, if one knows the joint and marginal distribution: see Chapter 5.

4.6 BOUNDS FOR DISTRIBUTION FUNCTIONS OF SUMS OF n RANDOM VARIABLES

The matter of the distribution function of the sum of r.v.s can be addressed in the multivariate case as well.

In the present setting, it has the following formulation: given n r.v.s with distribution functions F_i, $i = 1, 2, \ldots, n$, and having denoted with F_S the distribution function of their sum, find distribution functions F_L and F_U such that, for every $s \in \Re^*$

$$F_L(s) = \inf_{F \in \mathcal{F}} F_S(s) \qquad (4.11)$$

$$F_U(s) = \sup_{F \in \mathcal{F}} F_S(s) \qquad (4.12)$$

where $\mathcal{F}$ is the Fréchet class which has F_i, $i = 1, 2, \ldots, n$ as marginals, defined as in the bi-dimensional case.

Theorem 4.9 If one denotes with **1** the n-dimensional vector whose components are all equal to 1, and defines as $T(s)$ the set of vectors such that the sum of their components is equal to 1:

$$T(s) = \left\{ \mathbf{t} \in \Re^n : \mathbf{t1} = s \right\}$$

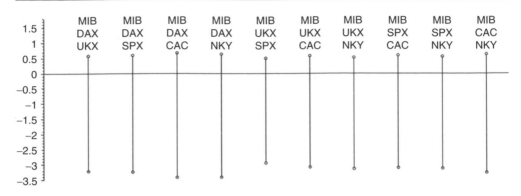

Figure 4.1   VaR bounds at the 95% level of confidence for equally weighted portfolios of three stock indices, the empirical quantiles

then the stochastic bounds on F_S are

$$F_L(s) = \sup_{\mathbf{t} \in T(s)} \max \left\{ \sum_1^n F_i(t_i) - (n-1), 0 \right\} \tag{4.13}$$

$$F_U(s) = \inf_{\mathbf{t} \in T(s)} \min \left\{ \sum_1^n F_i(t_i), 1 \right\} \tag{4.14}$$

As in the bi-dimensional case, apart from very special cases, the bounds do not have a closed form expression: however, Frank, Nelsen and Schweizer (1987) notice that they can be computed iteratively. The same iterative procedure can be adopted with the numerical algorithms of Williamson and Downs (1990).

An application: VaR bounds, Luciano & Marena, 2002a

The computation of the VaR bounds in Chapter 2 can be extended to larger portfolios. Luciano and Marena start by considering equally weighted portfolios of three assets, using the same data as in the three-dimensional case and adopting the numerical computation device in Williamson and Downs (1990). Figure 4.1 presents the portfolio VaR bounds, corresponding to Figure 2.9 in Chapter 2.

4.7   MULTIVARIATE DEPENDENCE

Some of the copula properties related to dependence measures may be extended to the multivariate case. For example, in three or more dimensions we have orthants as the generalization of quadrants: the extension of quadrant dependence is therefore the following orthant dependence concept.

Definition 4.10 [*Positively orthant dependence*]   Let $\mathbf{X} = (X_1, X_2, \ldots, X_n)$ be an n-dimensional random vector.

(1) $\mathbf{X}$ is said to be positively lower orthant dependent (PLOD) if for all $(x_1, x_2, \ldots, x_n)$ in $\Re^n$,

$$\Pr(X_1 \leqslant x_1, X_2 \leqslant x_2, \ldots, X_n \leqslant x_n) \geqslant \prod_{i=1}^{n} \Pr(X_i \leqslant x_i)$$

i.e. $C \succ C^{\perp}$.

(2) $\mathbf{X}$ is said to be positively upper orthant dependent (PUOD) if for all $(x_1, x_2, \ldots, x_n)$ in $\Re^n$,

$$\Pr(X_1 > x_1, X_2 > x_2, \ldots, X_n > x_n) \geqslant \prod_{i=1}^{n} \Pr(X_i > x_i)$$

i.e. $\bar{C} \succ \bar{C}^{\perp}$.

(3) $\mathbf{X}$ is said to be positively orthant dependent (POD) if for all $(x_1, x_2, \ldots, x_n)$ in $\Re^n$ it is both PLOD and PUOD.[2]

Negative lower orthant dependence (NLOD), negative upper orthant dependence (NUOD), and negative orthant dependence (NOD) are defined analogously by reversing the sense of the previous inequalities.

Many of the measures of concordance have a multivariate version. In general, however, each bivariate concordance and association measure has several multidimensional versions (see Joe, 1990, 1997; Wolff, 1981; Brindley & Thompson, 1972 and Block & Ting, 1981, for a further discussion of multivariate dependence concepts).

4.8 PARAMETRIC FAMILIES OF n-DIMENSIONAL COPULAS

4.8.1 The multivariate Gaussian copula

Definition 4.11 [*Multivariate Gaussian copula* (MGC)] Let R be a symmetric, positive definite matrix with $\text{diag}(R) = (1, 1, \ldots, 1)^T$ and Φ_R the standardized multivariate normal distribution with correlation matrix R. The MGC is defined as follows:

$$C_R^{\text{Ga}}(\mathbf{u}) = \Phi_R\left(\Phi^{-1}(u_1), \Phi^{-1}(u_2), \ldots, \Phi^{-1}(u_n)\right)$$

where Φ^{-1}, as usual, is the inverse of the standard univariate normal distribution function Φ.

As in the bivariate case, the Gaussian copula generates the standard Gaussian joint distribution function, whenever the margins are standard normal.

Proposition 4.1 The Gaussian copula generates the standard joint normal distribution function – via Sklar's theorem – iff the margins are standard normal.

From the definition of the Gaussian copula we can easily determine the corresponding density. Using the canonical representation, we have:

$$\frac{1}{(2\pi)^{\frac{n}{2}} |R|^{\frac{1}{2}}} \exp\left(-\frac{1}{2}\mathbf{x}^T R^{-1}\mathbf{x}\right) = c_R^{\text{Ga}}(\Phi(x_1), \Phi(x_2), \ldots, \Phi(x_n))$$

$$\times \prod_{j=1}^{n}\left(\frac{1}{\sqrt{2\pi}}\exp\left(-\frac{1}{2}x_j^2\right)\right)$$

---

[2] Since in the bi-dimensional case PLOD and PUOD coincide, we introduced PQD only.

where $|R|$ is the determinant of R. We deduce that:

$$c_R^{\text{Ga}}(\Phi(x_1), \Phi(x_2), \ldots, \Phi(x_n)) = \frac{\dfrac{1}{(2\pi)^{\frac{n}{2}} |R|^{\frac{1}{2}}} \exp\left(-\dfrac{1}{2} \mathbf{x}^T R^{-1} \mathbf{x}\right)}{\displaystyle\prod_{j=1}^{n} \left(\dfrac{1}{\sqrt{2\pi}} \exp\left(-\dfrac{1}{2} x_j^2\right)\right)}$$

Let $u_j = \Phi(x_j)$, so that $x_j = \Phi^{-1}(u_j)$. The density can be rewritten as follows:

$$c_R^{\text{Ga}}(u_1, u_2, \ldots, u_n) = \frac{1}{|R|^{\frac{1}{2}}} \exp\left(-\frac{1}{2} \varsigma^T (R^{-1} - I) \varsigma\right)$$

where $\varsigma = \left(\Phi^{-1}(u_1), \Phi^{-1}(u_2), \ldots, \Phi^{-1}(u_n)\right)^T$.

4.8.2 The multivariate Student's t copula

Definition 4.12 [*Multivariate Student's t copula* (MTC)]   Let R be a symmetric, positive definite matrix with $\text{diag}(R) = (1, 1, \ldots, 1)^T$ and $t_{R,\upsilon}$ the standardized multivariate Student's t distribution with correlation matrix R and υ degrees of freedom, i.e.

$$t_{R,\upsilon}(x_1, x_2, \ldots, x_n) = \int_{-\infty}^{x_1} \int_{-\infty}^{x_2} \cdots \int_{-\infty}^{x_n}$$

$$\times \frac{\Gamma\left(\dfrac{\upsilon + n}{2}\right) |R|^{-\frac{1}{2}}}{\Gamma\left(\dfrac{\upsilon}{2}\right) (\upsilon\pi)^{\frac{n}{2}}} \left(1 + \frac{1}{\upsilon} \mathbf{x}^T R^{-1} \mathbf{x}\right)^{-\frac{\upsilon+n}{2}} dx_1 dx_2 \ldots dx_n$$

The MTC is then defined as follows:

$$T_{R,\upsilon}(u_1, u_2, \ldots, u_n) = t_{R,\upsilon}(t_\upsilon^{-1}(u_1), t_\upsilon^{-1}(u_2), \ldots, t_\upsilon^{-1}(u_n))$$

$$= \int_{-\infty}^{t_\upsilon^{-1}(u_1)} \int_{-\infty}^{t_\upsilon^{-1}(u_2)} \cdots \int_{-\infty}^{t_\upsilon^{-1}(u_n)} \frac{\Gamma\left(\dfrac{\upsilon + n}{2}\right) |R|^{-\frac{1}{2}}}{\Gamma\left(\dfrac{\upsilon}{2}\right) (\upsilon\pi)^{\frac{n}{2}}} \left(1 + \frac{1}{\upsilon} \mathbf{x}^T R^{-1} \mathbf{x}\right)^{-\frac{\upsilon+n}{2}} dx_1 dx_2 \ldots dx_n$$

where t_υ^{-1} is the inverse of the univariate c.d.f. of Student's t with υ degrees of freedom.
   Using the canonical representation, it turns out that the copula density for the MTC is:

$$c_{R,\upsilon}(u_1, u_2, \ldots, u_n) = |R|^{-\frac{1}{2}} \frac{\Gamma\left(\dfrac{\upsilon + n}{2}\right)}{\Gamma\left(\dfrac{\upsilon}{2}\right)} \left(\frac{\Gamma\left(\dfrac{\upsilon}{2}\right)}{\Gamma\left(\dfrac{\upsilon + 1}{2}\right)}\right)^n \frac{\left(1 + \dfrac{1}{\upsilon} \varsigma^T R^{-1} \varsigma\right)^{-\frac{\upsilon+n}{2}}}{\displaystyle\prod_{j=1}^{n} \left(1 + \dfrac{\varsigma_j^2}{\upsilon}\right)^{-\frac{\upsilon+1}{2}}}$$

where $\varsigma_j = t_\upsilon^{-1}(u_j)$.

4.8.3 The multivariate dispersion copula

Definition 4.13 [*Multivariate dispersion copula* (MDC)]   Let $\boldsymbol{\mu} = (\mu_1, \mu_2, \ldots, \mu_n)^T$ be a position parameter, $\boldsymbol{\sigma}^2 = (\sigma_1^2, \sigma_2^2, \ldots, \sigma_n^2)^T$ a dispersion parameter and R a correlation matrix. We say that $\mathbf{X} \sim \mathrm{MDC}(\boldsymbol{\mu}, \boldsymbol{\sigma}^2, R)$ if

$$f(\mathbf{y}; \boldsymbol{\mu}, \boldsymbol{\sigma}^2, R) = \frac{1}{|R|^{\frac{1}{2}}} \exp\left(-\frac{1}{2}\boldsymbol{\varsigma}^T (R^{-1} - I)\boldsymbol{\varsigma}\right) \prod_{j=1}^{n} f_j\left(y_j; \mu_j, \sigma_j^2\right)$$

where

$$\varsigma_j = \Phi^{-1}\left(F_j\left(y_j; \mu_j, \sigma_j^2\right)\right) \quad \text{for } j = 1, 2, \ldots, n \quad \text{and}$$

$$f_j\left(y_j; \mu_j, \sigma_j^2\right) = \frac{\partial F_j\left(y_j; \mu_j, \sigma_j^2\right)}{\partial y_j} \quad \text{for every set of c.d.f. } F_j\left(y_j; \mu_j, \sigma_j^2\right)$$

Example 4.7   Just for a simple application of this definition, we can construct the MDC assuming Weibull margins. In such a case we have:

$$f(x) = \frac{\alpha x^{\alpha-1}}{\beta} \exp\left(-\frac{x^\alpha}{\beta}\right)$$

so we obtain the MDC density:

$$f(x_1, x_2, \ldots, x_n) = \frac{1}{|R|^{\frac{1}{2}}} \exp\left(-\frac{1}{2}\boldsymbol{\varsigma}^T (R^{-1} - I)\boldsymbol{\varsigma}\right) \prod_{j=1}^{n} \frac{\alpha_j x_j^{\alpha_j-1}}{\beta_j} \exp\left(-\frac{x_j^{\alpha_j}}{\beta_j}\right)$$

where

$$\varsigma_j = \Phi^{-1}\left(1 - \exp\left(-\frac{x_j^{\alpha_j}}{\beta_j}\right)\right)$$

4.8.4 Archimedean copulas

As in the bi-dimensional case, let us consider a generator function. Assume directly a strict generator:

$$\varphi(u) : [0, 1] \to [0, \infty]$$

continuous and strictly decreasing. Define its inverse as in Chapter 2.

The following theorem can be proved:

Theorem 4.10 (Kimberling, 1974)   Let φ be a generator. The function $C : [0, 1]^n \to [0, 1]$ defined by

$$C(u_1, u_2, \ldots, u_n) = \varphi^{-1}(\varphi(u_1) + \varphi(u_2) + \cdots + \varphi(u_n))$$

is a copula iff φ^{-1} is completely monotonic on $[0, \infty]$.

As a consequence of the previous theorem, we can give the following:

Definition 4.14 Let φ be a strict generator, with φ^{-1} completely monotonic on $[0, \infty]$. Then an n-variate Archimedean copula is the function

$$C(u_1, u_2, \ldots, u_n) = \varphi^{-1}(\varphi(u_1) + \varphi(u_2) + \cdots + \varphi(u_n))$$

As in the bi-dimensional case, an important source of generators for Archimedean n-copulas consists of the inverses of the Laplace transforms of c.d.f.s, as proved by the following theorem:

Theorem 4.11 (Feller, 1971) A function φ on $[0, \infty]$ is the Laplace transform of a c.d.f. F if and only if φ is completely monotonic and $\varphi(0) = 1$.

It is fairly simple to generate multivariate Archimedean copulas according to the previous definition: however, they have the limit that there are only one or two parameters to capture the dependence structure.[3]

Gumbel n-copula

The generator is given by $\varphi(u) = (-\ln(u))^{\alpha}$, hence $\varphi^{-1}(t) = \exp(-t^{\frac{1}{\alpha}})$; it is completely monotonic if $\alpha > 1$. The Gumbel n-copula is therefore:

$$C(u_1, u_2, \ldots, u_n) = \exp\left\{-\left[\sum_{i=1}^{n}(-\ln u_i)^{\alpha}\right]^{\frac{1}{\alpha}}\right\} \quad \text{with } \alpha > 1 \qquad (4.15)$$

Clayton n-copula

The generator is given by $\varphi(u) = u^{-\alpha} - 1$, hence $\varphi^{-1}(t) = (t + 1)^{-\frac{1}{\alpha}}$; it is completely monotonic if $\alpha > 0$. The Clayton n-copula is therefore:

$$C(u_1, u_2, \ldots, u_n) = \left[\sum_{i=1}^{n} u_i^{-\alpha} - n + 1\right]^{-\frac{1}{\alpha}} \quad \text{with } \alpha > 0 \qquad (4.16)$$

Frank n-copula

The generator is given by

$$\varphi(u) = \ln\left(\frac{\exp(-\alpha u) - 1}{\exp(-\alpha) - 1}\right)$$

hence

$$\varphi^{-1}(t) = -\frac{1}{\alpha}\ln\left(1 + e^{t}(e^{-\alpha} - 1)\right)$$

---

[3] A more general definition, overcoming this restriction, could also be given.

it is completely monotonic if $\alpha > 0$. The Frank n-copula is given by:

$$C(u_1, u_2, \ldots, u_n) = -\frac{1}{\alpha} \ln \left\{ 1 + \frac{\prod\limits_{i=1}^{n} \left(e^{-\alpha u_i} - 1\right)}{\left(e^{-\alpha} - 1\right)^{n-1}} \right\} \qquad \text{with } \alpha > 0 \text{ when } n \geqslant 3 \qquad (4.17)$$

Estimation and Calibration from Market Data

5.1 STATISTICAL INFERENCE FOR COPULAS

From a statistical point of view, a copula function is basically a very simple expression of a multivariate model and, as for most multivariate statistical models, much of the classical statistical inference theory is not applicable. The only theory that can be applied is the asymptotic maximum likelihood estimation (MLE). In addition, there are other possible ad hoc estimation methods that were proposed for overwhelming the hard computational efforts to get exact MLEs. These methods share, and also mix, concepts from non-parametric statistical inference and simulation techniques.

This section is devoted to statistical inference theory applied to copula models. We first describe the Exact Maximum Likelihood Estimator and introduce some deviations from that. Now, we would like to observe that every estimation method that we are going to describe often requires a numerical optimization of the objective function, because a copula is intrinsically a multivariate model and its likelihood involves mixed derivatives.

Copulas represent a powerful tool for tackling the problem of how to describe a joint distribution because, as evidenced in Chapter 2, they let the researcher deal separately with the needs of marginal and joint distribution modeling. Thus, one can choose for each data series the marginal distribution that best fits the sample, and afterwards put everything together using a copula function with some desirable properties. A potential problem comes from the simple fact that the number of combinations that can be made has virtually no limit, and one can easily get lost looking for the best combination of the marginals and the copula. This is why we will present some non-parametric methods to model both the margins and the copula. It is required that they have enough data since every non-parametric method performs much better when data are not scarce, and the main advantage is to let the dataset express the copula without any subjective choice.

In this chapter we will focus on continuous random variables. It should be noted that the assumption of continuity is not always required, but it simplifies some of the presentation. As in the previous chapters, we will denote throughout the cumulative distribution function (or c.d.f.) of a random variable (or r.v.) using an uppercase letter, and the corresponding probability density function (or p.d.f.) using a lowercase letter. We will still consider all r.v.s to be distributed in the extended real line.

When we extend this framework in a time series context, especially when we present some empirical application to financial time series, we will consider a strictly stationary stochastic process $\{\mathbf{Y}_t, t \in Z\}$ taking values in R^n and assume that our data consist in a realization of n-dimensional real vectors $\{\mathbf{Y}_t, t = 1, 2, \ldots, T\}$. These data, for example, may correspond to observed returns of n financial assets, say stock indexes, at different dates.

We denote by $f(\mathbf{y})$, $F(\mathbf{y})$, respectively, the (joint) p.d.f. and the (joint) c.d.f. of $\mathbf{Y}_t = (Y_{1t}, Y_{2t}, \ldots, Y_{nt})'$ at point $\mathbf{y} = (y_1, y_2, \ldots, y_n)'$.

The marginal (univariate) p.d.f. and c.d.f. of each element Y_{jt} at point y_j with $j = 1, 2, \ldots, n$ will be denoted by $f_j(y_j)$ and $F_j(y_j)$, respectively.

In the following we will consider the case where the marginals F_j are continuous.

5.2   EXACT MAXIMUM LIKELIHOOD METHOD

Before introducing this important estimation method it is worth recalling the following *canonical representation* presented in Chapter 4:

$$f(x_1, x_2, \ldots, x_n) = c(F_1(x_1), F_2(x_2), \ldots, F_n(x_n)) \cdot \prod_{j=1}^{n} f_j(x_j) \qquad (5.1)$$

where

$$c(F_1(x_1), F_2(x_2), \ldots, F_n(x_n)) = \frac{\partial^n(C(F_1(x_1), F_2(x_2), \ldots, F_n(x_n)))}{\partial F_1(x_1) \partial F_2(x_2) \ldots \partial F_n(x_n)} \qquad (5.2)$$

is the nth mixed partial derivative of the copula C, c is the copula density and f is the standard univariate probability density function.

This canonical representation for the multivariate density function permits us to say that, in general, a statistical modeling problem for copulas could be decomposed into two steps:

- identification of the marginal distributions;
- definition of the appropriate copula function.

This is an important point, to begin with, for estimation issues as we will see below.

Let $\aleph = \{x_{1t}, x_{2t}, \ldots, x_{nt}\}_{t=1}^{T}$ be the sample data matrix. Thus, the expression for the log-likelihood function is

$$l(\boldsymbol{\theta}) = \sum_{t=1}^{T} \ln c(F_1(x_{1t}), F_2(x_{2t}), \ldots, F_n(x_{nt})) + \sum_{t=1}^{T} \sum_{j=1}^{n} \ln f_j(x_{jt}) \qquad (5.3)$$

where $\boldsymbol{\theta}$ is the set of all parameters of both the marginals and the copula.

Hence, given a set of marginal p.d.f.s and a copula the previous log-likelihood may be written, and by maximization we obtain the maximum likelihood estimator:

$$\hat{\boldsymbol{\theta}}_{\text{MLE}} = \max_{\boldsymbol{\theta} \in \Theta} l(\boldsymbol{\theta}) \qquad (5.4)$$

Throughout this section, we assume that the usual regularity conditions (see Serfling, 1980 and Shao, 1999) for asymptotic maximum likelihood theory hold for the multivariate model (i.e. the copula) as well as for all of its margins (i.e. the univariate p.d.f.s). Under these regularity conditions the maximum likelihood estimator exists and it is consistent and asymptotically efficient; also, it verifies the property of asymptotically normal, and we have:

$$\sqrt{T}(\hat{\boldsymbol{\theta}}_{\text{MLE}} - \boldsymbol{\theta}_0) \to N(0, \Im^{-1}(\boldsymbol{\theta}_0)) \qquad (5.5)$$

with $\Im(\boldsymbol{\theta}_0)$ the usual Fisher's information matrix and $\boldsymbol{\theta}_0$ the usual true value.

The covariance matrix of $\hat{\boldsymbol{\theta}}_{\mathrm{MLE}}$ (Fisher's information matrix) may be estimated by the inverse of the negative Hessian matrix of the likelihood function.

5.2.1 Examples

Example 5.1 [*Multivariate Gaussian copula*]   Let R be a symmetric, positive definite matrix with $\mathrm{diag}(R) = (1, 1, \ldots, 1)'$, Φ_R the standardized multivariate normal distribution with correlation matrix R and let Φ denote the c.d.f. of a standard Gaussian or normal variable. The MGC, as defined in the previous chapter, is as follows:

$$C(u_1, u_2, \ldots, u_n; R) = \Phi_R(\Phi^{-1}(u_1), \Phi^{-1}(u_2), \ldots, \Phi^{-1}(u_n)) \qquad (5.6)$$

with density:

$$\frac{1}{(2\pi)^{\frac{n}{2}} |R|^{\frac{1}{2}}} \exp(-\tfrac{1}{2}\mathbf{x}' R^{-1} \mathbf{x}) = c(\Phi(x_1), \Phi(x_2), \ldots, \Phi(x_n)) \cdot \prod_{j=1}^{n} \left(\tfrac{1}{\sqrt{2\pi}} \exp(-\tfrac{1}{2}x_j^2) \right) \tag{5.7}$$

We deduce that:

$$c(\Phi(x_1), \Phi(x_2), \ldots, \Phi(x_n)) = \frac{\dfrac{1}{(2\pi)^{\frac{n}{2}} |R|^{\frac{1}{2}}} \exp(-\tfrac{1}{2}\mathbf{x}' R^{-1} \mathbf{x})}{\prod\limits_{j=1}^{n} \left(\tfrac{1}{\sqrt{2\pi}} \exp(-\tfrac{1}{2}x_j^2) \right)} \tag{5.8}$$

Let $u_j = \Phi(x_j)$, so $x_j = \Phi^{-1}(u_j)$ and we can rewrite as follows:

$$c(u_1, u_2, \ldots, u_n) = \frac{1}{|R|^{\frac{1}{2}}} \exp(-\tfrac{1}{2}\boldsymbol{\varsigma}'(R^{-1} - I)\boldsymbol{\varsigma}) \tag{5.9}$$

where $\boldsymbol{\varsigma} = \left(\Phi^{-1}(u_1), \Phi^{-1}(u_2), \ldots, \Phi^{-1}(u_n) \right)'$.

In this case, let $\aleph = \{x_{1t}, x_{2t}, \ldots, x_{nt}\}_{t=1}^{T}$ be the sample data matrix, and the expression for the log-likelihood function is:

$$l(\boldsymbol{\theta}) = -\frac{T}{2} \ln |R| - \frac{1}{2} \sum_{t=1}^{T} \boldsymbol{\varsigma}_t'(R^{-1} - I)\boldsymbol{\varsigma}_t \tag{5.10}$$

where $\boldsymbol{\theta}$ is the set of all parameters: R and $\boldsymbol{\varsigma}_t = \left(\Phi^{-1}(u_{1t}), \Phi^{-1}(u_{2t}), \ldots, \Phi^{-1}(u_{nt}) \right)'$.

The MLE of R is given by (refer to Magnus & Neudecker, 1980):

$$\hat{R}_{\mathrm{MLE}} = \frac{1}{T} \sum_{t=1}^{T} \boldsymbol{\varsigma}_t' \boldsymbol{\varsigma}_t \tag{5.11}$$

Example 5.2 [*Multivariate dispersion copula with Weibull margins*] As recalled in Chapter 4, let $\boldsymbol{\mu} = (\mu_1, \mu_2, \ldots, \mu_n)'$ be a position parameter, $\boldsymbol{\sigma}^2 = (\sigma_1^2, \sigma_2^2, \ldots, \sigma_n^2)'$ a dispersion parameter and R a correlation matrix.

We say that $\mathbf{X} \sim \text{MDC}(\boldsymbol{\mu}, \boldsymbol{\sigma}^2, R)$ if

$$f(y; \boldsymbol{\mu}, \boldsymbol{\sigma}^2, R) = \frac{1}{|R|^{\frac{1}{2}}} \exp(-\tfrac{1}{2}\boldsymbol{\varsigma}'(R^{-1} - I)\boldsymbol{\varsigma}) \prod_{j=1}^{n} f_j(y_j; \mu_j, \sigma_j^2) \qquad (5.12)$$

where

$$\varsigma_j = \Phi^{-1}(F_j(y_j; \mu_j, \sigma_j^2)) \quad \text{for } j = 1, 2, \ldots, n$$

and

$$f_j(y_j; \mu_j, \sigma_j^2) = \frac{\partial F_j(y_j; \mu_j, \sigma_j^2)}{\partial y_j} \quad \text{for every set of c.d.f. } F_j\left(y_j; \mu_j, \sigma_j^2\right)$$

Assuming Weibull margins, we saw in Chapter 4 that we obtain the MDC density:

$$f(x_1, x_2, \ldots, x_n) = \frac{1}{|R|^{\frac{1}{2}}} \exp(-\tfrac{1}{2}\boldsymbol{\varsigma}'(R^{-1} - I)\boldsymbol{\varsigma}) \prod_{j=1}^{n} \frac{\alpha_j x_j^{\alpha_j - 1}}{\beta_j} \exp\left(-\left(\frac{x_j^{\alpha_j}}{\beta_j}\right)\right) \qquad (5.13)$$

where $\varsigma_j = \Phi^{-1}\left(1 - \exp\left(-\frac{x_j^{\alpha_j}}{\beta_j}\right)\right)$.

In this case the log-likelihood function may be easily derived:

$$l(R, \boldsymbol{\alpha}, \boldsymbol{\beta}) = -\frac{T}{2}\ln|R| - \frac{1}{2}\sum_{t=1}^{T} \boldsymbol{\varsigma}_t'(R^{-1} - I)\boldsymbol{\varsigma}_t + \sum_{t=1}^{T}\sum_{j=1}^{n} \ln\left(\frac{\alpha_j x_{jt}^{\alpha_j - 1}}{\beta_j} \exp\left(-\frac{x_{jt}^{\alpha_j}}{\beta_j}\right)\right)$$

$$(5.14)$$

with $\varsigma_{jt} = \Phi^{-1}\left(1 - \exp\left(-\frac{x_{jt}^{\alpha_j}}{\beta_j}\right)\right)$.

This log-likelihood function has to be maximized with respect to all parameters (R, $\boldsymbol{\alpha}$, $\boldsymbol{\beta}$) by using a numerical optimization method.

5.3 IFM METHOD

The maximum likelihood method, previously shown, could be very computationally intensive, especially in the case of a high dimension, because it is necessary to estimate jointly the parameters of the marginal distributions and the parameters of the dependence structure represented by the copula. But, if the readers look more closely at the log-likelihood function, they will note that it is composed by two positive terms: one term involving the copula density and its parameters, and one term involving the margins and all parameters of the copula density. For that reason, Joe and Xu (1996) proposed that these set of parameters should be estimated in two steps:

1. As a first step, they estimate the margins' parameters θ_1 by performing the estimation of the univariate marginal distributions:

$$\hat{\theta}_1 = \text{ArgMax}_{\theta_1} \sum_{t=1}^{T} \sum_{j=1}^{n} \ln f_j(x_{jt}; \theta_1) \tag{5.15}$$

2. As a second step, given $\hat{\theta}_1$, they perform the estimation of the copula parameter θ_2:

$$\hat{\theta}_2 = \text{ArgMax}_{\theta_2} \sum_{t=1}^{T} \ln c(F_1(x_{1t}), F_2(x_{2t}), \ldots, F_n(x_{nt}); \theta_2, \hat{\theta}_1) \tag{5.16}$$

This method is called *inference for the margins* or IFM. The IFM estimator is defined as the vector:

$$\hat{\theta}_{\text{IFM}} = \left(\hat{\theta}_1, \hat{\theta}_2\right)' \tag{5.17}$$

We call l the entire log-likelihood function, l_j the log-likelihood of the jth marginal, and l_c the log-likelihood for the copula itself. Hence, the IFM estimator is the solution of:

$$\left(\frac{\partial l_1}{\partial \theta_{11}}, \frac{\partial l_2}{\partial \theta_{12}}, \ldots, \frac{\partial l_n}{\partial \theta_{1n}}, \frac{\partial l_c}{\partial \theta_2}\right) = \mathbf{0}' \tag{5.18}$$

while the MLE comes from solving

$$\left(\frac{\partial l}{\partial \theta_{11}}, \frac{\partial l}{\partial \theta_{12}}, \ldots, \frac{\partial l}{\partial \theta_{1n}}, \frac{\partial l}{\partial \theta_2}\right) = \mathbf{0}' \tag{5.19}$$

so, the equivalence of the two estimators, in general, does not hold.

The readers can note that for MGC with correlation matrix R and univariate $N(\mu_j, \sigma_j^2)$ margins, the two estimators coincide.

It is simple to see that the IFM estimator provides a good starting point for obtaining an exact MLE.

Since it is computationally easier to obtain the IFM estimator than the MLE, it is worth addressing a question about the IFM asymptotic efficiency compared with the MLE. Thus, one has to compare the asymptotic covariance matrix of the two estimators.

The IFM theory is a special case of using a set of appropriate inference equations to estimate a vector of parameters. In this case each equation is a score function (i.e. its left side is the partial derivative of the log-likelihood of each marginal density).

Joe (1997) proves that, like the MLE, the IFM estimator verifies, under regular conditions, the property of asymptotic normality, and we have:

$$\sqrt{T}\left(\hat{\theta}_{\text{IFM}} - \theta_0\right) \to N\left(0, \mathcal{G}^{-1}(\theta_0)\right) \tag{5.20}$$

with $\mathcal{G}(\theta_0)$ the Godambe information matrix.

Thus, if we define a score function

$$s(\boldsymbol{\theta}) = \left(\frac{\partial l_1}{\partial \theta_{11}}, \frac{\partial l_2}{\partial \theta_{12}}, \ldots, \frac{\partial l_n}{\partial \theta_{1n}}, \frac{\partial l_c}{\partial \theta_2} \right)'$$

splitting the log-likelihood in two parts $l_1, l_2, \ldots, l_n$ for each margin and l_c for the copula, the Godambe information matrix takes the following form:

$$\mathsf{G}(\boldsymbol{\theta}_0) = D^{-1} V (D^{-1})' \tag{5.21}$$

with

$$D = E \left[\frac{\partial s(\boldsymbol{\theta})}{\partial \boldsymbol{\theta}} \right] \quad \text{and} \quad V = E \left[s(\boldsymbol{\theta}) s(\boldsymbol{\theta})' \right]$$

The estimation of this covariance matrix requires us to compute many derivatives. Joe (1997) then suggests the use of the jacknife method or other bootstrap methods to estimate it. In a time series context, it may be useful to adopt a block-bootstrap, especially when the time series in hand show a low autocorrelation (see Efron & Tibshirani, 1993 and Shao & Tu, 1995, for a deeper and more formal explanation of these concepts).

Joe (1997) points out that the IFM method is highly efficient compared with the ML method. It is worth noting that the IFM method may be viewed as a special case of the generalized method of moments (GMM) with an identity weight matrix (Davidson & Mac-Kinnon, 1993).

5.3.1 Application: estimation of the parametric copula for market data

In this section we present an empirical application[1] of parametric copula modeling to the following five assets: DAX 30 index, S&P 500 index, 10-year total return index for the US bond market, 10-year total return index for the German bond market, and the DEM/USD exchange rate.

We use weekly (average) data from January 1992 to June 2001; in total we have a sample of 248 observations. Table 5.1 reports some descriptive statistics for each weekly return series. JB is the Jarque–Bera Gaussianity test statistic.

Table 5.1

	Dax30	S&P500	Ger10y	USA10y	DEM/$
Mean	0.53	0.43	0.30	0.27	0.16
Std	3.56	2.68	0.90	1.04	2.04
Skew	−0.40	−0.45	−0.55	−0.18	0.13
Kurtosis	3.22	4.00	3.44	2.75	3.38
JB Statistics	0.0288	0.0000	0.0007	0.3879	0.3204

[1] This example is borrowed from Cazzulani, Meneguzzo and Vecchiato (2001). The data have already been used in the previous chapters in order to compute some concordance measures. In the following, this example will be extended for further comments and more detailed discussions.

Results for the mean and standard deviations are reported in the table in percentage points. The Jarque–Bera test is the best-known normality test. Our strategy will be to model the joint dependence using a Frank copula because it is a simple Archimedean copula and, in the bivariate case, allows for both positive and negative dependence. As for the marginal behavior, we can consider the use of a Student t in order to capture a high kurtosis. Unfortunately the Student t is a symmetric distribution and it would fail to capture the negative skewness. At first sight, it may seem more appropriate then to use a non-central Student t, so that we can allow for a negative skewness. We present its p.d.f. below:

$$f(x) = \frac{(v)^{v/2} \exp\left[-\delta^2/2\right]}{\Gamma(v/2)\pi^{1/2}(v+x^2)^{(v+1)/2}} \cdot \sum_{i=0}^{\infty} \Gamma\left(\frac{v+i+1}{2}\right) \left(\frac{x\delta}{i!}\right)^i \left(\frac{2}{v+x^2}\right)^{i/2} \tag{5.22}$$

where Γ is the Euler function.

We, indeed, choose to adopt a non-central t density for a more general setting due to asymmetry and kurtosis sample characteristics.

Here δ is the non-centrality parameter, which can range between $-\infty$ and $+\infty$; and v is the usual parameter for the degrees of freedom. It is worth noting that a Student t distribution converges to the standard normal distribution when the degrees of freedom tend to infinity. We standardize our returns so that they have zero mean and unit standard deviation. We then fit a normal distribution, a Student's t and a non-central t distribution to these normalized data.

Table 5.2 gives the parameter estimates for the margins via MLE, first considering a non-central t and then considering a (central) standard t. All estimates, except δ, are statistically significant.

As can be seen in the table, the difference in the estimated degrees of freedom is small due to almost zero estimates for the non-centrality parameter. All degrees of freedom imply a marginal behavior close to normal.

We now turn our attention to the copula modeling, and, following the IFM estimation technique, we have estimated the relevant parameters for the marginal distributions (refer to Table 5.2), and we now estimate the Frank copula via maximum likelihood.

The optimization problem is as follows:

$$\max_{\alpha} L(\alpha) = \sum_{t=1}^{T} 2\log\left[1 - e^{-\alpha} - (1 - e^{-\alpha F(x_{1t}, v_1, \delta_1)})(1 - e^{-\alpha F(x_{2t}, v_2, \delta_2)})\right]$$

$$- \log(\alpha(1 - e^{-\alpha})) - \alpha\left[F(x_{1t}, v_1, \delta_1) + F(x_{2t}, v_2, \delta_2)\right] \tag{5.23}$$

Table 5.2 Marginal estimation – standardized returns

	DAX	S&P 500	GER10y	USA10y	DEM/USD
		NC Student t			
v	78.10	20.10	44.79	300.00	41.01
δ	0.00	0.01	0.00	0.00	−0.01
		Student t			
v	78.79	20.23	45.40	300.00	41.06

Table 5.3 Estimated α for the Frank copula with NC-t marginals

	DAX 30	S&P 500	GER10y	USA10y	DEM/USD
DAX 30	–				
S&P 500	5.12	–			
GER10y	1.17	1.03	–		
USA10y	0.23	1.32	3.72	–	
DEM/USD	2.05	1.28	0.44	−1.10	–

where x_{1t} and x_{2t} are the returns on the first and second asset considered, α is the copula parameter, F is the non-central t c.d.f., υ_1, υ_2, δ_1, δ_2 are respectively the degrees of freedom and non-centrality parameters for the two marginal distributions.

We report, in Table 5.3, the MLE estimates for the α parameter for the Frank copula. We draw the readers' attention to the substantial stability of these estimates between central and non-central Student t distributions. All estimates are statistically significant.

5.4   CML METHOD

We wish to remark that the copula parameters may be estimated without specifying the marginals. In fact, another estimation method consists in transforming the sample data $\{x_{1t}, x_{2t}, \ldots, x_{nt}\}_{t=1}^{T}$ into uniform variates $\{u_{1t}, u_{2t}, \ldots, u_{nt}\}_{t=1}^{T}$ and then estimating the copula parameters. This method may be described as follows:

1. First estimate the marginals using the empirical distributions (without assumptions on the parametric form for each of them), i.e. $\hat{F}_i(x_{it})$ with $i = 1, \ldots, n$.
2. Estimate via MLE the copula parameters

$$\hat{\boldsymbol{\theta}}_2 = \text{ArgMax}_{\boldsymbol{\theta}_2} \sum_{t=1}^{T} \ln c(\hat{F}_1(x_{1t}), \hat{F}_2(x_{2t}), \ldots, \hat{F}_n(x_{nt}); \boldsymbol{\theta}_2) \qquad (5.24)$$

This method is called the *Canonical Maximum Likelihood* or CML. In this case, the CML estimator could be viewed as an MLE, given the observed margins.

5.4.1   Application: estimation of the correlation matrix for a Gaussian copula

Using the dataset of the previous example, we wish to estimate the correlation matrix parameter of the Gaussian copula (MGC) with the CML method. We proceed as follows.

1. Transform the original data into Gaussian data:
   (i) estimate the empirical distribution functions (uniform transformation) using order statistics;
   (ii) generate Gaussian values by applying the inverse of the normal distribution to the empirical distribution functions.
2. Compute the correlation matrix of the transformed data.

The estimated correlation matrix is shown in Table 5.4.

Table 5.4 Estimated correlation matrix via CML method for MGC

	DAX 30	DEM/USD	GER10y	S&P 500	USA10y
DAX 30	1				
DEM/USD	0.3035	1			
GER10y	0.1998	0.0551	1		
S&P 500	0.6494	0.1501	0.1941	1	
USA10y	0.0019	−0.2144	0.4850	0.1585	1

5.5 NON-PARAMETRIC ESTIMATION

In this section we no longer assume a particular parametric copula. Our interest is in modeling the dependence structure with consistency to find, for example, an appropriate non-parametric method to estimate the copula form that is going to converge (in a certain formal probabilistic sense) to the underlying dependence structure.

5.5.1 The empirical copula

Here we present the notion of the empirical copula introduced by Deheuvels (1979, 1981).

Let $X_t = (X_{1t}, X_{2t}, \ldots, X_{nt}) \in \Re^n$ be an i.i.d. sequence with (continuous) c.d.f. F and (continuous) margins F_j. Let $\{x_1^{(t)}, x_2^{(t)}, \ldots, x_n^{(t)}\}$ be the order statistic and let $\{r_1^{(t)}, r_2^{(t)}, \ldots, r_n^{(t)}\}$ be the rank statistic of the sample, which are linked by the relationship $x_n^{(r_n^t)} = x_{nt}$, $t = 1, 2, \ldots, T$.

Definition 5.1 [*Deheuvels' empirical copula*] The empirical copula defined on the lattice

$$\ell = \left\{ \left(\frac{t_1}{T}, \frac{t_2}{T}, \ldots, \frac{t_n}{T} \right) : 1 \leqslant j \leqslant n, t_j = 0, 1, \ldots, T \right\} \tag{5.25}$$

is the following function:

$$\hat{C}\left(\frac{t_1}{T}, \frac{t_2}{T}, \ldots, \frac{t_n}{T} \right) = \frac{1}{T} \sum_{t=1}^{T} \prod_{j=1}^{n} \mathbf{1}\left(r_j^t \leqslant t_j \right) \tag{5.26}$$

where $\mathbf{1}$ is the indicator function that takes value equal to 1 when its argument condition is satisfied.

Deheuvels (1978, 1981) proves that the empirical copula converges uniformly to the underlying copula.

The analog of the Radon–Nikodym density for the empirical copula is the following *empirical copula frequency*, as defined by Nelsen (1999):

$$\hat{c}\left(\frac{t_1}{T}, \frac{t_2}{T}, \ldots, \frac{t_n}{T} \right) = \sum_{i_1=1}^{2} \sum_{i_2=1}^{2} \cdots \sum_{i_n=1}^{2} (-1)^{\sum_{j=1}^{n} i_j}$$

$$\times \hat{C}\left(\frac{t_1 - i_1 + 1}{T}, \frac{t_2 - i_2 + 1}{T}, \ldots, \frac{t_n - i_n + 1}{T} \right) \tag{5.27}$$

Nelsen (1999) notes that the concept of empirical copula permits us to define the sample version of many dependence measures and, also, the sample version of other concepts expressed in terms of copulas. Besides that, empirical copulas may also be used to construct non-parametric tests for independence (Deheuvels, 1981).

Polynomial approximation for copula

It is possible to use certain polynomial approximations that lead to a stronger convergence than uniform convergence in order to estimate the underlying dependence structure. For example, by using the Bernstein polynomial

$$B_{i,n}(x) = \binom{n}{i} x^i (1-x)^{n-i} \tag{5.28}$$

we can define a *Bernstein copula* as follows:

$$B_T(C)(u_1, u_2, \ldots, u_n) = \sum_{t_1=1}^{n} \sum_{t_2=1}^{n} \cdots \sum_{t_n=1}^{n} B_{t_1,T}(u_1) \cdot B_{t_2,T}(u_2) \cdots B_{t_n,T}(u_n)$$

$$\times \hat{C}\left(\frac{t_1}{T}, \frac{t_2}{T}, \ldots, \frac{t_n}{T}\right) \tag{5.29}$$

The Bernstein copula uniformly converges to the underlying copula (refer to Li et al., 1997).

5.5.2 Kernel copula

In statistics a lot of non-parametric estimation methods are based on a kernel structure (see Hardle, 1990, for a further explanation). *Kernel* means a functional form, usually chosen for its smooth properties, that is used as the building block to get the desired estimator.

Scaillet (2000) proposes a kernel-based approach to apply to a copula setup, that has the advantage of providing a smooth differentiable estimate of the copula function without assuming any particular parametric *a priori* on the dependence structure between marginals. The approach is developed in the context of multivariate stationary processes satisfying strong mixing conditions (see Serfling, 1980 and Shao, 1999). Once estimates of copulas (and their derivatives) are available, other concepts expressed in terms of copulas may be empirically analyzed. The most important point is the need for differentiability that dictates the choice of a kernel approach.

Non-parametric estimators of copulas may also lead to testing procedures for independence between margins in the same spirit as kernel-based methods to test for serial dependence for a univariate stationary time series (see Tjostheim, 1996).

Estimating a copula is indeed estimating values taken by a c.d.f. at m distinct points in $\Re^n$ by the formula:

$$C(u_1, u_2, \ldots, u_n) = F(F_1^{-1}(u_1), F_2^{-1}(u_2), \ldots, F_n^{-1}(u_n)) \tag{5.30}$$

where $F_1^{-1}, F_2^{-1}, \ldots, F_n^{-1}$ are quasi-inverses of $F_1, F_2, \ldots, F_n$.

For given $u_{ij} \in (0, 1)$, $i = 1, 2, \ldots, m$; $j = 1, 2, \ldots, n$, we assume that the c.d.f. F_j of Y_{jt} is such that equation $F_j(y) = u_{ij}$ admits a unique solution denoted by ξ_{ij}. As commonly known, kernels are real bounded and symmetric functions $k_{ij}(x)$ on $\Re$ such that

$$\int_{\Re} k_{ij}(x)\,dx = 1, \qquad i = 1, 2, \ldots, m; \quad j = 1, 2, \ldots, n \tag{5.31}$$

and

$$K_i(x; h) = \prod_{j=1}^{n} k_{ij}\left(\frac{x_j}{h_j}\right), \qquad i = 1, 2, \ldots, m \tag{5.32}$$

where the bandwidth h is a diagonal matrix with elements $\{h_j\}_{j=1,2,\ldots,n}$ and determinant $|h|$, while the individual bandwidth h_j are positive functions of T such that

$$|h| + \frac{1}{T|h|} \to 0 \text{ as } T \to \infty \tag{5.33}$$

The p.d.f. of Y_{jt} at y_{ij}, i.e. $f_j(y_{ij})$, will be estimated by

$$\hat{f}_j(y_{ij}) = \frac{1}{Th_j} \sum_{t=1}^{T} k_{ij}\left(\frac{y_{ij} - Y_{jt}}{h_j}\right) \tag{5.34}$$

while the joint p.d.f. of Y_t at $y_i = (y_{i1}, y_{i2}, \ldots, y_{in})'$ will be estimated by

$$\hat{f}(y_i) = \frac{1}{T|h|} \sum_{t=1}^{T} K_i(y_i - Y_t; h) = \frac{1}{T|h|} \sum_{t=1}^{T} \prod_{j=1}^{n} k_{ij}\left(\frac{y_{ij} - Y_{jt}}{h_j}\right) \tag{5.35}$$

Hence, the estimator of the c.d.f. of Y_{jt} at distinct points y_{ij} is obtained as

$$\hat{F}_j(y_{ij}) = \int_{-\infty}^{y_{ij}} \hat{f}_j(x)\,dx \tag{5.36}$$

while estimators of the c.d.f. of Y_t at $y_i = (y_{i1}, y_{i2}, \ldots, y_{in})'$ will be obtained as

$$\hat{F}(y_i) = \int_{-\infty}^{y_{i1}} \int_{-\infty}^{y_{i2}} \cdots \int_{-\infty}^{y_{in}} \hat{f}(x)\,dx \tag{5.37}$$

If a single Gaussian kernel $k_{ij}(x) = \varphi(x) = \frac{1}{\sqrt{2\pi}} \exp\left(-\frac{x^2}{2}\right)$ is adopted, we get

$$\hat{F}_j(y_{ij}) = \frac{1}{Th_j} \sum_{t=1}^{T} \Phi\left(\frac{y_{ij} - Y_{jt}}{h_j}\right) \tag{5.38}$$

and

$$\hat{F}(y_j) = \frac{1}{T|h|} \sum_{t=1}^{T} \prod_{j=1}^{n} \Phi\left(\frac{y_{ij} - Y_{jt}}{h_j}\right) \tag{5.39}$$

where φ and Φ denote, respectively, the p.d.f. and c.d.f. of a standard Gaussian variable.

In order to estimate the copula at distinct points $u_i, i = 1, 2, \ldots, m$ with $u_{ij} < u_{lj}$ for $i < l$, we use a "plug-in" method as follows:

$$\hat{C}(u_i) = \hat{F}\left(\hat{\xi}_i\right) \tag{5.40}$$

where

$$\hat{\xi}_i = \left(\hat{\xi}_{i1}, \hat{\xi}_{i2}, \hat{\xi}_{i3}, \ldots, \hat{\xi}_{in}\right)' \quad \text{and} \quad \hat{\xi}_{ij} = \inf_{y \in \Re}\left\{y : \hat{F}_j(y) \geqslant u_{ij}\right\}$$

The estimate $\hat{\xi}_{ij}$ corresponds to a kernel estimate of the quantile of Y_{jt} with probability level u_{ij}.

Scaillet (2000), following Robinson (1983), derives the asymptotic distribution (asymptotic normality), under regularity conditions, for these kernel estimators, and also derives the asymptotic distribution of kernel estimators of some bivariate dependence measures.

Indeed, Kendall's τ, Spearman's ρ, Gini's γ, Blomqvist's β have been written in copula terms in Chapter 3. Also Schweitzer–Wolff's σ and Hoeffding's ϕ may be expressed in terms of copula as follows:

$$\sigma = 12 \iint_{I^2} |C(u_1, u_2) - u_1 u_2| \, du_1 \, du_2 \tag{5.41}$$

$$\phi = 3\sqrt{10 \iint_{I^2} (C(u_1, u_2) - u_1 u_2)^2 \, du_1 \, du_2} \tag{5.42}$$

Other dependence concepts may also be expressed in terms of copula: as we saw in Chapter 3, positive quadrant dependency, the left tail decreasing property and upper tail dependency.

Once a copula is empirically estimated, it is easy to compute the kernel counterpart of all of these dependence measures, and all other properties may be checked at least locally.

Scaillet (2000) proves, under regular conditions (Robinson, 1983), that kernel estimators of Spearman's rho, Gini's gamma and Blomqvist's beta are asymptotically independent standard normal random variables.

Finally, we note that this non-parametric method may be combined with other parametric methods for estimating a copula and margins (commonly known as *mixed estimators*).

Application to equity market data

We are going to use this approach to estimate the copula using the previous sample dataset. Our finding is that this approach provides a better fit to the data and is also more flexible.

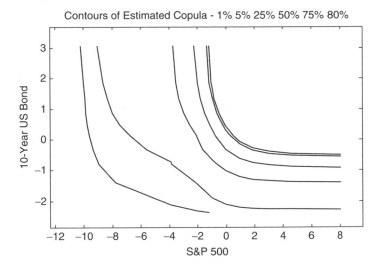

Figure 5.1 Contours for the non-parametric copula (contours of S&P 500–US bond 10y)

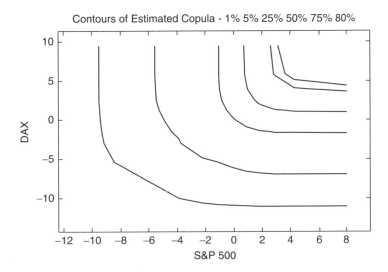

Figure 5.2 Contours for the non-parametric copula (contours of S&P 500–DAX)

The kernel approach requires a long series of data but it permits a more efficient estimate of the copula structure implied by the sample observations.

Figures 5.1 and 5.2 show the level curves from a copula estimated non-parametrically. It can be seen that while the estimated dependence between the two equity indexes is fairly regular, the dependence between total return on bonds and stock index is more irregular. An interesting point to be noted is that the normal distribution approximates well the middle of the distribution but performs very poorly on the tails; this point may be seen by looking at the lower contour and its irregular form.

Table 5.5 Spearman's rho calculated using non-parametric copula

	DAX 30	S&P 500	GER10y	USA10y	DEM/USD
DAX 30	–				
S&P 500	0.54	–			
GER10y	0.14	0.11	–		
USA10y	0.02	0.16	0.43	–	
DEM/USD	0.26	0.17	0.01	−0.15	–

In Table 5.5 we compute Spearman's rho implied by the non-parametric estimated copula. Readers will note that there are very small differences between the implied measures and their sample counterparts.[2]

In the following we report the graphs for the estimation of the PQD measures, the implied c.d.f.s for maximum and minimum, and also some other results such as the left tail decreasing property described in Chapter 3 (Figures 5.3–5.6). We also present the trace of a copula, defined as a function $C(u, u) = h(u)$ of a single variable $u \in [0, 1]$.

We note that, at first sight, the form of each copula may seem similar, but the readers should observe that each copula extends to different interval values for each axis. So, a given region in the plane has different probability induced by each estimated kernel copula, though their form is similar.

The same argument applies to all other diagrams.

We also report a trace of the non-parametric estimate for a copula for a trivariate case (S&P 500, 10-year US bond and 10-year German bond) whose values are reported in Figure 5.7.

Application to value at risk for an asset portfolio

Given these preliminary results we move on to estimate the *value at risk*, given a confidence level θ, for a portfolio of n assets. For instance, we consider a portfolio of two assets. Let x_1 and x_2 be their respective returns, and $\beta \in (0, 1)$ the allocation weight, so the portfolio return is given by $z_t = \beta x_{1t} + (1 - \beta) x_{2t}$ where, omitting the subscript t,

$$F(x_1, x_2) = \Pr(X_1 \leqslant x_1, X_2 \leqslant x_2)$$

$$= \Pr(F_1(X_1) \leqslant F_1(x_1), F_2(X_2) \leqslant F_2(x_2)) = C(F_1(x_1), F_2(x_2))$$

and by derivation, we express in term of p.d.f.s:

$$f(x_1, x_2) = c(F_1(x_1), F_2(x_2)) \cdot \prod_{j=1}^{2} f_j(x_j)$$

where c is the copula-density and f is the standard univariate probability density function.

---

[2] We discuss the sample dependence measure in the next section by introducing another useful estimation method.

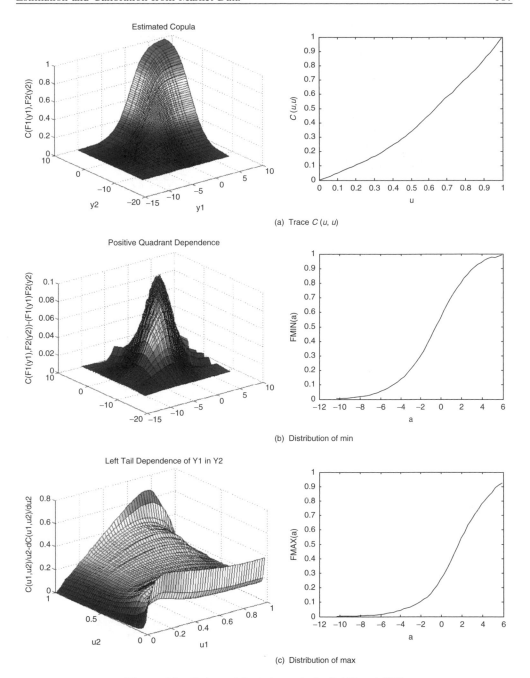

Figure 5.3 Estimated kernel copula for DAX and SPX

Measure of association implied by the copula

Spearman's Rho	Blomqvist's Beta	Gini's Gamma
0.5396	0.3737	0.4324

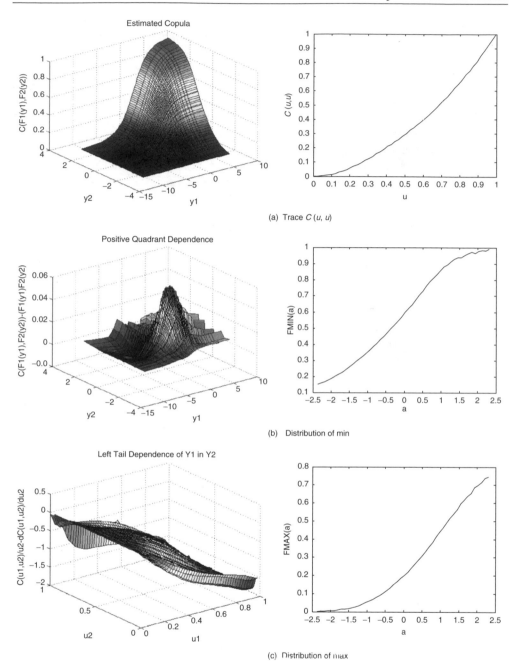

Figure 5.4   Estimated kernel copula for SPX and 10-year US bonds

Measure of association implied by the copula

Spearman's Rho	Blomqvist's Beta	Gini's Gamma
0.1595	0.1711	0.1517

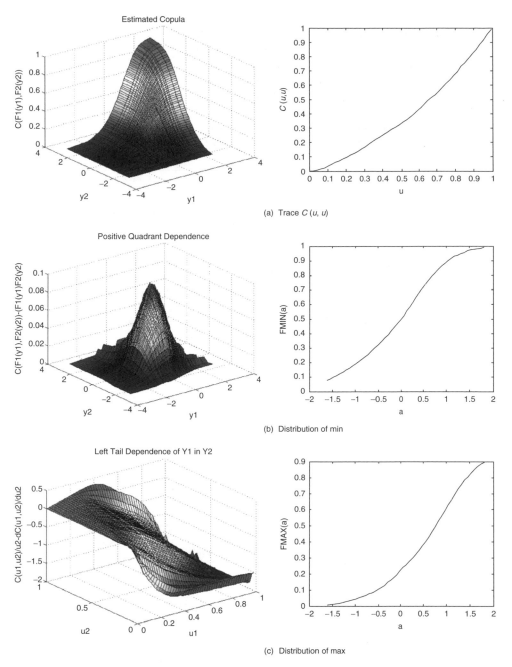

(a) Trace $C(u, u)$

(b) Distribution of min

(c) Distribution of max

Figure 5.5 Estimated kernel copula for 10-year German bonds and 10-year US bonds

Measure of association implied by the copula		
Spearman's Rho	Blomqvist's Beta	Gini's Gamma
0.4304	0.3402	0.3692

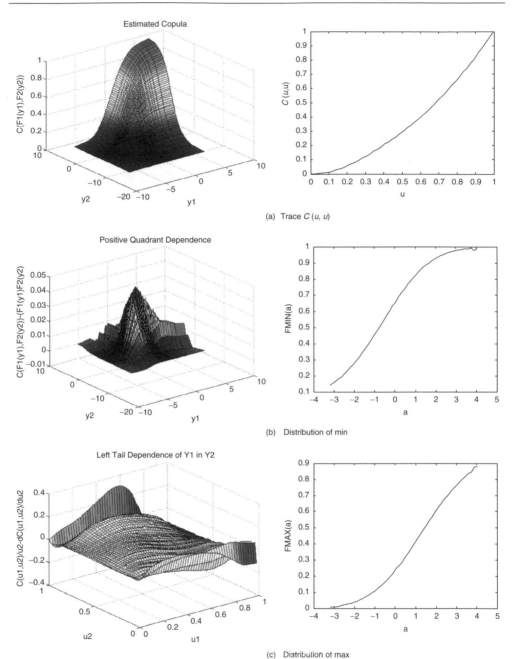

(a) Trace $C(u, u)$

(b) Distribution of min

(c) Distribution of max

Figure 5.6 Estimated kernel copula for DEM/USD and SPX

Measure of association implied by the copula

Spearman's Rho	Blomqvist's Beta	Gini's Gamma
0.1692	0.1470	0.1606

spx10	usbond10	ger10		spx10	usbond10	ger10	
u1	u2	u3	C(u1,u2,u3)	u1	u2	u3	C(u1,u2,u3)
0.01	0.01	0.01	0.0000	0.51	0.51	0.51	0.1619
0.02	0.02	0.02	0.0000	0.52	0.52	0.52	0.1715
0.03	0.03	0.03	0.0000	0.53	0.53	0.53	0.1834
0.04	0.04	0.04	0.0001	0.54	0.54	0.54	0.1895
0.05	0.05	0.05	0.0002	0.55	0.55	0.55	0.1984
0.06	0.06	0.06	0.0004	0.56	0.56	0.56	0.2067
0.07	0.07	0.07	0.0006	0.57	0.57	0.57	0.2181
0.08	0.08	0.08	0.0009	0.58	0.58	0.58	0.2284
0.09	0.09	0.09	0.0016	0.59	0.59	0.59	0.2358
0.10	0.10	0.10	0.0019	0.60	0.60	0.60	0.2477
0.11	0.11	0.11	0.0022	0.61	0.61	0.61	0.2578
0.12	0.12	0.12	0.0028	0.62	0.62	0.62	0.2681
0.13	0.13	0.13	0.0039	0.63	0.63	0.63	0.2785
0.14	0.14	0.14	0.0044	0.64	0.64	0.64	0.2933
0.15	0.15	0.15	0.0056	0.65	0.65	0.65	0.3039
0.16	0.16	0.16	0.0067	0.66	0.66	0.66	0.3186
0.17	0.17	0.17	0.0084	0.67	0.67	0.67	0.3287
0.18	0.18	0.18	0.0099	0.68	0.68	0.68	0.3469
0.19	0.19	0.19	0.0112	0.69	0.69	0.69	0.3553
0.20	0.20	0.20	0.0142	0.70	0.70	0.70	0.3699
0.21	0.21	0.21	0.0146	0.71	0.71	0.71	0.3884
0.22	0.22	0.22	0.0178	0.72	0.72	0.72	0.3970
0.23	0.23	0.23	0.0189	0.73	0.73	0.73	0.4098
0.24	0.24	0.24	0.0218	0.74	0.74	0.74	0.4283
0.25	0.25	0.25	0.0239	0.75	0.75	0.75	0.4486
0.26	0.26	0.26	0.0267	0.76	0.76	0.76	0.4575
0.27	0.27	0.27	0.0299	0.77	0.77	0.77	0.4818
0.28	0.28	0.28	0.0339	0.78	0.78	0.78	0.4979
0.29	0.29	0.29	0.0368	0.79	0.79	0.79	0.5134
0.30	0.30	0.30	0.0406	0.80	0.80	0.80	0.5284
0.31	0.31	0.31	0.0440	0.81	0.81	0.81	0.5523
0.32	0.32	0.32	0.0473	0.82	0.82	0.82	0.5774
0.33	0.33	0.33	0.0516	0.83	0.83	0.83	0.5908
0.34	0.34	0.34	0.0568	0.84	0.84	0.84	0.6032
0.35	0.35	0.35	0.0614	0.85	0.85	0.85	0.6228
0.36	0.36	0.36	0.0657	0.86	0.86	0.86	0.6569
0.37	0.37	0.37	0.0728	0.87	0.87	0.87	0.6740
0.38	0.38	0.38	0.0766	0.88	0.88	0.88	0.6938
0.39	0.39	0.39	0.0797	0.89	0.89	0.89	0.7167
0.40	0.40	0.40	0.0878	0.90	0.90	0.90	0.7425
0.41	0.41	0.41	0.0921	0.91	0.91	0.91	0.7680
0.42	0.42	0.42	0.1002	0.92	0.92	0.92	0.7919
0.43	0.43	0.43	0.1036	0.93	0.93	0.93	0.8180
0.44	0.44	0.44	0.1125	0.94	0.94	0.94	0.8505
0.45	0.45	0.45	0.1190	0.95	0.95	0.95	0.8669
0.46	0.46	0.46	0.1236	0.96	0.96	0.96	0.9064
0.47	0.47	0.47	0.1309	0.97	0.97	0.97	0.9226
0.48	0.48	0.48	0.1456	0.98	0.98	0.98	0.9462
0.49	0.49	0.49	0.1464	0.99	0.99	0.99	0.9872
0.50	0.50	0.50	0.1538				

Figure 5.7 Trace of the non-parametric copula for a trivariate case

Hence, the c.d.f. for the portfolio return Z is given by:

$$\mathfrak{H}(z) = \Pr\left(Z \leqslant z\right) = \Pr(\beta X_1 + (1 - \beta) X_2 \leqslant z)$$

$$\int_{-\infty}^{+\infty} \left\{ \int_{-\infty}^{\frac{1}{\beta}z - \frac{1-\beta}{\beta}x_2} c(F_1(x_1), F_2(x_2)) f_1(x_1)\, \mathrm{d}x_1 \right\} f_2(x_2)\, \mathrm{d}x_2$$

which is equivalent to the expression in section 2.5 of Chapter 2.

As recalled there, the VaR for the portfolio, at a confidence level $\theta \in (0, 1)$ and for a given weight $\beta \in (0, 1)$, is the solution z^* of the equation $\mathfrak{H}(z^*) = \theta$. This result may be extended straight to an n-variate case with the constraint that the n weights sum to 1.

We calculate the VaR both using the standard assumption that returns are distributed jointly as a normal and returns are jointly distributed as implied by our non-parametrically estimated copula.

We first estimate the copula using 250 days and with the same sample we estimate the VarCov matrix needed to calculate the normal VaR. From the copula we calculate the VaR. We then repeat the operation rolling the sample.

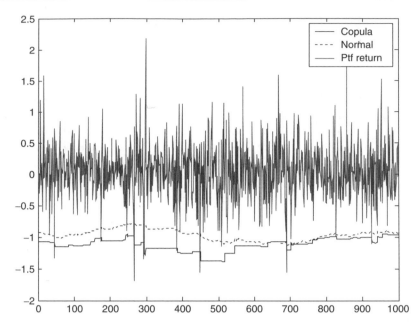

Figure 5.8 VaR with copulas (VaR at 99% for portfolio composed of 30% S&P 500, 70% US bond 10y)

We decided to use daily data because, to give to this exercise reasonable reliability, we need to perform the calculations on many samples. Using daily data we have a total of 1000 subsamples from August 18, 1997 to June 15, 2001.

Some graphical results are displayed in Figures 5.8, 5.9 and 5.10. It can be seen from these diagrams that the VaR calculated from the copula is able to capture the tail fatness and other non-normality features found in the data and, as expected, is overperformed with respect to the standard normal VaR.

The results we found point in the direction that, as we add in the portfolio more of the leptokurtotic asset and as we require a greater confidence level, the VaR based on the copula function performs better than the one calculated under normality.

5.6 CALIBRATION METHOD BY USING SAMPLE DEPENDENCE MEASURES

We introduce an idea pointed out by Genest and MacKay (1986) to calibrate an Archimedean copula, i.e. how to estimate the parameter α once a particular Archimedean copula has been chosen. This method is very simple compared with the previous ones, but it is limited to a bivariate setting because it makes inference on the dependence structure of the multivariate model from a chosen dependence coefficient.

First, sum up all sample information in the consistent estimator of Kendall's τ obtained from the two series S_{1t} and S_{2t} with $t = 1, \dots, T$ as follows:

$$\hat{\tau} = \frac{2}{T(T-1)} \sum_{i<j} \text{sgn} \left[\left(S_{1i} - S_{1j} \right) \left(S_{2i} - S_{2j} \right) \right] \tag{5.43}$$

where the sign function is defined as in the list of symbols.

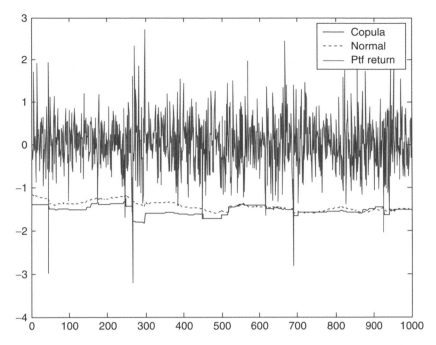

Figure 5.9 VaR with copulas (VaR at 99% for portfolio composed of 50% S&P 500, 50% US bond 10y)

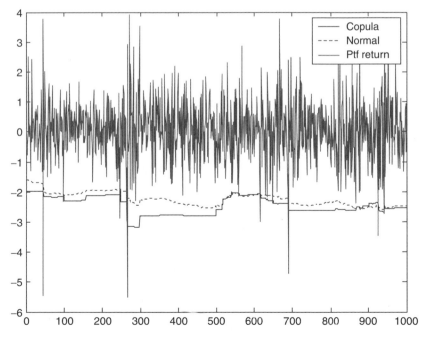

Figure 5.10 VaR with copulas (VaR at 99% for portfolio composed of 80% S&P 500, 20% US bond 10y)

Since we are considering a one-parameter family of Archimedean copulas, we use the relationship between α and τ in order to infer an estimate for the copula parameter α. We also can check for different Archimedean copulas how each of them fits the data by comparison with the empirical copula. This fitting test is performed through an (unobserved) auxiliary variable, $W = F(S_1, S_2)$, where F is the (unknown) joint distribution function of the two variables S_1 and S_2. We use the following algorithm based on Genest and Rivest (1993) (also described by Frees & Valdez, 1998):

- Denote by $K(w)$ the distribution of W, $K(w) : [0, 1] \to [0, 1]$ and that for Archimedean copulas whose generator is indicated by ψ_α

$$K(w) = w - \frac{1}{(\partial \ln \psi_\alpha(w))/\partial w} \tag{5.44}$$

hence, for each one-parameter Archimedean copula, construct an estimate of K substituting the estimate, previously obtained, for α.
- Define

$$Z_i = \frac{\text{Card}\left\{(S_{1j}, S_{2j}) : S_{1j} < S_{1i}, S_{2j} < S_{2i}\right\}}{T - 1} \tag{5.45}$$

and construct an empirical version of $K(w)$ as:

$$K_T(w) = \frac{\sum_{i=1}^T \mathbf{1}(w - Z_i)}{T} \tag{5.46}$$

where $\mathbf{1}$ is the commonly known indicator function.
- Finally, compare K_T and $K_{\hat{\alpha}}(w)$ graphically and via mean-square error.[3]

This method is simple to use and very easy to perform. Its main disadvantage is that it sums up all data information in the empirical, though consistent, estimator of the chosen association measure. Obviously, besides neglecting all other potential sources of statistical information that come from the data, it is strongly dependent on the particular associative measure chosen.

This method may be considered an estimation criteria based on sample dependence measures.

5.7 APPLICATION

Now we want to compare the empirical estimates of some dependence measures for the five series considered in our dataset. The readers should refer to Gibbons (1992) Chap. 12 for a formal definition and a more extensive explanation of measures of association for bivariate samples (sample estimates, large sample distribution, important relation between these measures, etc.); and to Chap. 13 for an extension in multiple classification.

---

[3] This method has been extended to the n-variate case for Archimedean copulas by Barbe et al. (1996), Frees and Valdez (1998) as reported by Durrleman, Nikeghbali and Roncalli (2000a).

Table 5.6 Sample Spearman's rho

	DAX 30	S&P 500	GER10y	USA10y	DEM/USD
DAX 30	–				
S&P 500	0.67	–			
GER10y	0.20	0.18	–		
USA10y	0.04	0.13	0.49	–	
DEM/USD	0.31	0.19	0.06	−0.22	–

Table 5.7 Spearman's rho calculated from Frank copula with NC Student t margins

	DAX 30	S&P 500	GER10y	USA10y	DEM/USD
DAX 30	–				
S&P 500	0.60	–			
GER10y	0.09	0.07	–		
USA10y	−0.08	0.12	0.46	–	
DEM/USD	0.24	0.11	−0.04	−0.08	–

Using the same data as in the previous examples (sections 3.1 and 5.2.1), we compute the sample Spearman's rho, and obtain the values given in Table 5.6. We also report in Table 5.7 the same index based on the estimated α from the Frank copula function. More precisely the relation that we use is

$$\rho_S = \left[\frac{12}{\alpha} D_2(-\alpha) - D_1(-\alpha) \right] - 1 \tag{5.47}$$

where D denotes the Debye function.[4] Rho depends, via a one-to-one relationship, on the Frank copula parameter α that we estimated via maximum likelihood. The copula is fitted for each pair of assets and the rho coefficient is then calculated. Most of the time this measure is quite close to the sample counterparty, but there are two notable exceptions: the correlation between the DAX index and the 10-year US bond is estimated to be negative when the copula is used, while the sample counterparty is (slightly) positive. The same can be said of the correlation between the 10-year German bond and the exchange rate.

Like above, we report in Table 5.8 some results obtained for Kendall's tau. Also, Kendall's tau (Table 5.9) is linked to α from the Frank copula, as recalled in Chapter 3:

$$\tau = \frac{4}{\alpha} \{ 1 - D_1(-\alpha) \} - 1 \tag{5.48}$$

In this case the estimated τ coefficient is closer to its sample counterparty than previously happened for Spearman's rho.

For the sake of completeness we also report the Pearson's correlation matrix in Table 5.10. The readers may note that this "correlation matrix" is very close to that estimated via the CML method, assuming a Gaussian copula.

---

[4] The Debye functions are defined in Chapter 3.

Table 5.8   Sample Kendall's tau

	DAX 30	S&P 500	GER10y	USA10y	DEM/USD
DAX 30	–				
S&P 500	0.44	–			
GER10y	0.13	0.12	–		
USA10y	0.03	0.14	0.35	–	
DEM/$	0.22	0.13	0.05	−0.11	–

Table 5.9   Kendall's tau implied by α from Frank copula

	DAX 30	S&P 500	GER10y	USA10y	DEM/USD
DAX 30	–				
S&P 500	0.47	–			
GER10y	0.13	0.12	–		
USA10y	0.03	0.15	0.38	–	
DEM/USD	0.23	0.14	0.05	−0.13	–

Table 5.10   Pearson correlation

	DAX 30	S&P 500	GER10y	USA10y	DEM/USD
DAX 30	–				
S&P 500	0.67	–			
GER10y	0.18	0.13	–		
USA10y	−0.02	0.13	0.50	–	
DEM/USD	0.30	0.14	0.06	−0.21	–

5.8   EVALUATION CRITERIA FOR COPULAS

Modeling a copula function means modeling both marginals and the joint distribution. Hence, measures of goodness of fit are important for evaluating the fit of a proposed copula and for testing the specification of the marginal distributions. As discussed above, the copula evaluation is a special case of the more general issue of evaluating multivariate density models. For such a problem, some methods have been proposed in the literature, and no single method has emerged as best (see Diebold et al., 1998, 1999).

This evaluation issue may be split into two distinct problems. First, one should evaluate the goodness of fit for each margin and then the overall goodness of fit given by the copula. The former problem may be easily faced by using the probability integral transform, thus, it has been shown that for the time series framework the sequence of probability integral transforms of the data will be i.i.d. Uniform (0, 1) if the sequence of densities is correct. It is worth noting that instead of testing, for each margin, whether its probability integral transform series $\{u_t\}_{t=1}^T$ be i.i.d. Uniform (0, 1), it is equivalently possible to test that the transformed series $\left\{z_t = \Phi^{-1}(u_t)\right\}_{t=1}^T$ be i.i.d. Normal (0, 1). The latter procedure is the most used in practice due to the large number of tests of normality available. Diebold et al.

(1998, 1999) propose some tests to check the independence of the transformed series by using the Kolmogorov–Smirnov test (see Shao, 1999, for the theory underlying this test) and other ad hoc tests by using their first moments. Diebold, Hahn and Tay (1999) extend the results of Diebold, Gunther and Tay (1998) to the evaluation of bivariate density models by testing the conditional c.d.f.s of X and Y.

As pointed out by the same authors, the issue to evaluate the joint c.d.f., such as the copula fitting, is much more difficult.

Patton (2001) proposes, for a bivariate case, an extension of the "Hit" regression of Christoffersen (1998) and Engle and Manganelli (1999) for evaluating interval forecasts, such as VaR forecasts (for an empirical application and a discussion about such statistical tests refer to Meneguzzo & Vecchiato, 2000). Briefly, the author builds up a test by decomposing the density model into a set of region models (interval models in the basic univariate case), each of which should be correctly specified under the null hypothesis that the entire multivariate density is correctly specified. The evaluation problem is so reconducted to test whether the model is adequately specified in each of the regions individually via tests of each binomial hypothesis (i.e. each hit or indicator function is a Bernoulli r.v.). Patton (2001) uses logistic regression, which yields more efficient parameter estimates, to test equivalent null hypothesis i.i.d. Bernoulli or Multinomial r.v.s. Following his method it is possible to build up a family of tests to evaluate if the model is correctly specified in a set of regions where it is defined.

5.9 CONDITIONAL COPULA

In econometric theory much attention has been reserved to conditional distribution modeling, i.e. conditional to all past information. This is mainly due to forecasting and fitting purposes (see Davidson & MacKinnon, 1993, for a further explanation).

For the bivariate case, Patton (2001) extends the standard definition of copula to the conditional case. Thus, he introduces the copula theory to model the time-varying conditional dependence. His interest consists in taking into account the well-known heteroskedastic pattern, widely reported in the financial literature, for the volatility of any financial return time series (see Engle, 1996, for an excellent survey). Further, there are many situations where the entire conditional joint density is required, such as the pricing of financial options with multiple underlying assets (see Rosemberg, 2000), or in the calculation of portfolio VaR, as previously discussed (also refer to Hull & White, 1998).

The extension to the conditional copula consists in expressing the Sklar's theorem for conditional c.d.f., i.e. conditional to a sigma algebra $\Im$ generated by all past information. For example, in a time series context

$$\Im_t = \sigma \{x_{1t-1}, x_{2t-1}, \ldots, x_{nt-1}, x_{1t-2}, x_{2t-2}, \ldots, x_{nt-2}, \ldots\} \quad \text{for } t = 1, \ldots, T \quad (5.49)$$

represents the past information up to time t. Hence, Sklar's theorem may be extended as follows:

$$F_t(x_{1t}, x_{2t}, \ldots, x_{nt} \mid \Im_t) = C_t(F_{1t}(x_{1t} \mid \Im_t), F_{2t}(x_{2t} \mid \Im_t), \ldots, F_{nt}(x_{nt} \mid \Im_t) \mid \Im_t) \quad (5.50)$$

where C_t has to be a copula function at all times t.

It is worth noting that the joint distribution of $(X_{1t}, X_{2t}, \ldots, X_{nt})$ may differ from the joint distribution of $(X_{1t-1}, X_{2t-1}, \ldots, X_{nt-1})$, and so on. Thus a sample data matrix $\aleph =$

$\{x_{1t}, x_{2t}, \ldots, x_{nt}\}_{t=1}^{T}$ may not represent T observations of the same joint distribution, but T observations from T different joint distributions. Besides that, note that the conditioning set for each marginal and for the conditional copula is the same; hence, each transformed variable must be independent of the information in the conditioning set of its marginal distribution. This condition allows us to build statistical tests.

Obviously, without assuming some functional structure it is impossible to estimate the form of each joint distribution. So, for example, one is forced to assume that the distributions remain constant over time, while some of their parameters vary according to some finite difference equation.

Patton (2001), in modeling the marginal distributions, assumes that the conditional means evolve according to an autoregressive process, and that the conditional variances evolve according to a GARCH(1, 1) process.

Similarly the evolution of C_t has to be assumed. Its possible paths may be the *degenerate case* (i.e. it does not vary at all), the *time-varying parameters case* (i.e. the functional form of the conditional copula is fixed, but its parameters evolve through time), or the complete *time-varying structure* (i.e. time variation involves changes in both the form of the conditional copula and its parameters). Nelsen (1999) shows that any convex linear combination of copulas is also a copula, and so a time-varying functional form for the conditional copula could be set to a convex sum (even with time-varying weights) of various types of copulas (even time-varying parameter copulas, as previously defined).

5.9.1 Application to an equity portfolio

We consider two sets of equity daily (last) price data (General Motors and IBM). In specifying the model for the bivariate density of the General Motors and the IBM stocks it is necessary to specify three models: two models for the marginal distributions of each stock and one model for the conditional copula.

The model that we choose for the marginal distributions is a GARCH(1, 1) with normal innovations, because it is the most frequently used model in the literature of applied financial econometrics (refer to Engle, 1996, for a survey) and is defined as:

$$X_t = \varepsilon_t \tag{5.51}$$

$$h_t^x = \omega_x + \beta_x h_{t-1}^x + \alpha_x \varepsilon_{t-1}^2 \tag{5.52}$$

$$\frac{\varepsilon_t}{\sqrt{h_t^x}} \rightsquigarrow N(0, 1) \tag{5.53}$$

where X_t represents the log-difference of the stock price.

In our particular case it happens that we only need univariate models for the two marginal distributions due to the fact that no lags of the other variables appear in the regression. This will not always be so.

In Tables 5.11 and 5.12 we present the results we have obtained using the GARCH(1, 1) model.

After having estimated the marginal distributions it is necessary to define the copula function in order to obtain the joint distribution of the two stocks. In this example we consider the Gaussian copula. We also assume that the correlation parameter of the copula,

Table 5.11 Results for the marginal distributions

IBM stock	ω_x	β_x	α_x
	0.0000	0.9302	0.0613
Standard error	0.0000	0.0000	0.0000
Robust standard error*	0.0000	0.0001	0.0001

*Quasi-likelihood standard errors which are robust to some forms of mis-specification (refer to White, 1984).

Table 5.12

GM Stock	ω_x	β_x	α_x
	0.0000	0.9134	0.0611
std. error	0.0000	0.0000	0.0000
robust std. error	0.0000	0.0001	0.0001

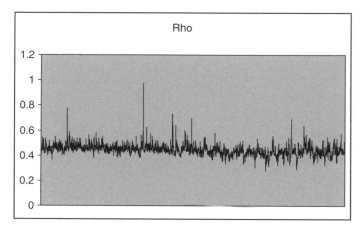

Figure 5.11 Time-varying conditional correlation in the normal copula

Results for the Gaussian copula		
ω_ρ	β_ρ	α_ρ
0.010731	−2.090770	−0.043261

ρ, varies according to the following evolution equation:

$$\rho_t = \Lambda\left(\omega_\rho + \beta_\rho \rho_{t-1} + \alpha_\rho \frac{1}{p}\sum_{j=1}^{p}\Phi^{-1}(u_{t-j})\Phi^{-1}(v_{t-j})\right) \qquad (5.54)$$

where $\Lambda(x)$ is the modified logistic (also known as hyperbolic tangent) function $\frac{1-e^{-x}}{1+e^{-x}}$ necessary to keep ρ_t belonging to the interval $(-1, 1)$.

The regression (5.53) includes the term ρ_{t-1} in order to capture the persistence in the dependence parameter, and the average sum

$$\frac{1}{p} \sum_{j=1}^{p} \Phi^{-1}(u_{t-j}) \Phi^{-1}(v_{t-j})$$

in order to capture any variation in dependence.

We choose to allow a time-varying correlation coefficient, instead of a constant one, for a more general setting.

In this empirical application, according to the data we are analyzing, we set p equal to 1 in the equation (5.54) and we report the results for the Gaussian copula below Figure 5.11 and in Figure 5.11 for the time varying correlation.

All estimates are statistically significant.

6

Simulation of Market Scenarios

6.1 MONTE CARLO APPLICATION WITH COPULAS

Simulation is a widely used tool for generating draws from a lot of stochastic models. In the following we describe some useful techniques in order to generate random scenarios from the copula set up. We start with the elliptical copulas – the Gaussian and Student t copulas – where the simulations are obtained easily even if their copula is not in closed form. As for other copulas, like the Archimedean ones, we describe the conditional method. This method may be applied for every chosen copula. Besides that, for some Archimedean copulas, a simple method proposed by Marshall and Olkin (1998) allows us to get simulations easily. We offer some illustrative examples.

Generally, once a copula has been decided upon, we may draw multivariate random samples.

6.2 SIMULATION METHODS FOR ELLIPTICAL COPULAS

Our attention is dedicated to the Gaussian and T copula because they are the most widely known and applied copulas to Empirical Finance. As we have seen previously, the form of their copula is not closed and easy to write down, but the simulation draws are very easy to obtain.

We provide the following algorithm in order to generate random variates from the Gaussian n-copula C_R^N:

- Find the Cholesky decomposition A of R
- Simulate n independent random variates $\mathbf{z} = (z_1, z_2, \ldots, z_n)'$ from $N(0, 1)$
- Set $\mathbf{x} = A\mathbf{z}$
- Set $u_i = \Phi(x_i)$ with $i = 1, 2, \ldots, n$ and where Φ denotes the univariate standard normal distribution function
- $(u_1, \ldots, u_n)' = (F_1(t_1), \ldots, F_n(t_n))'$ where F_i denotes the ith margin

The Student T copula is also easy to simulate. We provide the following algorithm in order to generate random variates from the n-copula $T_{R,\upsilon}$:

- Find the Cholesky decomposition A of R
- Simulate n i.i.d. $\mathbf{z} = (z_1, z_2, \ldots, z_n)'$ from $N(0, 1)$
- Simulate a random variate s from χ_υ^2 independent of $\mathbf{z}$
- Set $\mathbf{y} = A\mathbf{z}$
- Set $\mathbf{x} = \sqrt{(\upsilon/s)}\mathbf{y}$
- Set $u_i = T_\upsilon(x_i)$ with $i = 1, 2, \ldots, n$ and where T_υ denotes the univariate Student t distribution function
- $(u_1, \ldots, u_n)' = (F_1(t_1), \ldots, F_n(t_n))'$ where F_i denotes the ith margin

6.3   CONDITIONAL SAMPLING

A general method to simulate draws from a chosen copula is formulated by using a conditional approach (*conditional sampling*). Just to explain this concept in a simple way, let us assume a bivariate copula in which all of its parameters are known (fixed or estimated with some statistical methods). The task is to generate pairs (u, v) of observations of $[0, 1]$ uniformly distributed r.v.s U and V whose joint distribution function is C. To reach this goal we will use the conditional distribution

$$c_u(v) = \Pr(V \leqslant v | U = u) \tag{6.1}$$

for the r.v. V at a given value u of U.

Basically, we know that

$$c_u(v) = \Pr(F_2 \leqslant v | F_1 = u) = \lim_{\Delta u \to 0} \frac{C(u + \Delta u, v) - C(u, v)}{\Delta u} = \frac{\partial C}{\partial u} = C_u(v) \tag{6.2}$$

where $C_u(v)$ is the partial derivative of the copula. We know that $c_u(v)$ is a non-decreasing function and exists for almost all $v \in [0, 1]$.

With this result at hand, we generate the desired pair (u, v) in the following way:

- Generate two independent uniform r.v.s $(u, w) \in [0, 1]$. u is the first draw we are looking for.
- Compute the (quasi-)inverse function of $c_u(v)$. This will depend on the parameters of the copula and on u, which can be seen, in this context, as an additional parameter of $c_u(v)$. Set $v = c_u^{-1}(w)$ to obtain the second desired draw.[1]

The general procedure in a multivariate setting is as follows:

- Define $C_i = C(F_1, F_2, \ldots, F_i, 1, 1, \ldots, 1)$ for $i = 2, 3, \ldots, n$.
- Draw F_1 from the uniform distribution $U(0, 1)$.
- Next, draw F_2 from $C_2(F_2 | F_1)$.
- More generally, draw F_n from $C_n(F_n | F_1, \ldots, F_{n-1})$.

Putting it differently, let us consider the general setting for an n-copula $C = C(u_1, u_2, \ldots, u_n)$ and let $C_k(u_1, u_2, \ldots, u_k, 1, \ldots, 1)$ for $k = 2, \ldots, n - 1$ denote the k-dimensional margins of C, with $C_1(u_1) = u_1$ and $C_n(u_1, u_2, \ldots, u_n) = C(u_1, u_2, \ldots, u_n)$.

Since $U_1, U_2, \ldots, U_n$ have joint distribution function C, then the conditional distribution of U_k, given the values of $U_1, \ldots, U_{k-1}$, is given by

$$C_k(u_k | u_1, \ldots, u_{k-1}) = \Pr(U_k \leqslant u_k | U_1 = u_1, \ldots, U_{k-1} = u_{k-1})$$

$$= \frac{[\partial^{k-1} C_k(u_1, \ldots, u_k)]/[\partial u_1 \ldots \partial u_{k-1}]}{[\partial^{k-1} C_{k-1}(u_1, \ldots, u_{k-1})]/[\partial u_1 \ldots \partial u_{k-1}]} \tag{6.3}$$

with $k = 2, \ldots, n$. Obviously we assume that both the numerator and the denominator exist and that the denominator is not zero. Hence the algorithm may be rewritten as:

---

[1] Nelsen (1999, p. 35) calls this function the quasi-inverse of c_u.

- Simulate a random variate u_1 from $U(0, 1)$
- Simulate a random variate u_2 from $C_2(\cdot|u_1)$
- ...
- Simulate a random variate u_n from $C_n(\cdot|u_1, \ldots, u_{n-1})$

In order to simulate a value u_k from $C_k(\cdot|u_1, \ldots, u_{k-1})$ one has to draw v from $U(0, 1)$ from which $u_k = C_k^{-1}(v|u_1, \ldots, u_{k-1})$ can be obtained through the equation $v = C_k(u_k|u_1, \ldots, u_{k-1})$ by numerical rootfinding.[2]

The conditional approach is very elegant but it may not be possible to calculate the inverse function analytically. In this case one has to use a numerical algorithm to determine the desired draw. Obviously, this procedure may be computationally intensive.

In the case of Archimedean copulas this method may be rewritten as the following theorem states.

Theorem 6.1 Let $C(u_1, u_2, \ldots, u_n) = \varphi^{-1}(\varphi(u_1) + \varphi(u_2) + \cdots + \varphi(u_n))$ be an Archimedean n-variate copula with generator $\varphi(\cdot)$, then for $k = 2, \ldots, n$

$$C_k(u_k|u_1, \ldots, u_{k-1}) = \frac{\varphi^{-1(k-1)}(\varphi(u_1) + \varphi(u_2) + \cdots + \varphi(u_k))}{\varphi^{-1(k-1)}(\varphi(u_1) + \varphi(u_2) + \cdots + \varphi(u_{k-1}))} \qquad (6.4)$$

Proof: Since by definition $\varphi(1) = 0$ then, for $k = 2, \ldots, n-1$,

$$C_k(u_1, \ldots, u_k) = C(u_1, \ldots, u_k, 1, \ldots, 1) = \varphi^{-1}(\varphi(u_1) + \varphi(u_2) + \cdots + \varphi(u_k)) \qquad (6.5)$$

Besides $C_1(u_1) = \varphi^{-1}(\varphi(u_1)) = u_1$ and

$$C_n(u_1, \ldots, u_n) = C(u_1, u_2, \ldots, u_n) = \varphi^{-1}(\varphi(u_1) + \varphi(u_2) + \cdots + \varphi(u_n)) \qquad (6.6)$$

Moreover

$$C_k(u_k|u_1, \ldots, u_{k-1}) = \frac{[\partial^{k-1} C_k(u_1, \ldots, u_k)]/[\partial u_1 \ldots \partial u_{k-1}]}{[\partial^{k-1} C_{k-1}(u_1, \ldots, u_{k-1})]/[\partial u_1 \ldots \partial u_{k-1}]} \qquad (6.7)$$

and by derivation we have

$$\frac{\partial^{k-1} C_{k-1}(u_1, \ldots, u_k)}{\partial u_1 \ldots \partial u_{k-1}} = \frac{\partial^{k-1} \varphi^{-1}(\varphi(u_1) + \varphi(u_2) + \cdots + \varphi(u_{k-1}))}{\partial u_1 \ldots \partial u_{k-1}}$$

$$= \varphi^{-1(k-1)}(\varphi(u_1) + \varphi(u_2) + \cdots + \varphi(u_{k-1})) \cdot \prod_{j=1}^{k-1} \varphi^{(1)}(u_j) \qquad (6.8)$$

[2] For a detailed description of simulation procedures, see Genest (1987), Genest and Rivest (1993), Lee (1993), Frees and Valdez (1998), Marshall and Olkin (1988), and Embrechts, Lindskog and McNeil (2001).

and

$$\frac{\partial^{k-1} C_k(u_1, \ldots, u_k)}{\partial u_1 \ldots \partial u_{k-1}} = \frac{\partial^{k-1} \varphi^{-1} (\varphi(u_1) + \varphi(u_2) + \cdots + \varphi(u_k))}{\partial u_1 \ldots \partial u_{k-1}}$$

$$= \varphi^{-1(k-1)} (\varphi(u_1) + \varphi(u_2) + \cdots + \varphi(u_k)) \cdot \prod_{j=1}^{k-1} \varphi^{(1)}(u_j) \quad (6.9)$$

hence we obtain the following result

$$C_k(u_k | u_1, \ldots, u_{k-1}) = \frac{\varphi^{-1(k-1)}(c_k)}{\varphi^{-1(k-1)}(c_{k-1})} \quad (6.10)$$

where $c_k = \sum_{j=1}^{k} \varphi(u_j)$ and with $k = 2, \ldots, n$. $\qquad \square$

Now we would like to apply this important result to the most used Archimedean copulas. We present, in full detail, the particular cases for the Frank copula and for the Clayton copula, because they are the most frequently used and best known Archimedean copulas in empirical applications.

6.3.1 Clayton n-copula

The generator is given by $\varphi(u) = u^{-\alpha} - 1$, hence $\varphi^{-1}(t) = (t + 1)^{-\frac{1}{\alpha}}$. The Clayton n-copula, also known as Cook and Johnson's (1981) family, is given by:

$$C(u_1, u_2, \ldots, u_n) = \left[\sum_{i=1}^{n} u_i^{-\alpha} - n + 1 \right]^{-\frac{1}{\alpha}} \quad \text{with } \alpha > 0 \quad (6.11)$$

Let us compute the derivatives of the function $\varphi^{-1}(t)$. We have

$$\varphi^{-1(1)}(t) = -\frac{1}{\alpha}(t+1)^{-\frac{1}{\alpha}-1}, \quad \varphi^{-1(2)} = \frac{1}{\alpha}\frac{\alpha+1}{\alpha}(t+1)^{-\frac{1}{\alpha}-2}, \ldots,$$

$$\varphi^{-1(k)}(t) = (-1)^k \frac{(\alpha+1)(\alpha+2) \cdots \cdots (\alpha+k-1)}{\alpha^k}(t+1)^{-\frac{1}{\alpha}-k} \quad (6.12)$$

Hence, by applying the previous theorem, the following algorithm generates a random variate $(u_1, u_2, \ldots, u_n)'$ from the Clayton copula:

- Simulate n independent random variables $(v_1, v_2, \ldots, v_n)'$ from $U(0, 1)$
- Sct $u_1 = v_1$
- Set $v_2 = C_2(u_2 | v_1)$, hence

$$v_2 = \frac{\varphi^{-1(1)}(c_2)}{\varphi^{-1(1)}(c_1)} \quad \text{with } c_1 = \varphi(u_1) = u_1^{-\alpha} - 1 \text{ and } c_2 = \varphi(u_1) + \varphi(u_2)$$

$$= u_1^{-\alpha} + u_2^{-\alpha} - 2$$

so

$$v_2 = \left(\frac{u_1^{-\alpha} + u_2^{-\alpha} - 1}{u_1^{-\alpha}} \right)^{-\frac{1}{\alpha} - 1}$$

Finally

$$u_2 = \left(v_1^{-\alpha} \left(v_2^{-\frac{\alpha}{\alpha+1}} - 1 \right) + 1 \right)^{-\frac{1}{\alpha}} \tag{6.13}$$

- Set

$$v_3 = C_3(u_3|u_1, u_2) = \frac{\varphi^{-1(2)}(c_3)}{\varphi^{-1(2)}(c_2)} = \left(\frac{u_1^{-\alpha} + u_2^{-\alpha} + u_3^{-\alpha} - 2}{u_1^{-\alpha} + u_2^{-\alpha} - 1} \right)^{-\frac{1}{\alpha} - 2}$$

and solve it in u_3
- ...
- Solve in u_n the equation

$$v_n = \left(\frac{u_1^{-\alpha} + u_2^{-\alpha} + \cdots + u_n^{-\alpha} - n + 1}{u_1^{-\alpha} + u_2^{-\alpha} + \cdots + u_{n-1}^{-\alpha} - n + 2} \right)^{-\frac{1}{\alpha} - n + 1}$$

so we have:

$$u_n = \left\{ \left(u_1^{-\alpha} + u_2^{-\alpha} + \cdots + u_{n-1}^{-\alpha} - n + 2 \right) \cdot \left(v_n^{\frac{\alpha}{\alpha(1-n)-1}} - 1 \right) + 1 \right\}^{-\frac{1}{\alpha}} \tag{6.14}$$

6.3.2   Gumbel n-copula

The generator is given by $\varphi(u) = (-\ln(u))^{\alpha}$, hence $\varphi^{-1}(t) = \exp(-t^{\frac{1}{\alpha}})$. The Gumbel n-copula is given by:

$$C(u_1, u_2, \ldots, u_n) = \exp \left\{ - \left[\sum_{i=1}^{n} (-\ln u_i)^{\alpha} \right]^{\frac{1}{\alpha}} \right\} \qquad \text{with } \alpha > 1 \tag{6.15}$$

Let $w = t^{\frac{1}{\alpha}} \rightarrow t = w^{\alpha}$, so we have

$$\varphi^{-1}(w) = \exp(-w) \quad \text{and} \quad \frac{\partial w}{\partial t} = \frac{1}{\alpha} t^{\frac{1}{\alpha} - 1} = \frac{1}{\alpha} w^{1-\alpha}$$

Hence we have

$$\varphi^{-1(1)}(t) = \frac{\partial \varphi^{-1}}{\partial w} \frac{\partial w}{\partial t} = -e^{-w} \frac{1}{\alpha} w^{1-\alpha} \quad \text{and}$$

$$\varphi^{-1(2)}(t) = \frac{\partial \varphi^{-1(1)}}{\partial w} \frac{\partial w}{\partial t} = \frac{1}{\alpha^2} e^{-w} w^{1-2\alpha} (w - 1 + \alpha)$$

and so on. Unfortunately this is not a recursive formula.

The following algorithm generates a random variate $(u_1, u_2, \ldots, u_n)'$ from the Gumbel copula:

- Simulate n independent random variables $(v_1, v_2, \ldots, v_n)'$ from $U(0, 1)$
- Set $u_1 = v_1$
- Set $v_2 = C_2(u_2|v_1)$, hence

$$v_2 = \frac{\varphi^{-1(1)}(c_2)}{\varphi^{-1(1)}(c_1)} \quad \text{with } c_1 = \varphi(u_1) = (-\ln(u_1))^\alpha$$

and

$$c_2 = \varphi(u_1) + \varphi(u_2) = (-\ln(u_1))^\alpha + (-\ln(u_2))^\alpha$$

This equation has to be solved with respect to u_2.
- Set

$$v_3 = C_3(u_3|u_1, u_2) = \frac{\varphi^{-1(2)}(c_3)}{\varphi^{-1(2)}(c_2)}$$

and solve it in u_3
- ...

6.3.3 Frank n-copula

The generator is given by $\varphi(u) = \ln\left(\frac{\exp(-\alpha u)-1}{\exp(-\alpha)-1}\right)$, hence

$$\varphi^{-1}(t) = -\frac{1}{\alpha}\ln\left(1 + e^t(e^{-\alpha} - 1)\right)$$

The Frank n-copula is given by:

$$C(u_1, u_2, \ldots, u_n) = -\frac{1}{\alpha}\ln\left\{1 + \frac{\prod_{i=1}^{n}(e^{-\alpha u_i} - 1)}{(e^{-\alpha} - 1)^{n-1}}\right\} \quad \text{with } \alpha > 0 \text{ when } n \geqslant 3 \quad (6.16)$$

We will soon see why higher dimensions allow only positive dependence ($\alpha > 0$).
As for derivatives of $\varphi^{-1}(t)$, we have $\varphi^{-1(1)}(t) = -\frac{1}{\alpha}\frac{e^t(e^{-\alpha}-1)}{1+e^t(e^{-\alpha}-1)}$.
Let $w = \frac{e^t(e^{-\alpha}-1)}{1+e^t(e^{-\alpha}-1)}$ so we have

$$\frac{\partial w}{\partial t} = -w(w-1) \quad \text{and} \quad \varphi^{-1(1)}(t) = -\frac{1}{\alpha}w$$

Hence,

$$\varphi^{-1(2)}(t) = \frac{\partial}{\partial t}\left[\varphi^{-1(1)}(t)\right] = \frac{\partial}{\partial w}\left[\varphi^{-1(1)}\right]\frac{\partial w}{\partial t} = \frac{1}{\alpha}w(w-1)$$

analogously

$$\varphi^{-1(3)}(t) = \frac{\partial}{\partial w}\left[\varphi^{-1(2)}\right]\frac{\partial w}{\partial t} = -\frac{1}{\alpha}w(w-1)(2w-1)$$

In general we obtain:

$$\varphi^{-1(1)}(t) = -\frac{1}{\alpha}g_1(w) \quad \text{where } g_1(w) = w \tag{6.17}$$

and

$$\varphi^{-1(k)}(t) = (-1)^k\frac{1}{\alpha}g_k(w) \quad \text{where } g_k(w) = w(w-1)g_{k-1}^{(1)}(w) \tag{6.18}$$

with $g_{k-1}^{(1)}(w) = \frac{\partial g_{k-1}}{\partial w}$ and $k \geqslant 2$.

In such a way one can proceed to higher order derivatives.[3]

Finally, we give the following algorithm in order to generate a random variate $(u_1, u_2, \ldots, u_n)'$ from the Frank copula:

- Simulate n independent random variables $(v_1, v_2, \ldots, v_n)'$ from $U(0, 1)$
- Set $u_1 = v_1$
- Set $v_2 = C_2(u_2|v_1)$ hence

$$v_2 = \frac{\varphi^{-1(1)}(c_2)}{\varphi^{-1(1)}(c_1)} \quad \text{with } c_1 = \varphi(u_1) = \ln\left(\frac{\exp(-\alpha u_1) - 1}{\exp(-\alpha) - 1}\right)$$

and

$$c_2 = \varphi(u_1) + \varphi(u_2) = \ln\left(\frac{(\exp(-\alpha u_1) - 1)(\exp(-\alpha u_2) - 1)}{(\exp(-\alpha) - 1)^2}\right)$$

Hence

$$v_2 = e^{-\alpha u_1}\frac{\exp(-\alpha u_2) - 1}{\exp(-\alpha) - 1 + (\exp(-\alpha u_1) - 1)(\exp(-\alpha u_2) - 1)}$$

has to be solved with respect to u_2. We obtain:

$$u_2 = -\frac{1}{\alpha}\ln\left\{1 + \frac{v_2(1 - e^{-\alpha})}{v_2(e^{-\alpha u_1} - 1) - e^{-\alpha u_1}}\right\} \tag{6.19}$$

---

[3] From these expressions it is also possible to see that the Kimberling theorem may be invoked for higher dimensions if and only if $\alpha > 0$ in order to have a generator completely monotone. This means that the generators suitable for extension to arbitrary dimensions of Archimedean 2-copulas correspond to copulas that can model only positive dependence. In fact the readers may note that g_k is a polynomial of degree k with the leading term of positive sign. For $w < 0$ (hence $\alpha > 0$) the polynomials are positive for even k and negative for odd k. When $\alpha < 0$, then $0 < w < 1$, and it is easily verified that $\varphi^{-1(3)}(t)$ fails to be negative for all t.

Alternatively refer to Schweizer and Sklar (1983), Chap. 6, where it is proven that the inverse of a strict generator of an Archimedean n-copula C is completely monotone, then $C > \Pi$, where Π is the product (or independent) n-copula.

- Set

$$v_3 = C_3(u_3|u_1, u_2) = \frac{\varphi^{-1(2)}(c_3)}{\varphi^{-1(2)}(c_2)} \quad \text{with } c_2 = \ln\left(\frac{(\exp(-\alpha u_1) - 1)(\exp(-\alpha u_2) - 1)}{(\exp(-\alpha) - 1)^2}\right)$$

and

$$c_3 = \ln\left(\frac{(\exp(-\alpha u_1) - 1)(\exp(-\alpha u_2) - 1)(\exp(-\alpha u_3) - 1)}{(\exp(-\alpha) - 1)^3}\right)$$

Hence,

$$v_3 = (e^{-\alpha} - 1)[(e^{-\alpha} - 1) + (e^{-\alpha u_1} - 1)(e^{-\alpha u_2} - 1)]^2$$
$$\times \frac{e^{-\alpha u_3} - 1}{[(e^{-\alpha} - 1)^2 + (e^{-\alpha u_1} - 1)(e^{-\alpha u_2} - 1)(e^{-\alpha u_3} - 1)]^2} \qquad (6.20)$$

We obtain a polynomial equation of order 2 in the variable $x = e^{-\alpha u_3} - 1$ that has to be solved with respect to u_3

- And so on, obtaining each variate u_k involves solving a polynomial equation of degree $k - 1$.

6.4 MARSHALL AND OLKIN'S METHOD

We present a simulation algorithm proposed by Marshall and Olkin (1988) for the *compound construction of copulas*. This is a construction method of copulas involving the Laplace transform and its inverse function. Recall that the Laplace transform of a positive random variable γ is defined by:

$$\tau(s) = E_\gamma(e^{-s\gamma}) = \int_0^{+\infty} e^{-st} dF_\gamma(t) \qquad (6.21)$$

where F_γ is the distribution function of γ. This is also the moment generating function evaluated at $-s$; thus, knowledge of $\tau(s)$ determines the distribution. Laplace transforms have well-defined inverses. We saw that the inverse function τ^{-1} serves as the generator for an Archimedean copula.

Marshall and Olkin's (1988) method for constructing copulas may be described as follows. Suppose that X_i is a r.v. whose conditional, given a positive latent variable γ_i, distribution function is specified by $H_i(x|\gamma_i) = H_i(x)^{\gamma_i}$, where $H_i(.)$ is some baseline distribution function, for $i = 1, 2, \ldots, n$.

Marshall and Olkin (1988) considered multivariate distribution functions of the form:

$$F(x_1, x_2, \ldots, x_n) = E\left[K(H_1(x)^{\gamma_1}, H_2(x)^{\gamma_2}, \ldots, H_n(x)^{\gamma_n})\right] \qquad (6.22)$$

where K is a c.d.f. with uniform marginals, and the expectation is taken over $\gamma_1, \gamma_2, \ldots, \gamma_n$.

As a special case, we consider all latent variables equal to one another so that $\gamma_1 = \gamma_2 = \cdots = \gamma_n = \gamma$ and use c.d.f.s corresponding to independent marginals. Marshall and Olkin (1988) show that:

$$F(x_1, x_2, \ldots, x_n) = E(H_1(x)^{\gamma_1} \cdot H_2(x)^{\gamma_2} \cdot \cdots \cdot H_n(x)^{\gamma_n})$$

$$= \tau(\tau^{-1}(F_1(x_1)) + \tau^{-1}(F_2(x_2)) + \cdots + \tau^{-1}(F_n(x_n))) \qquad (6.23)$$

where F_i is the ith marginal c.d.f. of the joint c.d.f. F, and $\tau(.)$ is the Laplace transform of γ.

Generating outcomes from a compound copula

To generate $X_1, X_2, \ldots, X_n$ having a distribution (6.23), Frees and Valdez (1998) propose the following algorithm:

- Generate a (latent) r.v. γ having Laplace transform τ
- Independently of the previous step, generate $U_1, U_2, \ldots, U_n$ independent Uniform $(0, 1)$ r.v.s
- For $k = 1, 2, \ldots, n$, calculate $X_k = F_k^{-1}(U_k^*)$ where

$$U_k^* = \tau\left(-\frac{1}{\gamma} \ln U_k\right) \qquad (6.24)$$

This algorithm is straightforward for most copulas of interest that are generated by the compounding method. It can easily be implemented for high dimension. The only disadvantage is that it is necessary to simulate an additional r.v., γ. Needless to say, this additional variable is not always easy to simulate.

For example, if we recall that a generator for a strict Archimedean copula is the Laplace transform of some positive random variable, we may see that for the Clayton copula γ is a Gamma$(1, 1/\alpha)$ r.v., that is very easy to simulate; for the Gumbel copula γ is a $(1/\alpha)$-stable r.v.; and for the Frank copula γ is a logarithmic series r.v. defined on all natural numbers (see Marshall & Olkin, 1988). In the last case the simulation with this technique is not easy, and the conditional sampling should be preferred.

We report on how to obtain draws by using this method for the Clayton and the Gumbel copula, alternatively, to the conditional sampling technique previously discussed.

Clayton case

- Generate a r.v. γ Gamma$(1, 1/\alpha)$ (hence, γ has Laplace transform $\tau(s) = (1 + s)^{-\frac{1}{\alpha}}$)
- Independently of the previous step, generate $U_1, U_2, \ldots, U_n$ independent Uniform $(0, 1)$ r.v.s
- For $k = 1, 2, \ldots, n$ calculate $X_k = F_k^{-1}(U_k^*)$ where

$$U_k^* = \tau\left(-\frac{1}{\gamma} \ln U_k\right)$$

Gumbel case

- Generate a r.v. γ Stable(1, 0, 0) with parameter $1/\alpha$ (hence, γ has Laplace transform $\tau(s) = \exp\{-s^{\frac{1}{\alpha}}\})^4$;
- Independently of the previous step, generate $U_1, U_2, \ldots, U_n$ independent Uniform (0, 1) r.v.s
- For $k = 1, 2, \ldots, n$ calculate $X_k = F_k^{-1}(U_k^*)$ where

$$U_k^* = \tau\left(-\frac{1}{\gamma}\ln U_k\right)$$

A common procedure to obtain a draw from a Stable(1, 0, 0) with parameter β r.v. is based on the following result (Samorodnitsky & Taqqu, 1995, p. 42):

- Let υ be uniform on $\left(-\frac{\pi}{2}, \frac{\pi}{2}\right)$ and let ξ be exponential with mean 1 independently drawn. Then

$$\kappa = \frac{\sin(\beta\upsilon)}{(\cos\upsilon)^{\frac{1}{\beta}}} \cdot \left[\frac{\cos((1-\beta)\upsilon)}{\xi}\right]^{\frac{1-\beta}{\beta}} \tag{6.25}$$

is Stable(1, 0, 0) with parameter β.

In Figure 6.1 we present an example of 10 000 simulated draws, following the above algorithms, from a Gumbel copula with $\alpha = 2$. As can be seen, there is evidence of upper tail dependence.

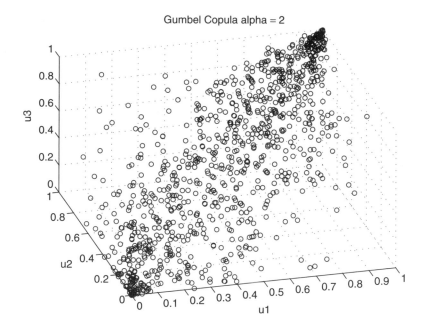

Figure 6.1   Gumbel copula with $\alpha = 2$

---

[4] For a detailed description of stable r.v.s and their properties we refer readers to the excellent book of Samorodnitsky and Taqqu (1995).

6.5 EXAMPLES OF SIMULATIONS

In this section we apply the previous algorithms to simulate some trivariate copulas. In Figure 6.2 we show the simulated Student t copula with 4 d.o.f. and correlation matrix given by daily equity series. We used daily returns series for ABN Amro, Bayer AG, Renault SA (January 2, 2001–July 30, 2002) having estimated their robust positive definite correlation matrix (by means of the Spearman's rho ρ_S), a univariate t-GARCH(1, 1) process for each series, and the T copula d.o.f. is found statistically significant around 4.

Using the conditional sampling technique, we simulate the trivariate Clayton and Frank copula with different values for the α parameter for the same data set. This parameter was estimated via the IFM technique, equal respectively to 0.53 for the Clayton copula and 1.61 for the Frank copula.

We remark that the α parameter in the Archimedean copulas is the only driver of the dependence. Indeed, we show in Figures 6.3–6.8 how different values for α induce stronger dependence. It can be seen from these figures that, in the Clayton copula, the lower tail dependence is much stronger than in the Frank copula, where there is no tail dependence.

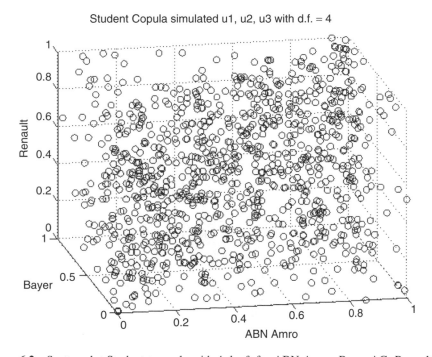

Figure 6.2   Scatter plot Student t copula with 4 d.o.f. for ABN Amro, Bayer AG, Renault SA

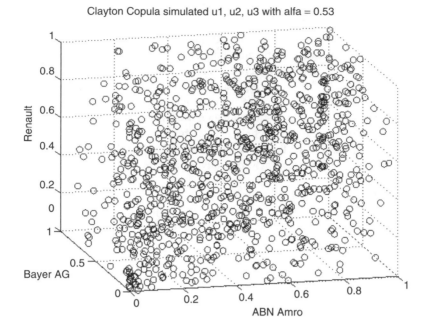

Figure 6.3   Clayton copula with $\alpha = 0.53$

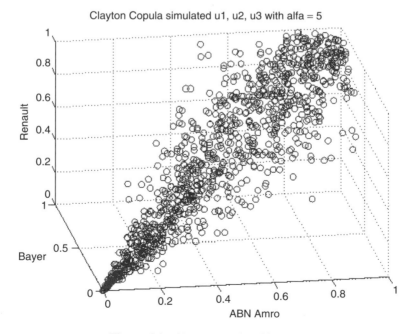

Figure 6.4   Clayton copula with $\alpha = 5$

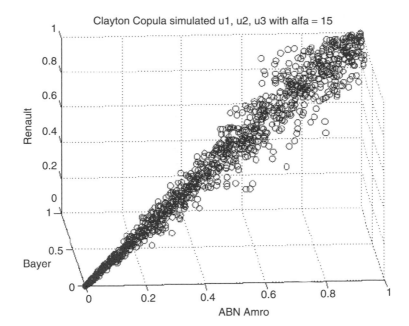

Figure 6.5   Clayton copula with $\alpha = 15$

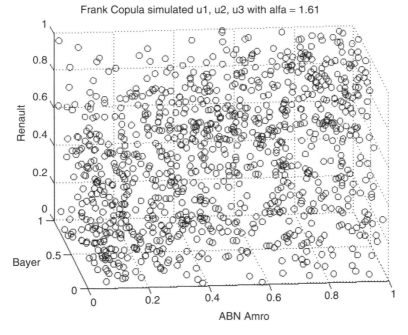

Figure 6.6   Frank copula with $\alpha = 1.61$

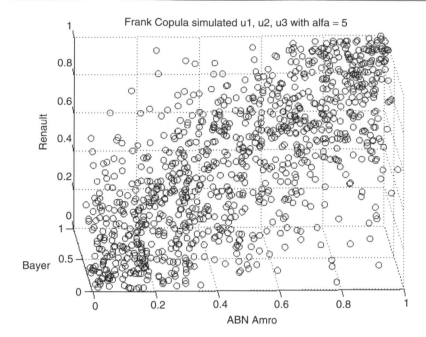

Figure 6.7   Frank copula with $\alpha = 5$

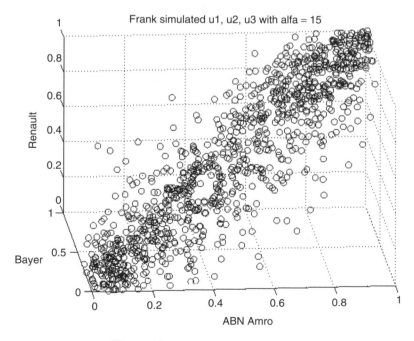

Figure 6.8   Frank copula with $\alpha = 15$

7

Credit Risk Applications

7.1 CREDIT DERIVATIVES

Credit derivatives are financial contracts that allow the transfer of credit risk from one market participant to another. In such a way, they facilitate greater efficiency in the pricing and distribution of credit risk among financial market participants.

Credit derivatives attracted attention through the use of credit default swaps in the early 1990s. Credit default swaps – the basic credit derivatives products – allow banks to hedge their credit risk associated with their loan and interest rate derivatives books without selling or otherwise transferring the underlying asset.

In recent years credit derivatives have become the main tool for transferring and hedging risk. The credit derivatives market has grown rapidly both in volume and in the type of instruments it offers. Innovations in this market have been growing at an unprecedented rate, and will likely persist in the near future.

Credit derivatives have experienced a lot of applications, ranging from hedging default risk, freeing up credit lines, reducing the regulatory capital requirements, to hedging dynamic credit exposure driven by market variables and diversifying financial portfolios by gaining access to otherwise unavailable credits.

As evidence of the huge growth of this market, the outstanding balance of credit derivatives contracts has increased from an estimated USD 50 billion in 1996 to almost USD 500 billion at the end of 2000. Volumes are continuing to grow: according to the latest survey by *Risk* magazine (Patel, 2003), the volume of the credit derivatives market has reached an outstanding notional of more than USD 2 trillion in February 2003. An extensive discussion of the credit derivatives market and the evolution of the market can be found in the J. P. Morgan "Guide to credit derivatives" (2000) and in Davies, Hewer and Rivett (2001).

The market is also developing outside the United States. According to a survey by the British Bankers' Association (BBA), the global credit derivatives market is estimated to be at least twice as large as the US market. The exact size of the global credit derivatives markets, however, is difficult to estimate, given the potential for overcounting when contracts involve more than one counterparty, and also that notional amounts outstanding considerably overstate the net exposure associated with those contracts.

Nowadays many new financial securities are being developed. Among the most complicated of these instruments are the multiple underlying ones. These are instruments with pay-offs that are contingent on the default realization in a portfolio of obligors. Default risk at the level of an individual security has been extensively modeled using both the structural and the reduced form approach.[1] However, default risk at the portfolio level is not as well understood. Default dependencies among many obligors in a large portfolio play a crucial role in the quantification of a portfolio's credit risk exposure for the effects caused by

---

[1] See the *structural models* of Merton (1974), Geske (1977), Leland (1994), Longstaff and Schwartz (1995), and the *reduced form models* of Duffie and Singleton (1999), Madan and Unal (1999), among others. We refer the reader also to Arvanitis and Gregory (2001) for an extensive survey of credit risk.

simultaneous defaults and by the joint dependency between them. This dependency may be due to both macroeconomic (the overall economy) and microeconomic (sectoral and even firm specific) aspects. These latter factors are referred to in the literature as *credit contagion*. As reported in Jarrow and Yu (2001) there has been evidence of credit contagion in the recent financial crisis in East Asia and in the USA where the downfall of a small number of firms had an economy-wide impact.

Recently the credit derivatives market offers more and more innovative products. From the simple single name credit default swaps, the market has proposed total return swaps, credit-linked notes, credit spread options, and multiple underlying products. This last category contains probably the most complex products to price and hedge, because their structure is linked to a portfolio of underlying credits and, hence, their pay-offs depend on the joint behavior of the underlying securities. Typical multiple underlying products are basket default swaps (BDSs) and collateralized debt obligations (CDOs).

The main users of credit derivatives are large financial institutions and banks, followed by securities firms and insurance companies. While banks and securities firms act both as sellers and buyers of protection, insurance companies, which have reportedly increased their market participation substantially in recent years, are primarily protection sellers, presumably using their expertise at evaluating risk. Corporate firms have increasingly come to the market, but primarily to buy protection to hedge their exposure in vendor financial deals. Hedge funds are also relatively active participants, arbitraging perceived mispricing between the cash and derivatives markets, and thus participating on both sides. Other participants include pension funds and mutual funds, although their participation in the market is very limited.

7.2 OVERVIEW OF SOME CREDIT DERIVATIVES PRODUCTS

We give an overview of some credit derivatives products. We refer interested readers to the recent guide provided by Davies, Hewer and Rivett (2001).

7.2.1 Credit default swap

A *credit default swap* is a bilateral contract where one counterparty buys default protection with respect to a reference entity. The contract has a given maturity, but will terminate early if the credit event occurs. In this contract one party, the protection seller, receives a premium (expressed in basis points per annum on the notional amount and received every quarter) from another party, the protection buyer, who will receive a payment upon the occurrence of the credit event in respect of the reference entity. The protection seller is buying credit risk while the protection buyer is selling credit risk. Since no asset is transferred, there is no need to fund the position.

A specific asset (i.e. bond or loan) may be cited for determining the occurrence of the credit event and payment upon default. If this is not so, there will be a deliverable option for the protection buyer in case of default. This is the main difference between a credit default swap and an asset default swap: in the latter case a specific asset has to be specified and in the former case there is the so-called deliverable option.

Normally, the default payment is given by the notional amount minus the recovery amount (net loss).

This contract allows a credit risky asset to be transformed into a credit risk-free asset by purchasing default protection referenced to this credit.

Usually, there are two methods of settlement: physical delivery and cash settlement. With physical delivery, the protection buyer delivers the defaulted asset in return for a payment equal to the notional value of that asset. With cash settlement, the protection seller pays the protection buyer an amount that is equal to the difference between the notional amount and the price of the defaulted reference asset. The recovery rate is commonly determined by a dealer survey.

In a *digital binary default swap*, the default payment is equal to a prespecified notional, irrespective of the recovery value.

The credit event, which triggers the payment of the amount due to the protection seller from the protection buyer, is defined in the documentation. The potential credit events are usually based on those specified in the new 2003 ISDA Credit Derivatives Definitions: i.e. bankruptcy, failure to pay (principal or interest), obligation default, obligation acceleration, repudiation/moratorium, and restructuring.

The most common methodology for the valuation of a credit default swap may be found in Arvanitis and Gregory (2001) Chap. 5 and in the excellent survey of Roncalli (2003).

Let us indicate the default time with the greek letter τ. $S(t)$ represents the survival function at time t

$$\overline{F}(t) = S(t) = \Pr(\tau > t) = E\left[\mathbf{1}\{\tau > t\}\right]$$

where $F(t)$ is the c.d.f. of τ.

For the sake of completeness, when we need to refer to an origin time t_0 we will indicate with $S(t_0, t) = \Pr(\tau > t | \tau > t_0) = S_{t_0}(t)$ the survival function between (t_0, t).

The protection buyer pays the premium (fixed) leg to the protection seller who will pay the default (floating) leg in the case of default. The premium leg is expressed as a margin on the notional amount of the contract. Let $t_1, t_2, \ldots, t_M$ be the payment dates for the premium leg. Since the margin is not paid after default, the present value of the premium leg is given by[2]

$$\text{PL}(t) = \sum_{t_m \geqslant t} W \cdot N\,(t_m - t_{m-1}) \cdot E[B(t, t_m) \cdot \mathbf{1}\{\tau > t_m\}]$$

where $T = t_M$ is the maturity of the credit default swap, W is the premium (also called the margin or the annuity), N is the notional amount of the contract, $B(t, t_m)$ indicates the discount factor between (t, t_m), $m = 2, \ldots, M$.

The present value of the default leg is given by

$$\text{DL}(t) = N \cdot E\left[(1 - R\,(\theta, \tau)) \cdot B(t, \tau) \cdot \mathbf{1}\{\tau \leqslant T\}\right]$$

where $R(\theta, \tau)$ indicates the recovery value, which may depend on default time τ and some other parameters θ related to both macroeconomic (the entire economy) and microeconomic (firm/business specific) factors. We assume independency between default times and recovery rates.

In the following we suppose that the recovery value is independent of the default time.[3]

---

[2] This expression is justified under a t_m-survival measure $\overline{P}_m$ as defined in Schönbucher (2000).
[3] Generally the mark to market procedures used by many large banks fix the recovery value to 30% for accounting evaluations.

We may express the present value of the credit default swap as the difference between the two legs. Hence, the fair (premium) spread is given by

$$
W = \frac{(1 - R) \cdot E\left[B(t, \tau) \cdot \mathbf{1}\{\tau \leqslant T\}\right]}{\displaystyle\sum_{t_m \geqslant t} (t_m - t_{m-1}) \cdot B(t, t_m) \cdot E\left[\mathbf{1}\{\tau > t_m\}\right]}
$$

In the real activity, traders know the market quote of the premium for each tradable reference entity. Hence, the mark to market evaluation of a credit default swap may be obtained through a *bootstrapping procedure* in order to get the survival probabilities at each payment date (or analogously constant-wise hazard rates) implied by the market spread curve for that reference entity.

7.2.2 Basket default swap

A *basket default swap* is a contract similar to a credit default swap, except that it is indexed to a basket of reference entities rather than a single reference asset. This contract will provide default protection on a number of entities in the basket of credits (typically from three to five names). Typically it is as follows.

- First to default: offers protection against the first default only (i.e. the contract triggers at the first default occurrence)
- Second to default: offers protection against the second to default only
- First k out of n to default: offers protection against the first k defaults
- Last j out of n to default: offers protection against the last j defaults

In the particular case of a *first-to-default basket* (1st to Def), it is the first credit in a basket of reference obligors whose default triggers a payment to the protection buyer. As in the case of a (single name) default swap, this payment may be cash settled. More commonly, it will involve physical delivery of the defaulted asset in return for a payment of the par amount in cash.

In return for protection against the 1st to Def, the protection buyer pays a *basket spread* to the protection seller as a set of regular accruing cash flows. As with a default swap, these payments terminate following the first credit event.

Similarly other credit products may be defined such as a *second-to-default basket* which triggers a credit event after two or more obligors have defaulted, and so on from the *nth-to-default basket* until the *last-to-default basket*.

Basket trades can permit substitutions whereby the reference obligations in the basket are not fixed and can be swapped in and out by the protection buyer. Normally, the protection buyer is only permitted to switch similar assets thereby maintaining, for example, a portfolio-weighted rating, industry or geographical concentration limits. Besides, there are usually some constraints on that if any default occurs.

This characteristic is usually pertained to the so-called *percentage loss* or first (or second, and so on) loss. In these cases the exposure is to a percentage of the notional amount of the underlying pool of reference obligations or up to a pre-agreed set amount, after which the contract will terminate.

7.2.3 Other credit derivatives products

A *credit spread option* has a strike price based on a credit spread above the risk-free rate. The option will be exercised if the credit spread of the underlying reference entity moves above or below this strike spread, depending on whether the contract is a put or a call option respectively. Credit spread options are not commonly traded and are privately negotiated.

In a *step-up credit default swap*, the premium paid by the protection buyer to the protection seller increases after an agreed term. At the step-up date, the protection buyer has the option of terminating the contract. If the contract is not terminated at the step-up date, the premium paid to the protection seller is increased significantly. These types of transactions have been used to reduce capital charges.

A *total return swap*, also known as the *total rate of return swap*, is an agreement under which one party ("the total return payer") transfers the economic risks and rewards associated with an underlying asset to another counterparty ("the total return receiver"). The transfer of risks and rewards is effected by way of an exchange of cash flows pertaining to any change in the value and any income derived from the underlying asset (i.e. the total return).

All total return swap contracts are over-the-counter contracts and currently there are no standard contractual definitions specific to the product.

In contrast to a credit default swap, a total return swap transfers both the credit risk and the market risk associated with an underlying asset. The economic effect for a total return receiver is the same as that derived from owning the asset.

A *credit linked note* is an instrument under which one party ("the issuer") issues a note to another party ("the investor") in return for consideration equal to the principal value (assuming that the note is issued at par) of the note. The coupon and the redemption of the note are linked both to the credit quality of the issuer and to an obligation ("the reference obligation") of a third party ("the reference entity").

Credit linked notes are often listed on a stock exchange. The issuer of a credit linked note is equivalent to the protection buyer in a fully funded credit default swap. The investor in a credit linked note is equivalent to the protection seller.

7.2.4 Collateralized debt obligation (CDO)

At a very simple level, a *collateralized debt obligation* (CDO) is a security backed by a pool of assets (loans, bonds, credit default swaps, etc.) which are packaged together as a portfolio and then tranched.

A CDO comprises a pool of underlying instruments (called *collateral*) against which notes of debt are issued with varying cash flow priority. These notes vary in credit quality depending on the subordination level. At inception when each note is issued, it usually receives a rating from an independent agency (Moody's, S&P, Fitch, etc.). The collateral of a CDO is typically a portfolio of corporate bonds (or sovereign bonds, emerging markets bonds as well) or bank loans or other types of financial facilities (residential or commercial mortgages, leasing, lending, revolving facilities, even other credit derivatives, etc.).

In such a way, CDOs create a customized asset class by allowing various investors to share the risk and return of an underlying pool of debt obligations. Hence, a CDO consists of a set of assets (its collateral portfolio) and a set of liabilities (the issued notes).

A CDO cash flow structure allocates interest income and principal repayment from a collateral pool of different debt instruments to a prioritized collection of securities notes, which are commonly called *tranches*. A standard prioritizing structure is a simple subordination, i.e. *senior* CDO notes are paid before *mezzanine* and lower subordinated notes are paid, with any residual cash flow, to an *equity* piece. The tranches are ordered so that losses in interest or principal of the collateral are absorbed first by the lowest level tranche and then in order to the next tranche, and so on. The lowest tranche is the riskiest one, and because it has to respond immediately to the incurred losses it is called the equity tranche. The mechanism for distributing the losses to the various tranches is called the *waterfall*. Losses occur when there is a certain kind of *credit event*, explicitly defined in the offering circular. A credit event is usually either a default of the collateral, or a failure to pay off the collateral or other specified event according to the latest ISDA agreements.[4] In either case, the market value of the collateral drops; and, consequently, the issued related notes are usually hit by a credit downgrade and by a market value slump.

Obviously, credit events are not independent, and their number is uncertain too. Clearly, a diversification helps to manage investors' risk and return profile, and an investor in a particular tranche would like to know the probability distribution of losses to the underlying pool of debt. The probability distribution depends on both the probability of a credit event and on the relationship between two or more credit events (the relationship between the default behavior of different obligors is called *hidden linkage*). Hence, the underlying dependence structure is fundamental for any quantitative analysis on potential losses.

In the financial markets there are many kinds of CDOs. The most well-known types of CDO are the cash flow CDOs, the market-value CDOs and the synthetic CDOs.

A *cash flow* CDO is one for which the collateral portfolio is not subject to active trading by the CDO manager. The uncertainty concerning the interest and principal repayments is determined by the number and timing of the collateral assets that default. Losses due to defaults are the main source of risk.

A *market-value* CDO is one in which the CDO tranches receive payments based essentially on the mark to market return of the collateral pool, as determined largely by the trading performance of the CDO manager. A potential investor needs to evaluate the ability of the manager and his or her institutional structure.

A *synthetic* CDO is one whose notes are synthetic, so the collateral portfolio is created synthetically (i.e. it is not held by the structure but remains in the originator's book). Each note pays a fixed spread (commonly, in these structures, the spread is a fixed premium added to a predetermined market floating rate, i.e. LIBOR rate).

Synthetic CDOs are very common in the so-called *SuperSenior* transactions. In this case the higher protected tranche in the reference CDO (called SuperSenior because its credit quality has to be higher than Aaa at inception) is the reference entity in a credit default swap contract. In this contract one counterparty buys default protection with respect to this SuperSenior tranche. The contract has a given maturity, but, obviously, it will terminate early if the credit event occurs. The protection seller receives a premium (expressed in basis points per annum on the notional amount) from the protection buyer that will receive a payment upon the occurrence of the credit event in respect of the reference entity, i.e. the SuperSenior tranche in the CDO structure. Normally, the default payment is given by the notional amount minus the recovery amount *(net loss)*. Since no asset is transferred, there is no need to fund the position. For this reason these transactions are unfunded.

---

[4] We refer readers to the J. P. Morgan "Guide to credit derivatives" (2000), and to O'Kane (2001) and Davies, Hewer and Rivett (2001) for an extensive discussion of these concepts.

We are interested here in synthetic or cash flow CDOs, thus avoiding an analysis of the trading behavior of CDO managers, because, otherwise, the analysis would take into account microeconomic utility functions and invoke other concepts from Game Theory.

Basket default swaps (BDSs) and CDOs are essentially default correlation products; hence, the main aspect for pricing and risk monitoring is to model the joint default dependency. The modeling of dependent defaults is difficult because there is very little historical data available about joint defaults and because the prices of these instruments are not quoted (i.e. there are usually no reliable quotes in the market). Therefore, the models cannot be calibrated, neither to defaults nor to prices.

Duffie and Garleanu (2001) address the risk analysis and market valuation of CDOs in a jump-diffusion setting for correlated default intensities. They capture the default dependence by assuming that each intensity process is given by the sum of two affine processes. One process models the common aspect of different obligors, and the other concerns the idiosyncratic default risk specific to each obligor. Their framework is theoretically appealing but there are some disadvantages: the default correlation that can be reached with this approach is typically too low when compared with empirical default correlations, and, furthermore, it is not easy to analyze the resulting default dependency structure.

An extension of this approach are the infectious default models by Davis and Lo (2001) and Jarrow and Yu (2001), which give more realistic default correlations. The major task in these models is undoubtedly the estimation and calibration to historical data.

Copula methods are emerging as the favored pricing approach due to the simplicity in simulation and calibration. Li (2000) proposes a methodology for the pricing of multi-names contingent securities. Li proposed the Gaussian copula to capture the joint default dependency in the collateral portfolio. Li's methodology has been implemented into RiskMetrics CDO Manager software, and may be seen as an extended version of the CreditMetrics framework.[5] Nowadays this product is well known in the financial environment and many financial institutions around the world use it for pricing and risk monitoring CDOs. Also Frey and McNeil (2001) analyze the effect of the choice of different copulas on the resulting return distribution of a loan portfolio, and Mashal and Zeevi (2002) investigate comovements between financial assets by introducing a T-copula structure and comparing this copula with the Gaussian one with a likelihood ratio test.

Schönbucher and Schubert (2001) present a method to incorporate dynamic default dependency in intensity-based default risk models. They use a copula for the times of default, which is combined with the individual intensity-based models for the defaults of the obligors. The authors do not offer an empirical comparison in order to select an appropriate copula function.

In this chapter, we would like to provide a framework that allows us to price these multiple underlying credit securities, and, also, to manage their risk. This approach is a reduced-form approach as it avoids an accurate definition of the underlying stochastic default process, concentrating instead on the dependence structure between pool obligors from a statistical perspective. Since these products are *correlation products*, i.e. investors are buying correlation risk, the dependence structure in the pool is essential for pricing, hedging and risk managing purposes. Our approach is to use an adequate measure of dependence for the collateralized portfolio, then to adopt multivariate survival and copulas frameworks to

---

[5] CreditMetrics is a widely used portfolio-based credit methodology. Refer to the *Credit Metrics Guide*. RiskMetrics Group http://www.riskmetrics.com.

define an underlying dependence structure. The model incorporates the clustering of default over time due to default correlation. By revisiting statistical survival analysis, it is possible to construct a model for correlated times until default that has to be simulated. Finally, our methodology allows us to price CDOs (and basket default swaps or percentage loss as well) and to manage their risk by applying the appropriate pay-off functions to each series of simulated times until default.

7.3 COPULA APPROACH

One of the main issues concerning credit risk is without doubt the modeling of joint distributions between default times. Li (2000) suggests that a Gaussian copula could be a suitable tool for such a problem. The key issue of this framework is to shift the focus from modeling the dependency between default events up to a fixed time horizon (i.e. discrete variables) to the dependency between default times which are continuous random variables and do not depend on an arbitrarily chosen time horizon.

We introduce the topic by briefly reviewing the survival time approach to single default modeling and its calibration, and then examining the joint ones.

7.3.1 Review of single survival time modeling and calibration

Li (2000) describes a default by a survival function $S(t) = \Pr(\tau > t)$, which indicates the probability that a security will attain age t, in the spirit of the reduced form models of Chapter 1. The survival time τ is called the time until default, or default time. If S is differentiable, by defining the hazard rate or intensity $h(u) = -S'(u)/S(u)$, the survival function can be expressed in terms of the hazard rate function

$$S(t) = \exp\left(-\int_0^t h(u)\,du\right)$$

and the default arrival is an inhomogeneous Poisson process.

A typical assumption is that the hazard rate is a constant, h. In this case, the survival time follows an exponential distribution with parameter h and the default arrival follows a homogeneous Poisson process.

The survival time distribution may be easily generalized by assuming a Weibull distribution.

Duffie and Singleton (1998) and Lando (1998) consider h as a (non-negative, continuous, adapted) stochastic process: in this case the process of default arrivals, as we recalled in Chapter 1, is a Cox process. Under a Cox process the default time τ can be equivalently characterized in one of the following ways:

$$\tau := \inf\left\{t : \int_0^t h_s\,ds \geq \theta\right\}$$

where θ is an exponential r.v. of parameter 1, independent of the intensity process, or:

$$\tau := \inf\left\{t \geq 0 : \check{N} > 0\right\}$$

where $\check{N}$ is the Cox process.

Under the Cox assumption, modeling a default process is equivalent to modeling the intensity process. As there are many similarities between the hazard and the short rate, many short rate processes may be borrowed to model the hazard rate. The affine class is particularly appealing (see Chapter 1).

In both the Poisson and Cox cases, the hazard rate function used to characterize the distribution of the survival time can be obtained for a given credit in many ways:

- From historical default rates provided by rating agencies;
- By using the Merton approach (refer to Delianedis & Geske, 1998);
- Extracting default probabilities by using market observable information, such as asset swap spread, credit default swap spread or corporate bond prices (refer to Li, 1998).

In the first case one obtains the intensity or intensity process under the historical measure, while in the second and third cases it is obtained under the risk neutral measure.

It is shown under the Duffie and Singleton (1998) approach that a defaultable instrument can be valued as if it were a default-free instrument by discounting the defaultable cash flow at a credit risk adjusted factor, as follows: let Y be a cash flow (random payment) contingent on no default occurrence before T. Its value at time t is under zero recovery

$$
E\left[\exp\left(-\int_t^T r_s \, ds\right) \mathbf{1}_{\{r > T\}} Y | \varsigma_t\right] = E\left[\exp\left(-\int_t^T (r_s + h_s) \, ds\right) Y | F_t\right] \tag{7.1}
$$

where the expectation is taken, as usual, under a risk-neutral probability

- ς_t is the market filtration, $\varsigma_t = F_t \vee H_t$
- H_t is the filtration generated by defaults: $H_t = \sigma(\tau_i \wedge s, s \leqslant t, i = 1, 2, \ldots, I)$
- F_t is the default-free filtration

and Y is F_T-measurable.

Formula (7.1) is crucial in two respects. First, loosely speaking, increasing the short rate by the intensity rate permits us to take default into account, and keep using the standard rule: take as fair value the expected discounted value of the final pay-off. Second, the replacement of the enlarged filtration ς_t with the default-free one turns out to be of particular usefulness in practical applications, for obvious reasons.

In addition, if the underlying factors affecting default and those affecting the interest rate are independent, the credit risk adjusted discount factor is the product of the risk-free discount factor, $E[\exp(-\int_t^T r_s \, ds)]$, and the pure credit discount factor, $E[\exp(-\int_t^T h_s \, ds)]$.

Under this framework, and the assumption of a piecewise constant hazard rate function (extracted from some market data, i.e. asset swap spread or credit default swap spread at different maturities), it is possible to specify the distribution of the survival time.

Our interest will be a credit portfolio of n assets and, in the following application, we will price some multi-name credit derivatives. Therefore, we need to analyze the corresponding multivariate problem and the joint survival times distribution.

7.3.2 Multiple survival times: modeling

Suppose you have I different firms, each with a Cox default arrival process, and define the default time or survival time of the ith firm, τ_i, together with its intensity at time s, h_s^i, and its threshold, θ_i. These quantities are related by the fact that

$$\tau_i := \inf\left\{t : \int_0^t h_s^i \, ds \geqslant \theta_i\right\}$$

Multiple default times and their association can be introduced in three different ways.

First, one can correlate directly the intensity processes of the I firms, $h_s^i, i = 1, \ldots, I$. However, as Jouanin et al. (2001) show, correlating intensities does not permit us to obtain high dependence between default times.

Second, one can adopt the approach of Li (2000): the joint survival function of the I firms,

$$S(t_1, t_2, \ldots, t_I) = \Pr(\tau_1 > t_1, \tau_2 > t_2, \ldots, \tau_I > t_I)$$

has, by the version of Sklar's theorem in section 2.6, Chapter 2, a (survival) copula representation,

$$S(t_1, t_2, \ldots, t_I) = \overline{C}_{\tau_1, \tau_2, \ldots, \tau_I}(S_1(t_1), S_2(t_2), \ldots, S_I(t_I))$$

Li models $\overline{C}$ directly using a Gaussian assumption.

Third, one can correlate the thresholds θ_i by assuming a specific copula for them:

$$\mathcal{S}(m_1, m_2, \ldots, m_I) = \Pr(\theta_1 > m_1, \theta_2 > m_2, \ldots, \theta_I > m_I)$$
$$= \overline{C}_{\theta_1, \theta_2, \ldots, \theta_I}(\mathcal{S}_1(m_1), \mathcal{S}_2(m_2), \ldots, \mathcal{S}_I(m_I))$$

where $\mathcal{S}_i$ is the survival function of θ_i, $\mathcal{S}$ is their joint one. This is the so-called threshold approach of Giesecke (2001) and Schönbucher and Schubert (2001). In this framework, one can derive the (survival) copula between the default times from the threshold one as follows:

$$\overline{C}_{\tau_1, \tau_2, \ldots, \tau_I}(S_1(t_1), \ldots, S_I(t_I))$$
$$= E\left[\overline{C}_{\theta_1, \theta_2, \ldots, \theta_I}\left(\exp\left(-\int_0^{t_1} h_s^1 \, ds\right), \ldots, \exp\left(-\int_0^{t_I} h_s^I \, ds\right)\right)\right]$$

In what follows we will not discuss which of the second and third approaches is "the better", since we will assume deterministic intensities, under which they coincide[6]:

$$\overline{C}_{\tau_1, \tau_2, \ldots, \tau_I} = \overline{C}_{\theta_1, \theta_2, \ldots, \theta_I}$$

In particular, we will refer to Li's approach, which can be specified as follows: the author extends the CreditMetrics model to a Gaussian copula model capturing the timing risk of default. In this setup the pairwise default correlation of survival times is taken by the pairwise asset correlation (refer to the CreditMetrics user manual). Each survival time for

---

[6] However, a comparison between the two approaches is given in Jouanin et al. (2001).

the ith credit in the portfolio, τ_i, has a distribution function, $F_i(t)$. Using a normal copula we obtain the joint distribution of the survival times as:

$$F(t_1, t_2, \ldots, t_n) = \Phi_n(\Phi^{-1}(F_1(t_1)), \Phi^{-1}(F_2(t_2)), \ldots, \Phi^{-1}(F_n(t_n)))$$

where Φ_n is the n-dimensional normal cumulative function with correlation matrix Σ (given by the asset correlation matrix).

In order to simulate correlated survival times we introduce another series of random variables $Y_1, Y_2, \ldots, Y_n$ such that

$$Y_i = \Phi^{-1}(F_i(t_i)) \quad \text{for } i = 1, 2, \ldots, n$$

There is a one-to-one mapping between Y and τ. Li (2000) sums up in the following scheme:

- Simulate $Y_1, Y_2, \ldots, Y_n$ from an n-dimensional normal distribution with correlation matrix given by the asset correlation of the underlying credit.
- Obtain $\tau_1, \tau_2, \ldots, \tau_n$ using the relation $\tau_i = F_i^{-1}(\Phi(Y_i))$ for $i = 1, 2, \ldots, n$.

With each simulation run it is possible to generate survival times for all credits in the portfolio. With this information one can price any credit derivatives structure written on the portfolio.

As for risk monitoring, one has to look at the distribution of losses and take its percentiles. Obviously, the simulation allows us to determine this distribution easily by taking into account the CDO's waterfall scheme and the simulated losses.

The ability to measure risk and assess prices relies on the details of each deal's liability structure (this point is very important, especially when one has to analyze a cash flow CDO where, sometimes, the waterfall structure is particularly tailored to the deal, and may involve a certain kind of overcollateralization test to be performed and other particularities that have to be taken into account).

This approach may be extended to other copula functions by applying the sampling algorithms described in Chapter 5.

7.3.3 Multiple defaults: calibration

If one could rely on no-arbitrage pricing of some multi-name credit derivative, it would be possible to infer the implied default correlation (or concordance measure, in general), in the same way as one could do with derivatives on multiple underlyings. However, we have already remarked that the multi-name credit derivatives market is – at the present stage – very illiquid. Therefore the relevant copulas can be calibrated in one of the following ways:

- Estimating discrete default correlations, i.e. the correlations between the default indicators at a given horizon, from historical joint default occurrences (see, for instance, Nagpal & Bahar, 2001, Erturk, 2000, and the joint default probabilities in Carty, 1997): this method is quite unsatisfactory, since the margins are Bernoulli r.v.s.

- Estimating from the same observations the survival time correlations, i.e. the correlations between the times to default, which are not Bernoulli.
- Using Moody's diversity score, as in Jouanin et al. (2001) or Giesecke (2001).
- "Approximating" them through equity correlation, in the spirit of structural models.

We will take the last approach, as in most market practice (see, for instance, CreditMetric^{TM} and KMV's Portfolio Manager^{TM}).

This approach may be extended to other copula functions by applying the sampling algorithms described in Chapter 5. Obviously for multiple underlying credit instruments the simulations from elliptical copulas, such as Gaussian and the Student t, are much easier than what happens for other copulas because it is often really difficult to derive recursive formulas to get the desired draws within a general n-variate setting.

In the following subsections we explain the pricing and risk monitoring for CDOs and BDSs. We follow the approach and notation explained in the factor copula approach (i.e. marginal distributions independent given a common latent factor) of Laurent and Gregory (2002).

7.3.4 Loss distribution and the pricing of CDOs

Our aim is to compute the fair price at time 0 as the expected pay-off at time 0 for a standard CDO. For simplicity, we also assume independence between default dates and interest rates, since the most important issue we address is the modeling of dependence between default dates. Similarly we assume that the recovery rates on the underlying assets are independent of default times and interest rates; hence, we would like to proceed as conditioned to the joint determination of the interest rates and recovery rates.

We consider n reference obligors with a nominal amount A_i and a recovery rate R_i with $i = 1, 2, \ldots, n$. $L_i = (1 - R_i)A_i$ will denote the loss given default (or net loss) for the ith credit. Let τ_i be the default time of the ith name and $N_i(t) = \mathbf{1}_{\{\tau_i < t\}}$ be the counting process which jumps from 0 to 1 at the default time of name i. Finally $L(t)$ will denote the cumulative loss on the collateral portfolio at time t:

$$L(t) = \sum_{i=1}^{n} L_i N_i(t) \tag{7.2}$$

which is thus a pure jump process.

Let us consider a tranche of a CDO, where the default payment leg pays all losses that occur on the collateral portfolio above a threshold C and below a threshold D, where $0 \leqslant C \leqslant D \leqslant \sum_{i=1}^{n} A_i$.

When $C = 0$ we consider the equity tranche; if $C > 0$ and $D < \sum_{i=1}^{n} A_i$ we speak of the mezzanine tranches, and when $D = \sum_{i=1}^{n} A_i$ we consider senior or SuperSenior tranches.

Let $M(t)$ be the cumulative losses on a given tranche, hence

$$M(t) = \begin{cases} 0 & \text{if } L(t) \leqslant C \\ L(t) - C & \text{if } C \leqslant L(t) \leqslant D \\ D - C & \text{if } L(t) \geqslant D \end{cases} \tag{7.3}$$

or equivalently:

$$M(t) = (L(t) - C)\mathbf{1}_{\{C,D\}}(L(t)) + (D - C)\mathbf{1}_{\{D,\sum_{i=1}^{n} A_i\}}(L(t))$$

We notice that as $L(t)$, $M(t)$ is a pure jump process. By using this framework the default payments are the increments on $M(t)$. Hence there is a payment on every jump of $M(t)$.

Since $M(t)$ is an increasing process, we can define Stieltjes integrals with respect to $M(t)$. But, $M(t)$ is constant apart from jump times, so any Stieltjes integral with respect to $M(t)$ turns out to be a discrete sum with respect to every jump time.

Let $B(0, t)$ be the discount factor for the maturity t, and let T denote the maturity of the CDO. Hence, we can write the price of the default payment leg of the given tranche as:

$$E^P\left[\int_0^T B(0, t)\, \mathrm{d}M(t)\right]$$

where P denotes a risk-neutral probability measure.[7]

The term within the square brackets is the sum of the discounted default payments on the tranche. By using the integration by parts and Fubini's theorem we have:

$$E^P\left[\int_0^T B(0, t)\, \mathrm{d}M(t)\right] = B(0, T)E^P[M(T)] + \int_0^T f(0, t)B(0, t)E^P[M(t)]\, \mathrm{d}t \quad (7.4)$$

where $f(0, t)$ denotes the instantaneous forward rate:

$$f(0, t)B(0, t) = -\frac{\mathrm{d}B(0, t)}{\mathrm{d}t}$$

The default leg may be discretized as follows[8]:

$$\sum_{i=1}^{\varkappa} B(0, t_i)\left[M(t_i) - M(t_{i-1})\right]$$

where $t_0 = 0$ and $t_{\varkappa} = T$, $\varkappa$ indicates the number of payment dates between successive defaults by the maturity T.

We would like to remark that we only need the first moment of the cumulative loss on the tranche. This can be computed when the distribution of total losses has been simulated via a pure Monte Carlo approach.

The fair spread (or equivalently the fair premium) of that tranche has to be found by putting into an equivalence the default leg with the premium leg.

---

[7] We observe that the risk-neutral measure P is not likely to be unique, since the market is incomplete in this setup without further assumptions on the structure of the market. What we have in mind, and what we need here, is that the market chooses some P that we take as given. The same observation will apply many times in what follows.

[8] We assume that the net default payments occur at $\varkappa$ discrete dates between 0 and T.

In this discrete time case the premium leg may be written as:

$$
E^P \left[\sum_{i=1}^{m} \Delta_{i-1,i} \cdot W \cdot B(0, t_i) \cdot [D - C] \cdot \mathbf{1}_{(L(t) \leqslant C)} \right.
$$

$$
\left. + \sum_{i=1}^{m} \Delta_{i-1,i} \cdot W \cdot B(0, t_i) \cdot [D - L(t)] \cdot \mathbf{1}_{(C \leqslant L(t) \leqslant D)} \right]
$$

where $D - C$ is the tranche size at inception, and where m denotes all premium payment dates, t_i denotes the premium payment date, $\Delta_{i-1,i}$ denotes the tenor between successive premium payment dates which takes into account the day count convention, W is the fair spread, $D - L(t)$ is the outstanding tranche notional at time $t \in [0, T]$ and, clearly, $0 \leqslant M(t) \leqslant D - C$ since $0 \leqslant L(t) \leqslant \sum_{i=1}^{n} A_i$ for all t.

This formula may be written also as:

$$
E^P \left[\sum_{i=1}^{m} \Delta_{i-1,i} \cdot W \cdot B(0, t_i) \min \{ \max [D - L(t), 0], D - C \} \right] \tag{7.5}
$$

In a continuous time setting, if we suppose that the premium is paid instantaneously, we may express the discounted value at time 0 of the premium leg of a CDO as

$$
W \cdot E^P \left[\int_0^T B(0, t) g(L(t)) \, \mathrm{d}t \right]
$$

where $g(L(t)) = \min \{ \max [D - L(t), 0], D - C \}$.

Hence, the fair (equilibrium) instantaneous spread (or premium) W is given by

$$
W = \frac{E^P \left[\int_0^T B(0, t) \, \mathrm{d}M(t) \right]}{E^P \left[\int_0^T B(0, t) g(L(t)) \, \mathrm{d}t \right]}
$$

We remark that the only thing we need in order to price each CDO tranche is to obtain the simulated counting process via the chosen copula framework.

Moreover we stress that we model the copula of the times to default of the different obligors, without considering the possible stochastic dynamics of the default intensities; since our default intensities are assumed to be deterministic functions of the time, i.e. constant stepwise functions where each step is given by the corresponding single name credit default swap at the analysis date (refer to section 7.5, Technical Appendix, for more details).

7.3.5 Loss distribution and the pricing of homogeneous basket default swaps

We consider the pricing of a basket default swap. In a first-to-default swap there is a default payment at the first-to-default time. In a k out of n basket default swap ($k \leqslant n$), where n denotes the number of obligors, there is a default payment at the kth default time. The payment corresponds to the non-recovered part of the defaulted asset.

If the notional amounts of all credits in the basket are equal then we refer to a homogeneous basket, i.e. $A_i = A$ for every $i = 1, 2, \ldots, n$.

As before, we compute separately the price of the premium leg and of the default leg. The basket premium is such that the prices of the two legs are equal.

We make the same assumptions as in the previous chapter for the interest rates and the recovery rates. Moreover, for simplicity, we do not take into account accrued premium payments between payment dates.

We use the same notation as before.

$N(t) = \sum_{i=1}^{n} N_i(t)$ denotes the counting process indicating the total number of defaults in the basket. If $N(t) \geqslant k$ the basket payments are exhausted. If $0 \leqslant N(t) < k$ the premium is paid on the outstanding notional for the ith underlying credit A for a homogeneous basket.

The discounted expectation of premium payment is given by:

$$E^P \left[\sum_{j=1}^{m} \Delta_{j-1,j} \cdot W \cdot B(0, t_j) \cdot A \cdot \mathbf{1}_{\{N(t) < k\}} \right] \tag{7.6}$$

The homogeneity assumption allows us to compute the price of the default payment leg knowing the distribution of the number of defaults only.

We denote by $S_k(t) = P(N(t) < k)$ the survival function of the kth default time $\tau_{(k)}$, i.e. $S_k(t) = P(N(t) < k) = P(\tau_{(k)} > t) = 1 - F_k(t)$; hence $dS_k(t) = S_k(t + dt) - S_k(t)$ is the probability that the kth default time occurs in $[t, t + dt)$.

Under previous assumptions on interest rates and recovery rates (for simplicity we assume that the recovery rate is the same for all names), we can then write the price of the kth-to-default payment leg as:

$$E^P[(1 - R) \cdot A \cdot B(0, \tau_k) \cdot \mathbf{1}_{(0 \leqslant \tau_{(k)} \leqslant T)}] = (1 - R) \cdot A \int_0^T B(0, t) \, dF_k(t) \tag{7.7}$$

where T is the maturity of the homogeneous k out of n default basket.

The default leg in brackets may also be written as follows:

$$- (1 - R) \cdot A \int_0^T B(0, t) \, dS_k(t)$$

$$= (1 - R) \cdot A \left(1 - S_k(T) B(0, T) + \int_0^T S_k(t) \, dB(0, t) \right)$$

$$= (1 - R) \cdot A \left(1 - S_k(T) B(0, T) - \int_0^T f(0, t) B(0, t) S_k(t) \, dt \right)$$

where, as before, $f(0, t)$ denotes the instantaneous forward rate:

$$f(0, t) B(0, t) = - \frac{dB(0, t)}{dt}$$

In the following empirical application we simulate via the copula framework the distribution of the times to default number and the distribution of each kth default time with $k = 1, 2, \ldots, n$.

Table 7.1   Collateral portfolio description

Initial portfolio par value	500 000 000 euros
Number of obligors	50
Moody's diversity score	29.25
Maturity date	18/05/2006

Table 7.2   Tranches of the CDO

Tranche name	Notional in euros
SS	437 500 000
A	11 000 000
B	19 500 000
C	20 000 000
Equity	12 000 000

As before, in a continuous time setting, we have:

$$W = \frac{E^P \left[(1 - R) \int_0^T B(0, t) \, dF_k(t) \right]}{E^P \left[\int_0^T B(0, t) F_k(t) \, dt \right]}$$

7.4   APPLICATION: PRICING AND RISK MONITORING A CDO

7.4.1   Dow Jones EuroStoxx50 CDO

In this section we extend the empirical example shown in Meneguzzo and Vecchiato (2004). This empirical application, as far as we know, is the first application to a real market CDO and a real market basket default swap (BDS).

We consider a synthetic CDO called *EuroStoxx50* because it is composed by 50 single name credit default swaps on 50 credits that belong to the DJ EuroStoxx50 equity index. Each reference credit has a notional equal to 10 million euros, hence the collateral portfolio has a nominal amount equal to 500 million euros. The inception date of this CDO was May 18, 2001, and it lasts 5 years with a maturity on May 18, 2006. This CDO is composed by five tranches with the standard prioritized scheme. The riskiest tranche is the equity tranche, which did not have a Moody's rating at inception, then, in order, we have four other tranches respectively rated at inception Baa3, Aa2, AAA and, finally, the less risky tranche called SuperSenior (SS). Tables 7.1 and 7.2 report the CDO structure. Up to now this CDO has not experienced any default.

The analysis date is set on August 30, 2002. We report some pictures depicting the collateral by rating at the analysis date, and the collateral description by industry sector (see Figures 7.1 and 7.2).

7.4.2   Application: basket default swap

The description of the basket default swap we are going to analyze may be found in Tables 7.3 and 7.4.

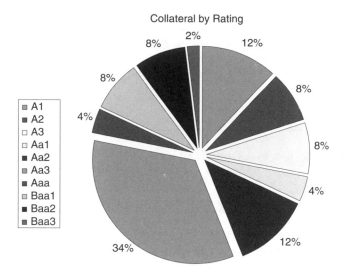

Figure 7.1   Collateral description by rating

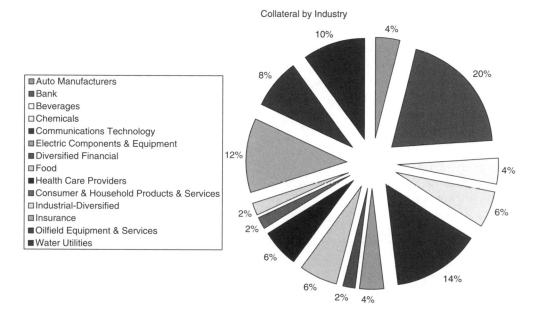

Figure 7.2   Collateral description by industry sector

Table 7.3   Basket default swap

Initial par value	40 000 000 euros
Number of obligors	4
Moody's diversity score	3.25
Maturity date	30/08/2007

Table 7.4   Basket default swap at August 30, 2002

Name	Amount (euros)	5y CDS spread	Country – Industry sector
ABN Amro	10 000 000	40	NL – Banking & Finance
Bayer AG	10 000 000	45	DE – Pharmaceutical
Renault	10 000 000	110	FR – Automotive
Telecom Italia	10 000 000	155	IT – Telecommunication

In this contract the first-to-default swap stated (contractual) spread has been fixed to 270 bps.

7.4.3   Empirical application for the EuroStoxx50 CDO

We follow the IFM method by using the corresponding equity prices for each obligor both in the CDO and in the default basket. Obviously this is a trick solution because, as may be seen, one cannot observe a time to default series, so one is compelled to use alternative proxies to get the desired parameter both for the marginals and for the copula itself. As always in the financial market, the equity prices are the best proxies for such a task.

In the following we report some graphs regarding the behavior of such equity returns. Daily equity returns for each reference credit go from September 1, 2000 to August 30, 2002 (Figures 7.3 and 7.4).

As can be seen, the returns pattern shows evidence of heteroskedasticity behavior common to all daily equity returns. We decide to overcome this fact by taking a GARCH(1, 1) filter with Student t error term in order to capture the fatness of the return series tails. For the sake of completeness we report this model as follows:

$$y_t = \sigma_t \varepsilon_t$$
$$\sigma_t^2 = \alpha + \beta y_{t-1}^2 + \gamma \sigma_{t-1}^2$$

where $\varepsilon_t \sim$ i.i.d. $t_\upsilon (0, 1)$.

The estimation method is the standard QMLE. We report some results in Table 7.5. These results (except Renault) are for the obligors that belong both to the EuroStoxx50 CDO and to the basket default swap.

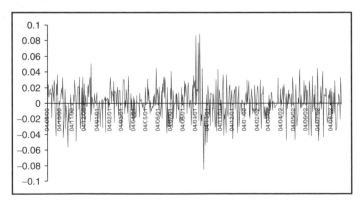

Figure 7.3   Daily equity returns: Telecom Italia

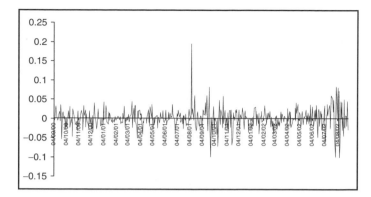

Figure 7.4   Daily equity returns: Bayer AG

Table 7.5   Estimated GARCH(1, 1) parameters and standard errors

	ABN Amro	Bayer AG	Renault	Telecom Italia
α	0.00002	0.00003	0.00005	0.00003
Std err.	0.00000	0.00000	0.00000	0.00000
β	0.15757	0.13798	0.10433	0.07372
Std err.	0.00092	0.00174	0.00037	0.00033
γ	0.81121	0.80056	0.83082	0.87794
Std err.	0.00061	0.00147	0.00032	0.00014
υ	7.67061	8.02422	6.25853	5.39743
Std err.	0.09881	0.06757	0.05987	0.06566

As expected, all GARCH parameters in Table 7.5 are statistically significant.

As for the joint behavior, we consider the normal, the Student t and two Archimedean copulas.

When we adopt the normal copula we only need to identify the variance–covariance matrix. An important point is to determine a robust estimate of that matrix. As noted by Lindskog (2000), the Pearson correlation estimator is not robust for heavy tailed distributions, so the author recommends the use of Kendall's tau, especially when the dimensionality increases. In our case, we have 50 dimensions, and all the equity prices show fatness in the tails. Hence, we adopt an estimation for the variance–covariance matrix obtained by computing the empirical Kendall tau coefficient between each pair of equity series.

The empirical Kendall's tau is computed as presented in section 7.5.

We report the scatter plot for some reference entities where it is possible to see more dispersion in the tails (Figures 7.5 and 7.6). For such a reason we consider a Student t copula.

When we use the Student t copula we need to identify the degrees of freedom parameter. We choose to estimate it by the IFM method since, previously, we had estimated all marginal distributions (Student t c.d.f. is applied to the standardized residuals obtained from the Student t–GARCH(1, 1) processes in order to map them on $[0, 1]^n$).

Figure 7.7 presents the graph of the likelihood function for different degrees of freedom. As can be seen, the MLE for the degrees of freedom parameter is approximately equal to 8.

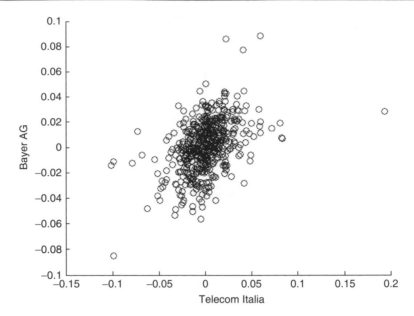

Figure 7.5   Scatter plot: Bayer AG–Telecom Italia

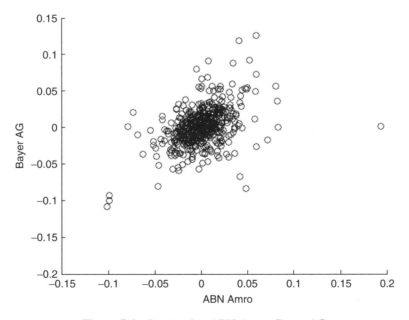

Figure 7.6   Scatter plot: ABN Amro–Bayer AG

We find statistical significance for this parameter by using a statistical bootstrap procedure (refer to Efron & Tibshirani, 1993).

The same approach has been applied to the Clayton copula after having determined its copula density (see section 7.5 for a formal derivation).

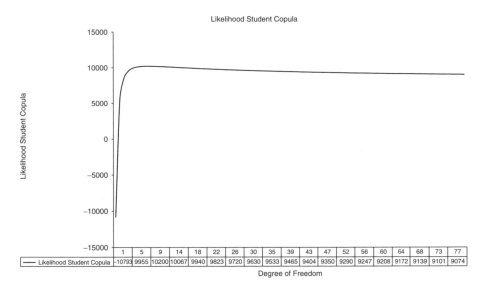

Figure 7.7   Student copula likelihood

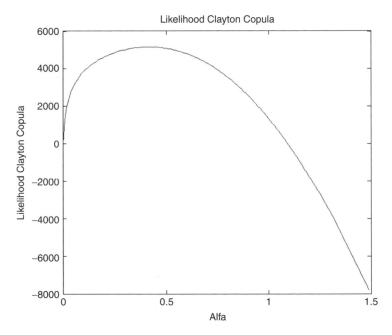

Figure 7.8   Clayton copula likelihood

As before we adopt the IFM method to obtain an estimate for the Archimedean copula parameter. In Figure 7.8 we present the form of the log-likelihood function.

The IFM estimator for alpha is equal to 0.48. As before, its significance is supported by a bootstrap procedure. In order to get the simulations for each obligor's time to default, we assume a marginal density for each obligor's time to default, according to an exponential density for which the hazard term has been derived by the credit default swap curve at

August 30, 2002, for each obligor in the collateral (see Table 7.6). Each hazard term is assumed as follows:

$$h_t = \frac{S_t}{1 - R}$$

where the recovery rate R is fixed to 30%, as is common practice, in order to price the credit default swap contract, and S_t represents the credit default swap spread at a given term t.

In Table 7.6 we report for each obligor the credit default swap curve as at August 30, 2002 (the analysis date).

We would like to refer the readers to section 7.5 for a more extensive discussion and further details about the time to default derivation, given the hazard rate.

We also present some histograms in order to show the simulated time to default distribution for some reference credit in the collateral (Table 7.7).

Since, for pricing purposes, we are interested in the number of defaults that may occur prior to maturity of the CDO, we report in Table 7.8 the percentage of these times, for some obligors, in 10 000 simulations before maturity, expressed in annual points (3.77 years).

7.4.4 EuroStoxx50 pricing and risk monitoring

In our empirical application we generate, for each reference credit in the collateral portfolio, an exogenous recovery rate from an independent, Beta distribution[9] that is across all obligors and independent from the times to default and the interest rates.

We report the results for each chosen copula in Tables 7.9, 7.10 and 7.11. The fair spread is computed by equaling the premium leg and the default leg of the contract for each chosen copula. Clearly, this is related to the expected loss as shown previously.

The loss statistics for each copula are reported in Tables 7.12, 7.13 and 7.14.

In the previous tables each level of VaR was computed from the percentile of each tranche's cumulative losses distribution. As can be seen, results from the elliptical copulas are close to each other. The Student copula is able to capture more fatness in the tail.

The results from the Clayton copula do not appear to be useful, because this copula is not able to capture the upper tail dependence. Tail dependence is important to obtain more simulated times to default before the deal matures. We will return to this point in the following basket default swap empirical analysis.

Finally, we present the Box–Wishart plot for the collateral losses. As can be seen, the Student copula gives more losses than any other simulated copula (Figure 7.9).

---

[9] The Beta distribution has a range $0 \leqslant x \leqslant 1$ and shape parameters $v > 0$, $\omega > 0$. Its density is given by:

$$\frac{x^{v-1}(1-x)^{\omega-1}}{B(v, \omega)}$$

where $B(v, \omega) = \int_0^1 u^{v-1}(1-u)^{\omega-1} du$.

Its mean is equal to $v/(v + \omega)$ and its variance is equal to $v\omega/[(v + \omega)^2(v + \omega + 1)]$.

We choose the parameters v, ω by fixing the mean equal to 50% and variance equal to 30% (these data are reported in a latest Moody's study on recoveries from defaulted corporate bonds).

Table 7.6 Collateral obligors and mid-market CDS 1-, 3- and 5-year spreads at August 30, 2002

Obligors	1 yr	3 yr	5 yr	Obligors	1 yr	3 yr	5 yr
ABN Amro	20	30	40	Generali	40	55	60
Aegon NV	150	230	230	HypoVereinsbank	20	25	32
Ahold	140	150	160	ING Groep	30	35	49
Air Liquide	35	50	50	LVMH	170	180	195
Alcatel SA	1500	1500	1500	L'Oreal	15	22	30
Allianz AG	40	50	75	Munich Re	50	70	75
Aventis	25	40	45	Nokia	100	140	140
Axa	130	200	200	Philips	130	160	170
Basf	15	30	30	Pinault-Printemps	420	420	420
Bayer AG	27	35	45	Repsol YPF	525	525	525
BBVA	25	40	45	Royal Dutch Petrol.	10	20	25
BNP Paribas	20	25	30	Royal KPN NV	250	290	315
BSCH	45	60	65	RWE	30	45	65
Carrefour	40	50	65	San Paolo-IMI	20	25	40
DaimlerChrysler	110	140	155	Sanofi-Synthelabo	30	40	50
Danone	15	30	30	Siemens	45	60	70
Deutsche Bank	22	35	40	Société Generale	25	30	38
Deutsche Telecom	300	345	335	SUEZ	50	70	95
Dresdner Bank	20	30	40	Telecom Italia	135	155	155
E.on	35	60	60	Telefonica	160	170	205
Endesa SA	75	100	100	TotalFinaElf	10	15	25
Enel Spa	40	50	60	Unicredito	20	30	37
ENI	15	25	32	Unilever	25	35	45
Fortis	30	40	45	Vivendi Universal	975	1150	1150
France Telecom	435	460	470	Volkswagen	50	65	78

Table 7.7 Histogram of simulated default times for Bayer AG and Air Liquide

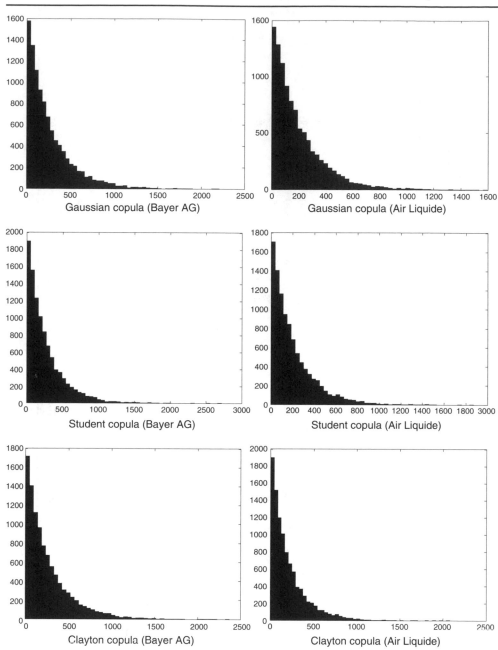

Table 7.8   Percentage of default times before CDO maturity

	Gaussian	Student	Clayton
Air Liquide	0.0154%	0.0177%	0.0137%
Pinault-Printemps	0.1968%	0.1983%	0.1415%
Bayer AG	0.0133%	0.0137%	0.0106%
BNP Paribas	0.0101%	0.0108%	0.0094%

Table 7.9   Results: Gaussian copula

Tranche	Fair spread	Expected loss
SS	0.03%	496 364
A	0.77%	346 588
B	1.93%	1 509 068
C	6.97%	5 142 699
Equity	23.07%	7 607 209

Table 7.10   Results: Student copula 8 d.o.f.

Tranche	Fair spread	Expected loss
SS	0.04%	795 313
A	0.97%	430 133
B	2.10%	1 628 398
C	6.61%	4 893 133
Equity	22.04%	7 474 042

Table 7.11   Clayton copula $\alpha = 0.48$

Tranche	Fair spread	Expected loss
SS	0.00%	3,523
A	0.04%	16 350
B	0.34%	281 028
C	4.04%	3 267 464
Equity	18.53%	7 224 680

Table 7.12   Loss statistics: Gaussian copula

Statistics	SS	A	B	C	Equity
Median	0	0	0	0	9 858 666
Mean	496 364	346 588	1 509 068	5 142 699	7 607 209
Std. dev.	4 165 898	1 833 116	4 676 705	7 453 992	4 934 804
Min	0	0	0	0	0
Max	89 465 261	11 000 000	19 500 000	20 000 000	12 000 000
95% VaR	0	0	16 618 167	20 000 000	12 000 000
99% VaR	20 072 488	11 000 000	19 500 000	20 000 000	12 000 000

Table 7.13   Loss statistics: Student copula 8 d.o.f.

Statistics	SS	A	B	C	Equity
Median	0	0	0	0	9 360 774
Mean	795 313	430 133	1 628 398	4 893 133	7 474 042
Std. dev.	6 432 416	2 044 136	4 918 527	7 407 938	4 916 958
Min	0	0	0	0	0
Max	133 924 467	11 000 000	19 500 000	20 000 000	12 000 000
95% VaR	0	0	19 045 358	20 000 000	12 000 000
99% VaR	28 117 222	11 000 000	19 500 000	20 000 000	12 000 000

Table 7.14   Loss statistics: Clayton copula $\alpha = 0.48$

Statistics	SS	A	B	C	Equity
Median	0	0	0	0	8 717 641
Mean	3 523	16 350	281 028	3 267 464	7 224 680
Std. dev.	184 585	350 643	1 810 103	5 706 847	4 884 579
Min	0	0	0	0	0
Max	13 951 110	11 000 000	19 500 000	20 000 000	12 000 000
95% VaR	0	0	0	18 434 870	12 000 000
99% VaR	0	0	10 689 314	20 000 000	12 000 000

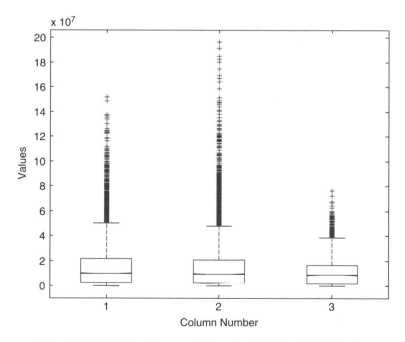

Figure 7.9   Collateral losses: 1. Gaussian 2. Student t 3. Clayton

7.4.5 Pricing and risk monitoring of the basket default swaps

Many previous discussions may be tailored to the basket default swap case. As before we report in Tables 7.15, 7.16 and 7.17 the results obtained for each chosen copula. Due to its smaller dimensions we also introduce the Frank copula in the analysis. In section 7.5 we derive the Frank copula density (Table 7.18 reports the results) in order to get the MLE of its parameter.

As for the loss statistics we report the results in Tables 7.19–7.22.

In Figures 7.10, 7.11 and 7.12 we show the likelihood function for each estimated copula from the corresponding equity series returns. We estimated that the d.o.f. of the Student t

Table 7.15 Gaussian copula

Tranche	Fair spread
Last-to-default	0.00%
3rd-to-default	0.01%
2nd-to-default	0.12%
1st-to-default	2.34%

Table 7.16 T-copula 4 d.o.f.

Tranche	Fair spread
Last-to-default	0.00%
3rd-to-default	0.00%
2nd-to-default	0.14%
1st-to-default	2.53%

Table 7.17 Clayton copula $\alpha = 0.53$

Tranche	Fair spread
Last-to-default	0.00%
3rd-to-default	0.00%
2nd-to-default	0.07%
1st-to-default	1.93%

Table 7.18 Frank copula $\alpha = 1.61$

Tranche	Fair spread
Last-to-default	0.00%
3rd-to-default	0.00%
2nd-to-default	0.09%
1st-to-default	2.03%

Table 7.19   Gaussian copula

Statistics	First-to-default
Median	0
Mean	1 111 719
Std. dev.	2 604 153
Min	0
Max	10 000 000
95% VaR	8 253 625
99% VaR	10 000 000

Table 7.20   Student copula 4 d.o.f.

Statistics	First-to-default
Median	0
Mean	1 190 738
Std. dev.	2 680 928
Min	0
Max	10 000 000
95% VaR	8 398 548
99% VaR	10 000 000

Table 7.21   Clayton copula $\alpha = 0.53$

Statistics	First-to-default
Median	0
Mean	951 800
Std. dev.	2 411 352
Min	0
Max	10 000 000
95% VaR	7 666 130
99% VaR	10 000 000

Table 7.22   Frank copula $\alpha = 1.61$

Statistics	First-to-default
Median	0
Mean	1 002 489
Std. dev.	2 479 172
Min	0
Max	10 000 000
95% VaR	7 919 957
99% VaR	10 000 000

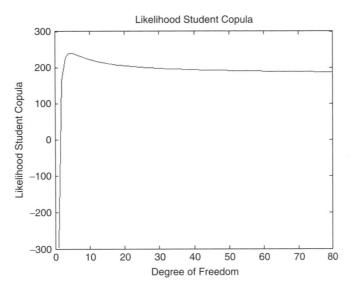

Figure 7.10 Log-likelihood Student t copula

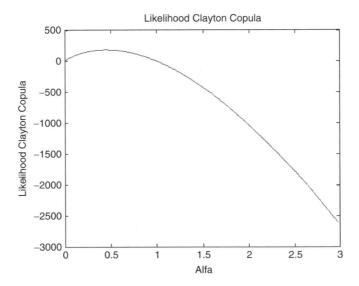

Figure 7.11 Log-likelihood Clayton copula

copula was approximately equal to 4; the alpha for the Clayton copula was equal to 0.53, and the alpha for the Frank copula was equal to 1.61. All estimates, as before, are significant. All comments previously made still apply.

In Figure 7.13 we show the scatter plot implied by the Gaussian copula with Kendall's tau dependence matrix for ABN Amro, Bayer AG and Renault SA; the Student t copula for the same companies can be seen in Figure 7.14.

We conclude this application stressing that there is no standard way to model multiple defaults. We have considered a pure Monte Carlo approach by using a copula framework

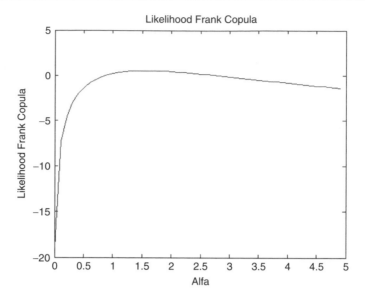

Figure 7.12   Log-likelihood Frank copula

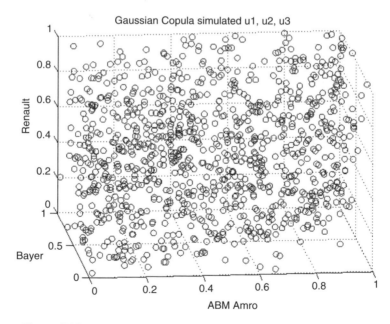

Figure 7.13   Gaussian copula for ABN Amro, Bayer AG, Renault SA

as the choice of the copula function is crucial for pricing, hedging and risk monitoring. As for credit risk purposes, the copula has often to be assumed, so we propose to select the copula that allows us to obtain results closer to those found in the real market activity. In such a way, we found that the choice of a Student t copula allows us to obtain more reliable results.

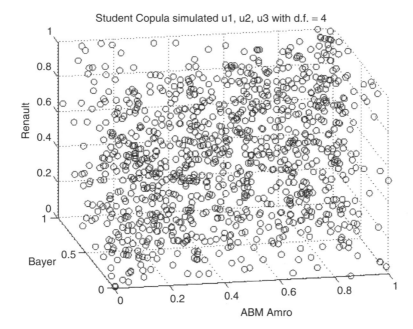

Figure 7.14   Student t copula with 4 d.o.f. for ABN Amro, Bayer AG, Renault SA

7.5   TECHNICAL APPENDIX

7.5.1   Derivation of a multivariate Clayton copula density

An n-variate Clayton copula is given by:

$$C(u_1, u_2, \ldots, u_n) = \left(\sum_{i=1}^{n} u_i^{-\alpha} - n + 1 \right)^{-\frac{1}{\alpha}}$$

where $\alpha > 0$.

The Clayton copula density is given by:

$$\frac{\partial^n C}{\partial u_1 \partial u_2 \ldots \partial u_n} = \alpha^n \frac{\Gamma\left(\frac{1}{\alpha} + n\right)}{\Gamma\left(\frac{1}{\alpha}\right)} \left(\prod_{i=1}^{n} u_i^{-\alpha-1} \right) \left(\sum_{i=1}^{n} u_i^{-\alpha} - n + 1 \right)^{-\frac{1}{\alpha} - n}$$

where Γ indicates the usual Euler Γ function.

The derivation is very easy because it offers a recursive formula.

In the 4-variate case, as is necessary for the empirical application to the basket default swap we have considered, we have the following density:

$$(1 + \alpha)(1 + 2\alpha)(1 + 3\alpha) u_1^{-\alpha-1} u_2^{-\alpha-1} u_3^{-\alpha-1} u_4^{-\alpha-1} \left(u_1^{-\alpha} + u_2^{-\alpha} + u_3^{-\alpha} + u_4^{-\alpha} - 3 \right)^{-\frac{1}{\alpha} - 4}$$

7.5.2 Derivation of a 4-variate Frank copula density[10]

A 4-variate Frank copula is given by:

$$C(u_1, u_2, u_3, u_4) = -\frac{1}{\alpha} \ln \left\{ 1 + \frac{w_1 w_2 w_3 w_4}{\left(e^{-\alpha} - 1\right)^3} \right\}$$

where $\alpha > 0$ and $w_i = e^{-\alpha u_i} - 1$ for $i = 1, 2, 3, 4$.

We have:

$$\frac{\partial w_i}{\partial u_i} = -\alpha e^{-\alpha u_i} = -\alpha \left(w_i + 1\right) \quad \text{for } i = 1, 2, 3, 4$$

and

$$\frac{\partial C}{\partial w_1} = -\frac{1}{\alpha} \frac{\left(e^{-\alpha} - 1\right)^3}{\left(e^{-\alpha} - 1\right)^3 + w_1 w_2 w_3 w_4} \cdot \frac{w_2 w_3 w_4}{\left(e^{-\alpha} - 1\right)^3}$$

hence

$$\frac{\partial C}{\partial u_1} = \frac{\left(w_1 + 1\right) w_2 w_3 w_4}{\left(e^{-\alpha} - 1\right)^3 + w_1 w_2 w_3 w_4}$$

Continuing by derivation:

$$\frac{\partial^2 C}{\partial u_1 \partial u_2} = \frac{\partial}{\partial u_2} \left(\frac{\partial C}{\partial u_1} \right) = -\alpha \left(w_1 + 1\right) \left(w_2 + 1\right) w_3 w_4 \cdot \frac{\left(e^{-\alpha} - 1\right)^3}{\left[\left(e^{-\alpha} - 1\right)^3 + w_1 w_2 w_3 w_4\right]^2}$$

and

$$\frac{\partial^3 C}{\partial u_1 \partial u_2 \partial u_3} = \frac{\partial}{\partial u_3} \left(\frac{\partial^2 C}{\partial u_1 \partial u_2} \right) = \alpha^2 \left(w_1 + 1\right) \left(w_2 + 1\right) \left(w_3 + 1\right) w_4 \left(e^{-\alpha} - 1\right)^3$$

$$\cdot \frac{\left[\left(e^{-\alpha} - 1\right)^3 - w_1 w_2 w_3 w_4\right]}{\left[\left(e^{-\alpha} - 1\right)^3 + w_1 w_2 w_3 w_4\right]^3}$$

Finally the copula density is given by:

$$\frac{\partial^4 C}{\partial u_1 \partial u_2 \partial u_3 \partial u_4} = \frac{\partial}{\partial u_4} \left(\frac{\partial^3 C}{\partial u_1 \partial u_2 \partial u_3} \right) = -\alpha^3 \left(w_1 + 1\right) \left(w_2 + 1\right) \left(w_3 + 1\right) \left(w_4 + 1\right) \left(e^{-\alpha} - 1\right)^3$$

$$\cdot \frac{\left[\left(e^{-\alpha} - 1\right)^6 - 4 \left(e^{-\alpha} - 1\right)^3 w_1 w_2 w_3 w_4 + w_1^2 w_2^2 w_3^2 w_4^2\right]}{\left[\left(e^{-\alpha} - 1\right)^3 + w_1 w_2 w_3 w_4\right]^4}$$

It is really cumbersome to write down but it is easily maximized w.r. α.

The derivation of a general n-variate Frank copula may be obtained as previously done for the 4-variate case, though it requires an overweight algebra.

---

[10] W. Vecchiato would like to thank Lanhua Yu (Imperial College, London UK) for pointing out some imperfections in an earlier version of this derivation.

7.5.3 Correlated default times

In our applications we do not focus on whether default occurs over the risk horizon (i.e. the time to maturity of the credit derivatives contract), but on the precise time when the default occurs. We are not concerned with rating migrations, but only with defaults. For each credit in the collateral portfolio we have to determine its default time probability distribution function. We choose to specify the default time distribution from the hazard rates implied by the observed credit default swap (CDS) for terms of 1 year, 3 years and 5 years, at the analysis date, for each underlying single name credit. We choose this way because the credit spreads can be observed from both the CDS market and the asset swap market. With the explosive growth in the credit derivatives markets, the movement of the credit spreads reflects more timely the market-based assessments of credit quality and the market perception of both market and credit risk of each specific credit.

We can derive hazard rates from credit spreads as follows:

$$h_t = \frac{S_t}{1 - R}$$

where h_t is the hazard rate, S_t is the CDS spread at term t and R is a recovery rate.

To understand the relationship presented we have to consider the cash flows exchanged during a CDS. A fair valuation requires that the total amount of payment received by the protection seller should equal the expected loss the seller has to pay the buyer when a credit event (i.e. for simplicity the default) occurs (adjusting everything by the probability of occurrence and discounting). This means that the expected payments have to be equal to the expected loss.

First we discuss the payment (or premium) leg. Let W_t be a given CDS spread as a function of time, hence the amount the protection seller receives in each tiny interval is $W_t \, dt$. The probability that this payment will be received is equal to the probability that the underlying credit has not defaulted by time t, i.e. $1 - F(t)$. Discounting by the risk-free factor $B(0, t)$ and integrating over the whole time T of the deal, we obtain the total expected payment to the protection seller:

$$\int_0^T B(0, t) W_t \, [1 - F(t)] \, dt$$

Now we examine the other side of the equation, i.e. the expected loss. Let R be a given exogenous default rate. In each tiny interval of time the amount of money the protection seller would pay to the protection buyer if the default occurs is equal to $(1 - R) \, dt$. The probability that this payment will be due is equal to the unconditional probability that the underlying credit defaults between time t and time $t + dt$, hence $F(t + dt) - F(t)$. Discounting and integrating as before, we arrive at the total expected loss of the protection seller:

$$(1 - R) \int_0^T B(0, t) \, [F(t + dt) - F(t)] \, dt = (1 - R) \int_0^T B(0, t) h_t \, [1 - F(t)] \, dt$$

where h_t is the hazard rate given by $dF(t)/[1 - F(t)]$.

Thus, for any given time t, the relationship $h_t(1 - R) = W_t$ holds.[11]

---

[11] It holds for any non-degenerate case.

Moreover, it is well known that the relation between the hazard rate and the cumulative default probability (c.d.p.) is given by:

$$F(t) = 1 - \exp\left[-\int_0^t h(s)\,\mathrm{d}s\right]$$

In the real world we do not have observations of the hazard rate for all periods of time, but for only a finite set of times. In our application we have three observed points implied by the single name credit default swap premium at terms of 1 year, 3 years and 5 years. In general, we can have N points in time $t_1, t_2, \ldots, t_N$. Hence, we consider a stepwise constant function of the time for each hazard rate by using the observable values of h. We can then rewrite the continuous form of the c.d.f. for each obligor's time to default into:

$$F(t) = 1 - \exp\left(-\sum_{j=1}^k h_j \Delta_j\right)$$

where $h_j = h\left(t_j\right)$, $\Delta_j = t_j - t_{j-1}$ and

$$k = \begin{cases} 1 & \text{if } t \leqslant t_1 \\ 2 & \text{if } t_1 < t \leqslant t_2 \\ \vdots & \\ N & \text{if } t > t_{N-1} \end{cases}$$

This methodology has been used for each reference credit in the collateral portfolio in order to obtain the draws for each time to default, after having generated draws from the chosen copula.

These marginals may be easily extended to Weibull distributions by inserting a shape parameter.

7.5.4 Variance–covariance robust estimation

As is well known for elliptical distributions, linear correlation is a natural measure of dependence. However, a linear correlation estimator such as the Pearson standard correlation estimator has shown a very poor performance for heavier tailed or contaminated data. Therefore, robust estimators are needed – where "robust" means to be insensitive to contamination and to maintain a high efficiency for heavier tailed elliptical distributions as well as for multivariate normal distributions. Lindskog (2000) gives an overview of techniques for a robust linear correlation estimation and for comparing contaminated and uncontaminated elliptical distributions. Moreover, he shows that Kendall's tau has the necessary robustness properties and is an efficient (low variance) estimator for all elliptical distributions. For this reason, in our application, we choose to adopt the empirical Kendall's tau matrix (after having checked that positive definiteness holds) instead of the standard Pearson variance–covariance matrix estimator. We determine this matrix from the equity return data for each obligor in the collateral portfolio, and we adopt it to obtain draws from each elliptical copula we have considered.

For the sake of completeness we present the empirical Kendall's tau for a chosen pair of variables.

The consistent estimator of Kendall's τ obtained from the two series S_{1t} and S_{2t} with $t = 1, \ldots, T$ is defined as follows:

$$\hat{\tau} = \frac{2}{T(T-1)} \sum_{i<j} \mathrm{sgn}\left[(S_{1i} - S_{1j})(S_{2i} - S_{2j})\right] \tag{7.8}$$

where the sign function is defined as commonly known:

$$\mathrm{sgn}(x) = \begin{cases} 1 & \text{if } x \geqslant 0 \\ -1 & \text{if } x < 0 \end{cases}$$

Another robust dependence measure is Spearman's rho, also called rank correlation, which may be seen to be the standard Pearson's linear correlation between the ranks of two series.

Let X and Y be r.v.s with c.d.f. respectively F_X and F_Y and joint c.d.f. F. Spearman's rho is given by

$$\rho_S(X, Y) = \rho_P(F_X(X), F_Y(Y))$$

where ρ_P is the standard Pearson linear correlation.

The generalization of ρ_S to $n > 2$ dimensions can be done analogously to that of linear correlation. In such a way we obtain a Spearman's correlation matrix that is positive definite by construction, without applying the so-called eigenvalue method, i.e. the negative eigenvalue has to be replaced by an arbitrary small positive number (see Rousseuw & Molenberghs, 1993), as must be done for a high-dimensional extension of Kendall's tau.

A consistent estimator of Spearman's rho may be obtained by the use of the standard empirical correlation coefficient between the sample ranks of each series, hence

$$\hat{\rho}_S = \hat{\rho}_P\left[\hat{F}_X(x_i), \hat{F}_Y(y_i)\right]$$

7.5.5   Interest rates and foreign exchange rates in the analysis

One of the inputs used in the application is the par swap rate term structures for all currencies involved in the CDO and in the BDS. Using the par swap rates it is possible to derive discount factors for every maturity (i.e. commonly this procedure is termed as bootstrapping). After deriving discount factors, one can determine forward interest rates for any needed period and maturity. Since our focus is on effects due to collateral default, we do not simulate interest rate and/or foreign exchange rates. But, one can choose to make these simulations by calibrating the chosen models to observed variables for use in Monte Carlo analysis. For example, one can assume that short-term forward interest rates follow a lognormal process over time, and when simulating interest rates across multiple currencies one has to find estimates for the correlations between the interest rates of different currencies; it is important to assume that these processes are exogenous from the copula framework, otherwise this task would involve higher and higher dimensionality problems.

8
Option Pricing with Copulas

8.1 INTRODUCTION

In this chapter we show how to use copula functions to solve the pricing problem of multivariate contingent claims. The purpose is to derive pricing formulas which are valid for very general distribution settings, beyond the standard Black and Scholes framework under which closed form solutions are available for almost all the pricing problems. We know that the assumptions on the basis of the Black–Scholes model have been challenged on the grounds of two major arguments. The first is non-normality of returns, as implied by the smile and term structure effects of implied volatility. The second is market incompleteness, and the difficulty of providing exact replication strategies for all the contingent claims and a unique pricing kernel for their prices. Both of these problems are amplified in a multivariate setting. On the one hand, non-normality of the returns implies that the standard linear correlation figure that has been currently used to recover the price is a biased tool; and as shown in Chapter 3, in the presence of smile effects, linear correlation may turn out to be smaller than 1 even in the case of perfect dependence between the markets. On the other hand, market incompleteness in a multivariate setting is made more involved because of the difficulty of recovering implied information concerning the dependence structure among the assets. So, evaluating multivariate contingent claims in incomplete markets poses a two-stage problem: choosing a pricing kernel for each and every asset in the underlying basket and picking out the copula function representing the dependence structure among them. Nowadays, multivariate contingent claims are widely used by financial institutions, particularly to design structured finance products: on the one hand, it is all the more usual to find multi-asset features in index-linked bonds and digital notes, providing the investor with a diversified product; on the other hand, multicurrency options have been around for a long time and have represented a relevant risk management service provided by banks to corporate borrowers and investors.

The increasing trend in structured finance has highlighted the relevance of the multivariate contingent claim pricing problem through a second important channel. In the structured finance business, the financial institutions face the problem of hedging a large variety of different risks, connected to derivative products which are often exotic and written on underlying assets that might not be actively traded on liquid markets. As a result, the hedging activity may heavily rely on transactions on the OTC market, where the counterparty risk component can be relevant. Notice that accounting for counterparty risk in a derivative transaction directly casts the problem in a multivariate setting. Intuitively, in fact, the value of the derivative contract depends on two events: the first, that the contract ends in the money; the second, that the counterparty survives until the contract is exercised. Taking into consideration both the marginal probability of these two events and their dependence structure may make both the evaluation and the hedging strategy of these products more accurate and safe, and it is not difficult to foresee that copula functions can be of great help to reach this goal.

8.2   PRICING BIVARIATE OPTIONS IN COMPLETE MARKETS

Let us consider a derivative contract that is written on two underlying assets, which we denote as S_1 and S_2. The information structure is represented in the usual way by a filtered probability space $\{\Omega, \Im_t, P\}$ generated by the stochastic processes $S_1(t)$ and $S_2(t)$, $t \in [0, T]$. Throughout the discussion, we will assume that $S_1(t)$, $S_2(t)$ are continuous random variables with non-negative support. If, for the sake of simplicity, we take the bivariate derivative to be European, its pay-off may be written in full generality as $G(S_1(T), S_2(T), T)$, a function defined $\mathfrak{R}_+^3 \to \mathfrak{R}$. Our problem is to recover a pricing function $g(S_1(t), S_2(t), t)$ which would rule out arbitrage opportunities in the market. In the case in which the market is complete, we know that this product, as any other one, can be exactly replicated, and its price is uniquely determined. This unique price also corresponds to a unique risk-neutral probability distribution $Q(S_1, S_2 \mid \Im_t)$, whose density function is denoted $q(S_1, S_2 \mid \Im_t)$, which represents the pricing kernel of the economy. The price of the bivariate contingent claim can then be represented in integral form as

$$g(S_1(t), S_2(t), t)$$
$$= B(t, T) \int_0^\infty \int_0^\infty G(S_1(T), S_2(T), T) q(S_1(T), S_2(T) \mid \Im_t) \, dS_1(T) \, dS_2(T)$$

where $B(t, T)$ is the risk-free discount factor. Throughout the analysis the risk-free rate is assumed to be non-stochastic or independent of the underlying assets. The extension to the more general case is, however, straightforward if we change the measure to the forward risk-neutral one, as described in Chapter 1.

Let us denote by $Q_1(S_1 \mid \Im_t)$ and $Q_2(S_2 \mid \Im_t)$ the marginal conditional distributions of S_1 and S_2 respectively, with densities $q_1(S_1 \mid \Im_t)$ and $q_2(S_2 \mid \Im_t)$. They are also derived from the bivariate pricing kernel by definition

$$q_1(S_1 \mid \Im_t) = \int_0^\infty q(S_1(T), S_2(T) \mid \Im_t) \, dS_2(T)$$

$$q_2(S_2 \mid \Im_t) = \int_0^\infty q(S_1(T), S_2(T) \mid \Im_t) \, dS_1(T)$$

Prices of univariate contingent claims are obtained as discounted expected values under the relevant marginal risk-neutral distribution. So, if $G(S_1(T), S_2(T), T) = G(S_1(T), T)$, so that a contingent claim is written on asset S_1 only we have

$$g(S_1(t), t) = B(t, T) \int_0^\infty G(S_1(T), T) \int_0^\infty q(S_1(T), S_2(T) \mid \Im_t) \, dS_1(T) \, dS_2(T)$$

$$= B(t, T) \int_0^\infty G(S_1(T), T) q_1(S_1(T) \mid \Im_t) \, dS_1(T)$$

8.2.1   Copula pricing kernels

In this complete market setting it is quite easy to write the pricing relationship of bivariate contingent claims in terms of copula functions and marginal distributions. We only need the extension of Sklar's theorem to conditional distributions.

Theorem 8.1 For any joint conditional distribution $Q(S_1, S_2 \mid \Im_t)$ there exists a copula function $C(u, v)$ such that

$$Q(S_1, S_2 \mid \Im_t) = C\left(Q_1(S_1 \mid \Im_t), Q_2(S_2 \mid \Im_t)\right)$$

and, conversely, given two conditional distributions $Q_1(S_1 \mid \Im_t)$ and $Q_2(S_2 \mid \Im_t)$ and a copula function $C(u, v)$ the function $C\left(Q_1(S_1 \mid \Im_t), Q_2(S_2 \mid \Im_t)\right)$ is a joint conditional distribution function.

The proof is in Patton (2001). Notice that the result holds if the conditioning information $\Im_t$ is the same for both marginal distribution and joint distributions. The copula obtained in this way corresponds to the dependence structure in the risk-neutral probability distribution, and is the risk-neutral copula.

Using copula functions enables us to separate the effects of the marginal pricing kernels and the dependence structure of the underlying assets. This is very important because it makes it possible to check the consistency of prices of multivariate and univariate contingent claims, particularly with respect to the no-arbitrage requirement. As a simple example, let us take digital options, as in the examples presented in Chapter 2. Remember that digital options pay a fixed sum, which we may set equal to one unit of currency without loss of generality, if some event takes place. The event may be that the price of the underlying asset is higher than some strike level (call digital option). A put digital option instead pays a unit of value if the value of the underlying asset is lower than a strike level. So, in a complete market, the prices of univariate digital options, that is options written on a single asset, are equal to the discounted values of risk-neutral probability distributions.

Call digital options DC_i written on our assets S_1 and S_2 are priced as

$$DC_1(K_1) = B(t, T)\,\overline{Q}_1(K_1 \mid \Im_t), \qquad DC_2(K_2) = B(t, T)\,\overline{Q}_2(K_2 \mid \Im_t)$$

where we recall that $\overline{Q}_i(u) \equiv 1 - Q_i(u)$. Of course, the corresponding put digital options are priced by arbitrage as $DP_i = B - DC_i$. Consider now the case of bivariate digital options paying one unit of currency if both assets S_1 and S_2 are higher than strike prices K_1 and K_2 respectively. Options like these are sometimes used in particular structured finance products such as digital bivariate notes. Denoting D_{HH} this digital option, we can write it as a copula function taking the forward values of univariate digital options as arguments:

$$D_{\mathrm{HH}}(K_1, K_2) = B(t, T)\,C_{\mathrm{HH}}\left(\frac{DC_1}{B(t, T)}, \frac{DC_2}{B(t, T)}\right)$$

where $C_{\mathrm{HH}}(u, v)$ is a copula function: in particular, this is the survival copula discussed in Chapter 2. Once such a copula function has been chosen, the other digital options for the same strikes are determined by arbitrage. For example, the digital option D_{HL} paying one unit if $S_1 > K_1$ and $S_2 \leqslant K_2$ is determined by the relation

$$D_{\mathrm{HL}}(K_1, K_2) = DC_1 - D_{\mathrm{HH}}(K_1, K_2)$$

$$= DC_1 - B(t, T)\,C_{\mathrm{HH}}\left(\frac{DC_1}{B}, \frac{DC_2}{B}\right)$$

We remind the reader (see Chapter 2) that if $C_{HH}(u, v)$ is a copula function, then $C_{HL}(u, 1 - v) = u - C_{HH}(u, v)$ is also a copula function, representing the probability that the first uniform marginal be higher than u and the second be lower than v. The price of the digital option D_{HL} can then be written as

$$D_{HL}(K_1, K_2) = B(t, T) \left[\frac{DC_1(K_1)}{B(t, T)} - C_{HH} \left(\frac{DC_1(K_1)}{B(t, T)}, \frac{DC_2(K_2)}{B(t, T)} \right) \right]$$

$$= B(t, T) C_{HL} \left(\frac{DC_1(K_1)}{B(t, T)}, \frac{DP_2(K_2)}{B(t, T)} \right)$$

where we have exploited $DP_2 = B(t, T) - DC_2$. By the same token, we have

$$D_{LH}(K_1, K_2) = DC_2(K_2) - D_{HH}(K_1, K_2)$$

$$= B(t, T) C_{LH} \left(\frac{DP_1(K_1)}{B}, \frac{DC_2(K_2)}{B} \right)$$

with $C_{LH}(1 - u, v) = v - C_{HH}(u, v)$ representing the joint probability that the first marginal be lower than u and the second be higher than v. Finally, the put bivariate digital, paying one unit if $S_1 \leqslant K_2$ and $S_2 \leqslant K_2$ is obtained by arbitrage from

$$D_{LL}(K_1, K_2) = B(t, T) - D_{HL}(K_1, K_2) - D_{LH}(K_1, K_2) - D_{HH}(K_1, K_2)$$

$$= B(t, T) - DC_1(K_1) - DC_2(K_2) + D_{HH}(K_1, K_2)$$

Again, remembering that $C_{LL}(1 - u, 1 - v) = 1 - u - v + C_{HH}(u, v)$ is a copula function we have

$$D_{LL}(K_1, K_2) = B(t, T) \left[1 - \frac{DC_1(K_1)}{B(t, T)} - \frac{DC_2(K_2)}{B(t, T)} + C_{HH} \left(\frac{DC_1(K_1)}{B(t, T)}, \frac{DC_2(K_2)}{B(t, T)} \right) \right]$$

$$= B C_{LL} \left(\frac{DP_1(K_1)}{B(t, T)}, \frac{DP_2(K_2)}{B(t, T)} \right)$$

All of this proves that, just as in the univariate case, digital options paying under some events are linked to those paying under the complement, and this induces a no-arbitrage relation among copula functions. These relationships will be particularly useful in some of the applications that we cover in the rest of this chapter. For the time being, this result states that the requirement that a bivariate pricing kernel be a copula function is necessary but not sufficient. Moreover, in general the shape of copulas C_{HH}, C_{HL}, C_{LH} and C_{LL} will be different. We say in general because it is not difficult to find a counterexample: we leave the readers to verify that the product copula $C_{HH}(u, v) = uv$ is such a case.

Representing the bivariate pricing kernel by a copula function enables us to specify the dependence structure of the underlying assets and to gauge its effect on the price of the bivariate contingent claim. Sticking to the simplest case of the bivariate digital option, we have that

$$B\left(t,T\right)C^{-}\left(\frac{DC_1(K_1)}{B\left(t,T\right)},\frac{DC_2(K_2)}{B\left(t,T\right)}\right)\leqslant D_{\mathrm{HH}}(K_1,K_2)$$

$$\leqslant B\left(t,T\right)C^{+}\left(\frac{DC_1(K_1)}{B\left(t,T\right)},\frac{DC_2(K_2)}{B\left(t,T\right)}\right)$$

where C^{-} and C^{+} represent the Fréchet bounds of copulas corresponding to the cases of perfect negative and positive dependence respectively. Using such bounds we obtain

$$\max\left(DC_1(K_1)+DC_2(K_2)-B\left(t,T\right),0\right)\leqslant D_{\mathrm{HH}}(K_1,K_2)$$

$$\leqslant \min\left(DC_1(K_1),DC_2(K_2)\right)$$

So, the price of a bivariate call digital option reaches its maximum value in the case of perfect positive dependence, in which case it is worth the minimum of the univariate digital options. Going back to the arbitrage arguments above, readers may verify that if the value of such an option is maximum, i.e. $D_{\mathrm{HH}}=\min\left(DC_1,DC_2\right)$, the price of the digital option D_{HL}, i.e. the option paying if $S_1 > K_1$ and $S_2 \leqslant K_2$, is minimum: $D_{\mathrm{HL}} = \max\left(DC_1+DP_2-1,0\right)$. On the question of the bivariate digital put option, paying one unit if $S_1 \leqslant K_1$ and $S_2 \leqslant K_2$, we leave the simple answer to the readers.

8.2.2 Alternative pricing techniques

In the previous analysis we showed that a pricing kernel may be written in terms of copula functions. In a complete market setting, the argument follows in quite a straightforward way from the unique probability measure and an extension of Sklar's theorem to the case of conditional distributions. The same result obviously applies to incomplete market models in which a specific probability measure is selected to compute the price. Throughout the following sections, we will see whether the result carries over to more general pricing models in an incomplete setting. Prior to that, we would like to explore the techniques that can be applied to make the copula pricing kernel approach most effective. These approaches will then represent the set of tools among which to choose the most effective to solve the specific pricing problems that will be addressed at the end of this chapter.

The probability density approach

The most straightforward way to represent the price of a contingent claim is to use the standard integral representation involving the joint conditional density $q(S_1, S_2 \mid \Im_t)$. The representation can be written in terms of copulas, remembering the relationship

$$q(S_1, S_2 \mid \Im_t) = c\left(Q_1, Q_2 \mid \Im_t\right) q_1\left(S_1 \mid \Im_t\right) q_2\left(S_2 \mid \Im_t\right)$$

where we recall that $c\left(v, z\right)$ is the density associated to the copula function. In other words, the joint density is equal to the cross-derivative of the copula function times the marginal densities. Using this result we have that the price $g(S_1, S_2, t)$ of our bivariate contingent claim can be written

$$g(S_1(t), S_2(t), t) = B(t, T) \int_0^\infty \int_0^\infty G(S_1(T), S_2(T), T) c(Q_1, Q_2 \mid \Im_t)$$
$$\times q_1(S_1(T) \mid \Im_t) q_2(S_2(T) \mid \Im_t) \, dS_1(T) \, dS_2(T)$$

Unfortunately, this representation of price does not lead to any simplification of the price representation, as in most cases the formula for the cross-derivative of the copula function turns out to be quite involved and difficult to handle, so that computing the double integral may not come as an easy task. So, this representation can only be useful in cases in which such cross-derivative is very easy to calculate, such as in the case of the product copula, for which we have $C_{12} = 1$.

The probability distribution approach

An alternative to the integral representation above can be of some help in many cases. To introduce this approach, it may be useful to go back to the univariate setting for a short digression. Consider the case of a European option written on the underlying asset Z, for strike price K and exercise date T. Let us denote $\mathrm{CALL}(Z, t; K, T)$ the price of the option at time t. We recall the famous result due to Breeden and Litzenberger (1978), discussed in Chapter 1

$$-\frac{\partial \mathrm{CALL}(Z, t; K, T)}{\partial K} \frac{1}{B(t, T)} = \overline{Q}_Z(K \mid \Im_t)$$

so that the derivative of the price of the call option with respect to the strike divided by the discount factor is equal to the risk-neutral probability of exercising the option (apart from a change in sign). Integrating both sides from K to infinity we may write the price of the option as

$$\mathrm{CALL}(Z, t; K, T) = B(t, T) \int_K^\infty \overline{Q}_Z(u \mid \Im_t) \, du$$

Likewise, for put options we have

$$\frac{\partial \mathrm{PUT}(Z, t; K, T)}{\partial K} \frac{1}{B(t, T)} = Q_Z(K \mid \Im_t)$$

and, integrating from zero to K, we get

$$\mathrm{PUT}(Z, t; K, T) = B(t, T) \int_0^K Q_Z(u \mid \Im_t) \, du$$

Notice that in the representations above the prices of call and put options are obtained by computing the integral of the distribution function, rather than the density function.

Let us now go back to a bivariate problem. Assume, for example, that the pay-off function of a contingent claim is of the kind

$$G(S_1(T), S_2(T), T) = \max \left[f(S_1(T), S_2(T), T) - K, 0 \right]$$

and set $Z(T) = f(S_1(T), S_2(T))$. We may then use the integral representation above to recover the price of this contingent claim as

$$\text{CALL}\,(S_1(t), S_2(t), t; K, T) = B\,(t, T) \int_K^\infty \Pr\left(f(S_1(T), S_2(T), T) > u \mid \Im_t\right) \mathrm{d}u$$

where the probability is computed under the risk-neutral measure Q.

Likewise, for pay-off functions of the put type

$$G(S_1(T), S_2(T), T) = \max \left[K - f(S_1(T), S_2(T), T), 0 \right]$$

we may write the price of the contingent claim as

$$\text{PUT}\,(S_1(t), S_2(t), t; K, T) = B\,(t, T) \int_0^K \Pr\left(f\,(S_1(T), S_2(T), T) \leqslant u \mid \Im_t\right) \mathrm{d}u$$

The pricing representations reported above may be particularly useful in all cases in which the probability distribution of $f(S_1(T), S_2(T), T)$ is easy to handle analytically or by simulation. Below, we will show some cases in which such a function is in fact a copula function. Here we show a different example just to fix ideas.

Compo option. Take an option in which the value of the pay-off and the strike price are denoted in a currency that is different from that of the underlying asset. An example is an option written on Vodaphone stocks denominated in British pounds with a strike price in euros. The pay-off of this option, say a call, is then written as

$$G(S(T), e(T), T) = \max \left[S(T)e(T) - K, 0 \right]$$

where S is the price of the underlying asset (Vodaphone in our case) denominated in foreign currency and e is the exchange rate, determining the number of euros to be exchanged for one pound. So, the method described above can be applied setting $f(S(T), e(T)) = S(T)e(T)$. We have

$$\text{CALL}\,(S(t), e(t), t; K, T) = B \int_K^\infty \Pr(S(T)e(T) > u \mid \Im_t) \mathrm{d}u$$

In cases in which the distribution of the product of the two variables is known or easy to simulate, the above formula can be used. For example, we know that if S and e are lognormally distributed, their product will also have log-normal distribution: it is not surprising that the integral will have a closed form solution of the type of the Black–Scholes formula. Unfortunately, beyond this case there are not many general results available for the product of random variables, and the distribution will generally have to be reconstructed by simulation.

The conditional distribution approach

A third approach to the pricing of bivariate contingent claims consists in evaluating the contingent claim conditional on one of the two variables and integrating the result with respect to the other one. As an example, consider again the case in which the pay-off function is of the kind: $\max[f(S_1(T), S_2(T)) - K, 0]$. Intuitively the idea is quite simple. Assuming that one knows the value of one of the two variables, say $S_2(T) = s$, one is able to recover the value of the derivative. We have, for example

$$\text{CALL}\,(S_1(t), t; S_2(T) = s, K, T) = B\,(t, T) \int_K^\infty \Pr(f(S_1(T), s) > u \mid \Im_t)\,\mathrm{d}u$$

Then the price of the bivariate contingent claim can be recovered by integrating this "conditional" price over the whole domain of S_2. We then have

$$\text{CALL}\,(S_1(t), S_2(t), t; K, T) = B\,(t, T) \int_0^\infty \text{CALL}\,(S_1(t), t; S_2(T), K, T)$$

$$\times q_2(S_2(T) \mid \Im_t)\,\mathrm{d}S_2(T)$$

Even in this case the use of copula functions can be of some help. We recall in fact from Chapter 2 that

$$Q(S_1 \mid S_2 = s, \Im_t) = \frac{\partial C\,(Q_1, Q_2\,(s))}{\partial Q_2\,(s)}$$

and the probability distribution of one of the two variables, conditional on a given value of the other, is equal to the derivative of the copula function with respect to the marginal distribution of the latter evaluated at that value.

Stochastic volatility. As an example, assume a pricing model in which both the price and the volatility of the underlying asset are stochastic. The use of copulas may be particularly useful to account for the dependence structure between price and volatility. Denote by Q_S and Q_σ the marginal probability distributions of the price of the underlying asset and its volatility. The joint conditional distribution can then be written as $Q(S, \sigma \mid \Im_t) = C(Q_S, Q_\sigma \mid \Im_t)$. Consider the problem of pricing a put option for strike K and exercise T. It is clear that, conditional on a given value of volatility, $\sigma = s$, the value of the option could be written

$$\text{PUT}\,(S(t), t; \sigma(T) = s, K, T) = B\,(t, T) \int_0^K \Pr(S(T) \leqslant u \mid \sigma(T) = s, \Im_t)\,\mathrm{d}u$$

Using the copula function representation we could write

$$\text{PUT}\,(S(t), t; \sigma(T) = s, K, T) = B\,(t, T) \int_0^K \frac{\partial C\,(Q_1, Q_\sigma\,(s) \mid \Im_t)}{\partial Q_\sigma\,(s \mid \Im_t)}\,\mathrm{d}u$$

The price of the put option would then be

$$\text{PUT}\,(S(t), t, \sigma(t); K, T) = B\,(t, T) \int_0^\infty \left[\int_0^K \frac{\partial C\,(Q_1, Q_\sigma\,(s) \mid \Im_t)}{\partial Q_\sigma\,(s \mid \Im_t)}\,\mathrm{d}u \right] q_\sigma(s \mid \Im_t)\,\mathrm{d}s$$

The model is then able to capture the dependence structure between volatility and price of the underlying asset. From this point of view, it may be checked that it is an extension of the Hull–White model. In fact, if we take Q_S to be the log-normal distribution and $C(u, v) = uv$ the product copula, we obtain

$$\text{PUT}\,(S(t), t, \sigma(t); K, T) = \int_0^\infty \text{PUT}_{\text{BS}}\,(S, t; \sigma(t) = s, K, T)\, q_\sigma(s \mid \Im_t)\, ds$$

where $\text{PUT}_{\text{BS}}(.)$ is the Black–Scholes pricing formula for put options.

8.3 PRICING BIVARIATE OPTIONS IN INCOMPLETE MARKETS

We begin by recalling the terms of the incomplete market problem. In this setting, a general contingent claim $g(S, t)$, with pay-off $G(S, T)$, where S is a univariate variable, can be priced computing

$$g\,(S, t) = B\,(t, T)\, E_Q\left[G\,(S, T)\,;\, Q \in \wp \mid \Im_t\right]$$

where E_Q represents the expectation with respect to a risk-neutral measure Q. The set $\wp$ contains the risk-neutral measures and describes the information available on the underlying asset. If it is very precise, and the set $\wp$ contains a single probability measure, we are in the standard complete market pricing setting tackled above. In the case in which we do not have precise information – for example, because of limited liquidity of the underlying asset – we have the problem of choosing a single probability measure, or some pricing strategy. So, in order to price the contingent claim g in this incomplete market setting, we have to define: (i) the set of probability measures $\wp$ and (ii) a set of rules describing a strategy to select the appropriate measure and price. One could resort to expected utility to give a preference rank for the probabilities in the set, picking out the optimal one. As an alternative, or prior to that, one could instead rely on some more conservative strategy, selecting a range of prices: the bounds of this range would yield the highest and lowest price consistent with the no-arbitrage assumption, and the replicating strategies corresponding to these bounds are known as super-replicating portfolios. In this case we have

$$g^-\,(S, t) = B \inf E_Q\left[G\,(S, T)\,;\, Q \in \wp\right]$$
$$g^+\,(S, t) = B \sup E_Q\left[G\,(S, T)\,;\, Q \in \wp\right]$$

As we have discussed in Chapter 1, the market incompleteness issue emerges as a problem that is very involved even at the one-dimension level. We have seen that the solution can also involve non-additive pricing kernels, technically known as *capacities* (more precisely, the subset of convex capacities). The copula pricing result which, as we saw, is fairly straightforward in a complete market setting, has to be derived carefully in a setting in which even at the univariate level the pricing kernel may not be represented by probability measures. Following Cherubini and Luciano (2002a), we are going to show that the same results that were obtained for a complete market setting carry over easily to the case in which the market is incomplete, both at the univariate and multivariate levels. Moreover, deriving the pricing kernel result without reference to probability arguments will help to highlight the arbitrage arguments.

8.3.1 Fréchet pricing: super-replication in two dimensions

We are now going to discuss how the same approach can be generalized to the bivariate pricing problem. As we did in the complete market setting, we start with the bivariate digital products. This time, however, we are going to drop any reference to Sklar's theorem as well as to any other probability theory argument. Our only guideline will be to check that the pricing relationships rule out arbitrage opportunities. We now focus our discussion on the properties that are to be imposed on the pricing kernel to achieve this task.

In financial terms, modeling the pricing kernel means recovering the forward value of a digital option, i.e. an option that pays one unit of value if some event occurs. Likewise, in our bivariate setting, recovering the pricing kernel amounts to pricing a digital option that pays one unit if two events take place. So, our problem is to find a replicating strategy for the bivariate digital option. An interesting question is whether it is possible to use univariate digital options to hedge the bivariate one.

In order to focus on the bivariate feature of the pricing problem, we assume that we may replicate and price two univariate digital options with the same exercise date T written on the underlying markets S_1 and S_2 for strikes K_1 and K_2 respectively. Our problem is then to use these products to replicate a bivariate option which pays one unit if $S_1 > K_1$ and $S_2 > K_2$ and zero otherwise.

As a starting point, it is quite natural to break the sample space into the four relevant regions and to construct a map that could facilitate the proofs of some static arbitrage relationship (Table 8.1).

So, a bivariate call digital option pays one unit only if both of the assets are in state H, that is, in the upper left cell of the table. The single digital options written on assets 1 and 2 pay in the first row and the first column respectively. In Table 8.2 below we sum up the pay-offs of these different assets and determine which prices are observed in the market. We recall that DC_1, DC_2 and $B(t, T)$ denote the prices of the univariate digital options and the risk-free asset respectively.

Our problem is to use no-arbitrage arguments to recover information on the price of the bivariate digital option. In particular, we may begin to investigate the pricing bounds for the bivariate digital, that is its super-replication portfolio. To this aim, some interesting

Table 8.1 Breaking down the sample space for the digital option

	State H	State L
State H	$S_1 \geqslant K_1, S_2 \geqslant K_2$	$S_1 \geqslant K_1, S_2 < K_2$
State L	$S_1 < K_1, S_2 \geqslant K_2$	$S_1 < K_1, S_2 < K_2$

Table 8.2 Prices and pay-offs for digital options

	Price	HH	HL	LH	LL
Digital option asset 1	DC_1	1	1	0	0
Digital option asset 2	DC_2	1	0	1	0
Risk-free asset	$B(t, T)$	1	1	1	1
Bivariate digital option	?	1	0	0	0

no-arbitrage implications can easily be obtained by comparing its pay-off with that of portfolios of the univariate digital options and the risk-free asset. The following proposition states such bounds for the price.

Proposition 8.1 The no-arbitrage price $D_{HH}(K_1, K_2)$ of a bivariate digital option is bounded by the inequality

$$\max(DC_1 + DC_2 - B(t, T), 0) \leqslant D_{HH}(K_1, K_2) \leqslant \min(DC_1, DC_2)$$

Proof: Assume first that the right hand side of the inequality is violated. Say that, without loss of generality, it is $D_{HH}(K_1, K_2) > DC_1$; in this case selling the bivariate digital option and buying the single digital option would allow a free lunch in the state $[S_1 > K_1, S_2 \leqslant K_2]$. As for the left hand side of the inequality, it is straightforward to see that D must be non-negative. There is also a bound $DC_1 + DC_2 - B(t, T)$. Assume in fact that $DC_1 + DC_2 - B(t, T) > D_{HH}(K_1, K_2)$; in this case buying the bivariate digital option and a risk-free asset and selling the two univariate digital options would allow a free lunch in the current date with non-negative pay-off in the future (actually, the pay-off could even be positive if state $[S_1 \leqslant K_1, S_2 \leqslant K_2]$ occurred). $\qquad \square$

The proposition exploits a static super-replication strategy for the bivariate digital option: the lower and upper bounds have a direct financial meaning, as they describe the pricing bounds for long and short positions in the bivariate options. The result may sound even more suggestive if we use forward prices. As we know, the forward prices are defined as $D_{HH}(K_1, K_2)/B(t, T)$, $DC_1/B(t, T)$ and $DC_2/B(t, T)$ for the double and single digital options respectively. We have then

$$\max\left(\frac{DC_1}{B(t, T)} + \frac{DC_2}{B(t, T)} - 1, 0\right) \leqslant \frac{D_{HH}(K_1, K_2)}{B(t, T)} \leqslant \min\left(\frac{DC_1}{B(t, T)}, \frac{DC_2}{B(t, T)}\right)$$

and it is easy to recognize that the two bounds constraining the forward price of the double digital option are the Fréchet bounds taking the forward prices of the single digital options as arguments. Let us observe and stress that these bounds emerged from no-arbitrage considerations only. Furthermore, it must be recalled that the Fréchet bounds fulfill the conditions defining copula functions, suggesting that this arbitrage-based result could hide a more general finding that is going to be proved in the following section.

8.3.2 Copula pricing kernel

We now take one step further and investigate the features of the no-arbitrage forward price of the bivariate digital option. From our previous findings of Fréchet-like pricing bounds, we are naturally led to conjecture that such a bivariate kernel is a copula function, i.e. a function of the kind

$$D_{HH}(K_1, K_2)/B(t, T) = C(DC_1/B(t, T), DC_2/B(t, T))$$

The following proposition proves that this conjecture is true.

Proposition 8.2 The bivariate pricing kernel is a function $C_{HH}(v, z)$ taking the univariate pricing kernels as arguments. In order to rule out arbitrage opportunities the function must fulfill the following requirements:

- it is defined in $I^2 = [0, 1] \times [0, 1]$ and takes values in $I = [0, 1]$
- for every v and z of I^2, $C_{HH}(v, 0) = 0 = C(0, z)$, $C_{HH}(v, 1) = v$, $C_{HH}(1, z) = z$
- for every rectangle $[v_1, v_2] \times [z_1, z_2]$ in I^2, with $v_1 \leqslant v_2$ and $z_1 \leqslant z_2$

$$C_{HH}(v_2, z_2) - C_{HH}(v_2, z_1) - C_{HH}(v_1, z_2) + C_{HH}(v_1, z_1) \geqslant 0$$

Proof: The first condition is trivial: the prices of the digital options cannot be higher than the risk-free asset B, implying that the forward prices of both the univariate and bivariate digital are bounded in the unit interval. The second condition follows directly from the no-arbitrage inequality in Proposition 8.2, by substituting the values 0 and 1 for $v = DC_1/B(t, T)$ or $z = DC_2/B(t, T)$. As for the last requirement, consider taking two different strike prices $K_{11} > K_{12}$ for the first security, and $K_{21} > K_{22}$ for the second. Denote with v_1 the forward price of the first digital corresponding to the strike K_{11} – with v_2 that of the first digital for the strike K_{12} – and use an analogous notation for the second security. Then, the third condition above can be rewritten as

$$D_{HH}(K_{12}, K_{22}) - D_{HH}(K_{12}, K_{21}) - D_{HH}(K_{11}, K_{22}) + D_{HH}(K_{11}, K_{21}) \geqslant 0$$

As such, it implies that a spread position in bivariate options paying one unit if the two underlying assets end in the region $[K_{12}, K_{11}] \times [K_{22}, K_{21}]$ cannot have negative value.

$\square$

To sum up our results, we may match the two propositions above with the mathematical definitions given in Chapter 2, so giving a characterization of the requirements that have to be imposed on the bivariate pricing kernel in order to rule out arbitrage opportunities.

Proposition 8.3 The arbitrage-free pricing kernel of a bivariate contingent claim is a copula function taking the univariate pricing kernels as arguments

$$\frac{D_{HH}(K_1, K_2)}{B(t, T)} = C_{HH}\left(\frac{DC_1(K_1)}{B(t, T)}, \frac{DC_2(K_2)}{B(t, T)}\right)$$

and the corresponding super-replication strategies are represented by the Fréchet bounds:

$$\max\left(\frac{DC_1(K_1)}{B(t, T)} + \frac{DC_2(K_2)}{B(t, T)} - 1, 0\right) \leqslant C_{HH}\left(\frac{DC_1(K_1)}{B(t, T)}, \frac{DC_2(K_2)}{B(t, T)}\right)$$

$$\leqslant \min\left(\frac{DC_1(K_1)}{B(t, T)}, \frac{DC_2(K_2)}{B(t, T)}\right)$$

It must be stressed again that in order to prove the result we did not rely on any assumption concerning the probabilistic nature of the arguments of the pricing function: these are only required to be no-arbitrage prices of single digital options. In this respect, our results carry over to the more general incomplete market pricing models based on the use of convex *capacities*, that we discussed above.

It is worth while noticing how the market incompleteness question is complicated in a bivariate setting, and in a multivariate setting in general. We may say that we have a market incompleteness problem in one dimension, which has to do with the issues discussed above and may lead to pricing bounds for the digital options. So, we may have, for example,

$$B(t, T) Q_i^-(K_i \mid \Im_t) \leqslant DC_i(K_i) \leqslant B(t, T) Q_i^+(K_i \mid \Im_t)$$

for $i = 1, 2$. There is then a second dimension of the market incompleteness problem for bivariate and, in general, multivariate claims, beyond that of the univariate problem. The problem of selecting prices for the univariate products is compounded by the choice of copula function, which has to do with the dependence structure of the underlying assets. At this level, the Fréchet bounds represent the natural choice if the conservative pricing strategy is selected. In this case we have

$$B[\max(Q_1^- + Q_2^- - 1, 0)] \leqslant D_{HH}(K_1, K_2) \leqslant B \min(Q_1^+, Q_2^+)$$

where, for the sake of simplicity, we omitted the arguments of the probability bounds.

8.4   PRICING VULNERABLE OPTIONS

The massive growth of the structured finance, and the increasing practice of financial institutions to resort to the OTC market to hedge the derivatives exposures incurred to supply these products, has made counterparty risk in derivatives a major reason of concern. When a derivative contract is negotiated in the OTC market, one has to account for the possibility that the counterparty could go bust during the life of the contract. This poses a problem both to the risk management of the position and the pricing of the contract. As for risk management, the institution has to take into account that some capital must be allocated to hedge the risk connected to default of the counterparties. As for pricing, the evaluation of each derivative contract has to take into account the credit standing of the counterparty, as well as the dependence between its default and the dynamics of the underlying asset.

Copula functions are particularly well suited to address the pricing and hedging problem of vulnerable derivatives – that is, contracts in which the counterparty may not be able to make good its obligation. In fact, evaluating vulnerable derivatives is an intrinsically bivariate problem, as the pay-off is conditional on two events: the first is that the derivative ends up in the money, the second is survival of the counterparty, as well as dependence between its default and the dynamics of the underlying asset. The approach proposed in Cherubini and Luciano (2002b), which we follow here, exploits copula functions to yield a flexible framework, extending and encompassing the specific models proposed in the literature. Well-known models such as Johnson and Stulz (1987), Hull and White (1995) and Klein (1996), for example, are built under the assumption of the log-normal distribution of the underlying asset and a structural model for the credit risk of the counterparty. Other papers, such as Jarrow and Turnbull (1995) and Barone, Barone-Adesi and Castagna (1998), deal with counterparty risk in bond options applying different term structure models, and both prefer a reduced form specification for counterparty risk. We are going to show that copula functions enable us to choose the most suitable specification for both market and counterparty risk, as well as a flexible representation of the dependence structure between the two risks.

8.4.1 Vulnerable digital options

We start our analysis from the simplest products, that is digital options. This will both make the building blocks of the application clearer and open the way to more complex applications, that will follow. We remind the reader that from the previous section we denote as $DC_i(K_i)$ the default-free price of a call digital option, i.e. a contract paying one unit if and only if at the exercise date T we observe $S_i \geqslant K_i$ for a given strike K_i. Assume now that a digital option is written by a counterparty A, which is subject to default risk: the option will pay one unit under the joint event of the option ending in the money and survival of the counterparty A; it will be worth R_A, the *recovery rate* for maturity T, if it expires in the money and counterparty A defaults; it will be worth zero otherwise. We will denote this option as V-$DC_i(K_i)$. Our task is to characterize the arbitrage-free value of such an option. We assume we are able to observe or estimate the value of a defaultable zero-coupon bond issued by counterparty A, or by some issuer of the same risk class, for the same maturity T. We denote its market value by $P_A(t, T)$. The value of the default-free zero-coupon bond for the same maturity is denoted by $B(t, T)$, as above. We also define some quantities that are often used by practitioners to assess the credit risk of a debt issue, and that will be useful in this analysis. In particular, we define Del_A the discounted expected loss on the zero-coupon issued by A for maturity T, computed as $Del_A = B(t, T) - P_A(t, T)$, and the corresponding expected loss $El_A = Del_A/B(t, T)$. We may also define the *loss given default* figure $Lgd_A = 1 - R_A$: throughout the analysis, we will assume that this figure is non-stochastic (or independent of the events of exercise of the option and default of the counterparty).

To recover the price of the vulnerable option we first partition the sample space at the expiration time T into the states shown in Table 8.3, and we may write down the pay-off matrix (Table 8.4) for all the products defined above.

Notice that the framework of the analysis is similar to that used in the previous section to price bivariate digital options. In order to apply that analysis, we can easily pivot the pay-off matrix in the following way. Let us build the following two portfolios: the first consists in a long and a short position in $1/(1 - R_A)$ units of the default-free and defaultable bond respectively; the second is made up by a long and a short position in $1/(1 - R_A)$ units

Table 8.3 Breaking down the sample space for the vulnerable digital option

	State H	State L
State H	$S_i \geqslant K_i$ and A survives	$S_i \geqslant K_i$ and A defaults
State L	$S_i < K_i$ and A survives	$S_i < K_i$ and A defaults

Table 8.4 Prices and pay-offs for bonds and digital options

	Price	HH	HL	LH	LL
Defaultable bond company A	$P_A(t, T)$	1	R_A	1	R_A
Risk-free asset	$B(t, T)$	1	1	1	1
Univariate digital option	$DC_i(K_i)$	1	1	0	0
Vulnerable digital option	V-$DC_i(K_i)$	1	R_A	0	0

Table 8.5 Prices and pay-offs for portfolios of assets in Table 8.4

Price	HH	HL	LH	LL
$[B(t, T) - P_A(t, T)]/(1 - R_A)$	0	1	0	1
$B(t, T)$	1	1	1	1
$DC_i(S_i \geqslant K_i)$	1	1	0	0
$[DV_i(K_i) - V\text{-}D_i(K_i)]/(1 - R_A)$	0	1	0	0

of the default-free and vulnerable digital option. Including these portfolios in the pay-off matrix we get the values shown in Table 8.5.

The pricing problem is now exactly the same as that of a bivariate digital option, and we can apply the results in the propositions above. The arbitrage-free price of the second portfolio described above (long the default-free option and short the vulnerable one) has to be equal to the discounted value of a copula function taking the forward values of the default-free digital option and the first portfolio as arguments. Rearranging terms, it is straightforward to show

Corollary 8.1 The price of a vulnerable call digital option, $V\text{-}DC_i$, is given by

$$V\text{-}DC_i(K_i) = DC_i(K_i) - B(t, T)(1 - R_A)C_{HL}\left(\frac{DC_i(K_i)}{B(t, T)}, \frac{B(t, T) - P_A(t, T)}{B(t, T)(1 - R_A)}\right)$$

where $C_{HL}(x, y)$ is a copula function.

The corollary allows us to split the vulnerable digital price into the non-vulnerable digital price, $D_i(K_i)$, minus **counterparty risk**:

$$B(t, T)(1 - R_A)C_{HL}\left(\frac{DC_i(K_i)}{B(t, T)}, \frac{B(t, T) - P_A(t, T)}{B(t, T)(1 - R_A)}\right) = B(t, T)Lgd_A$$

$$\times C_{HL}\left(\frac{DC_i(K_i)}{B(t, T)}, \frac{El_A}{Lgd_A}\right)$$

Denoting by $Q_A(T \mid \Im_t)$ the default probability of counterparty A by time T, conditional on the information available at time t, we have that $El_A = Lgd_A * Q_A(T \mid \Im_t)$. The price of the vulnerable call option can then be written

$$V\text{-}DC_i(K_i) = DC_i(K_i) - B(t, T)Lgd_A C_{HL}(\overline{Q}_i(K_i), Q_A(T) \mid \Im_t)$$

and it is clear why the price involves a copula function, taking the risk-neutral probability of exercise of the option and the risk-neutral probability of default of the counterparty as arguments.

By the same argument, the price of a defaultable digital put option can be priced as

$$V\text{-}DP_i(K_i) = DP_i(K_i) - B(t, T)Lgd_A C_{LL}(Q_i(K_i), Q_A(T) \mid \Im_t)$$

Notice that using the relationship between copulas

$$C_{LL}(Q_i(K_i), Q_A(\dot{T})) = Q_A(T \mid \Im_t) - C_{HL}(\overline{Q}_i(K_i), Q_A(T) \mid \Im_t)$$

we may rewrite

$$
\begin{aligned}
\text{V-}DP_i(K_i) &= DP_i(K_i) - B(t, T) Lgd_A C_{LL}(Q_i(K_i), Q_A(T) \mid \Im_t) \\
&= DP_i(K_i) - B(t, T) Lgd_A [Q_A(T \mid \Im_t) - C_{HL}(\overline{Q}_i(K_i), Q_A(T) \mid \Im_t)] \\
&= B(t, T) - DC_i(K_i) + C_{HL}(\overline{Q}_i(K_i), Q_A(T) \mid \Im_t) \\
&\quad - B(t, T) Lgd_A Q_A(T \mid \Im_t) \\
&= B(t, T) - \text{V-}DC_i(K_i) - B(t, T) Lgd_A Q_A(T \mid \Im_t) \\
&= B(t, T) [1 - Lgd_A Q_A(T \mid \Im_t)] - \text{V-}DC_i(K_i) \\
&= P_A(t, T) - \text{V-}DC_i(K_i)
\end{aligned}
$$

where we have used $DC_i(K_i) + DP_i(K_i) = B(t, T)$. In this way we recovered an obvious put−call parity relationship between vulnerable digital options. Buying a digital call and a digital put from the same counterparty amounts to buying a defaultable zero-coupon bond issued by the counterparty:

$$DC_i(K_i) + DP_i(K_i) = P_A(t, T)$$

8.4.2 Pricing vulnerable call options

We now use the results obtained above for digital options to evaluate counterparty risk in a typical derivative contract such as a European option. As suggested above, we resort to the Breeden and Litzenberger (1978) idea of considering an option as an integral sum of digital contracts. We recall that according to their approach, the value at time t of a default-free call option written on S_i with time to expiration T and strike K may be written as

$$\text{CALL}(S_i, t : K, T) = \int_K^\infty DC_i(u) \, du = B(t, T) \int_K^\infty \overline{Q}_i(u) \, du$$

This representation can be easily extended to the vulnerable case, and it is natural to use the results obtained in the previous section, concerning the vulnerable pricing kernel, to recover

$$
\begin{aligned}
\text{V-CALL}(S_i, t : K, T) &= \int_K^\infty \text{V-}DC_i(u) \, du \\
&= \int_K^\infty \left[DC_i(u) - B(t, T) Lgd_A C_{HL}\left(\frac{DC_i(u)}{B}, \frac{El_A}{Lgd_A} \right) \right] du
\end{aligned}
$$

where V-CALL denotes the vulnerable call option. Using the no-arbitrage pricing relationship $D_i(u) = B(t, T) \overline{Q}(u)$, it is now straightforward to obtain the following:

Proposition 8.4   The no-arbitrage price of a vulnerable call option is given by

$$\text{V-CALL}(S_i, t : K, T) = \text{CALL}(S_i, t : K, T) - B(t, T) Lgd_A \int_K^\infty C_{HL}\left(Q_i(u), \frac{El_A}{Lgd_A}\right) du$$

where $C_{HL}(x, y)$ is a copula function.

So, computing **counterparty risk**, which is now

$$B(t, T) Lgd_A \int_K^\infty C_{HL}\left(\overline{Q}_i(u), \frac{El_A}{Lgd_A}\right) du$$

requires to evaluate an integral of the copula function, with respect to the first argument, that is the pricing kernel. This integral is not generally available in closed form. Three interesting cases, however, represent notable exceptions, as we show below.

- The case of independence between the underlying asset and default of the counterparty is computed directly using the product copula, which enables us to exploit factorization of the terms in the integral to yield

$$\text{V-CALL}(S_i, t; K, T) = \text{CALL}(S_i, t; K, T)(1 - El_A)$$

Notice that in the case of independence the loss given default figure is dropped from the formula, and all we need is the aggregate expected loss figure, which is typically provided by the rating agencies.
- The second relevant case is perfect positive dependence. It is noticeable to observe that even in this instance we may recover a closed form solution, whenever a closed form solution exists for the corresponding default-free option price

$$\text{V-CALL}(S_i, t; K, T) = \text{CALL}(S_i, t; K, T) - \max\left(K^* - K, 0\right)$$
$$\times Del_A - Lgd_A \text{CALL}\left(S_i, t; \max\left(K, K^*\right), T\right)$$

where $K^* = \overline{Q}_i^{-1}(El_A/Lgd_A)$, that is the strike of a call option whose exercise probability is equal to the default probability of the counterparty.[1] For practical purposes, it is useful to notice that K^* corresponds to a far out-of-the-money option: as a result, the value of the corresponding default-free option is usually very close to zero. Since in

---

[1] It may be worthwhile to discuss how this formula is recovered. When $K < K^*$ the problem is to compute

$$BLgd_A \int_K^\infty \min\left(Q(\eta), \frac{El_A}{Lgd_A}\right) d\eta = BLgd_A\left[\int_K^{K^*} \frac{El_A}{Lgd_A} d\eta + \int_{K^*}^\infty Q(\eta) d\eta\right]$$
$$= (K^* - K)Del_A + Lgd_A C(S_i, t; K^*, T)$$

where the last equality uses the definition of discounted expected loss and the integral representation for the call option discussed above. Consideration of the case $K^* < K$ is trivial, and immediately leads to the formula in the text.

most applications we have $K^* \geqslant K$, counterparty risk in the case of perfect dependence will be effectively approximated by the quantity $(K^* - K)Del_A$, which is very easy to compute. If $K^* < K$ the value of the vulnerable option is simply $R_A C(S_i, t; K, T)$ and credit risk tends to zero with the option value.

• The case of perfect negative dependence may also be easily computed using the same strategy to get

$$\text{V-CALL}(S_i, t; K, T) = (1 - Lgd_A)\,\text{CALL}(S_i, t; K, T)$$
$$+ Lgd_A \text{CALL}\left(S_i, t; \max\left(K, K^{**}\right), T\right)$$
$$- \max\left(K^{**} - K, 0\right)\left(B(t, T)\,Lgd_A - Del_A\right)$$

with $K^{**} = \overline{Q}_i^{-1}(1 - (El_A/Lgd_A))$, that is the strike of a very deep-in-the-money option, whose exercise probability is equal to the survival probability of the counterparty. It is straightforward to check that if (as in most practical applications) $K^{**} \leqslant K$, the value of the vulnerable option is the same as that of the corresponding default-free contract. In the case $K < K^{**}$ counterparty risk is instead evaluated as

$$Lgd_A \left[\text{CALL}(S_i, t; K, T) - \text{CALL}\left(S_i, t; K^{**}, T\right) + \left(K^{**} - K\right)\left(B(t, T) - \frac{Del_A}{Lgd_A}\right)\right]$$

The formulas above provide very straightforward hedging strategies for the counterparty risk in a vulnerable call option. In the case of perfect positive dependence, the hedging strategy would call for being long $\max(K^* - K, 0)$ of a default put and Lgd_A of a call with strike $\max(K^*, K)$. Since usually, as we argued above, the value of this option is very close to zero, the credit derivative is a sufficient hedge. Correspondingly, under perfect negative dependence and with $K < K^{**}$ the hedge consists of being long Lgd_A call spreads written on strikes K and K^{**}, long $(K^{**} - K)\,R_A$ of the riskless bonds and short $(K^{**} - K)$ of P_A. These hedging strategies refer to extreme dependence cases, and represent the super-replication strategies corresponding to the Fréchet bounds discussed above.

8.4.3 Pricing vulnerable put options

The same approach can be applied to evaluate vulnerable put options. In this case, the starting point is given by the representation

$$\text{V-PUT}(S_i, t : K, T) = \int_0^K \text{V-}DP_i(u)\,\mathrm{d}u$$
$$= \int_0^K \left[DP_i(u) - B(t, T)\,Lgd_A C_{\text{LL}}\left(\frac{DP_i(u)}{B(t, T)}, \frac{El_A}{Lgd_A}\right)\right]\mathrm{d}u$$
$$= \text{PUT}(S_i, t : K, T) - B(t, T)\int_0^K Lgd_A C_{\text{LL}}\left(Q_i(u), \frac{El_A}{Lgd_A}\right)\mathrm{d}u$$

$$(8.1)$$

where V-PUT denotes the vulnerable put price, and the second addendum in (8.1) represents **counterparty risk**. Using the same strategy as before we can compute the value of the option in closed form for the three benchmark cases. Namely, we get

$$\text{V-PUT}(S_i, t; K, T) = \text{PUT}(S_i, t; K, T)(1 - El_A)$$

for the independence case,

$$\text{V-PUT}(S_i, t; K, T) = \text{PUT}(S_i, t; K, T) - \max\left(K - K^{**}, 0\right)$$
$$\times Del_A - Lgd_A\text{PUT}(S_i, t; \min\left(K^{**}, K\right), T)$$

for perfect positive dependence, and finally

$$\text{V-PUT}(S_i, t; K, T) = (1 - Lgd_A)\,\text{PUT}(S_i, t; K, T)$$
$$+ Lgd_A\text{PUT}\left(S_i, t; \min\left(K, K^*\right), T\right)$$
$$- \max\left(K - K^*, 0\right)(BLgd_A - Del_A)$$

for perfect negative correlation. Notice that the values K^* and K^{**} are the same as in the call option case above.

As for the case of vulnerable digital options, we can use the no-arbitrage relationship derived for digital call and put options to write

$$C_{LL}\left(Q(u), \frac{El_A}{Lgd_A}\right) = \frac{El_A}{Lgd_A} - C_{HL}\left(\overline{Q}(u), \frac{El_A}{Lgd_A}\right)$$

and to recover a relationship between the price of vulnerable call and put options as in the following.

Proposition 8.5 [*Vulnerable put–call parity*] In order to rule out arbitrage opportunities, the relationship between vulnerable call and put options must be

$$\text{V-PUT}(S_i, t : K, T) + S_i(t) = \text{V-CALL}(S_i, t : K, T) + K P_A(t, T)$$
$$+ B(t, T) Lgd_A \int_0^\infty C_{HL}\left(Q(u), \frac{El_A}{Lgd_A}\right) du$$

Proof:

$$\text{V-PUT}(S_i, t : K, T) + S_i(t) = \text{PUT}(S_i, t : K, T)$$
$$+ S_i(t) - B(t, T) Lgd_A \int_0^K C_{LL}\left(Q(u), \frac{El_A}{Lgd_A}\right) du$$
$$= \text{CALL}(S_i, t : K, T) + K B(t, T)$$
$$- B(t, T) Lgd_A \int_0^K \left[\frac{El_A}{Lgd_A} - C_{HL}\left(\overline{Q}(u), \frac{El_A}{Lgd_A}\right)\right] du$$

$$= \text{CALL}(S_i, t : K, T) + K(B(t, T) - Del_A)$$

$$+ B(t, T) Lgd_A \int_0^K C_{\text{HL}} \left(\overline{Q}(u), \frac{El_A}{Lgd_A} \right) du$$

$$= \text{V-CALL}(S_i, t : K, T) + K P_A(t, T)$$

$$+ B(t, T) Lgd_A \int_0^\infty C_{\text{HL}} \left(\overline{Q}(u), \frac{El_A}{Lgd_A} \right) du$$

$\square$

8.4.4 Pricing vulnerable options in practice

We now report some concrete examples of copula pricing applications to vulnerable options. Let us first notice that the approach guarantees the maximum flexibility concerning the choice of: (i) the option pricing model; (ii) the credit evaluation approach; and (iii) the dependence structure. As for the first choice, we stick here to the standard Black–Scholes for a matter of illustration of the approach. The credit assessment choice is, of course, crucial: one can choose either a structural approach based on the stock market value and volatility of the counterparty or a reduced form based on corporate bonds or credit derivatives information. Having firm specific information is obviously preferable if one wants to have some idea on the dependence between default risk of the counterparty and dynamics of the underlying asset of the vulnerable contract. If such information is not available, one could rely on figures from the rating agencies and assume some scenario concerning the dependence structure. Finally, a good choice to gauge the relevance of the dependence structure for counterparty risk is to resort to the Fréchet family of copulas. As these copulas are obtained as linear combinations of the perfect positive and negative dependence and the product one, it follows that they can be priced in closed form using the formulas derived in the paragraph above for each of these cases. In particular, it is very useful to use mixture copulas based on the perfect dependence and the independence cases.

The effect of counterparty risk on the prices of options

In Figure 8.1 we report the counterparty risk figure in a one-year digital option for a Baa3 rated counterparty, as a function of the Kendall's *tau* statistic. Use is made of the mixture copula described above. The relationship is reported for different levels of the probability of exercise, i.e. for different levels of moneyness. Based on Moody's data, the issuer has expected loss (El_A) equal to 0.231% and a recovery rate (R_A) of 55%. For the sake of simplicity, we select a 20% constant value of volatility of the underlying asset and zero risk-free rate. It may be checked that the relationship between counterparty risk and the dependence statistics is increasing.

   The prices of vulnerable call options are obtained by integration of the pricing kernel depicted above, and vulnerable put options are recovered by arbitrage. Figures 8.2 and 8.3 present the counterparty risk in vulnerable call and put options respectively. The current price of the underlying asset is assumed to be equal to 1 and the relationship is reported for levels of the strike ranging from 0.6 through 1.4. As before, we assume a time of one year to expiration, a 20% constant volatility and zero risk-free rate. As for the counterparty, we

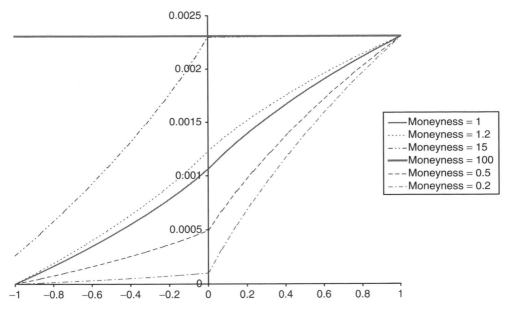

Figure 8.1   Counterpart risk in digital options

Vulnerable Call Options-Mixture Copulas

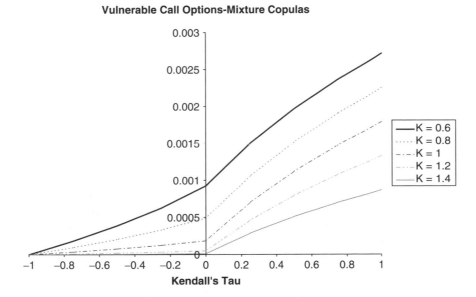

Figure 8.2   Counterpart risk in call options

consider an expected loss figure of 0.231%, corresponding to a Baa3 writer of the option. As a consequence, the values K^* and K^{**} used to represent positive and negative dependence turned out to be 1.727 and 0.556 respectively.

As for call options, the schedules of the relationship are shifted upwards as the strike price decreases. Concerning the amounts involved, we reckon that, for any billion of underlying

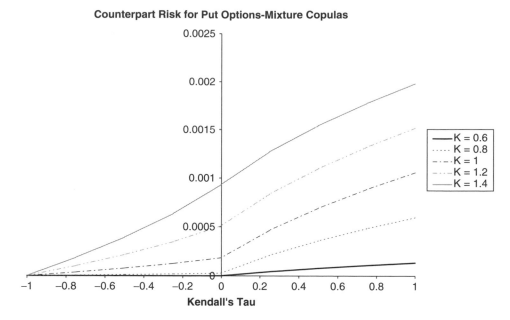

Figure 8.3 Counterpart risk in put options

Table 8.6 Counterpart risk as a percentage of the value of option

Kendall τ	AAA	Aaa3	A3	Baa3	Ba3	B3	Caa3
1	0.00117%	0.02700%	0.27620%	2.24963%	10.88450%	30.93574%	59.66535%
0.75	0.00094%	0.02200%	0.22594%	1.85151%	9.04262%	26.09492%	53.42897%
0.50	0.00069%	0.01639%	0.16946%	1.40410%	6.97275%	20.65490%	46.42065%
0.25	0.00040%	0.00984%	0.10365%	0.88277%	4.56084%	14.31590%	38.25417%
0	0.00003%	0.00166%	0.02137%	0.23100%	1.54550%	6.39100%	28.04461%
−0.25	0.00002%	0.00112%	0.01447%	0.15642%	1.04650%	4.32750%	18.98969%
−0.50	0.00001%	0.00070%	0.00895%	0.09676%	0.64735%	2.67694%	11.74680%
−0.75	0.00001%	0.00033%	0.00421%	0.04556%	0.30481%	1.26046%	5.53108%
−1	0.00000%	0.00000%	0.00000%	0.00000%	0.00000%	0.00000%	0.00000%

assets, in the case of independence counterparty risk is worth 924 603, 184 005 and 10 396 for deep-in-the-money ($K = 0.6$), at-the-money and far-out-of-the-money ($K = 1.4$) contracts. The figures increase with dependence up to 2 715 961, 1 791 961 and 867 961 respectively; counterparty risk tends to zero with perfect negative dependence, since the strike is higher than the upper level $K^* = 1.727$.

Finally, to have an idea concerning the effect of dependence for different rating classes of the counterparty we report, in Table 8.6, the value of counterparty risk as a percentage of the value of the corresponding default-free call option. The option is assumed to be at-the-money, with one year to the exercise date and a volatility parameter of 20%.

Hedging counterparty risk in options

Notice that in the analysis above for the particular cases of independence and perfect dependence the evaluation of vulnerable options only calls for knowledge of the pricing formulas for the corresponding default-free products. More precisely, in the case of perfect dependence, counterparty risk is represented by a short position in the spread $B(t, T) - P_A(t, T) = Del$, that can be traded in the market using a credit derivative contract, i.e. a default put option, and a short position in a default-free option. The same structure applies for put options. On the other hand, in the case of independence we have that the amount of the position in the spread turns out to be equal to the $CALL(.)/B(t, T)$, i.e. the forward value of the default-free call option. This suggests very straightforward hedging strategies for extreme dependence scenarios, that is the super-hedging strategies. The hedging strategy in the independence case is immediate. Instead, under the worst case scenario of perfect dependence, the counterparty risk of a call option can be hedged by entering a long position in default put options for an amount equal to $\max(K^* - K, 0)$ and by buying Lgd call options with strike K^*. By the same token, the super-hedging strategy for put options involves long positions in $\max(K - K^{**}, 0)$ default put options and Lgd put options with strike K^{**}.

To make a concrete example, consider a 1 million euro position in one of the call options studied above. Say it is at-the-money, exercised in one year, and is issued by a Baa3 counterparty. We recall that the one-year default probability is 0.231% and the recovery rate is 55%. Furthermore, the value K^* was found equal to 1.727. For the sake of simplicity, we assume the risk-free rate to be equal to zero. The perfect positive dependence super-hedge consists of

- buying protection for a 727 000 nominal exposure to the counterparty for an up-front payment equal to 755.72 euros;
- buying 450 000 default-free call options with strike equal to 1.727 against an up-front payment of 122.80 euros.

The total cost of the hedge is then 878.52 out of a default-free value of the option position of 79 655.79.

The independence super-hedge requires instead buying protection for a nominal value of 79 655.79 for a cost of 82.80 euros. Taking linear combinations of the extreme cases enables us to account for imperfect positive dependence. For example, corresponding to a Spearman ρ_S figure equal to 50%, the cost of the hedge is $(0.5 \times 878.52) + (0.5 \times 82.80) = 480.66$.

8.5 PRICING RAINBOW TWO-COLOR OPTIONS

Rainbow options are multivariate contingent claims whose underlying asset is the maximum or minimum in a set of assets. So, the typical pay-off for a bivariate, or two-color, rainbow option is

$$G(S_1(T), S_2(T), T) = \max[\min(S_1(T), S_2(T)) - K, 0]$$

which is the call option on the minimum between two assets, or

$$G(S_1(T), S_2(T), T) = \max[K - \max(S_1(T), S_2(T)), 0]$$

that is, the put option on the maximum between two assets. Once these options are priced, the evaluation of other similar products, such as call options on the maximum and put options on the minimum of two assets, can be recovered by arbitrage, as pointed out by Stulz (1982). His paper also provided closed form solutions for these options in a Black–Scholes world. We will see here that the use of copula functions enables us to extend these results quite naturally to a more general setting. In fact, we are going to show that the price of the two options described above has a straightforward interpretation in terms of copula functions, and that these representations easily lead to analytical super-replication hedges.

8.5.1 Call option on the minimum of two assets

The basic argument that allows us to write down, in terms of copulas, the price of a call option on the minimum of two underlying assets is quite easy to understand by exploiting the analogy with the univariate plain vanilla option. We know that, in that case,

$$\text{CALL}(Z, t; K, T) = B(t, T) \int_K^\infty \overline{Q}_Z(u \mid \Im_t) \, du$$

Applying the probability distribution technique described above, with $Z = f(S_1, S_2) = \min(S_1, S_2)$ we may write

$$\text{CALL}(S_1, S_2, t; K, T) = B(t, T) \int_K^\infty \Pr(\min(S_1(T), S_2(T)) > u \mid \Im_t) \, du$$

where probability is computed under the risk-neutral measure. So, the relevant pricing kernel is that of the minimum of the two risky assets S_1 and S_2. Consider their joint survival probability, for any threshold u: $\Pr(S_1(T) > u, S_2(T) > u \mid \Im_t)$. Obviously, stating that, at time T, both of the prices will be higher than u is equivalent to saying that the lower of the two will be above that threshold. So, the price of the option becomes

$$\text{CALL}(S_1, S_2, t; K, T) = B(t, T) \int_K^\infty \Pr(S_1(T) > u, S_2(T) > u \mid \Im_t) \, du$$

$$= B(t, T) \int_K^\infty \overline{Q}(u, u \mid \Im_t) \, du$$

It is now easy to check that the copula function approach can be particularly useful to give a flexible representation of this kind of product. In fact, using the general result discussed above for bivariate digital options

$$D_{\text{HH}}(u, u) = B(t, T) \overline{Q}(u, u \mid \Im_t)$$

$$= B(t, T) C_{\text{HH}}(\overline{Q}_1(u), \overline{Q}_2(u) \mid \Im_t)$$

we may write

$$\text{CALL}(S_1, S_2, t; K, T) = B(t, T) \int_K^\infty C_{\text{HH}}(\overline{Q}_1(u), \overline{Q}_2(u) \mid \Im_t) \, du$$

In this way, we are able to separate the marginal distributions, and thus the marginal pricing kernels, from the dependence structure, which is represented by the copula function C_{HH}.

Using the copula function representation we may also check how the problem of market incompleteness is compounded in a multidimensional setting. First, the market for each underlying asset may have incompleteness problems. In this case we would have

$$\text{CALL}\,(S_1, S_2, t; K, T) = B\,(t, T) \int_K^\infty C_{HH}(\overline{Q_1}\,(u), \overline{Q_2}\,(u) \mid \Im_t)\, du$$

Second, even if the market for each underlying asset is complete, so that the marginal distributions are uniquely determined, it may be the case that the dependence structure cannot be precisely identified. In other words, it may happen (and it happens often) that the joint pricing kernel cannot be uniquely determined. We know that if the marginal pricing kernels are continuous, each candidate joint pricing kernel can be associated to a specific copula function. So, solving the pricing problem in an incomplete market amounts to selecting a specific copula function. As in the univariate approach, one could then select one specific copula, following some strategy of choice. Alternatively, or prior to that, one could follow a conservative approach, and evaluate pricing bounds, corresponding to extreme dependence assumptions, and the corresponding copula functions. As we are going to show, by using Fréchet copulas it is also easy to design super-replication portfolios corresponding to these conservative scenarios.

Dependence structure and super-replicating portfolios

We now try to recover the pricing bounds of the call option on the minimum between two underlying assets. In order to focus the analysis on the dependence structure issue, we may assume that the markets of each of the underlying assets are complete, so that the marginal pricing kernels are uniquely identified. Then, the only source of market incompleteness has to do with the dependence structure between the two assets. We may then apply the Fréchet bounds for copulas

$$\max(\overline{Q}_1\,(u) + \overline{Q}_2\,(u) - 1, 0 \mid \Im_t) \leqslant C_{HH}(\overline{Q}_1\,(u), \overline{Q}_2\,(u) \mid \Im_t)$$

$$\leqslant \min(\overline{Q}_1\,(u), \overline{Q}_2\,(u) \mid \Im_t)$$

Substituting in the pricing formula above we obtain

$$\text{CALL}^+\,(S_1, S_2, t; K, T) = B\,(t, T) \int_K^\infty \min(\overline{Q}_1\,(u), \overline{Q}_2\,(u) \mid \Im_t)\, du$$

as the upper bound for the price, corresponding to perfect positive dependence of the underlying assets. We also obtain

$$\text{CALL}^-\,(S_1, S_2, t; K, T) = B\,(t, T) \int_K^\infty \max(\overline{Q}_1\,(u) + \overline{Q}_2\,(u) - 1, 0 \mid \Im_t)\, du$$

as the lower price corresponding to perfect negative dependence.

These pricing bounds are particularly useful because they can be computed analytically and can be expressed in terms of univariate call options. In such a way, they are directly referred to specific super-replication strategies for the product. Let us start with the upper bound CALL$^+$. To compute the integral we first recover a strike price K^* such that $\overline{Q}_1 (K^*) = \overline{Q}_2 (K^*)$. Assume, without loss of generality, that for $u < K^*$ we have $\overline{Q}_1 (u) < \overline{Q}_2 (u)$. Then we have two cases. If $K \geqslant K^*$ the joint pricing kernel will coincide with the marginal pricing kernel $\overline{Q}_2 (u)$, which will be lower than $\overline{Q}_1 (u)$ for any $u > K$. As a result, the price of the call option on the minimum will be the same as that of a univariate plain vanilla call option written on S_2. If instead we have $K < K^*$ the integral can be split in two yielding a call spread on asset S_1 and a call option on S_2 with a higher strike. Analytically we have

$$\text{CALL}^+ (S_1, S_2, t; K, T) = \mathbf{1}_{\{K^* \geqslant K\}} B (t, T) \int_K^{K^*} (\overline{Q}_1 (u) \mid \Im_t) \, du$$

$$+ B (t, T) \int_{\max[K, K^*]}^{\infty} (\overline{Q}_2 (u) \mid \Im_t) \, du$$

where $\mathbf{1}_{\{K^* \geqslant K\}}$ is the indicator function assigning a value of 1 to the case $K \geqslant K^*$. As for the financial meaning of the formula, the first term is a call spread on asset S_1 for strike prices K and K^*; the second term is a call option on asset S_2 for strike price equal to $\max[K, K^*]$. So, the super-replication portfolio for the call option on the maximum is

$$\text{CALL}^+ (S_1, S_2, t; K, T) = \mathbf{1}_{\{K^* \geqslant K\}}[\text{CALL}(S_1, t; K, T) - \text{CALL}(S_1, t; K^*, T)]$$

$$+ \text{CALL}(S_2, t; \max[K, K^*], T)$$

Following the same strategy we can compute the lower bound of the price, and the corresponding super-replication portfolio. In this case, we define a strike price K^{**} such that $\overline{Q}_1 (K^{**}) + \overline{Q}_2 (K^{**}) = 1$. Of course, as both $\overline{Q}_1 (u)$ and $\overline{Q}_2 (u)$ are strictly decreasing, we would have that $\overline{Q}_1 (u) + \overline{Q}_2 (u) \leqslant 1$ for any $u \geqslant K^{**}$. So, remembering that the joint pricing kernel is $\max[\overline{Q}_1 (u) + \overline{Q}_2 (u) - 1, 0]$ it will be equal to zero for any such $u \geqslant K^{**}$. Now consider two cases. If it is $K \geqslant K^{**}$ the value of the option will be identically zero. If instead we have $K < K^{**}$ the integral can again be split in two yielding

$$\text{CALL}^- (S_1, S_2, t; K, T) = \mathbf{1}_{\{K^{**} \geqslant K\}} B (t, T) \left[\int_K^{K^{**}} (\overline{Q}_1 (u) \mid \Im_t) \, du \right.$$

$$\left. + \int_K^{K^{**}} (\overline{Q}_2 (u) \mid \Im_t) \, du - [K^{**} - K] \right]$$

Notice that in this case we have two call spreads in the two assets S_1 and S_2, both with strike prices K^{**} and K, plus a debt position for an amount equal to $K^{**} - K$. In other words, we have

$$\text{CALL}^- (S_1, S_2, t; K, T) = \mathbf{1}_{\{K^{**} \geqslant K\}}[\text{CALL}(S_1, t; K, T) - \text{CALL}(S_1, t; K^{**}, T)$$

$$+ \text{CALL}(S_2, t; K, T) - \text{CALL}(S_2, t; K^{**}, T)$$

$$- B(t, T)[K^{**} - K]]$$

For some pair of assets, the assumption that they can be negatively dependent may be an implausible assumption. In this case it may be useful to limit the analysis to the positive dependence orthant, so that the relevant lower bound will be the independence case. We would have, in this case,

$$
\text{CALL}^{\perp}(S_1, S_2, t; K, T) = B(t, T) \int_K^{\infty} (\overline{Q}_1(u)\,\overline{Q}_2(u) \mid \Im_t)\, du
$$

Unfortunately, however, the solution is not directly available in closed form, apart from very special cases.

8.5.2 Call option on the maximum of two assets

The call option on the maximum of two assets can be recovered by arbitrage as suggested in Stulz (1982). Define this call option by the pay-off

$$
G(S_1(T), S_2(T), T) = \max[\max(S_1(T), S_2(T)) - K, 0]
$$

It is easy to see that this pay-off can be exactly replicated by

$$
\max[\max(S_1(T), S_2(T)) - K, 0] = \max[S_1(T) - K, 0] + \max[S_2(T) - K, 0]
$$
$$
- \max[\min(S_1(T), S_2(T)) - K, 0]
$$

In fact, if we have $S_1(T) > S_2(T) > K$ the option is worth $S_1(T) - K$, while in the case $S_2(T) > S_1(T) > K$ we get $S_2(T) - K$. Checking equivalence of the pay-off in the other cases is trivial.

In order to rule out arbitrage opportunities, we must then have

$$
\overline{\text{CALL}}(S_1, S_2, t; K, T) = \text{CALL}(S_1, t; K, T) + \text{CALL}(S_2, t; K, T)
$$
$$
- \text{CALL}(S_1, S_2, t; K, T)
$$

Remark 8.1 Notice that the call option on the maximum of two assets can also be written using the dual of the survival copula C_{HH}. In fact, applying the definition given in Chapter 2 we have

$$
\overline{\text{CALL}}(S_1, S_2, t; K, T) = B(t, T) \int_K^{\infty} (\overline{Q}_1(u) \mid \Im_t)\, du + B(t, T) \int_K^{\infty} (\overline{Q}_2(u) \mid \Im_t)\, du
$$
$$
- B(t, T) \int_K^{\infty} C_{\text{HH}}(\overline{Q}_1(u), \overline{Q}_2(u) \mid \Im_t)\, du
$$
$$
= B(t, T) \int_K^{\infty} [(\overline{Q}_1(u) \mid \Im_t) + (\overline{Q}_2(u) \mid \Im_t)
$$
$$
- C_{\text{HH}}(\overline{Q}_1(u), \overline{Q}_2(u) \mid \Im_t)]\, du
$$
$$
= B(t, T) \int_K^{\infty} \widetilde{C}_{\text{HH}}(\overline{Q}_1(u), \overline{Q}_2(u) \mid \Im_t)\, du
$$

Alternatively, it is easy to check that the price could also be written in terms of the co-copula of copula C_{LL}. In fact, as shown in Chapter 2, the dual of a survival copula C_{HH} generated by a copula C_{LL} corresponds to the co-copula of the latter copula. This enables us to use the discussion in Chapter 2 to spell the basic intuition behind this result. The pricing kernel of the call option on the maximum of two assets is the risk-neutral probability that either S_1 or S_2 at time T is greater than a threshold value u:

$$\overline{\text{CALL}}\,(S_1, S_2, t; K, T) = B\,(t, T) \int_K^\infty \Pr(S_1\,(T) \text{ or } S_2\,(T) > u, \mid \Im_t)\,du$$

8.5.3   Put option on the maximum of two assets

We now approach the symmetric problem of two-color put options. In particular, symmetry suggests to start from the put option written on the maximum of two assets, whose pay-off is written as

$$G(S_1(T), S_2(T), T) = \max\,[K - \max(S_1(T), S_2(T), 0]$$

Along the same lines followed for the case of the call option, we obtain

$$\overline{\text{PUT}}\,(S_1, S_2, t; K, T) = B\,(t, T) \int_0^K \Pr(\max\,(S_1\,(T)\,, S_2\,(T)) \leqslant u \mid \Im_t)\,du$$

Again, saying that the maximum price of the underlying assets is lower than a given threshold u is the same as stating that both the prices are below that threshold. Analytically, we can write

$$\Pr\,(\max\,(S_1\,(T)\,, S_2\,(T)) \leqslant u \mid \Im_t) = \Pr\,(S_1\,(T) \leqslant u, S_2\,(T) \leqslant u \mid \Im_t)$$

so that we have

$$\overline{\text{PUT}}\,(S_1, S_2, t; K, T) = B\,(t, T) \int_0^K \Pr(S_1\,(T) \leqslant u, S_2\,(T) \leqslant u \mid \Im_t)\,du$$

Going back again to the general results obtained for bivariate digital options

$$D_{LL}\,(u, u) = B\,(t, T)\,Q\,(u, u \mid \Im_t)$$
$$= B\,(t, T)\,C_{LL}\,(Q_1\,(u)\,, Q_2\,(u) \mid \Im_t)$$

we may write

$$\overline{\text{PUT}}\,(S_1, S_2, t; K, T) = B\,(t, T) \int_0^K C_{LL}(Q_1\,(u)\,, Q_2\,(u) \mid \Im_t)\,du$$

and the price of the put option is the integral of a copula function. We could obviously apply the same techniques shown above to recover closed form solutions for the pricing bounds of this rainbow put option and the corresponding super-replication portfolios. While leaving this development to the readers, we want to focus attention on the fact that the copula function in the put option formula is different from that appearing in the call price representation. A closer inspection of the formula suggests, however, a precise relationship between the two functions, which we are going to explore in more detail in the next section.

Rainbow put/call parity

Let us restate in financial terms the results recovered for rainbow options of the call and put type. In sum, we applied to these options the same principle that Breeden and Litzenberger (1978) suggested for univariate options. Call options on the minimum between two assets can then be represented as the integral of bivariate digital call options, the integral being computed from the strike K to infinity. Symmetrically, the price of a put option on the maximum of two assets is the integral of bivariate digital put options, the integral running from zero to the strike K. We saw at the beginning of this chapter that bivariate digital call and put options are linked by precise arbitrage relationships. Intuitively, building on these findings must be possible to recover arbitrage relationships between call and put rainbow options.

We remind the readers that bivariate call and put digital options are linked by the no-arbitrage relationship

$$D_{\text{LL}}(K_1, K_2) = B(t, T) - DC_1(K_1) - DC_2(K_2) + D_{\text{HH}}(K_1, K_2)$$

which corresponds to the relationship between one copula and its survival:

$$C_{\text{LL}}(1 - u, 1 - v) = 1 - u - v + C_{\text{HH}}(u, v)$$

So, in our case we have

$$C_{\text{LL}}(Q_1(S_1(T) \leqslant u), Q_2(S_2(T) \leqslant u) \mid \Im_t)$$
$$= 1 - Q_1(S_1(T) > u \mid \Im_t) - Q_2(S_2(T) > u \mid \Im_t)$$
$$+ C_{\text{HH}}(S_1(T) > u, S_2(T) > u \mid \Im_t)$$

Based on this relationship it is now straightforward to derive a no-arbitrage link between the put option on the maximum and the call option on the minimum.

Proposition 8.6 [*Rainbow put–call parity*]   A put option on the maximum of two assets with strike price K and exercise date T is linked to the call option on the minimum of the same assets, with the same strike and exercise date by the relationship

$$\overline{\text{PUT}}(S_1, S_2, t; K, T) + S_1 + S_2 = \overline{\text{CALL}}(S_1, S_2, t; K, T) + B(t, T)K$$
$$+ \text{CALL}(S_1, S_2, t; 0, T)$$

Proof: Adding and subtracting 1 to the right-hand side of the relationship between C_{LL} and its survival copula and considering $1 - \overline{Q_i}(u \mid \Im_t) = Q_i(u \mid \Im_t)$ we have

$$C_{\text{LL}}(Q_1(u), Q_2(\leqslant u) \mid \Im_t) = Q_1(u \mid \Im_t) + Q_2(u \mid \Im_t)$$
$$-1 + C_{\text{HH}}(\overline{Q}_1(u), \overline{Q}_2(u) \mid \Im_t)$$

We now compute

$$\overline{\text{PUT}}\,(S_1, S_2, t; K, T) = B\,(t, T) \int_0^K C_{\text{LL}}(Q_1\,(u)\,, Q_2\,(u) \mid \Im_t)\,du$$

$$= \int_0^K B\,(t, T)\,Q_1\,(u \mid \Im_t)\,du + \int_0^K B\,(t, T)\,Q_2(u \mid \Im_t)\,du$$

$$- \int_0^K B(t, T)\,du + \int_0^K B\,(t, T)\,C_{\text{HH}}(u, u \mid \Im_t)\,du$$

$$= \int_0^K B\,(t, T)\,Q_1\,(u \mid \Im_t)\,du + \int_0^K B\,(t, T)\,Q_2(u \mid \Im_t)\,du$$

$$- \int_0^K B(t, T)\,du + \int_0^\infty BC_{\text{HH}}(\overline{Q}_1\,(u)\,, \overline{Q}_2\,(u) \mid \Im_t)\,du$$

$$- \int_K^\infty BC_{\text{HH}}(\overline{Q}_1\,(u)\,, \overline{Q}_2\,(u) \mid \Im_t)\,du$$

$$= \text{PUT}\,(S_1, t; K, T) + \text{PUT}\,(S_2, t; K, T) - K B\,(t, T)$$

$$+ \text{CALL}\,(S_1, S_2, t; 0, T) - \text{CALL}\,(S_1, S_2, t; K, T)$$

If we now use the univariate put–call parity

$$\text{PUT}\,(S_i, t; K, T) + S_i = \text{CALL}\,(S_i, t; K, T) + K B$$

and we reorder terms, we have

$$\overline{\text{PUT}}\,(S_1, S_2, t; K, T) + S_1 + S_2 = \text{CALL}\,(S_1, t; K, T) + \text{CALL}\,(S_2, t; K, T) + B K$$

$$+ \text{CALL}\,(S_1, S_2, t; 0, T) - \text{CALL}\,(S_1, S_2, t; K, T)$$

Finally, if we consider the relationship proved in the previous section

$$\overline{\text{CALL}}\,(S_1, S_2, t; K, T) = \text{CALL}\,(S_1, t; K, T) + \text{CALL}\,(S_2, t; K, T)$$

$$- \text{CALL}\,(S_1, S_2, t; K, T)$$

we obtain the result in the proposition. $\square$

Remark 8.2 Notice that using the same relationship between call options on the maximum and minimum between two assets and the fact that

$$\text{CALL}\,(S_i, t; 0, T) = S_i\,(t)$$

for $i = 1, 2$ the put–call parity relationship in the proposition can be written as

$$\overline{\text{PUT}}\,(S_1, S_2, t; K, T) = \overline{\text{CALL}}\,(S_1, S_2, t; K, T) + B\,(t, T)\,K$$

$$- \overline{\text{CALL}}\,(S_1, S_2, t; 0, T)$$

as in Stulz (1982), page 167.

8.5.4 Put option on the minimum of two assets

Finally, let us come to evaluate the put option on the minimum between two assets. The pay-off of the option is

$$G\left(S_1\left(T\right), S_2\left(T\right), T\right) = \max\left[K - \min\left(S_1\left(T\right), S_2\left(T\right)\right), 0\right]$$

Again by arbitrage arguments, it is easy to check that the same parity relationship above holds, and by symmetry we have

$$\text{PUT}\left(S_1, S_2, t; K, T\right) = \text{CALL}\left(S_1, S_2, t; K, T\right) + B\left(t, T\right)K$$
$$- \text{CALL}\left(S_1, S_2, t; 0, T\right)$$

However, it may be instructive to derive the result directly by using copula duality. Intuitively, this put option may end up in the money if either $S_1\left(T\right) \leqslant K$ or $S_2\left(T\right) \leqslant K$. It is then natural to write the price as

$$\text{PUT}\left(S_1, S_2, t; K, T\right) = B\left(t, T\right) \int_0^K \Pr(S_1 \leqslant u \text{ or } S_2 \leqslant u \mid \Im_t)\, du$$

where the probability is computed under the risk-neutral measure Q. Remember that

$$\Pr\left(S_1 \leqslant u, S_2 \leqslant u \mid \Im_t\right) = C_{\text{LL}}\left(Q_1\left(u\right), Q_2\left(u\right) \mid \Im_t\right)$$

and from Chapter 2

$$\Pr\left(S_1 \leqslant u \text{ or } S_2 \leqslant u \mid \Im_t\right) = \widetilde{C}_{\text{LL}}\left(Q_1\left(u\right), Q_2\left(u\right) \mid \Im_t\right)$$
$$= Q_1\left(u \mid \Im_t\right) + Q_2\left(u \mid \Im_t\right) - C_{\text{LL}}\left(Q_1\left(u\right), Q_2\left(u\right) \mid \Im_t\right)$$

where $\widetilde{C}_{\text{LL}}$ is the dual of copula C_{LL}. Using this we obtain a relationship between put options on the minimum and the maximum between two assets

$$\text{PUT}\left(S_1, S_2, t; K, T\right) = B\left(t, T\right) \int_0^K \widetilde{C}_{\text{LL}}(Q_1\left(u\right), Q_2\left(u\right) \mid \Im_t)\, du$$

$$= B\left(t, T\right) \int_0^K [Q_1\left(u \mid \Im_t\right) + Q_2\left(u \mid \Im_t\right)$$
$$- C_{\text{LL}}\left(Q_1\left(u\right), Q_2\left(u\right) \mid \Im_t\right)]\, du$$
$$= \text{PUT}\left(S_1, t; K, T\right) + \text{PUT}\left(S_2, t; K, T\right) - \overline{\text{PUT}}\left(S_1, S_2, t; K, T\right)$$

Substituting put–call parities we finally have

$$\text{PUT}\left(S_1, S_2, t; K, T\right) = 2B\left(t, T\right)K - S_1\left(t\right) - S_2\left(t\right)$$
$$+ \text{CALL}\left(S_1, t; K, T\right) + \text{CALL}\left(S_2, t; K, T\right)$$
$$+ S_1\left(t\right) + S_2\left(t\right) - \overline{\text{CALL}}\left(S_1, S_2, t; K, T\right)$$
$$- \text{CALL}\left(S_1, S_2, t; 0, T\right) - B\left(t, T\right)K$$
$$= B\left(t, T\right)K - \text{CALL}\left(S_1, S_2, t; 0, T\right)$$
$$+ \text{CALL}\left(S_1, S_2, t; K, T\right)$$

where again we used the relationship between call options on the maximum and minimum between two assets.

8.5.5   Option to exchange

The price of the option to exchange one asset for another was originally derived – for log-normal distributions – by Margrabe (1978). It can be considered as a portfolio of one underlying asset and a zero-strike call option on the minimum. Consider the option to exchange the first asset for the second, for instance.[2] The pay-off of this exchange option is

$$G(S_1(T), S_2(T), T) = \max(S_1(T) - S_2(T), 0)$$

which can be rewritten as

$$G(S_1(T), S_2(T), T) = S_1(T) - \max(\min(S_1, S_2), 0)$$

Recalling that the risk-neutral expected value of the underlying asset at maturity is the forward price, it follows that the exchange option price (OEX) is the current value of the first underlying asset minus the price of the option on the minimum between the two, with strike equal to zero. So,

$$\text{OEX}(S_1, S_2, t; T) = S_1(t) - \text{CALL}(S_1, S_2, t; 0, T)$$

It is then straightforward to design super-replication bounds for this product. The bounds used in the call option on the minimum simplify substantially, at least in notation, because we obviously have $K^{**} \geqslant K = 0$. In fact, the upper bound is

$$
\begin{aligned}
\text{OEX}^+(S_1, S_2, t; T) &= S_1(t) - \text{CALL}^-(S_1, S_2, t; 0, T) \\
&= S_1(t) - \big[\text{CALL}(S_1, t; 0, T) - \text{CALL}(S_1, t; K^{**}, T) \\
&\quad + \text{CALL}(S_2, t; 0, T) - \text{CALL}(S_2, t; K^{**}, T) - B(t, T)[K^{**} - 0]\big] \\
&= S_1(t) - S_1(t) + \text{CALL}(S_1, t; K^{**}, T) - S_2(t) \\
&\quad + \text{CALL}(S_2, t; K^{**}, T) + B(t, T) K^{**} \\
&= \text{CALL}(S_1, t; K^{**}, T) + \text{CALL}(S_2, t; K^{**}, T) + B K^{**} - S_2(t) \\
&= \text{CALL}(S_1, t; K^{**}, T) + \text{PUT}(S_2, t; K^{**}, T)
\end{aligned}
$$

where we recall that a strike price K^{**} is such that $Q_1(K^{**}) + Q_2(K^{**}) = 1$. On the other hand, the lower bound turns out to be

$$
\begin{aligned}
\text{OEX}^-(S_1, S_2, t; T) &= S_1(t) - \text{CALL}^+(S_1, S_2, t; 0, T) \\
&= S_1(t) - \big[\text{CALL}(S_1, t; 0, T) - \text{CALL}(S_1, t; K^*, T)\big] \\
&\quad - \text{CALL}(S_2, t, K^*, T)
\end{aligned}
$$

---

[2] It is also a particular case of the spread option, with $K = 0$.

$$= S_1(t) - S_1(t) + \text{CALL}\left(S_1, t; K^*, T\right) + \text{CALL}\left(S_2, t;, K^*, T\right)$$

$$= \text{CALL}\left(S_1, t; K^*, T\right) + \text{CALL}\left(S_2, t;, K^*, T\right)$$

with K^* defined in such a way that $Q_1(K^*) = Q_2(K^*)$.

Summing up, the super-replication bounds of the option to exchange are represented by

$$\text{CALL}\left(S_1, t; K^*, T\right) - \text{CALL}\left(S_2, t;, K^*, T\right) \leqslant \text{OEX}\left(S_1, S_2, t; T\right)$$

$$\leqslant \text{CALL}\left(S_1, t; K^{**}, T\right) + \text{PUT}\left(S_2, t; K^{**}, T\right)$$

8.5.6 Pricing and hedging rainbows with smiles: Everest notes

Consider a concrete example of an index-linked product whose coupon is linked to the minimum or maximum return of two assets measured over the investment horizon from t to T, provided this figure is higher than some assigned threshold K. The value of the coupon is then, for example,

$$\max\left(\min\left(\frac{S_1(T)}{S_1(t)}, \frac{S_2(T)}{S_2(t)}\right), K\right) = K + \max\left(\min\left(\frac{S_1(T)}{S_1(t)}, \frac{S_2(T)}{S_2(t)}\right) - K, 0\right)$$

and the problem involves the evaluation of a call option on the minimum of two assets. For example, setting $K = 1$ we ensure against the possibility of a negative coupon. Our task is to provide a solution to the problem that could be sufficiently general to account for different shapes of the risk-adjusted distributions of the two assets or indexes involved and for a general dependence structure. We are particularly interested in checking extreme dependence scenarios and the corresponding super-replication strategies. Our example uses information on the Italian blue chip index, Mib 30 and the Japanese index, Nikkei 225.

We apply the following procedure. We first estimate the implied risk-neutral distribution from option data. We then compute the super-replication strategies and the pricing bounds for the product. We finally show how to construct a mixture copula to account for imperfect dependence and maintain a closed form solution for the hedging strategy and the price.

Retrieving the implied probability from market prices

We start by extracting the risk-neutral distributions from the option data taken from Bloomberg. The implied volatility smile for both the markets was fitted using a quadratic interpolation technique as suggested by Shimko (1994). The fitted smile curves are presented in Figure 8.4. The strikes were normalized by the observed value of the underlying index on the day of evaluation, so that the value 1 on the horizontal axis corresponds to the *at-the-money* volatility.

Volatility interpolation is used to reconstruct call spreads approximating the implied cumulative risk-neutral distributions. The resulting probability distributions are given in Figure 8.5. For any level of one underlying asset, which is again normalized by its current value, we depict the probabilities that over the next six months that market is growing more than or less than the threshold. Using the previous notation, the decreasing schedules are referred to the decumulative distributions $\overline{Q}_i$ and the increasing ones describe the cumulative probabilities Q_i.

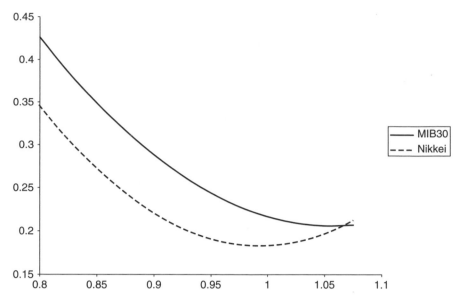

Figure 8.4 Smiles of Nikkei 225 and Mib 30

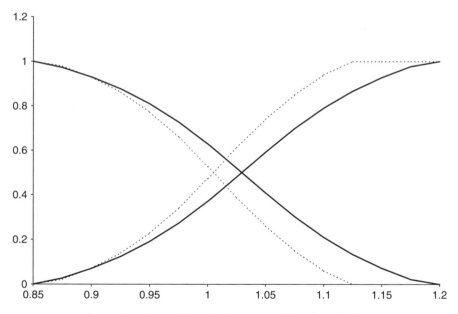

Figure 8.5 Probability distributions of Nikkei and Mib 30

We notice that both distributions give negligible value to the event of a decrease of the markets 15% below the current value. Furthermore, the probability of the Mib 30 index increasing or falling by a given percentage is always lower than the corresponding probability for the Nikkei 225 index (first-order stochastic dominance). This implies, of course,

$$\min(\overline{Q}_{\text{Mib}}(K), \overline{Q}_{\text{Nikkei}}(K)) = \overline{Q}_{\text{Nikkei}}(K)$$

for any threshold return K and the perfect positive dependence pricing kernel for call options coincides with that of the Nikkei.

In order to recover the perfect negative dependence pricing kernel we notice instead that the cumulative distribution of returns on the Mib 30 index crosses the decumulative distribution of the Nikkei slightly above the current values of the indexes. More precisely, we have

$$Q_{Mib}\,(1.00676) = \overline{Q}_{Nikkei}\,(1.00676)$$

In other terms, the risk-neutral probability of the Italian index to grow less than 67.6 basis points is equal to the probability of the Japanese index growing more than the same figure. We have then that $K^{**} = 1.00676$, and the lower bound of the pricing kernel is zero beyond that level.

Pricing the rainbow option

We are now in a position to price and hedge the rainbow option and the index-linked product. Based on the above analysis, we have that the upper bound pricing kernel corresponds to the Nikkei pricing kernel. The lower pricing kernel for strike prices $K < 1.00676$ is instead equal to two call spreads on the strike prices K and $K^{**} = 1.00676$ and a debt position equal to $K^{**} - K$, while it is equal to zero for all the other prices. The pricing kernels are depicted in Figure 8.6.

In the figure we also report linear combinations of the upper and lower pricing kernels, which are consistent with imperfect dependence between the markets: the corresponding copula functions are special cases of the Fréchet family of copulas.

Finally, in Figure 8.7 we present the pricing schedules of the index-linked product with respect to different return protection rates, i.e. for different strikes of the rainbow option.

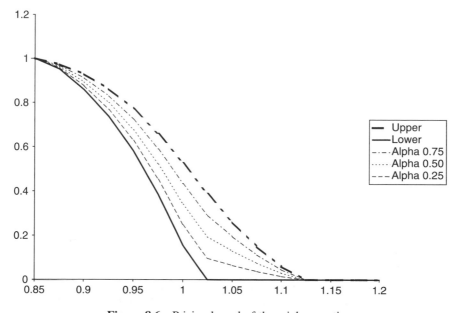

Figure 8.6 Pricing kernel of the rainbow option

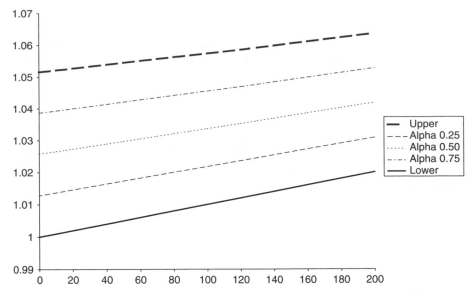

Figure 8.7   Price of the rainbow equity-linked note

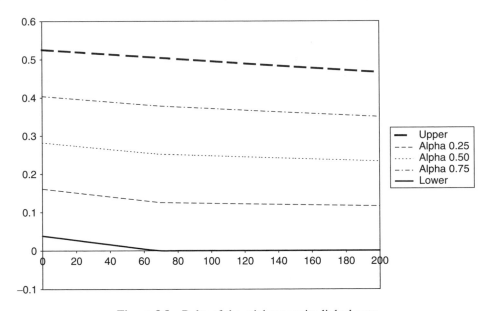

Figure 8.8   Delta of the rainbow equity-linked note

The pricing schedules are reported for the different pricing kernels depicted above. The pricing schedules look almost linear and increase with the degree of dependence between the markets. To give a figure, the cost of providing zero return protection on a 1 million investment in the product ($K = 1$) is almost worthless if the two markets are perfectly negatively dependent (it is 24 cents), while it amounts to 51 546.31 in the case of perfect positive dependence. In the case of independence the cost is about half that, scoring 25 773.27.

To conclude, we report in Figure 8.8 the value of the delta of the contracts with respect to movements of the two markets. The sensitivity to the market increases with dependence and decreases with moneyness, that is, with the increase in the protection threshold offered.

8.6 PRICING BARRIER OPTIONS

Barrier options are contingent claims in which the exercise is conditional on the event that the value of the underlying asset has been above or below a given value over a given reference period. In the standard plain vanilla cases, barrier options are classified according to whether an option is activated (knocked-in) or deactivated (knocked-out) if some upper or lower barrier level is reached over the whole life of the option. We may then have down-and-out, up-and-out, down-and-in and up-and-in options both of the call and put type. Typically, a fixed payment R may be given to the holder of the option if it is not activated: this payment is called "rebate". These options have closed form solutions under the standard Black–Scholes setting, and the readers are referred to the standard option pricing literature for these results.

Here we want to show how to apply the copula function pricing technique for a general treatment of barrier options, accounting for more complex cases. In fact, the pricing problem of barrier options may get involved if some of the assumptions concerning either the dynamics of the underlying asset are made more general or the structure of the contract is made more complex than in the standard plain vanilla case. The first problem has to do with the fact that while closed form solutions for barrier options are available under the standard Black–Scholes assumption of constant volatility, the reality of markets shows clear evidence against such hypotheses of normally distributed returns. So, even for standard options one would like to cast the pricing problem in a more general setting in order to account for models in which the conditional distribution of the underlying asset can be chosen to be consistent with some stochastic volatility dynamics. As barriers are generally used to reduce the cost of the option for the buyer and the premium earned by the counterparty who writes it, it is particularly relevant for the counterparty to assess the risk of this option under realistic dynamics of the underlying asset.

A general setting would also enable one to address the case of complex barrier option contracts. A simple example is given by barriers in options with exotic pay-offs. Consider the case of rainbow or basket options or path-dependent contingent claims including barriers: in all of these cases the closed form solutions obtained under the standard Black–Scholes setting can only be taken as arbitrary approximations to the "fair value" of the contract.

The structure of the barrier can also be much more sophisticated than it is in the standard cases. A first source of complexity can be represented by the fact that the barrier may be referred to a variable which is different from the underlying asset: this is the case, for example, of barrier swaptions, whose underlying asset we recall is the forward swap rate, with barriers referred to the LIBOR rate. In cases like these the important question is how the dependence structure between the underlying asset and the barrier variable (the swap rate and the LIBOR rate in the example above) impacts on the determination of the joint probability that the option ends in the money and the barrier is hit or not. Another source of complexity could be represented by the way in which the event of reaching or crossing a barrier is linked to activation or deactivation of the contingent claim. In some cases the option may be knocked-out or knocked-in only if the reference variable has been below or above some given barrier for a period of time longer than a given interval. Such an interval can be referred to the whole length of the time to exercise, as in the so-called parisian options, or it may be itself stochastic, and referred to the time difference between the exercise date and the date on which the barrier is crossed (caution time), as in the so-called edokko options. Furthermore, the period the reference variable has been below or above the barrier can be computed as the length of time it has continuously been beyond the barrier or the overall time spent in that region: the latter case is called cumulative parisian or edokko option. The idea behind these structures is to make manipulation of the trigger variable market more difficult.

To understand how copula functions can be usefully employed to price barrier options, consider that, from a fully general perspective, a barrier option can be seen as a contingent claim that provides a positive pay-off if two events take place. Beside the standard event that the option ends up in the money at the time of exercise, there is a second event which acts as a "trigger" to activate and deactivate the option. In a broad sense, pricing a barrier option involves the evaluation of the joint probability of the exercise and the trigger event, and that is where copula functions can help.

8.6.1 Pricing call barrier options with copulas: the general framework

As a first example, consider a European call option written on asset S with strike K and exercise time T which can be exercised if some trigger event h occurs, and provides a rebate R otherwise. For the sake of simplicity we assume that the rebate is paid at the exercise date. Considering the rebate to be paid at the time the trigger event occurs would only make the treatment more involved, calling for a specification of the probability density of the time when it takes place. Say, the trigger variable is a boolean variable taking value 1 if the event takes place and 0 otherwise. The relevant pricing kernel in this case is represented by the joint probability $\overline{Q}(u, 1) = \Pr(S(T) > u, h = 1)$. Using the probability distribution approach we may write the price of the option as

$$\text{CALL}\,(S(t), t; K, T, h = 1, R) = B \int_K^\infty \overline{Q}(u,\,1 \mid \Im_t)\,\mathrm{d}u + B\,(t, T)\,Q_h(\Im_t)R$$

where Q_h is the marginal conditional probability of the trigger event $h = 0$ and we recall that $\overline{Q}_h = 1 - Q_h$ is the probability of the complement. This bivariate distribution interpretation is well suited for the application of copula functions. We have in fact

$$\text{CALL}\,(S(t), t; K, T, h = 1, R) = B\,(t, T) \int_K^\infty C_{\text{HH}}[\overline{Q}_S\,(u),\,\overline{Q}_h \mid \Im_t)]\,\mathrm{d}u$$
$$+ B\,(t, T)\,Q_h(\Im_t)R$$

The same technique could be applied to price a call option with the same strike and exercise date, but with exercise conditioned on the event that the trigger is not activated. In this case the option can be exercised if $h = 0$ and the rebate R is paid otherwise. The price will be

$$\text{CALL}\,(S(t), t; K, T, h = 0, R) = B\,(t, T) \int_K^\infty C_{\text{HL}}[\overline{Q}_S\,(u),\,Q_h \mid \Im_t)]\,\mathrm{d}u$$
$$+ B\,(t, T)\,\overline{Q}_h(\Im_t)R$$

We may again verify that no-arbitrage requires the relationship $C_{\text{HL}}(u, 1 - v) = u - C_{\text{HH}}(u, v)$, so that

$$\text{CALL}\,(S(t), t; K, T, h = 0, R)$$

$$= B\,(t, T) \int_K^\infty [\overline{Q}_S(u) - C_{\text{HH}}(\overline{Q}_S\,(u)\,, \overline{Q}_h \mid \Im_t)]\,\mathrm{d}u + B\,(t, T)\,\overline{Q}_h(\Im_t)R$$

$$= \text{CALL}\,(S(t), t; K, T) - \text{CALL}\,(S(t), t; K, T, h = 1, R) + B\,(t, T)\,R$$

In fact, buying a barrier option that can be exercised under some set of states of the world, i.e. some trigger condition, and an equal option whose exercise is conditioned on the complement set, amounts to removing the effect of the barrier. So, the result is the same as to buy an option that can be exercised irrespective of the condition plus a fixed sum, the rebate, which is received for sure.

$$\text{CALL}\,(S(t), t; K, T, h = 0, R) + \text{CALL}\,(S(t), t; K, T, h = 1, R)$$

$$= \text{CALL}\,(S(t), t; K, T) + B\,(t, T)\,R$$

Remark 8.3 It is worthwhile checking what would happen if the rebate were paid at the time the trigger event takes place. Notice that in this case there would be an asymmetry in the treatment. In fact, for the option conditioned on the event $h = 1$, the rebate could only be paid at expiration (it is a knock-in barrier option). On the contrary, the option conditioned on the event that the trigger is not activated, that is $h = 0$, would typically pay a rebate at the time in which the event actually takes place (it is a knock-out barrier option). Let us define $\theta = \inf(s; h(s) = 1, s \geqslant t)$ the time of the trigger event and $B(t, \theta)$ the corresponding risk-free discount factor. In this case the value of the rebate would be $E_Q\left(B(t, \theta)\,\mathbf{1}_{\{t \leqslant \theta \leqslant T\}}\right) R$. Accordingly, in the relationship between knock-in and knock-out options we would recover

$$B\,(t, T)\,Q_h(\Im_t)R + E_Q\left(B\,(t, \theta)\,\mathbf{1}_{\{t \leqslant \theta \leqslant T\}}\right) R$$

instead of $B\,(t, T)\,R$. Substituting this term for $B\,(t, T)\,R$ would not, however, change the proofs reported below.

Before going on it may be worth considering a very special case that will be useful in the development of this discussion. Take the case of a barrier call option with a strike $K = 0$. We have

$$\text{CALL}\,(S(t), t; 0, T, h = 1, R) = B\,(t, T) \int_0^\infty C_{\text{HH}}\left[\overline{Q}_S\,(u), \overline{Q}_h \mid \Im_t)\right]\mathrm{d}u$$

$$+ B\,(t, T)\,Q_h(\Im_t)R$$

$$\text{CALL}\,(S(t), t; 0, T, h = 0, R) = B\,(t, T) \int_0^\infty C_{\text{HL}}\left[Q_S\,(u),\, Q_h \mid \Im_t)\right]\mathrm{d}u$$

$$+ B\,(t, T)\,\overline{Q}_h(\Im_t)R$$

and

$$\text{CALL}\,(S(t), t; 0, T, h = 0, R) + \text{CALL}\,(S(t), t; 0, T, h = 1, R) = S\,(t) + B\,(t, T)\,R$$

It is clear that the value of a barrier call option with strike equal to zero is an option delivering the asset at exercise date T if the trigger event occurs, and the rebate R if it does not. If the rebate is assumed to be zero, this contingent claim is known as digital, or one touch, asset-or-nothing (AoN) option. So, we define

$$DCAoN\,(S(t), t; T, h = 0) = CALL\,(S(t), t; 0, T, h = 0, 0)$$

$$DCAoN\,(S(t), t; T, h = 1) = CALL\,(S(t), t; 0, T, h = 1, 0)$$

By the same token, imagine a contract that pays a unit of cash at the exercise time T if the trigger event occurs. We may call this contingent claim a digital, or one touch, cash-or-nothing (CoN) option, and we may define

$$DCCoN\,(S(t), t; T, h = 0, 0) = B\,(t, T)\, Q_h(\Im_t)$$

$$DCCoN\,(S(t), t; T, h = 1, 0) = B\,(t, T)\, \overline{Q}_h(\Im_t)$$

8.6.2 Pricing put barrier option: the general framework

We are now going to show that the copula arbitrage relationship also enables us to establish a relationship between call and put options. Consider a put option with strike K and exercise time T. The exercise is again conditioned on the trigger $h = 1$ with rebate R. The price is

$$PUT\,(S(t), t; K, T, h = 1, R) = B\,(t, T) \int_0^K C_{LH}\,[Q_S\,(u),\ Q_h \mid \Im_t)]\,du$$

$$+ B\,(t, T)\, \overline{Q}_h(\Im_t)R$$

Using the no-arbitrage relationship, $C_{LH}(1 - u, v) = v - C_{HH}(u, v)$, we have

$$PUT(S(t), t; K, T, h = 1, R) = B(t, T) \int_0^K [\overline{Q}_h(\Im_t) - C_{HH}[\overline{Q}_S(u),\ \overline{Q}_h \mid \Im_t)]]\,du$$

$$+ B(t, T) Q_h(\Im_t)R$$

$$= B(t, T)K\overline{Q}_h(\Im_t) - B(t, T) \int_0^K C_{HH}[\overline{Q}_S(u),\ \overline{Q}_h \mid \Im_t)]\,du$$

$$+ B(t, T)Q_h(\Im_t)R$$

$$= B(t, T)K\overline{Q}_h(\Im_t) - B(t, T) \int_0^\infty C_{HH}[\overline{Q}_S(u),\ \overline{Q}_h \mid \Im_t)]\,du$$

$$+ B(t, T) \int_K^\infty C_{HH}[\overline{Q}_S(u),\ \overline{Q}_h \mid \Im_t)] + B(t, T)Q_h(\Im_t)R$$

$$= B(t, T)K Q_h(1 \mid \Im_t) + CALL(S(t), t; K, T, h = 1, R)$$

$$- B(t, T) \int_0^\infty C_{HH}[Q_S(u),\ Q_h(1) \mid \Im_t)]\,du$$

We now turn to the case in which the put option, with the same strike and time to exercise, is subject to the trigger $h = 0$ with rebate R. As in the case of call options, ruling out arbitrage opportunities requires

$$\text{PUT}(S(t), t; K, T, h = 0, R) + \text{PUT}(S(t), t; K, T, h = 1, R)$$
$$= \text{PUT}(S(t), t; K, T) + B(t, T) R$$

Using the put–call parity relationships we have finally

$$\text{PUT}(S(t), t; K, T, h = 0, R) = \text{PUT}(S(t), t; K, T) + B(t, T) R$$
$$- \text{PUT}(S(t), t; K, T, h = 1, R)$$
$$= \text{CALL}(S(t), t; K, T) + B(t, T) K - S(t)$$
$$+ B(t, T) R - \text{PUT}(S(t), t; K, T, h = 1, R)$$
$$= \text{CALL}(S(t), t; K, T) + B(t, T) K - S(t) + B(t, T) R$$
$$- B(t, T) K \overline{Q}_h(\Im_t) - \text{CALL}(S(t), t; K, T, h = 1, R)$$
$$+ B(t, T) \int_0^\infty C_{\text{HH}}[\overline{Q}_S(u), Q_h \mid \Im_t)] \, du$$
$$= B(t, T) K Q_h(\Im_t)$$
$$+ \text{CALL}(S(t), t; K, T, h = 0, R)$$
$$- B(t, T) \int_0^\infty C_{\text{HL}}[\overline{Q}_S(u), Q_h \mid \Im_t)] \, du$$

The final step is obtained using the no-arbitrage relationships between the barrier call options and the martingale property. In fact, we in turn exploit

$$\text{CALL}(S(t), t; K, T, h = 0, R) = \text{CALL}(S(t), t; K, T)$$
$$+ B(t, T) R - \text{CALL}(S(t), t; K, T, h = 1, R)$$

and

$$B(t, T) \left[\int_0^\infty C_{\text{HH}}[Q_S(u), Q_h(1) \mid \Im_t)] \, du \right.$$
$$\left. + \int_0^\infty C_{\text{HL}}[Q_S(u), 1 - Q_h(1) \mid \Im_t)] \, du \right] = S(t)$$

If the readers remember our definitions of digital asset-or-nothing and cash-or-nothing options, it is then immediate to obtain that the relationship between barrier put and call options can be summarized in very general terms as follows:

Proposition 8.7 [*Barrier options put–call parity*]   Denote by $\text{CALL}\,(S(t), t; K, T, h, R)$ the price of a barrier call option with strike K, exercise time T, trigger event h and rebate R. Then the barrier put option with the same terms is priced by

$$\text{PUT}\,(S(t), t; K, T, h, R) + DC\text{AoN}\,(S(t), t; T, h)$$

$$= \text{CALL}\,(S(t), t; K, T, h, R) + K\,DC\text{CoN}\,(S(t), t; T, h)$$

Let us note that the put–call parity for barrier options closely resembles the relationship between plain vanilla options, apart from the fact that the underlying asset and the discounted strike are substituted by digital asset-or-nothing and cash-or-nothing respectively. Furthermore, the relationship is very general and extends from standard barrier options to the more complex cases, such as parisian options.

8.6.3   Specifying the trigger event

We now relate the general approach above to special cases of barrier options. Of course the approach is not useful in cases in which the joint distribution of the exercise and trigger events are known in closed form. Unfortunately, this is true only for geometric brownian motions (BMs), and in general for standard products. The approach can instead be fruitfully applied to cases in which this joint distribution is not known or is not easily computed. As in the other applications the advantage of the approach lies in the possibility of modeling the marginal distributions of the two events separately from the dependence structure. In barrier option applications, however, a word of caution is in order. Indeed, the flexibility of the approach may turn into a flaw and lead to inconsistent results. The basic problem is that the dependence structure between the trigger event and the exercise event must be consistent with the dependence structure of the reference variable of the trigger event and the underlying asset. To understand the point, assume that we apply an arbitrary copula to the evaluation of a standard barrier option, in which the underlying asset is also the reference variable of the trigger event, and assume that it follows a geometric BM. This is a case in which the flexibility of the approach would result in a wrong price. While in this example the inconsistency shows up very clearly, mostly because we can compute the price in closed form, the same basic problem may be found in every barrier option application. Getting the copula function choice right is then particularly relevant in such applications.

In the following section we suggest some techniques that may be applied to estimate the marginal distribution of the trigger event and the dependence relationship with the exercise event.

Marginal probability of the trigger event

The trigger event is activated when the reference variable hits a prespecified level or stays beyond that level longer than a given period of time. Consider the case in which the reference variable is assumed to follow a geometric BM under the risk-neutral measure, that is

$$dS = rS\,dt + \sigma S\,dz$$

where z is a Wiener process, and r and σ are constant parameters. In this case, the marginal probability of the trigger event may be known in closed form. Take the simplest example in which the trigger event is defined as the case in which an upper or lower barrier H ($H \in \Re_+$) is hit. It may be useful to briefly review the basic principles behind the proof, because the same ideas will be used to extend the application to more complex cases for which the closed form solution cannot be obtained and must be computed by simulation. First, we introduce the ratio process $S(t)/H$ and change the stochastic process into an arithmetic BM defining $X(t) = \ln(S(t)/H)$. We have

$$dX = \upsilon \, dt + \sigma \, dz$$

with $\upsilon = r - \sigma^2/2$ and $X(0) = \ln(S(0)/H)$. It is clear that evaluating the probability that the process $S(t)$ will or will not hit the barrier H by a certain time T is the same as assessing the probability that an arithmetic BM starting at $X(0)$ will hit the zero barrier. That is, if for example $S(t) > H$

$$S(t) \geqslant H \Longleftrightarrow X(0) + \int_0^t \upsilon \, du + \int_0^t \sigma z(u) \geqslant 0$$

$$\Longleftrightarrow \int_0^t \upsilon \, du + \int_0^t \sigma z(u) \geqslant -X(0)$$

for all $t > 0$. By the same token, the event that the barrier will be attained from below, starting from $S(t) < H$, is equivalent to

$$S(t) \leqslant H \Longleftrightarrow X(0) + \int_0^t \upsilon \, du + \int_0^t \sigma z(u) \leqslant 0$$

$$\Longleftrightarrow \int_0^t \upsilon \, du + \int_0^t \sigma z(u) \leqslant -X(0)$$

We introduce two processes M_X and m_X denoting, respectively, the running maximum and minimum of the stochastic process X, i.e.

$$M_X(t) \equiv \{\max X(u); 0 \leqslant u \leqslant t\}$$

$$m_X(t) \equiv \{\min X(u); 0 \leqslant u \leqslant t\}$$

It is clear that the event of an upper or lower barrier H not being hit ($h = 0$) by time T may then be characterized as

$$h = 0 \Longleftrightarrow M_X(T) \leqslant y$$

$$h = 0 \Longleftrightarrow m_X(T) \geqslant y$$

with $y = -X(0)$. The probability that the barrier will not be hit is then given by the formulas

$$Q_h = Q(M_X(T) \leqslant y) = N\left(\frac{y - \upsilon t}{\sigma\sqrt{t}}\right) - \exp\left(\frac{2\upsilon y}{\sigma^2}\right) N\left(\frac{-y - \upsilon t}{\sigma\sqrt{t}}\right)$$

$$Q_h = Q(m_X(T) \geqslant y) = N\left(\frac{-y + \upsilon t}{\sigma\sqrt{t}}\right) - \exp\left(\frac{2\upsilon y}{\sigma^2}\right) N\left(\frac{y + \upsilon t}{\sigma\sqrt{t}}\right)$$

and the probability of the complement ($h = 1$) is of course

$$\overline{Q}_h = 1 - Q_h = N \left(\frac{-y + \upsilon t}{\sigma \sqrt{t}} \right) + \exp \left(\frac{2\upsilon y}{\sigma^2} \right) N \left(\frac{-y - \upsilon t}{\sigma \sqrt{t}} \right)$$

$$\overline{Q}_h = 1 - Q_h = N \left(\frac{y - \upsilon t}{\sigma \sqrt{t}} \right) + \exp \left(\frac{2\upsilon y}{\sigma^2} \right) N \left(\frac{y + \upsilon t}{\sigma \sqrt{t}} \right)$$

Remark 8.4 The formulas are obtained by, first, changing the measure in such a way as to transform the stochastic process followed by $X(t)$ into a standard BM (i.e. with no drift), and then applying the reflection principle. This principle determines the joint probability that a standard BM will hit a barrier y and will end above a given value k.

Pricing barrier options

Substituting $y = -X(t) = \ln(H/S(t))$ we may reconduct the probabilities above to the probability of the trigger event under the original geometric BM, and compute the prices of digital contracts representing the event of the barrier being hit (one touch) or not (no-touch).

For example, the risk-neutral exercise probability of a no-touch, i.e. an option that pays one unit of currency if an upper or lower barrier is not reached, is given by

$$Q(S(\theta) \leqslant H; t \leqslant \theta \leqslant T \mid \Im_t) = N \left(\frac{\ln(H/S(t)) - \upsilon(T - t)}{\sigma \sqrt{T - t}} \right)$$

$$- \frac{H}{S(t)} \exp \left(\frac{2\upsilon}{\sigma^2} \right) N \left(\frac{\ln(S(t)/H) - \upsilon(T - t)}{\sigma \sqrt{T - t}} \right)$$

$$Q(S(\theta) \geqslant H; t \leqslant \theta \leqslant T \mid \Im_t) = N \left(\frac{\ln(S(t)/H) + \upsilon(T - t)}{\sigma \sqrt{T - t}} \right)$$

$$- \frac{H}{S(t)} \exp \left(\frac{2\upsilon}{\sigma^2} \right) N \left(\frac{\ln(H/S(t)) + \upsilon(T - t)}{\sigma \sqrt{T - t}} \right) \tag{8.2}$$

The corresponding price is obtained if we multiply by the discount factor $B(t, T)$.

If one wants to price the corresponding digital put or call option, which pays one unit of currency if the upper or lower barrier is reached and the underlying asset is below or above a fixed strike, an analogous procedure must be followed. Consider, for instance, the down-and-out digital, which pays if and only if the minimum of the underlying process S does not go below the barrier H and the underlying asset is not below the strike K at maturity. The risk-neutral probability needed is

$$Q(m_S(T) \geqslant H, S(T) \geqslant K \mid \Im_t) = N \left(\frac{\ln(S(t)/K) + \upsilon(T - t)}{\sigma \sqrt{T - t}} \right)$$

$$- \frac{H}{S(t)} \exp \left(\frac{2\upsilon}{\sigma^2} \right) N \left(\frac{\ln(H^2/KS(t)) + \upsilon(T - t)}{\sigma \sqrt{T - t}} \right) \tag{8.3}$$

Let us use the usual notation

$$d_2(K) = \frac{\ln(S(t)/K) + \upsilon(T - t)}{\sigma\sqrt{T - t}}$$

which implies

$$\frac{\ln(H^2/KS(t)) + \upsilon(T - t)}{\sigma\sqrt{T - t}} = d_2(K) - 2\frac{\ln(S(t)/H)}{\sigma\sqrt{T - t}}$$

and note that

$$\frac{H}{S(t)}\exp\left(\frac{2\upsilon}{\sigma^2}\right) = \exp\left(\frac{2\upsilon}{\sigma^2}\ln\frac{H}{S(t)}\right) = \left(\frac{H}{S(t)}\right)^{a-1}$$

where $a = 2r/\sigma^2$. Probability (8.3) can be written, in a more concise way, as

$$N(d_2(K)) - \left(\frac{H}{S(t)}\right)^{a-1} N\left(d_2(K) - 2\frac{\ln(S(t)/H)}{\sigma\sqrt{T - t}}\right) \tag{8.4}$$

Knowing the digital price one can, in turn, reconstruct the down-and-out call price, following the procedure used several times before.

So far we have described the case of a standard barrier option, whose pay-off may be described as

$$\mathbf{1}_{\min S(\theta; t \leqslant \theta \leqslant T) > H} \max(S(T) - K, 0)$$

where we refer to a down-and-out call option as an example. More complex trigger events could be given by the general form

$$f(\tau^-)\max(S(T) - K, 0)$$

where τ^- is the amount of time during the option life that the underlying price was lower than a barrier H. This general approach was suggested by Linetsky (1999) as a way to address a large class of exotic barrier options. In particular, he proposes the use of standard linear or exponential discount functions, such as

$$\exp(-\delta\tau^-)\max(S(T) - K, 0)$$

where δ is a prespecified discount intensity. These products are called step options and include standard plain vanilla options and standard barrier options as extreme examples. Another choice would be instead

$$\mathbf{1}_{\tau^- < \alpha(T-t)}\max(S(T) - K, 0)$$

This option is called a cumulative parisian option by Chesney et al. (1997). For all of these options, the probability distribution of the amount of time spent below (or above) a given barrier, technically called "occupation time", can be recovered in closed form for the arithmetic and geometric BM cases. In cases in which the reference variable is represented by the underlying asset, we are also able to recover closed form solutions for the option price. Knowing the probability distribution of the occupation time, however, enables us to use the copula function approach for more general applications.

8.6.4 Calibrating the dependence structure

In order to provide a flexible characterization of the price of barrier options, defined in a broad sense, it may be useful to analyze the case in which the underlying and the trigger variable coincide and are represented by a geometric BM. Indeed, we are going to show that this case enables us to construct a new kind of copula, linked to the closed form solutions originating from the reflection principle. This dependence structure will be called a *reflection copula* and it will permit us to extend the pricing technique to more complex problems. Let us look at two examples: (i) the case of an option written on a variable different from that used as a trigger, and (ii) the case in which the underlying asset is not described by a geometric BM, while the trigger variable is. In cases like these, it may be intuitively appealing to use this copula to represent the dependence structure between the underlying and the triggering variable.

8.6.5 The reflection copula

We know that under the standard assumption of a process following a geometric BM, closed formulas for standard barrier options are available: from these one can extract the implied information concerning the dependence structure between the trigger event and the exercise of the option. In order to do this, we focus without loss of generality on the down-and-out case: from the no-arbitrage price of such options, we want to extract, for given variance of the underlying and riskless rate, the implied correlation between a geometric BM S and its running minimum, $m_S(T)$.

We start by rewriting the probability of the joint event $\{m_S(T) \geqslant H, S(T) \geqslant K\}$, which characterizes the down-and-out digital price, in terms of a copula function: assuming a complete market, Sklar's theorem can be applied, allowing us to state that the joint probability in (8.4) is a copula, written in the marginal probabilities of the events $\{S(T) \geqslant K\}$ and $\{m_S(T) \geqslant H\}$. The latter can be easily evaluated:

$$\Pr(S(T) \geqslant K \mid \Im_t) = N(d_2(K)) \tag{8.5}$$

and

$$\Pr(m_S(T) \geqslant H \mid \Im_t) = N(d_2(H)) - \left(\frac{H}{S(t)}\right)^{a-1} N\left(d_2(H) - 2\frac{\ln(S(t)/H)}{\sigma\sqrt{T-t}}\right) \tag{8.6}$$

For the sake of simplicity, let us denote as $l(H)$ the function

$$l(H) = d_2(H) - 2\frac{\ln(S(t)/H)}{\sigma\sqrt{T-t}}$$

Sklar's theorem allows us to state that there exists a unique (due to the continuity of S) implied copula, i.e. a unique function C_{HH} which gives (8.4) in terms of the marginals:

$$N(d_2(K)) - \left(\frac{H}{S(t)}\right)^{a-1} N\left(d_2(K) - 2\frac{\ln(S(t)/H)}{\sigma\sqrt{T-t}}\right)$$

$$= C_{HH}\left(N(d_2(K)), N(d_2(H)) - \left(\frac{H}{S(t)}\right)^{a-1} N(l(H))\right)$$

One can verify that the unique copula involved is

$$C_{HH}(v, z) = v + \frac{z - N(d_2(h(z)))}{N(l(h(z)))} N\left(d_2(g(v)) - 2\frac{\ln(S(t)/h(z))}{\sigma\sqrt{T-t}}\right) \tag{8.7}$$

where the functions $H = h(z)$ and $K = g(v)$ represent H and K as functions of the marginal probabilities z and v. They are obtained from the inverses, $v = g^{-1}(K)$ and $z = h^{-1}(H)$, where

$$z = h^{-1}(H) = N(d_2(H)) - \left(\frac{H}{S(t)}\right)^{a-1} N(l(H))$$

$$v = N(d_2(K))$$

or $K = d_2^{-1}(N^{-1}(v))$, since both N and d_2 are monotone.

In turn, one can verify that the function C_{HH} satisfies the definition of a copula function given in Chapter 2.

Figure 8.9 presents the copula (8.7) for the case $S(t) = 1$, $K = 1.1$, $r = 5\%$, $\sigma = 20\%$, $T - t = 1$, $H = \frac{1}{2}$.

Implied correlation

Once we have extracted the reflection copula implied in a down-and-out price (8.7), we can use it in order to reconstruct the Spearman correlation between $S(T)$ and $m_S(T)$, which, as

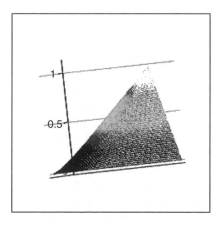

Figure 8.9   The reflection copula

recalled in Chapter 3, can be calculated from the copula as follows:

$$\rho_S = 12 \int \int_{I^2} C(v, z) \, dv \, dz - 3$$

By discretizing the latter integral and evaluating numerically the implied copula, we obtain, for instance, in the case $S(t) = 1, r = 15\%, \sigma = 20\%, T - t = 5, H = 0.7, K = 1.1$, a value of the Spearman $\rho_S = 0.5842$. By letting the moneyness and maturity of the option vary, while keeping the barrier H, the riskless rate r and the underlying (initial value and volatility) fixed, one obtains the following correlation values:

Cash position	K	T	ρ_S
ITM	0.9	1	0.741
ITM	0.9	5	0.5842
OTM	1.1	5	0.5842
OTM	1.1	10	0.473

The readers can note that for given maturity (in our example, 5 years) the implied correlation does not vary with the moneyness, as expected: one can infer this from either OTM or ITM options. The correlation itself is decreasing with maturity.

8.7 PRICING MULTIVARIATE OPTIONS: MONTE CARLO METHODS

To complete our review of copula function applications to option pricing problems, we take a look at more involved issues, in which simulation approaches are the only techniques that can be applied. We saw that copula functions yield valuation solutions that are particularly easy to apply and flexible for bivariate problems, and for problems in which the pricing kernel can be directly written as a copula function: as in the case of call options on the minimum among a set of assets or put options on the maximum. In other cases in which the underlying asset is represented by some general function of prices – such as, basket options based on the linear or geometric average of returns on a set of securities – it is not possible to derive closed form solutions even at the bivariate level. A look at the treatment of the problem in Chapter 2 shows that even at this level one has to resort to numerical integration. It is well known, however, that, as the dimension of the problem increases, Monte Carlo simulation remains the most effective technique. We know from Chapter 6 that copula functions may be of great help to implement Monte Carlo simulation in the most flexible way. In particular, it enables us to simulate joint distributions that are consistent with different marginals for the returns on different markets (fitting, for example, different smile curves), and with particular dependence structures among them.

The easiest approach is to specify the marginal distributions based on time series analyses or implied information and to fit a Student t copula to represent tail dependence. At this point, readers should be already familiar with the technical estimation and simulation issues involved in this procedure, and, for this reason, we only provide the example of a real world application developed with those tools.

8.7.1 Application: basket option

We consider a basket option written on the average quarterly return of five equity indexes. The equity indexes are: S&P 500, FTSE 100, DAX 30, Nikkei (NKY) and Amsterdam Exchange (AEX). The option has to be valued on March 31, 2003, with an expiry date of June 30, 2003, and strike equal to 3% quarterly return.

As for the specification of the marginal distributions, we could have used both implied information, selecting some technique to fit the smile in the markets, or a time series analysis based on historical data, trying to filter out the risk-premia from the time series.

Here we followed the latter approach and used a quarterly return series for all five indexes from June 29, 1984, to March 31, 2003. For each series we estimated a t-GARCH(1, 1), that is a model with time varying volatility and Student t conditional distribution. We found that all series except AEX did not show heteroskedastic effects. Only the AEX series presented a very weak heteroskedastic effect, and the persistence coefficient for the lagged volatility was estimated at around 0.38. This result will not come as a surprise to anyone familiar with the econometrics of financial time series, in which the GARCH effects are mainly recovered at very high frequencies, namely for daily or weekly returns. Nevertheless, the use of a Student t conditional distribution showed that AEX, DAX 30 and FTSE 100 displayed a fat-tail behavior: the estimated d.o.f. of the marginal t-GARCH was respectively around 4, 3 and 8. Contrary to that, S&P 500 and NKY showed a more normal behavior: the estimated d.o.f. of the marginal t-GARCH was around 13 for both series.

The next step was to specify the dependence structure among the markets. For this purpose, we estimated the Spearman variance–covariance matrix from filtered residuals from each marginal distribution. The estimated covariance matrix was used to simulate data from a T-copula distribution.

We compared three ways for pricing the option under analysis:

- historical simulation from empirical data;
- T-copula with t-GARCH marginals;
- T-copula with normal marginals.

The historical simulation approach is very easy, i.e. the value of the option is obtained by computing the pay-offs (i.e. max(average return, 3%, 0)) for each historical quarter and averaging them. The price in this case is equal to 0.021.

The T-copula estimated with t-GARCH margins gives a d.o.f. of around 10 – more akin to the behavior of a normal copula.

The T-copula estimated with normal marginal gives a d.o.f. around 2; so the fat-tails in some of the margins were transferred to the dependence function.

In these two cases we simulated 10 000 Monte Carlo runs and obtained the value of the mentioned option by computing the average over all of the simulated pay-offs. In the case of the T-copula with t-GARCH margins, the simulated price is equal to 0.013, while in the other case the value was equal to 0.020, quite close to that obtained by historical simulation.

Clearly, this exercise has to be taken as a simple example, and direct application of the model would call for specification of the risk-premia in the different markets. Nevertheless, it was enough to highlight the power of copula functions to effectively separate information concerning the marginal distributions and the dependence structure among the markets. More explicitly, even accounting for fat-tails at the multivariate level, using a T-copula specification did not give any significant improvement in the accuracy of the price over that computed by historical simulation. On the contrary, by disentangling the fat-tail problem at the univariate level and at the dependence structure level, we could come up with a price that was much more precise. In other words, the product turned out to be much more sensitive to fat-tails than to tail dependence in the marginal distributions.

Bibliography

Anderson, R. & Sundaresan, S. (1996) "Design and valuation of debt contracts", *Rev. Finan. Stud.*, **9**, 37–68.

Arvanitis, A. & Gregory, J. (2001) *Credit: The Complete Guide to Pricing, Hedging and Risk Management*. Risk Books, London.

Avellaneda, M. & Paràs, A. (1996) "Managing the volatility risk of portfolios of derivative securities: the Lagrangian uncertain volatility model", *Appl. Math. Finance*, **3**, 21–52.

Avellaneda, M., Levy, A. & Paràs, A. (1995) "Pricing and hedging derivative securities in markets with uncertain volatilities", *Appl. Math. Finance*, **2**, 73–78.

Barbe, P., Genest, C., Ghoudi, K. & Rèmillard, B. (1996) "On Kendall's process", *J. Multivar. Anal.*, **58**, 197–229.

Barone, E., Barone-Adesi, G. & Castagna, A. (1998) "Pricing bonds and bond options with default risk", *Europ. Finan. Manage.*, **4**, 231–282.

Barone-Adesi, G. & Giannopoulos, K. (1996), "A simplified approach to the conditional estimation of Value-at-Risk", *Fut. Opt. World*, October, 68–72

Black, F. & Cox, J.C. (1976) "Valuing corporate securities: some effects of bond indenture provisions", *J. Finance*, **31**, 351–367.

Black, F. & Scholes, M. (1973) "The pricing of options and corporate liabilities", *J. Polit. Econ.*, **81**, 637–654.

Block, H.W. & Ting, M.L. (1981) "Some concepts of multivariate dependence", *Comm. Statist. A – Theory Methods*, **10**, 749–762.

Block, H., Savits, T. & Shaked, M. (1982) "Some concepts of negative dependence", *Ann. Prob.*, **10**, 765–772.

Blomqvist, N. (1950) "On a measure of dependence between two random variables", *Ann. Math. Statist.*, **21**, 593–600.

Bouyè, E., Durrleman, V., Nikeghbali, A., Riboulet, G. & Roncalli, T. (2000) *Copulas for Finance – A Reading Guide and Some Applications*. Groupe de Recherche Opèrationelle, Crédit Lyonnais, working paper.

Breeden, D.T. & Litzenberger, R.H. (1978) "Prices of state-contingent claims implicit in option prices", *J. Business*, **51**, 621–651.

Brigo, D. & Mercurio, F. (2001) "Displaced and mixture diffusions for analytically tractable smile models", in H. Geman, D. Madan, S. Pliska & T. Vorst (eds), *Mathematical Finance, Proceedings of the Bachelier Congress 2000*.

Brindley, E.C. & Thompson Jr. W.A. (1972) "Dependence and aging aspects of multivariate survival", *J. Amer. Statist. Assoc.*, **67**, 822–830.

Cambanis, S., Huang, S. & Simons, G. (1981) "On the theory of elliptically contoured distributions", *J. Multivar. Anal.*, **11**, 368–385.

Carty, L.V. (1997) *Moody's Rating Migration and Credit Quality Correlation, 1920–1996*. Moody's Investor Service Special Report, July.

Cazzulani, L., Meneguzzo, D. & Vecchiato, W. (2001) *Copulas: A Statistical Perspective with Empirical Applications*. IntesaBCI Risk Management Department, working paper.

Cherubini, U. (1997) "Fuzzy measures and asset prices", *Appl. Math. Finance*, **4**, 135–149.

Cherubini, U. & Della Lunga, G. (2001) "Liquidity and credit risk", *Appl. Math. Finance*, **8**, 79–95.

Cherubini, U. & Luciano, E. (2001) "Value at risk trade-off and capital allocation with copulas", *Econ. Notes*, **30**, (2), 235–256.

Cherubini, U. & Luciano, E. (2002a) "Bivariate option pricing with copulas", *Appl. Math. Finance*, **8**, 69–85.

Cherubini, U. & Luciano, E. (2002b) "Copula vulnerability", *Risk*, October, **15**, 83–86.

Chesney, M., Jeanblank-Piqué, M. & Yor, M. (1997) "Brownian excursions and Parisian barrier options", *Advances in Applied Probability*, **29**, 165–184.

Christoffersen, P.F. (1998) "Evaluating interval forecasts", *Internat. Econ. Rev.*, **39** (4), 841–862.

Clayton, D.G. (1978) "A model for association in bivariate life tables and its application in epidemiological studies of familial tendency in chronic disease incidence", *Biometrika*, **65**, 141–151.

Coles, S., Currie, J. & Tawn, J. (1999) *Dependence Measures for Extreme Value Analysis*. Dept. of Mathematics and Statistics, Lancaster University, working paper.

Cook, R.D. & Johnson, M.E. (1981) "A family of distributions for modeling non-elliptically symmetric multivariate data", *J. Roy. Statist. Soc. Ser. B*, **43**, 210–218.

Cook, R.D. & Johnson, M.E. (1986) "Generalized Burr–Pareto-logistic distributions with applications to a uranium exploration data set", *Technometrics*, **28**, 123–131.

Cox, D.R. & Oakes, D. (1984) *Analysis of Survival Data*. Chapman & Hall, London.

Cox, J.C., Ingersoll, J. & Ross, S. (1985) "A theory of the term structure of interest rates", *Econometrica*, **53**, 385–407.

CreditMetrics Manual, RiskMetrics Group, available at http://www.riskmetrics.com

Davidson, R. & MacKinnon, J. (1993) *Estimation and Inference in Econometrics*. Oxford University Press, Oxford.

Davies, J., Hewer, J. & Rivett, P. (2001) *A Guide to Credit Derivatives*. PriceWaterHouseCoopers, The Financial Jungle Series.

Davis, M. & Lo, V. (2001) "Infectious defaults", *Quantitative Finance*, **1**, 382–386.

Deheuvels, P. (1978) "Caractérisation complète des Lois Extrèmes Multivariées et de la Convergence des Types Extrèmes", *Pub. l'Institut de Statist. l'Université de Paris*, **23**, 1–36.

Deheuvels, P. (1979) "La function de dépendance empirique et ses propriétés. Un test non paramétriquen d'indépendance", *Acad. Roy. Belg. Bull. Cl. Sci.*, **65** (5), 274–292.

Deheuvels, P. (1981) *A Nonparametric Test for Independence*. Université de Paris, Institut de Statistique.

Delbaen, F. & Schachermayer, W. (1994) "A general version of the fundamental theorem of asset pricing", *Math. Ann.*, **300**, 463–520.

Delianedis, G. & Geske, R. (1998) *Credit Risk and Risk Neutral Default Probabilities: Information about Rating Migrations and Defaults*. UCLA, The Anderson School, working paper.

Derman, E. & Kani, I. (1994) "Riding on a Smile", *Risk*, July, 32–39

Devroye, L. (1986) *Non-Uniform Random Variate Generation*. Springer-Verlag, New York.

Dhaene, J., Denuit, M., Goovaerts, M.J., Kaas, R. & Vyncke, D. (2002) "The concept of comonotonicity in actuarial science and finance: theory", *Insur.: Math. Econ.*, **31**, 3–33.

Diebold, F.X., Gunther, T. & Tay, A.S. (1998) "Evaluating density forecasts with applications to financial risk management", *Internat. Econ. Rev.*, **39**, 863–883.

Diebold, F.X., Hahn, J. & Tay, A.S. (1999) "Multivariate density forecast evaluation and calibration in financial risk management", *Rev. Econ. Statist.*, **81** (4), 661–673.

Duffie, D. & Garleanu, N. (2001) "Risk and valuation of collateralized debt obligations", *Finan. Anal. J.*, **57** (1), 41–59.

Duffie, D. & Kan, R. (1996) "A yield factor model of interest rates", *Mathematical Finance*, **6** (4), 379–406.

Duffie, D. & Lando, D. (2001) "The term structure of credit spreads with incomplete accounting information", *Econometrica*, **69**, 663–664.

Duffie, D.J. & Singleton, K.J. (1998) "Modeling term structures of defaultable bonds", *Rev. Finan. Stud.*, **12**, 687–720.

Duffie, D.J. & Singleton, K.J. (1999) *Simulating Correlated Defaults*. Stanford University, Graduate School of Business, working paper.

Durbin, J. & Stuart, A. (1951) "Inversions and rank correlations", *J. Roy. Statist. Soc., Series B*, **2**, 303–309.

Durrleman, V., Nikeghbali, A. & Roncalli, T. (2000a) *Copulas Approximation and New Families*. Groupe de Recherche Opèrationelle, Crédit Lyonnais, working paper.

Durrleman, V., Nikeghbali, A. & Roncalli, T. (2000b) *Which Copula is the Right One?* Groupe de Recherche Opèrationelle, Crédit Lyonnais, working paper.

Efron, B. & Tibshirani, R.J. (1993) *An Introduction to Bootstrap*. Chapman & Hall, London.

Embrechts, P., Klüppenberg, P. & Mikosch, T. (1997) *Modeling Extremal Event for Insurance and Finance*. Springer, Berlin.

Embrechts, P., McNeil, A.J. & Straumann, D. (1999) *Correlation and Dependency in Risk Management: Properties and Pitfalls*. Department of Mathematik, ETHZ, Zurich, working paper. Now in M.A.H. Dempster (ed.) (2002), *Risk Management: Value at Risk and Beyond* (pp. 176–223). Cambridge University Press, Cambridge.

Embrechts, P., Lindskog, F. & McNeil, A. (2001) *Modelling Dependence with Copulas and Applications to Risk Management*. Department of Mathematik, ETHZ, Zurich, working paper CH–8092. Now in S. Rachev (2003) *Handbook of Heavy Tailed Distributions in Finance* (pp. 329–384). Elsevier.

Engle, R.F. (ed.) (1996) *ARCH Selected Readings*. Oxford University Press, Oxford.

Engle, R.F. & Manganelli, S. (1999) *CAViaR: Conditional Autoregressive Value at Risk by Regression Quantiles*. UCSD Dept. of Economics, working paper.

Erturk, E. (2000) "Default correlation among investment-grade borrowers", *J. Fixed Income*, March, **9**, 55–59.

Evans, M., Hastings, N. & Peacock, B. (1993) *Statistical Distributions*. John Wiley & Sons, New York.

Fang, K.T., Kotz, S. & Ng, W. (1990) *Symmetric Multivariate and Related Distributions*. Chapman & Hall, London.

Feller, W. (1968) *An Introduction to Probability Theory and Its Applications*, Vol. I. John Wiley & Sons, New York.

Feller, W. (1971) *An Introduction to Probability Theory and Its Applications*, Vol. II. John Wiley & Sons, New York.

Ferguson, T.S. (1995) "A class of symmetric bivariate uniform distributions", *Statist. Papers*, **36**, 31–40.

Féron, R. (1956) "Sur les tableaux de corrélation dont les marges sont donées, cas de l'espace a trois dimensions", *Publ. Inst. Statist. Univ. Paris*, **5**, 3–12.

Finger, C. (ed.) (2003) *Credit Grades*. Technical Document.

Finger, C.C., Finkelstein, V., Lardy, J.-P., Pan, G., Ta, T. & Tierney, J. (2002) CreditGrades[TM] technical document, RiskMetrics Group Working Paper.

Follmer, H. & Schweitzer, M. (1991) "Hedging of contingent claims under incomplete information", in M.H.A. Davis & R.J. Elliot (eds), *Applied Stochastic Analysis*. Stochastics Monograph 5. Gordon Breach, London and New York, pp. 389–414.

Frank, M.J. (1979) "On the simultaneous associativity of $F(x, y)$ and $x + y - F(x, y)$", *Aequationes Math.*, **19**, 194–226.

Frank, M.J. & Schweizer, B. (1979) "On the duality of general infimal and supremal convolutions", *Rend. Math.*, **12**, 1–23.

Frank, M.J., Nelsen, R. & Schweizer, B. (1987) "Best-possible distributions of a sum – a problem of Kolmogorov", *Prob. Th. Rel. Fields*, **74**, 199–211.

Fréchet, M. (1935) "Généralisations du théorème des probabilités totales", *Fund. Math.*, **25**, 379–387.

Fréchet, M. (1951) "Sur le tableaux de corrélation dont les marges sont données", *Ann. Univ. Lyon*, **9**, Sect. A, 53–77.

Fréchet, M. (1958) "Remarques au sujet de la note précédente", *C.R. Acad. Sci. Paris*, **246**, 2719–2720.

Frees, E.W. & Valdez, E. (1998) "Understanding relationship using copulas", *N. Amer. Actuarial J.*, **2**, 1–25.

Frey, R. & McNeil, A.J. (2001) *Modeling Dependent Defaults*. Dept. of Mathematics, ETH Zurich, working paper.

Frittelli, M. (2000) "The minimal entropy martingale measure and the valuation problem in incomplete markets", *Math. Finance*, **10**, 39–52.

Fujita, T. & Miura, R. (2002) "Edokko options: a new framework of barrier options", *Asia-Pacific Financial Markets*, **9**, 141–151.

Genest, C. (1987) "Frank's family of bivariate distributions", *Biometrika*, **74**, 549–555.

Genest, C. & MacKay, J. (1986) "The joy of copulas: bivariate distributions with uniform marginals", *Amer. Statist.*, **40**, 280–283.

Genest, C. & Rivest, L. (1993) "Statistical inference procedures for bivariate Archimedean copulas", *J. Amer. Statist. Assoc.*, **88**, 1034–1043.

Georges, P., Lamy, A., Nicolas, E., Quibel, G. & Roncalli, T. (2001) *Multivariate Survival Modelling: A Unified Approach with Copulas*. Groupe de Recherche Opèrationelle, Crédit Lyonnais, working paper.

Geman, H. (1989) *The Importance of the Forward Risk Neutral Probability in a Stochastic Approach of Interest Rates*. Working paper, ESSEC.

Geske, R. (1977) "The valuation of corporate liabilities as compound options", *J. Finan. Quant. Anal.*, **12**, 541–552.

Gibbons, J.D. (1992) *Nonparametric Statistical Inference*. Marcel Dekker, New York.

Giesecke, K. (2001) *Structural Modelling of Correlated Defaults with Incomplete Information*. Humboldt University, working paper.

Gilboa, I. (1989) "Duality in non-additive expected utility theory", in P. Fishburn & I.H. LaValle (eds), *Choice under Uncertainty, Annals of Operations Research*. J.C. Baltzer, Basel, pp. 405–414

Gilboa, I. & Schmeidler, D. (1989) "Maxmin expected utility with non-unique prior", *J. Math. Econ.*, **18**, 141–153.

Gumbel, E.J. (1960) "Bivariate exponential distributions", *J. Amer. Statist. Assoc.*, **55**, 698–707.

Hardle, W. (1990) *Applied Nonparametric Regression*. ESM, Cambridge University Press, Cambridge.

Heath, D.C., Jarrow, R.A. & Morton, A. (1990) "Bond pricing and the term structure of interest rates: a discrete time approximation", *J. Finan. Quant. Anal.*, **25**, 419–440.

Heath, D.C., Jarrow, R.A. & Morton, A. (1992) "Bond pricing and the term structure of interest rates: a new methodology for contingent claim valuation", *Econometrica*, **60**, 77–105.

Heston, S.L. (1993) "A closed form solution for options with stochastic volatility with applications to bond and currency options", *Rev. Finan. Stud.*, **6**, 327–343.

Hoeffding, W. (1940) "Masstabinvariante Korrelationstheorie", *Schriften des Mathematischen Instituts und des Instituts für Angewandte Mathematik der Universität Berlin*, **5**, 179–233.

Hougaard, P. (1986) "A class of multivariate failure time distributions", *Biometrika*, **73**, 671–678.

Hull, J. & White, A. (1987) "The pricing of options on assets with stochastic volatility", *J. Finance*, **42**, 281–300.

Hull, J. & White, A. (1995) "The impact of default risk on the prices of options and other derivative securities", *J. Bank. Finance*, **19**, 299–322.

Hull, J. & White, A. (1998) "Value at Risk when daily changes in market variables are not normally distributed", *J. Derivatives*, **5** (3), 9–19.

Hull, J. & White, A. (2000) "Valuing credit default swap: no counterparty default risk", *J. Derivatives*, **8**, 29–40.

Hutchinson, T.P. & Lai, C.D. (1990) *Continuous Bivariate Distributions, Emphasising Applications*. Rumsby Scientific Publishing, Adelaide.

Ingersoll, J.E. (2000) "Digital contracts: simple tools for pricing complex derivatives", *J. Business*, **73** (1), 62–88.

Jamshidian, F. (1989) "An exact bond option pricing formula", *J. Finance*, **44**, 205–209.

Jamshidian, F. (1997) "LIBOR and swap market models and measures", *Finan. Stochast.*, **1**, 293–330.

Jarrow, R. & Turnbull, S. (1995) "Pricing derivatives on financial securities subject to credit risk", *J. Finance*, **50**, 53–85.

Jarrow, R.A. & Yu, F. (2001) "Counterparty risk and the pricing of defaultable securities", *J. Finance*, **56** (5), 555–576.

Joag-Dev, K. (1984) "Measures of dependence", in P.R. Krishnaiak (ed.), *Handbook of Statistics*, Vol. 4. North-Holland Elsevier, New York, pp. 79–88.

Joe, H. (1990) "Multivariate concordance", *J. Multivar. Anal.*, **35**, 12–30.

Joe, H. (1997) *Multivariate Models and Dependence Concepts*. Chapman & Hall, London.

Joe, H. & Hu, T. (1996) "Multivariate distributions from mixtures of max-infinitely divisible distributions", *J. Multivar. Anal.*, **57**, 240–265.

Joe, H. & Xu, J.J. (1996) *The Estimation Method of Inference Functions for Margins for Multivariate Models*. Dept. of Statistics University of British Columbia, Tech. Rept. 166.

Johnson, H. & Stulz, R. (1987) "The pricing of options with default risk", *J. Finance*, **42**, 267–280.

Jouanin, J.F., Rapuch, G., Riboulet, G. & Roncalli, T. (2001) *Modelling Dependence for Credit Derivatives with Copulas*. Groupe de Recherche Opèrationelle, Crédit Lyonnais, working paper.

J.P. Morgan (2000) "Guide to credit derivatives", *Risk*.

Karlin, S. & Taylor, H.M. (1981) *A Second Course in Stochastic Processes*. Academic Press, New York.

Kendall, M.G. (1938) "A new measure of rank correlation", *Biometrika*, **30**, 81–93.

Kimberling, C.H. (1974) "A probabilistic interpretation of complete monotonicity", *Aequationes Math.*, **10**, 152–164.

Kimeldorf, G. & Sampson, A.R. (1975) "Uniform representation of bivariate distributions", *Commun. Statist.*, **4**, 617–627.

Klein, P. (1996) "Pricing Black and Scholes options with correlated credit risk", *J. Bank. Finance*, **20**, 1211–1230.

Konijn, H.S. (1959) "Positive and negative dependence of two random variables", *Sankhyà*, **21**, 269–280.

Lando, D. (1998) "On Cox processes and credit risky securities", *Rev. Deriv. Res.*, **2**, 99–120.

Laurent, J.P. & Gregory, J. (2002) *Basket Default Swaps, CDOs and Factor Copulas*. October, BNP Paribas and University of Lyon, working paper.

Lee, A.J. (1993) "Generating random binary deviates having fixed marginal distributions and specified degrees of association", *Amer. Statist.*, **47**, 209–215.

Lehmann, E. (1966) "Some concepts of dependence", *Ann. Math. Statist.*, **37**, 1137–1153.

Lehmann, E. & Casella, G. (1998) *Theory of Point Estimation*. Springer-Verlag, New York.

Leland, H.E. (1994) "Corporate debt value, bond covenants and optimal capital structure", *J. Finance*, **49**, 1213–1252.

Li, D.X. (1998) "Constructing a credit curve", *Risk*. Special report on Credit Risk, Nov. 1988, 40–44.

Li, D.X. (2000) "On default correlation: a copula function approach", *J. Fixed Income*, **9**, 43–54.

Li, X., Mikusinski, P., Sherwood, H. & Taylor, M.D. (1997) "On approximation of copulas", in G. Dall'Aglio, S. Kotz & G. Salinetti (eds), *Distributions with Given Marginals and Moment Problems*. Kluwer Academic Publishers, Dordrecht.

Lindskog, F. (2000) *Linear Correlation Estimation*. RiskLab ETH, working paper.

Lindskog, F., McNeil, A. & Schmock, U. (2001) *A Note on Kendall's Tau for Elliptical Distribution*. ETH Zurich, working paper.

Linetsky, V. (1999) "Step options", *Math. Finance*, **9** (1), 55–96.

Ling, C.H. (1965) "Representation of associative functions", *Publ. Math. Debrecen*, **12**, 189–212.

Longstaff, F.A. & Schwartz, E.S. (1992) "Interest rate volatility and the term structure: a two-factor general equilibrium model", *J. Finance*, **47**, 1259–1282.

Longstaff, F.A. & Schwartz, E.S. (1995) "A simple approach to valuing risky fixed and floating rate debt", *J. Finance*, **50**, 789–819.

Luciano, E. & Marena, M. (2002a) "Portfolio value at risk bounds", *Internat. Trans. Oper. Res.*, **9** (5), 629–641.

Luciano, E. & Marena, M. (2002b) "Value at risk bounds for portfolios of non-normal returns", in C. Zopoudinis (ed.), *New Trends in Banking Management*. Physica-Verlag, Berlin, pp. 207–222.

Luciano, E. & Marena, M. (2003) "Copulae as a new tool in financial modelling", *Operational Research: An International Journal*, **2**, 139–155.

Madan, D. & Unal, H. (1999) "Pricing the risks of default", *Rev. Derivat. Res.*, 121–160.

Madan, D.B. & Unal, H. (2000) "A two-factor hazard rate model for pricing risky debt and the term structure of credit spreads", *J. Finan. Quant. Anal.*, **35**, 43–65.

Magnus, J.R. & Neudecker, H. (1980) *Matrix Differential Calculus with Applications in Statistics and Econometrics*. John Wiley & Sons, New York.

Makarov, G.D. (1981) "Estimates for the distribution function of a sum of two random variables when the marginal distributions are fixed", *Theory Prob. Appl.*, **26**, 803–806.

Margrabe, W. (1978): "The value of an option to exchange an asset for another", *J. Finance*, **33**, 177–186.

Marshall, A.W. & Olkin, I. (1967a) "A generalized bivariate exponential distribution", *J. Appl. Prob.*, **4**, 291–302.

Marshall, A.W. & Olkin, I. (1967b) "A multivariate exponential distribution", *J. Amer. Statist. Assoc.*, **62**, 30–44.

Marshall, A.W. & Olkin, I. (1988) "Families of multivariate distributions", *J. Amer. Statist. Assoc.*, **83**, 834–841.

Mashal, R. & Zeevi, A. (2002) *Beyond Correlation: Extreme Co-movements between Financial Assets.* Columbia Business School, working paper.

Meneguzzo, D. & Vecchiato, W. (2000) "Improvement on Value at Risk measures by combining conditional autoregressive and extreme value approaches", *Review in International Business and Finance.* Special Issue on Financial Risk and Financial Risk Management, Vol. **16**, Chap. **12**, pp. 275–324. Elsevier Science Ltd. April 2002.

Meneguzzo, D. & Vecchiato, W. (2004) "Copula sensitivity in Collateralized Debt Obligations and Basket Default Swaps". *The Journal of Future Markets*, **24**, 37–70.

Merton, R.C. (1974) "On the pricing of corporate debt: the risk structure of interest rates", *J. Finance*, **29**, 449–470.

Mikusinski, P., Sherwood, H. & Taylor, M.D. (1992) "Shuffles of min", *Stochastica*, **13**, 61–74.

Moody's Investor Service Global Credit Research (Feb. 2001) *Default and Recovery Rates of Corporate Bond Issuer: 2000.*

Moore, D.S. & Spruill, M.C. (1975) "Unified large-sample theory of general chi-squared statistics for tests of fit", *Ann. Statist.*, **3**, 599–616.

Moynihan, R., Schweizer, B. & Sklar, A. (1978) "Inequalities among binary operations on probability distribution functions", *General Inequalities*, **1**, 133–149.

Muller, A. & Scarsini, M. (2000) "Some remarks on the supermodular order", *J. Multivar. Anal.*, **73** (1), 107–119.

Nagpal, K. & Bahar, R. (2001) "Measuring default correlation", *Risk*, March, 129–132.

Nelsen, R.B. (1991) "Copulas and association", in G. Dall'Aglio, S. Kotz & G. Salinetti (eds), *Advances in Probability Distributions with Given Marginals.* Kluwer Academic Publishers, Dordrecht, pp. 51–74.

Nelsen, R.B. (1999) "An introduction to copulas", *Lecture Notes in Statistics.* Springer-Verlag, New York.

Oakes, D. (1982) "A model for association in bivariate survival data", *J. Roy. Statist. Soc. Ser. B*, **44**, 414–422.

Oakes, D. (1986) "Semiparametric inference in a model for association in bivariate survival data", *Biometrika*, **73**, 353–361.

O'Kane, D. (2001) *Credit Derivatives Explained.* Lehman Brothers, research paper.

Patel, N. (2003) "Flow business booms", *Risk Magazine*, February, **16** 20–23.

Patton, A.J. (2001) *Modelling Time-Varying Exchange Rate Dependence using the Conditional Copula.* UCSD Dept. of Economics, working paper.

Pearson, N.D. & Sun, T.S. (1994) "Exploiting the conditional density in estimating the term structure: an application to the Cox–Ingersoll–Ross Model", *J. Finance*, **49**, 1279–1304.

Plackett, R.L. (1965) "A class of bivariate distributions", *J. Amer. Statist. Assoc.*, **60**, 516–522.

Rényi, A. (1959) "On measures of dependence", *Acta Math. Acad. Sci. Hungar.*, **10**, 441–451.

Robinson, P. (1983) "Nonparametric estimators for time series", *J. Time Series Anal.*, **4**, 185–207.

Roncalli, T. (2001) *Copulas: A Tool for Dependence in Finance.* Groupe de Recherche Opèrationelle, Crèdit Lyonnais, working paper.

Roncalli, T. (2002) *Gestiondes Risques Multiples. Cours ENSAI de 3e année.* Groupe de Recherche Opèrationelle, Crèdit Lyonnais, working paper.

Roncalli, T. (2003) *Gestion des Risques Multiples: Le Risque de Credit 2ème partie.* Groupe de Recherche Opèrationelle, Crèdit Lyonnais, working paper.

Rosemberg, J.V. (2000) *Nonparametric Pricing of Multivariate Contingent Claims.* Stern School of Business, working paper.

Rousseuw, P. & Molenberghs, G. (1993) "Transformations of non-positive semidefinite correlation matrices", *Comm. Statist. – Theory and Methods*, **22** (4), 965–984.

Rubinstein, M. (1994) "Implied binomial trees", *J. Finance*, **49**, 771–818.

Ruschendorf, L., Schweizer, B. & Taylor, M.D. (eds) (1996) *Distributions with Fixed Marginals and Related Topics*. Institute of Mathematical Statistics, Hayward.

Samorodnitsky, G. & Taqqu, M.S. (1995) *Stable Non-Gaussian Random Processes. Stochastic Models with Infinite Variance*. Chapman & Hall, New York and London.

Scaillet, O. (2000) *Nonparametric Estimation of Copulas for Time Series*. IRES, working paper.

Scarsini, M. (1984) "On measures of concordance", *Stochastica*, **8**, 201–218.

Schönbucher, P. (2000) *A Libor Market Model with Default Risk*. Bonn University, Dept. of Statistics, working paper.

Schönbucher, P. & Schubert, D. (2001) *Copula-dependent Default Risk in Intensity Models*. University of Bonn, Germany, working paper.

Schweizer, B. (1991) "Thirty years of copulas", in G. Dall'Aglio, S. Kotz & G. Salinetti (eds), *Advances in Probability Distributions with Given Marginals*. Kluwer Academic Publishers, Dordrecht, pp. 13–50.

Schweizer, B. & Sklar, A. (1961) "Associative functions and statistical triangle inequalities", *Publ. Math. Debrecen.*, **8**, 169–186.

Schweizer, B. & Sklar, A. (1974) "Operations on distribution functions not derivable from operations on random variables", *Studia Mathematica*, **52**, 43–52.

Schweizer, B. & Sklar, A. (1983) *Probabilistic Metric Spaces*. Elsevier Science, New York.

Schweizer, B. & Wolff, E. (1976) "Sur une mesure de dépendance pour les variables aléatoires", *C.R. Acad. Sci. Paris*, **283**, 659–661.

Schweizer, B. & Wolff, E. (1981) "On non-parametric measures of dependence for random variables", *Ann. Statist.*, **9**, 879–885.

Serfling, R.J. (1980) *Approximation Theorems of Mathematical Statistics*. John Wiley & Sons, New York.

Shao, J. (1999) *Mathematical Statistics*. Springer-Verlag, New York.

Shao, J. & Tu, D. (1995) *The Jacknife and Bootstrap*. Springer-Verlag, New York.

Shimko, D.C. (1993) "Bounds of probability", *Risk*, **6**, 33–37.

Sklar, A. (1959) "Fonctions de repartition à *n* dimensions et leurs marges", *Pub. Inst. Statist. Univ. Paris*, **8**, 229–231.

Sklar, A. (1973) "Random variables, distribution functions, and copulas", *Kybernetica*, **9**, 449–460.

Sklar, A. (1996) "Random variables, distribution functions, and copulas – a personal look backward and forward", in L. Ruschendorf, B. Schweizer & M.D. Taylor (eds), *Distributions with Fixed Marginals and Related Topics*. Institute of Mathematical Statistics, Hayward, pp. 1–14.

Sklar, A. (1998) Personal communication.

Song, P. (2000) "Multivariate dispersion models generated from Gaussian copula". *Scandinavian J. Statistics*, **27**, 305–320.

Stulz, R.M. (1982) "Options on the minimum and maximum of two risky assets", *J. Finance*, **10**, 161–185.

Tjostheim, D. (1996) "Measures of dependence and tests of independence", *Statistics*, **28**, 249–284.

Vasicek, O. (1977) "An equilibrium characterization of the term structure", *J. Finan. Econ.*, **5**, 177–188.

Wang, S.S. (1998) *Aggregation of Correlated Risk Portfolios: Models – Algorithms*. CAS Committee on Theory of Risk, working paper.

White, H. (1984) *Asymptotic Theory for Econometricians*. Academic Press, New York.

Williamson, R.C. (1989) *Probabilistic Arithmetic*. PhD Thesis, University of Queensland.

Williamson, R.C. & Downs, T. (1990) "Probabilistic arithmetic I: Numerical methods for calculating convolutions and dependency bounds", *Internat. J. Approx. Reason.*, **4**, 89–158.

Wolff, E.F. (1981) "*N*-dimensional measures of dependence", *Stochastica*, **4**, 175–188.

Zangari, P. (1996) "A VaR methodology for portfolios that include options", *RiskMetrics Monitor*, first quarter, 4–12.

Zhou, C. (1996) *A Jump-Diffusion Approach to Modeling Credit Risk and Evaluating Defaultable Securities*. Federal Reserve Board, Washington, working paper.

Index